MW01014022

20

Changes | An Insider's View

cpt®

current procedural
terminology

AMA
AMERICAN MEDICAL
ASSOCIATION

Contents

Foreword

The American Medical Association is pleased to offer *CPT® Changes 2015: An Insider's View*. Since this book was first published in 2000, it has served as the definitive text on additions, revisions, and deletions to the CPT code set.

In developing this book, it was our intention to provide CPT users with a glimpse of the logic, rationale, and proposed function of CPT changes that resulted from the decisions of the CPT Editorial Panel and the yearly update process. The American Medical Association (AMA) staff members have the unique perspective of being both participants in the CPT editorial process and users of the CPT code set.

CPT Changes is intended to bridge understanding between clinical decisions made at the CPT Editorial Panel regarding appropriate service or procedure descriptions with functional interpretations of coding guidelines, code intent, and code combinations necessary for users of the CPT code set. A new edition of this book, like the codebook, is published annually.

To assist CPT users in applying new and revised CPT codes, this book includes clinical examples that describe the typical patient who might undergo the procedure and detailed descriptions of the procedure. Both of these are required as a part of the CPT code change proposal process and are used by the CPT Editorial Panel in crafting language, guidelines, and parenthetical notes associated with the new or revised codes. In addition, many of the clinical examples and descriptions of the procedures are used in the AMA/Specialty Society Relative Value Scale (RVS) Update (RUC) process for conducting surveys on physician work and in developing work relative value recommendations to the Centers for Medicare and Medicaid Services (CMS) as part of the Medicare Physician Fee Schedule (MPFS).

We are confident that the information contained in *CPT Changes* each year will prove to be a valuable resource to CPT users not only as they apply changes for the year of publication, but also as a resource for frequent reference as they continue their education in CPT coding. The AMA makes every effort to be a voice of clarity and consistency in an otherwise confusing system of health care claims and payment, and *CPT Changes 2015: An Insider's View* demonstrates our continued commitment to assist users of the CPT code set.

AMA|store

Take a quick survey and get $25 off your next AMA Store purchase!

Help us enhance *CPT® Changes 2016: An Insider's View*. Visit the link below to take our short, ten-minute survey and receive a promotion code for $25 off your next purchase on amastore.com upon completion.

We appreciate your input and look forward to enhancing our products to better meet your needs!

Take the survey now at:
surveymonkey.com/s/cptchanges2015

Using This Book

This book is designed to serve as a reference guide to understanding the changes contained in *Current Procedural Terminology (CPT®) 2015* and is not intended to replace the CPT codebook. Every effort is made to ensure accuracy, however, if differences exist, you should always defer to the information in the *CPT 2015* codebook.

The Symbols

This book uses the same coding conventions that appear in the CPT nomenclature.

- ● Indicates that a new procedure number was added to the CPT nomenclature

- ▲ Indicates that a code revision has resulted in a substantially altered procedure descriptor

- ✚ Indicates a CPT add-on code

- ⊘ Indicates a code that is exempt from the use of modifier 51 but is not designated as a CPT add-on procedure or service

- ▶◀ Indicates revised guidelines, cross-references, and/or explanatory text

- ⊙ Indicates a code that typically includes moderate sedation

- ⫫ Indicates a code for a vaccine that is pending FDA approval

- # Indicates a resequenced code. Note that rather than deleting and renumbering, resequencing allows existing codes to be relocated to an appropriate location for the code concept, regardless of the numeric sequence. Numerically placed references (ie, Code is out of numerical sequence. See…) are used as navigational alerts in the CPT codebook to direct the user to the location of an out-of-sequence code, therefore, remember to refer to the CPT codebook for these references.

- ○ Indicates a reinstated or recycled code

Whenever possible, complete segments of text from the CPT codebook are provided; however in some instances, only pertinent and truncated texts are included.

The Rationale

After listing each change or series of changes from the codebook, a rationale is provided. The rationale is intended to provide a brief clarification and explanation of the changes. Nevertheless, it's important to note that they may not address every question that may arise as a result of the changes.

Reading the Clinical Examples

The clinical examples and their procedural descriptions, which are descriptions of typical clinical examples and procedures, are included in this text with many of the codes to provide practical situations for which the new and/or revised codes in the CPT 2015 code set would be appropriately reported. It is important to note that these examples do not suggest limiting the use of a code; instead, they are meant to represent the typical patient and service or procedure, as previously stated. In addition, they do not describe the universe of patients for whom the service or procedure would be appropriate. It is important to also note that third-party payer reporting policies may differ.

The Tabular Review of the Changes

The table beginning on page 366 provides a quick overall review of all of the code changes. By reviewing the table, you can easily determine the level to which your particular field of interest has been affected by the changes in the CPT 2015 codebook.

CPT Codebook Text and Guidelines

In CPT Changes 2015, guidelines and revised CPT codebook text are set in red indented type. Any revised text, guidelines, and/or headings are indicated with the ►◄ symbols. This convention matches the style used in the codebook, ie, the revised or new text symbol is placed at the beginning and end of a paragraph that contains a revision or revisions.

Evaluation and Management (E/M) Services

Numerous changes have been made in the Evaluation and Management Services (E/M) section, some of which includes: (1) addition of "military history" to the social-history element in the E/M guidelines; (2) revision of inpatient neonatal and pediatric critical care guidelines to clarify appropriate reporting of these services; (3) deletion of intensive care services codes 99481 and 99482 and addition of new code 99184, which combines these services into a single code; (4) a section title has been changed from "Complex Chronic Care Coordination" to "Care Management Services" with an addition of a new subsection "Chronic Care Management Services" to better reflect the management services described by new code 99490; (5) addition of another new subsection, "Complex Chronic Care Management Services," with deletion of code 99488 and revisions of two codes 99487 and 99489. Guidelines have been significantly revised because of these two new subsections. In addition, a new subsection, guidelines, and codes 99497 and 99498 have been added for advance care planning.

Evaluation and Management (E/M) Services Guidelines

Definitions of Commonly Used Terms

Social History

▶An age appropriate review of past and current activities that includes significant information about:

■ Marital status and/or living arrangements

■ Current employment

■ Occupational history

■ Military history

■ Use of drugs, alcohol, and tobacco

■ Level of education

■ Sexual history

■ Other relevant social factors ◀

Rationale

The social-history element of history documentation in the E/M guidelines has been revised to include determination of any history of military service. The addition of this element will assist with diagnosing, assessing, and treating service members, veterans, and their families.

Evaluation and Management

Inpatient Neonatal Intensive Care Services and Pediatric and Neonatal Critical Care Services

Pediatric Critical Care Patient Transport

Codes 99466, 99467 are used to report the physical attendance and ...

Code 99485 is used to report the first 30 minutes of non-face-to-face supervision of an interfacility transport of a critically ill or critically injured pediatric patient and should be reported only once per date of service. Only the communication time spent by the supervising physician with the specialty transport team members during an interfacility transport should be reported. Code 99486 is used to report each additional 30 minutes beyond the initial 30 minutes. Non-face-to-face interfacility transport of 15 minutes or less is not reported.

▶(For total body and selective head cooling of neonates, use 99184)◀

99466   **Critical care** face-to-face services, during an interfacility transport of critically ill or critically injured pediatric patient, 24 months of age or younger; first 30-74 minutes of hands-on care during transport

Rationale
The parenthetical note for pediatric critical care patient transport guidelines regarding the appropriate use of total body and selective head cooling of neonates codes has been revised to replace deleted codes 99481 and 99482 with code 99184.

Inpatient Neonatal and Pediatric Critical Care

The same definitions for critical care services apply for the adult, child, and neonate.

▶Codes 99468, 99469 are used to report the services of directing the inpatient care of a critically ill neonate or infant 28 days of age or younger. They represent care starting with the date of admission (99468) to a critical care unit and subsequent day(s) (99469) that the neonate remains critical. These codes may be reported only by a single individual and only once per day, per patient, per hospital stay in a given facility. If readmitted to the neonatal critical care unit during the same day **or stay**, report the subsequent day(s) code 99469 for the first day of readmission to critical care, and 99469 for each day of critical care following readmission.◀

The initial day neonatal critical care code (99468) can be used in addition to 99464 or 99465 as appropriate, when the physician or other qualified health care professional is present for the delivery (99464) or resuscitation (99465) is required. Other procedures performed as a necessary part of the resuscitation (eg, endotracheal intubation [31500]) are also reported separately when performed as part of the pre-admission delivery room care. In order to report these procedures separately, they must be performed as a necessary component of the resuscitation and not simply as a convenience before admission to the neonatal intensive care unit.

⦸=Modifier 51 Exempt   ⊙=Moderate Sedation   ✚=Add-on Code   ⋀=FDA approval pending

▶Codes 99471-99476 are used to report direction of the inpatient care of a critically ill infant or young child from 29 days of postnatal age through less than 6 years of age. They represent care starting with the date of admission (99471, 99475) to all subsequent day(s) (99472, 99476) the infant or child remains critical. These codes may be reported only by a single individual and only once per day, per patient in a given setting. Services for the critically ill or critically injured child 6 years of age or older would be reported with the time based critical care codes (99291, 99292). Report 99471, 99475 only once per hospital stay in a given facility. If readmitted to the pediatric critical care unit during the same **day or** stay, report 99472 or 99476 for the first day of readmission to critical care and 99472 for each day of critical care following readmission.◀

▶Any services performed that are not included in these listings may be reported separately. For initiation of selective head or total body hypothermia in the critically ill neonate, report 99184. Facilities may report the included services separately.◀

99468 **Initial inpatient neonatal critical care,** per day, for the evaluation and management of a critically ill neonate, 28 days of age or younger

Initial and Continuing Intensive Care Services

99480 **Subsequent intensive care,** per day, for the evaluation and management of the recovering infant (present body weight of 2501-5000 grams)

▶(99481, 99482 have been deleted. To report, use 99184)◀

Rationale

The inpatient neonatal and pediatric critical care guidelines have been revised to clarify appropriate reporting for services provided subsequent to initial services that are provided on the same day or during the same stay.

Codes 99481 and 99482 have been deleted and replaced with code 99184, which has combined both selective head and total body hypothermia of neonates into a single defined description that includes all of the service components required of this procedure. A parenthetical note has been added following codes 99477-99480 to direct users to code 99184 for reporting hypothermia in the critically ill neonate. For more information, see Rationale for code 99184 in the Medicine section.

▶Care Management Services◀

▶Care management services are management and support services provided by clinical staff, under the direction of a physician or other qualified health care professional, to a patient residing at home or in a domiciliary, rest home, or assisted living facility. Services may include establishing, implementing, revising, or monitoring the care plan, coordinating the care of other professionals and agencies, and educating the patient or caregiver about the patient's condition, care plan, and prognosis. The physician or other qualified health care professional provides or oversees the management and/or coordination of services, as needed, for all medical conditions, psychosocial needs, and activities of daily living.

A plan of care must be documented and shared with the patient and/or caregiver. A care plan is based on a physical, mental, cognitive, social, functional, and environmental assessment. It is a comprehensive plan of care for all health problems. It typically includes, but is not limited to, the following elements: problem list, expected outcome and prognosis, measurable treatment goals, symptom management, planned interventions, medication management, community/social services ordered, how the services of agencies and specialists unconnected to the practice will be directed/coordinated, identification of the individuals responsible for each intervention, requirements for periodic review, and, when applicable, revision of the care plan.

Codes 99487, 99489, 99490 are reported only once per calendar month and may only be reported by the single physician or other qualified health care professional who assumes the care management role with a particular patient for the calendar month.

The face-to-face and non-face-to-face time spent by the clinical staff in communicating with the patient and/or family, caregivers, other professionals, and agencies; revising, documenting, and implementing the care plan; or teaching self-management is used in determining the care management clinical staff time for the month. Only the time of the clinical staff of the reporting professional is counted. Only count the time of one clinical staff member when two or more clinical staff members are meeting about the patient. **Note:** Do not count any clinical staff time on a day when the physician or qualified health care professional reports an E/M service (office or other outpatient services 99201, 99202, 99203, 99204, 99205, 99211, 99212, 99213, 99214, 99215, domiciliary, rest home services 99324, 99325, 99326, 99327, 99328, 99334, 99335, 99336, 99337, home services 99341, 99342, 99343, 99344, 99345, 99347, 99348, 99349, 99350).

Care management activities performed by clinical staff typically include:

- communication and engagement with patient, family members, guardian or caretaker, surrogate decision makers, and/or other professionals regarding aspects of care;

- communication with home health agencies and other community services utilized by the patient;

- collection of health outcomes data and registry documentation;

- patient and/or family/caregiver education to support self-management, independent living, and activities of daily living;

- assessment and support for treatment regimen adherence and medication management;

- identification of available community and health resources;

- facilitating access to care and services needed by the patient and/or family;

- management of care transitions not reported as part of transitional care management (99495, 99496);

- ongoing review of patient status, including review of laboratory and other studies not reported as part of an E/M service, noted above;

- development, communication, and maintenance of a comprehensive care plan.

The care management office/practice must have the following capabilities:

- provide 24/7 access to physicians or other qualified health care professionals or clinical staff including providing patients/caregivers with a means to make contact with health care professionals in the practice to address urgent needs regardless of the time of day or day of week;

⊘=Modifier 51 Exempt   ⊙=Moderate Sedation   ✚=Add-on Code   𝒩=FDA approval pending

- provide continuity of care with a designated member of the care team with whom the patient is able to schedule successive routine appointments;

- provide timely access and management for follow-up after an emergency department visit or facility discharge;

- utilize an electronic health record system so that care providers have timely access to clinical information;

- use a standardized methodology to identify patients who require care management services;

- have an internal care management process/function whereby a patient identified as meeting the requirements for these services starts receiving them in a timely manner;

- use a form and format in the medical record that is standardized within the practice;

- be able to engage and educate patients and caregivers as well as coordinate care among all service professionals, as appropriate for each patient.

E/M services may be reported separately by the same physician or other qualified health care professional during the same calendar month. Care management services include care plan oversight services (99339, 99340, 99374-99380), prolonged services without direct patient contact (99358, 99359), anticoagulant management (99363, 99364), medical team conferences (99366, 99367, 99368), education and training (98960, 98961, 98962, 99071, 99078), telephone services (99366, 99367, 99368, 99441, 99442, 99443), on-line medical evaluation (98969, 99444), preparation of special reports (99080), analysis of data (99090, 99091), transitional care management services (99495, 99496), medication therapy management services (99605, 99606, 99607) and, if performed, these services may not be reported separately during the month for which 99487, 99489, 99490 are reported. All other services may be reported. Do not report 99487, 99489, 99490 if reporting ESRD services (90951-90970) during the same month. If the care management services are performed within the postoperative period of a reported surgery, the same individual may not report 99487, 99489, 99490.

Care management may be reported in any calendar month during which the clinical staff time requirements are met. If care management resumes after a discharge during a new month, start a new period or report transitional care management services (99495, 99496) as appropriate. If discharge occurs in the same month, continue the reporting period or report Transitional Care Management Services. Do not report 99487, 99489, 99490 for any post-discharge care management services for any days within 30 days of discharge, if reporting 99495, 99496.◄

►Chronic Care Management Services◄

►Chronic care management services are provided when medical and/or psychosocial needs of the patient require establishing, implementing, revising, or monitoring the care plan. Patients who receive chronic care management services have two or more chronic continuous or episodic health conditions that are expected to last at least 12 months, or until the death of the patient, and that place the patient at significant risk of death, acute exacerbation/decompensation, or functional decline. Code 99490 is reported when, during the calendar month, at least 20 minutes of clinical staff time is spent in care management activities.◄

#●99490   Chronic care management services, at least 20 minutes of clinical staff time directed by a physician or other qualified health care professional, per calendar month, with the following required elements:

- multiple (two or more) chronic conditions expected to last at least 12 months, or until the death of the patient,

- chronic conditions place the patient at significant risk of death, acute exacerbation/ decompensation, or functional decline,

- comprehensive care plan established, implemented, revised, or monitored.

▶(Chronic care management services of less than 20 minutes duration, in a calendar month, are not reported separately)◀

▶Complex Chronic Care Management Services◀

▶Complex chronic care management services are provided during a calendar month that includes criteria for chronic care management services as well as establishment or substantial revision of a comprehensive care plan; medical, functional, and/or psychosocial problems requiring medical decision making of moderate or high complexity; and clinical staff care management services for at least 60 minutes, under the direction of a physician or other qualified health care professional. Physicians or other qualified health care professionals may not report complex chronic care management services if the care plan is unchanged or requires minimal change (eg, only a medication is changed or an adjustment in a treatment modality is ordered). Medical decision making as defined in the Evaluation and Management (E/M) guidelines is determined by the problems addressed by the reporting individual during the month.

Patients who require complex chronic care management services may be identified by practice-specific or other published algorithms that recognize multiple illnesses, multiple medication use, inability to perform activities of daily living, requirement for a caregiver, and/or repeat admissions or emergency department visits. Typical adult patients who receive complex chronic care management services are treated with three or more prescription medications and may be receiving other types of therapeutic interventions (eg, physical therapy, occupational therapy). Typical pediatric patients receive three or more therapeutic interventions (eg, medications, nutritional support, respiratory therapy). All patients have two or more chronic continuous or episodic health conditions that are expected to last at least 12 months, or until the death of the patient, and that place the patient at significant risk of death, acute exacerbation/decompensation, or functional decline. Typical patients have complex diseases and morbidities and, as a result, demonstrate one or more of the following:

- need for the coordination of a number of specialties and services;

- inability to perform activities of daily living and/or cognitive impairment resulting in poor adherence to the treatment plan without substantial assistance from a caregiver;

- psychiatric and other medical comorbidities (eg, dementia and chronic obstructive pulmonary disease or substance abuse and diabetes) that complicate their care; and/or

- social support requirements or difficulty with access to care.◀

⃠=Modifier 51 Exempt ⊙=Moderate Sedation ✚=Add-on Code 〰=FDA approval pending

Total Duration of Staff Care Management Services	Complex Chronic Care Management
Less than 60 minutes	Not reported separately
60 to 89 minutes (1 hour - 1 hr. 29 min.)	99487
90 - 119 minutes (1 hr. 30 min. - 1 hr. 59 min.)	99487 and 99489 X 1
120 minutes or more (2 hours or more)	99487 and 99489 X 2 and 99489 for each additional 30 minutes

▲99487   Complex chronic care management services, with the following required elements:

- multiple (two or more) chronic conditions expected to last at least 12 months, or until the death of the patient;

- chronic conditions place the patient at significant risk of death, acute exacerbation/decompensation, or functional decline;

- establishment or substantial revision of a comprehensive care plan;

- moderate or high complexity medical decision making;

- 60 minutes of clinical staff time directed by a physician or other qualified health care professional, per calendar month.

►(Complex chronic care management services of less than 60 minutes duration, in a calendar month, are not reported separately)◄

►(99488 has been deleted. To report one or more face-to-face visits by the physician or other qualified health care professional that are performed in the same month as 99487, use the appropriate E/M code[s])◄

+▲99489   each additional 30 minutes of clinical staff time directed by a physician or other qualified health care professional, per calendar month (List separately in addition to code for primary procedure)

►(Report 99489 in conjunction with 99487)◄

►(Do not report 99489 for care management services of less than 30 minutes additional to the first 60 minutes of complex chronic care management services during a calendar month)◄

►(Do not report 99487, 99489, 99490 during the same month with 90951-90970, 98960-98962, 98966-98969, 99071, 99078, 99080, 99090, 99091, 99339, 99340, 99358, 99359, 99363, 99364, 99366-99368, 99374-99380, 99441-99444, 99495, 99496, 99605-99607)◄

Rationale

The Complex Chronic Care Coordination Services section has been revised, beginning with the section title, which has changed to "Care Management Services" to better reflect the management services described by these codes. The guidelines have been revised because of the addition of two new subsections, which have their own headings, guidelines, and codes. The first new subsection, "Chronic Care Management," includes guidelines and new code 99490 to report provision of chronic care management services. The addition of this subsection allows for chronic care management services to be reported for patients who receive these services at least 20 minutes per calendar month. This is in contrast to at least 60 minutes of complex chronic care management services that would be reported by revised codes 99487 and 99489. Codes 99487 and 99489 have been placed under the second new subsection, "Complex Chronic Care Management Services," and these codes are specific to complex chronic care management. The subsection guidelines include information on the identification of patients who receive this type of complex care, as well as examples of typical patients. As with code 99490, the descriptors of codes 99487 and 99489 include required elements for the reporting of these codes. As part of the revisions to this subsection, code 99488 has been deleted because the care management codes no longer reference the requirement of face-to-face visits. To report one or more face-to-face visits, use the appropriate E/M code.

Chronic care management services of less than 20 minutes in a calendar month are not reported separately. Likewise, complex chronic care management services of less than 60 minutes in a calendar month are not reported separately. The add-on code 99489 should not be reported for services of less than 30 minutes in addition to the first 60 minutes of complex chronic care management services during a calendar month.

Clinical Example (99490)

The patient is a 75-year-old male with diabetes, claudication, and mild congestive heart failure, status post myocardial infarction with mild dementia who had a peripheral arterial stent placed six weeks ago during hospitalization for treatment of a foot ulcer. He lives with his daughter, participates in remote monitoring programs, and is being treated by two specialists in addition to his primary care physician.

Description of Procedure (99490)

Chronic care management services are management and support services provided by clinical staff, under the direction of a physician or other qualified health care professional, to a patient residing at home or in a domiciliary, rest home, or assisted living facility. These services typically involve clinical staff implementing a care plan directed by the physician or other qualified health care professional when medical and/or psychosocial needs of the patient require establishing and implementing, revising, or monitoring the care plan. Services typically include establishing, implementing, revising, or monitoring the care plan; coordinating the care of other professionals and agencies; and educating the patient or caregiver about the patient's condition, care plan, and prognosis. The physician or other qualified health care professional provides or oversees the management and/or coordination of services, as needed, for all medical conditions, psychosocial needs, and activities of daily living.

A plan of care must be documented and shared with the patient and/or caregiver. A care plan is based on a physical, mental, cognitive, social, functional, and environmental assessment. It is a comprehensive plan of care for all health problems. It typically includes, but is not limited to, the following elements: problem list; expected outcome and prognosis; measurable treatment goals; symptom management; planned interventions; medication management; community and social services ordered; how the services of agencies and specialists unconnected to the practice will be directed and coordinated; identification of the individuals

⊘=Modifier 51 Exempt   ⊙=Moderate Sedation   ✚=Add-on Code   *N*=FDA approval pending

responsible for each intervention; requirements for periodic review; and, when applicable, revision of the care plan.

The care management office/practice must have the following capabilities:

Provide 24/7 access to physicians or other qualified health care professionals or clinical staff, including providing patients and caregivers with a means to make contact with health care professionals in the practice to address urgent needs regardless of the time of day or day of week; provide continuity of care with a designated member of the care team with whom the patient is able to schedule successive routine appointments; provide timely access and management for follow up after an emergency department visit or facility discharge; utilize an electronic health record system so that care providers have timely access to clinical information; use a standardized methodology to identify patients who require care management services; have an internal care management process/function whereby a patient identified as meeting the requirements for these services starts receiving them in a timely manner; use a form and format in the medical record that is standardized within the practice; and be able to engage and educate patients and caregivers, as well as coordinate care among all service professionals, as appropriate for each patient.

▶Advance Care Planning◀

▶Codes 99497, 99498 are used to report the face-to-face service between a physician or other qualified health care professional and a patient, family member, or surrogate in counseling and discussing advance directives, with or without completing relevant legal forms. An advance directive is a document appointing an agent and/or recording the wishes of a patient pertaining to his/her medical treatment at a future time should he/she lack decisional capacity at that time. Examples of written advance directives include, but are not limited to, Health Care Proxy, Durable Power of Attorney for Health Care, Living Will, and Medical Orders for Life-Sustaining Treatment (MOLST).

When using codes 99497, 99498, no active management of the problem(s) is undertaken during the time period reported.

Codes 99497, 99498 may be reported separately if these services are performed on the same day as another Evaluation and Management service (99201-99215, 99217, 99218, 99219, 99220, 99221, 99222, 99223, 99224, 99225, 99226, 99231, 99232, 99233, 99234, 99235, 99236, 99238, 99239, 99241, 99242, 99243, 99244, 99245, 99251, 99252, 99253, 99254, 99255, 99281, 99282, 99283, 99284, 99285, 99304, 99305, 99306, 99307, 99308, 99309, 99310, 99315, 99316, 99318, 99324, 99325, 99326, 99327, 99328, 99334, 99335, 99336, 99337, 99341, 99342, 99343, 99344, 99345, 99347, 99348, 99349, 99350, 99381-99397, 99495, 99496).◀

●99497   Advance care planning including the explanation and discussion of advance directives such as standard forms (with completion of such forms, when performed), by the physician or other qualified health care professional; first 30 minutes, face-to-face with the patient, family member(s), and/or surrogate

+●99498   each additional 30 minutes (List separately in addition to code for primary procedure)

►(Use 99498 in conjunction with 99497)◄

►(Do not report 99497 and 99498 on the same date of service as 99291, 99292, 99468, 99469, 99471, 99472, 99475, 99476, 99477, 99478, 99479, 99480)◄

Rationale

A new E/M subsection, guidelines, and codes 99497 and 99498 have been added for advance care planning, which involves counseling and discussing advance directives. As defined in the guidelines, an advance directive is a document that appoints an agent and/or records the wishes of a patient pertaining to his or her medical treatment at a future time should he or she lack decisional capacity at that time. To report the code(s), the patient need not be present as the discussion can also be between a physician or qualified healthcare professional and a family member or surrogate. Because the purpose of the visit is the discussion, no active management of the problem(s) is undertaken during this time period. Completion of relevant legal forms is also not required at the time of the discussion. It is important to note that this service is limited to advance care planning. As stated in the guidelines, certain E/M services performed on the same day may be reported separately. As stated in the exclusionary parenthetical note following code 99498, critical care codes 99291 and 99292, the neonatal and pediatric critical care codes 99468-99476, and the Initial and Continuing Intensive Care Service codes 99477-99480 should not be reported with codes 99497 and 99498.

Codes 99497 and 99498 are time-based codes with code 99497 reported for the first 30 minutes and add-on code 99498 reported for each additional 30 minutes.

Clinical Example (99497)

A 68-year-old male with heart failure and diabetes on multiple medications is seen with his wife to discuss advanced care planning.

Description of Procedure (99497)

The physician or other qualified health care professional performs a cognitive evaluation to determine the patient's capacity to understand risks, benefits, and alternatives to advance care–planning choices. There is discussion of the risks, benefits, and alternatives to the various advance care planning tools (eg, living will, durable power of attorney). The physician or other qualified health care professional gives the patient and/or family member/surrogate an opportunity to view a blank advance care directive and a blank physician orders for life-sustaining treatment (POLST) form. The physician or other qualified health care professional explains and discusses advance directives with the patient and family member/surrogate. This includes a discussion of the patient's values and overall goals for treatment. As appropriate for the patient's conditions, they talk about palliative care options, ways to avoid hospital readmission, and the patient's desire for care if he suffers a health event that adversely affects his decision-making capacity. The latter includes a discussion of the role of a designated agent as a substitute decision maker if the patient loses decisional capacity. The physician or other qualified health care professional answers the patient's and family member/surrogate's questions. The patient may complete and sign the form at the visit or may take it home.

Clinical Example (99498)

A 68-year-old male with heart failure and diabetes on multiple medications, who was recently discharged from the intensive care unit, is seen with his wife to discuss advance care planning.

Description of Procedure (99498)

The work of this service is an extension of the work of 99497. This service is performed when the time required to perform 99497 is greater than 45 minutes. There is additional discussion of the patient's condition and prognosis due to the presence of a new, unexpected, or sudden illness; complicated family dynamics; or disagreement or controversy over advance directives or shared decision making for an adult not competent to make his own decisions. Extra time is needed to explain and discuss the advance care–direction options and to resolve any personal or family issues.

Anesthesia

The changes in the Anesthesia section involve the deletion of codes that describe services that have low utilization, which have been identified by the CPT Code Set Review process.

Anesthesia

Thorax (Chest Wall and Shoulder Girdle)

00450   Anesthesia for procedures on clavicle and scapula; not otherwise specified

►(00452 has been deleted)◄

00454   biopsy of clavicle

🖎 Rationale

As part of an effort to ensure that the CPT code set reflects current clinical practice, code 00452 has been deleted due to low utilization.

Spine and Spinal Cord

00620   Anesthesia for procedures on thoracic spine and cord, not otherwise specified

►(00622 has been deleted)◄

00630   Anesthesia for procedures in lumbar region; not otherwise specified

00632   lumbar sympathectomy

►(00634 has been deleted)◄

🖎 Rationale

As part of an effort to ensure that the CPT code set reflects current clinical practice, codes 00622 and 00634 have been deleted due to low utilization.

Surgery

In the Surgery section, several codes have been added, revised, and deleted.

In the Musculoskeletal System section, codes were added and revised for arthrocentesis procedures and ablation therapy procedures. New codes were also added for open treatment of rib fractures and new guidelines and codes were added for percutaneous vertebroplasty and vertebral augmentation procedures.

A large number of changes have been made in the Cardiovascular System section. This includes but is not limited to changes to guidelines and addition and revision of codes for pacemaker and implantable defibrillator services, a new subsection for reporting extracorporeal membrane oxygenation or extracorporeal life support services, and revised guidelines and codes for endovascular revascularization services.

Extensive changes to the Digestive System section involve the lower endoscopy codes, including new guidelines and codes for stomal endoscopy procedures and in the renamed Colon and Rectum subsection. Changes have also been made to reconcile similar language across the upper and lower endoscopy guidelines, parenthetical notes, and codes for consistency.

Changes in the Nervous System section include new injection codes for myelography and for transversus abdominis plane block.

Surgery Guidelines

CPT Surgical Package Definition

►By their very nature, the services to any patient are variable. The CPT codes that represent a readily identifiable surgical procedure thereby include, on a procedure-by-procedure basis, a variety of services. In defining the specific services "included" in a given CPT surgical code, the following services related to the surgery when furnished by the physician or other qualified health care professional who performs the surgery are included in addition to the operation per se:

- Evaluation and Management (E/M) service(s) subsequent to the decision for surgery on the day before and/or day of surgery (including history and physical)

- Local infiltration, metacarpal/metatarsal/digital block or topical anesthesia

- Immediate postoperative care, including dictating operative notes, talking with the family and other physicians or other qualified health care professionals

- Writing orders

- Evaluating the patient in the postanesthesia recovery area

- Typical postoperative follow-up care◄

🖉ᴅ Rationale

The CPT Surgical Package Definition subsection included in the Surgery guidelines has been revised to address the inclusive Evaluation and Management (E/M) service to reflect changes in current practice patterns. Specifically, the CPT Surgical Package Definition was revised to include clarification as to who can perform these services and identify what other services are included, in addition to the operation.

Surgery

Destruction

MOHS MICROGRAPHIC SURGERY

Mohs micrographic surgery is a technique for the removal of complex or ill-defined skin cancer with histologic examination of 100% of the surgical margins. It requires the integration of an individual functioning in two separate and distinct capacities: surgeon and pathologist. If either of these responsibilities is delegated to another physician or other qualified health care professional who reports the services separately, these codes should not be reported. The Mohs surgeon removes the tumor tissue and maps and divides the tumor specimen into pieces, and each piece is embedded into an individual tissue block for histopathologic examination. Thus a tissue block in Mohs surgery is defined as an individual tissue piece embedded in a mounting medium for sectioning.

If repair is performed, use separate repair, flap, or graft codes. If a biopsy of a suspected skin cancer is performed on the same day as Mohs surgery because there was no prior pathology confirmation of a diagnosis, then report diagnostic skin biopsy (11100, 11101) and frozen section pathology (88331) with modifier 59 to distinguish from the subsequent definitive surgical procedure of Mohs surgery.

▶(If additional special pathology procedures, stains or immunostains are required, see 88311-88314, 88342)◀

🖉 Rationale

A cross-reference parenthetical note has been added following the Mohs Micrographic Surgery guidelines to instruct users that for any additional special pathology procedures, stains, or immunostains required, refer to codes 88311-88314 and 88342.

Musculoskeletal System

General

EXCISION

20220 Biopsy, bone, trocar, or needle; superficial (eg, ilium, sternum, spinous process, ribs)

20225 deep (eg, vertebral body, femur)

▶(Do not report 20225 in conjunction with 22510, 22511, 22512, 22513, 22514, 22515, 0200T, 0201T, when performed at the same level)◀

(For bone marrow biopsy, use 38221)

(For radiologic supervision and interpretation, see 77002, 77012, 77021)

⊘=Modifier 51 Exempt ⊙=Moderate Sedation ✚=Add-on Code ⊮=FDA approval pending

Rationale

An exclusionary parenthetical note has been added following code 20225 to restrict the use of this code in conjunction with codes 22510, 22511-22515, 0200T, and 0201T when performed at the same level.

INTRODUCTION OR REMOVAL

▲20600   Arthrocentesis, aspiration and/or injection, small joint or bursa (eg, fingers, toes); without ultrasound guidance

●20604   with ultrasound guidance, with permanent recording and reporting

        ►(Do not report 20600, 20604 in conjunction with 76942)◄

        ►(If fluoroscopic, CT, or MRI guidance is performed, see 77002, 77012, 77021)◄

▲20605   Arthrocentesis, aspiration and/or injection, intermediate joint or bursa (eg, temporomandibular, acromioclavicular, wrist, elbow or ankle, olecranon bursa); without ultrasound guidance

●20606   with ultrasound guidance, with permanent recording and reporting

        ►(Do not report 20605, 20606 in conjunction with 76942)◄

        ►(If fluoroscopic, CT, or MRI guidance is performed, see 77002, 77012, 77021)◄

▲20610   Arthrocentesis, aspiration and/or injection, major joint or bursa (eg, shoulder, hip, knee, subacromial bursa); without ultrasound guidance

●20611   with ultrasound guidance, with permanent recording and reporting

        ►(Do not report 20610, 20611 in conjunction with 27370, 76942)◄

        ►(If fluoroscopic, CT, or MRI guidance is performed, see 77002, 77012, 77021)◄

Rationale

Ultrasound as an imaging technology in musculoskeletal medicine is often used as an extension of the physical examination for accuracy of intra-articular placement of the needle for safety and better patient outcomes. It is for this reason that three new codes for reporting ultrasound guidance for arthrocentesis procedures (20604, 20606, and 20611) have been added.

To accommodate these new procedures in the CPT code set, existing codes 20600, 20605, and 20610 have been revised as parent codes, and codes 20604, 20606, and 20611 have been added as child codes. Codes 20600, 20605, and 20610 are restricted to those arthrocentesis procedures performed without ultrasound guidance, and codes 20604, 20606, and 20611 require ultrasound guidance to be performed with the arthrocentesis procedure. It is also important to note that codes 20604, 20606, and 20611 require that the ultrasound guidance be recorded and the report included in the patient's permanent record.

Two parenthetical notes have been added following codes 20604, 20606, and 20611. The first parenthetical note following each of these codes restricts reporting code 76942 in conjunction with codes 20604, 20606, and 20611. (Note: The exclusionary parenthetical note that follows code 20611 additionally restricts its use with code 27370. See the Rationale for that code for more information.) The second parenthetical note following each of these codes instructs users to report codes 77002, 77012, or 77021 if fluoroscopic computed tomography (CT) or magnetic resonance imaging (MRI) guidance is performed. For consistency purposes and for accurate reporting, the exclusionary parenthetical note following ultrasound guidance code 76942 has also been updated to restrict the use of new codes 20604, 20606, and 20611. In support of these changes, the instructional note following code 20610 regarding imaging guidance has been deleted.

An additional revision has been made to clarify the intended use of code 20610 to allow differentiation of reporting for arthrocentesis, aspiration, and/or injection of a major joint (such as the knee) versus injection of contrast agent(s) into the knee for the purpose of arthrography (as identified by code 27370). Codes 20610 and 20611 should be reported to identify arthrocentesis procedures for major joints or bursas (eg, shoulder, hip, or knee) when they are performed without the use of ultrasound guidance (20610) and when ultrasound is needed to guide the needle into the correct location in the joint (20611). As is noted in the descriptor for these codes, aspiration and/or injection are both inherently included as part of the service. Therefore, either code may be reported once to identify the procedure performed. These codes are not intended to identify the injection of contrast materials into the knee. Instead, code 27370 is intended to be used specifically for this purpose. To exemplify this intent, the descriptor for code 27370 has been revised, adding the phrase "of contrast" to the descriptor to specify use for contrast agent injection only and exclude use for other injection types or aspiration procedures of the knee. An instructional parenthetical note has also been placed to direct users to the appropriate code to use to identify contrast injection of the knee. The exclusionary parenthetical note that follows the listing of these codes (20610, 20611) reflects the intended use of these codes.

Clinical Example (20604)

A 50-year-old patient presents with inflammation of a small joint (eg, metacarpophalangeal, metatarsophalangeal) and is treated with a steroid injection, utilizing ultrasound guidance.

Description of Procedure (20604)

Ultrasound: Perform a focused ultrasound evaluation. Obtain, label, and interpret images in multiple planes through the specific area of concern, focusing on best approach for injection. Document the normal anatomic structure and any pathologic findings. Utilize imaging to direct the needle to joint or bursa, avoiding bony prominences, blood vessels, or other vulnerable structures. Dictate report for the patient's chart.

Injection: Palpate joint. Infiltrate local anesthetic at the injection site, as indicated. Using ultrasound guidance, insert needle for aspiration and injection into the applicable joint or bursa. Inject the medication slowly but with consistent pressure. Visualize the injected medication and joint distention. Remove the needle.

 **Clinical Example (20606)**

A 50-year-old patient presents with inflammation of an intermediate joint (eg, wrist, ankle) and is treated with a steroid injection, utilizing ultrasound guidance.

Description of Procedure (20606)

Ultrasound: Perform a focused ultrasound evaluation. Obtain, label, and interpret images in multiple planes through the specific area of concern, focusing on best approach for injection. Document the normal anatomic structure and any pathologic findings. Utilize imaging to direct the needle to joint or bursa, avoiding bony prominences, blood vessels, or other vulnerable structures. Dictate report for the patient's chart.

Wrist Injection: Locate the radiocarpal joint just distal to Lister's tubercle. Infiltrate local anesthetic at the injection site, as indicated. Using ultrasound guidance, insert the needle for aspiration and injection into the joint proximal to the scapholunate ligaments and just distal to the radial articular surface. Inject the medication slowly but with consistent pressure. Visualize the injected medication and joint distention. Remove the needle.

Ankle Injection: Palpate the ankle joint. Infiltrate local anesthetic at the injection site, as indicated. Under ultrasound guidance, insert the needle for aspiration and injection into the anterior aspect of the joint, lateral to the common extensor tendon. Inject the medication slowly but with consistent pressure. Visualize the injected medication and joint distention. Remove the needle.

 Clinical Example (20611)

A 50-year-old patient presents with inflammation of a major joint (eg, shoulder, hip, knee) and is treated with a steroid injection, utilizing ultrasound guidance.

Description of Procedure (20611)

Ultrasound: Perform a focused ultrasound evaluation. Obtain, label, and interpret images in multiple planes through the specific area of concern, focusing on best approach for injection. Document the normal anatomic structure and any pathologic findings. Utilize imaging to direct the needle to joint or bursa, avoiding bony prominences, blood vessels, or other vulnerable structures. Dictate report for the patient's chart.

Injection: Palpate the joint. Infiltrate local anesthetic at the injection site, as indicated. Using ultrasound guidance, insert the needle for aspiration and injection into the applicable joint or bursa. Inject the medication slowly but with consistent pressure. Visualize the injected medication and joint distention. Remove the needle.

Shoulder Injection: The glenohumeral joint can be injected from an anterior, posterior, or lateral approach. Infiltrate local anesthetic at the injection site, as indicated. Using ultrasound guidance, insert the needle for aspiration and injection into the applicable joint or bursa. Anterior approach: Place the needle just medial to the head of the humerus and 1 cm lateral to the coracoid process. Direct the needle posteriorly and slightly superiorly and laterally. Posterior approach: Insert the needle 2 cm to 3 cm inferior to the posterolateral corner of the acromion and directed anteriorly in the direction of the coracoid process. Lateral approach: Insert the needle superior and distal to the affected distal subacromial-subdeltoid (SASD) bursal and supraspinatus and directed laterally to medially into the SASD bursal space distally. For all approaches, inject the medication slowly but with consistent pressure. Visualize the injected medication and joint distention. Remove the needle.

Subacromial Injection: Palpate the distal, lateral, and posterior edges of the acromion. Using ultrasound guidance, insert a needle just inferior to the posterolateral edge of the acromion and direct toward the opposite nipple. Inject the medication slowly but with consistent pressure. Visualize the injected medication and joint distention. Remove the needle.

Knee Injection: Using ultrasound guidance, insert a needle into the suprapatellar pouch, from the lateral aspect above the patella and direct medially. Inject the medication slowly but with consistent pressure. Visualize the injected medication and joint distention. Remove the needle.

Trochanteric Bursa Injection: Using ultrasound guidance, insert a needle through the posterolateral approach superior to the greater trochanteric bursa. Inject the medication slowly but with consistent pressure. Visualize the injected medication and joint distention. Remove the needle.

OTHER PROCEDURES

⊙▲**20982**   Ablation therapy for reduction or eradication of 1 or more bone tumors (eg, metastasis) including adjacent soft tissue when involved by tumor extension, percutaneous, including imaging guidance when performed; radiofrequency

⊙●**20983**   cryoablation

▶(Do not report 20982, 20983 in conjunction with 76940, 77002, 77013, 77022)◀

 Rationale

Codes 20982 and 20983 have been revised and added, respectively, to report the ablation of bone tumors using radiofrequency (20982) or cryoablation (20983). As is noted within the code descriptor, the intent of these codes is to include any efforts needed to extend the ablation procedure to the soft tissue areas that may be incorporated within the tumor margins when extension of the ablation borders is needed. The procedure inherently includes image guidance when performed. As a result, an exclusionary parenthetical note has been added following codes 20982 and 20983 to restrict the reporting of these codes in conjunction with ultrasound (76940), fluoroscopic (77002), computed tomography (77013), and magnetic resonance (77022) guidance.

In addition, both codes have been listed with the moderate sedation symbol ⊙ to note that moderate sedation is inherently included as part of the procedure. As a result, moderate sedation services should not be reported separately.

⦸=Modifier 51 Exempt   ⊙=Moderate Sedation   ✚=Add-on Code   ◢=FDA approval pending

Clinical Example (20983)

A 61-year-old male with a history of bronchogenic lung carcinoma has a painful metastasis to the iliac bone. He has had prior radiation, and his pain is unresponsive to medical therapy.

Description of Procedure (20983)

Following discussion of risks and benefits, obtain informed consent. Place the patient in the prone position on the CT gantry table. Perform a time out. Place the patient on physiologic monitors. Administer moderate conscious sedation. Prepare and drape the right hip region in sterile fashion, and give local anesthetic. Move the patient in and out of the gantry ensuring that the anesthesia leads, intravenous (IV) lines, and cryoablation cables are not tethered or potentially snagged. Review CT imaging again to plan needle placement for cryoablation.

Perform preliminary CT scan to ensure appropriate positioning of the patient in the CT gantry. Anesthetize the skin. Use a bone biopsy device to gain access to the intact bone tumor using intermittent CT guidance. Remove the biopsy device, place the 17-gauge cryoablation probe in the tract under CT guidance, and confirm the position with additional targeted CT scan. Insert two other 17-gauge cryoablation probes directly into the lesion using intermittent CT guidance in the same manner. After probe placement is confirmed, initiate the cryoablation procedure with simultaneous activation of the cryoablation probes. After placement of multiple probes, using imaging guidance, the procedure transitions to an active monitoring of the growing ablation zone. During the active ablation, which typically involves cycles of a 10-minute freeze, 5-minute thaw, 10-minute freeze, and then a final approximate 3-minute thaw (minimum total treatment phase 28 minutes) to remove probes, perform repeated CT imaging to assess the zone, vital structures in proximity, and evidence of hemorrhage. Continuously assess the skin for evidence of thermal injury. Remove the cryoablation probes. Evaluate neurologic function to confirm no change in function. Apply sterile occlusive dressings, and perform a final scan to exclude bleeding. Transport the patient to the recovery room for hemodynamic monitoring and pain control.

Head

REPAIR, REVISION, AND/OR RECONSTRUCTION

▶(For cranioplasty, see 21179, 21180 and 62120, 62140-62147)◀

21120   Genioplasty; augmentation (autograft, allograft, prosthetic material)

Rationale

In accordance with the deletion of code 62116, the cross-reference parenthetical note that appears before code 21120 has been revised with the removal of this code.

Neck (Soft Tissues) and Thorax

FRACTURE AND/OR DISLOCATION

▶(21800 has been deleted)◀

▶(To report closed treatment of an uncomplicated rib fracture, use the Evaluation and Management codes)◀

▶(21810 has been deleted. For external rib fixation, use 21899)◀

●**21811** Open treatment of rib fracture(s) with internal fixation, includes thoracoscopic visualization when performed, unilateral; 1-3 ribs

▶(For bilateral procedure, report 21811 with modifier 50)◀

●**21812** 4-6 ribs

▶(For bilateral procedure, report 21812 with modifier 50)◀

●**21813** 7 or more ribs

▶(For bilateral procedure, report 21813 with modifier 50)◀

Rationale

As standard of practice has evolved over the years to the point that strapping of a rib belt is no longer applied, code 21800 has been deleted. A parenthetical note has been added to direct users to refer to the Evaluation and Management services codes to report closed treatment of an uncomplicated rib fracture.

Due to low utilization, code 21810 also has been deleted. A parenthetical note has been added to direct users to report the unlisted procedure, neck or thorax code (21899) for external rib fracture procedures.

Category III codes 0245T-0248T have been converted to three Category I codes (21811-21813) to report internal fixation of rib fracture(s). Each code is distinguished by the number of ribs treated. Code 21811 describes open treatment requiring internal fixation including thoracoscopic visualization, when performed, of 1 to 3 ribs; code 21812 is reported for 4 to 6 ribs; and code 21813 is reported for 7 or more ribs. These codes are considered unilateral procedural codes. For bilateral procedures, report the primary code (21811-21813) with modifier 50 appended.

Clinical Example (21811)

A 72-year-old female presents with multiple displaced fractures of ribs 5, 6, and 7 on the right side after a fall resulting in intractable pain and an inability to maintain adequate oxygenation. On postinjury day three, open reduction and internal fixation of the rib fractures is performed.

Description of Procedure (21811)

Make a small incision over the displaced rib, dividing the skin, subcutaneous tissue, and muscle and exposing the ribs. Deflate the lung with the dual lumen endotracheal tube. Place a thoracoscope through a small separate incision in the pleural cavity, and visualize the area of the fractured ribs. Make additional similar

⊘=Modifier 51 Exempt ⊙=Moderate Sedation ✚=Add-on Code ⊿=FDA approval pending

small skin incisions over the fracture sites as identified by thoracoscopic visualization. Identify and separate the intercostal nerve bundles. Using thoracoscopic visualization, fit the drill guide and plate or splint to the rib overlying the fracture. Drill the screw holes for attachment of the plate or splint insertion in each fracture site of the rib. Secure the splint or plate to the rib with locking screws to fix the hardware in place over the fracture. Repeat this procedure at each rib and/or fracture site. Remove the thoracoscope, inflate the lung, and close the wounds in layers.

Clinical Example (21812)

A 55-year-old male involved in a high-speed motor vehicle crash suffers segmental fractures of ribs 5 through 9 on the left side resulting in severe pain, progressive atelectasis, and enlarging hemothorax. Open reduction and internal fixation of the rib fractures is performed.

Description of Procedure (21812)

Make a small incision over the displaced rib, dividing the skin, subcutaneous tissue, and muscle and exposing the ribs. Deflate the lung with the dual lumen endotracheal tube. Place a thoracoscope through a small separate incision in the pleural cavity, and visualize the area of the fractured ribs. Make additional similar small skin incisions over the fracture sites as identified by thoracoscopic visualization. Identify and separate the intercostal nerve bundles. Using thoracoscopic visualization, fit the drill guide and plate or splint to the rib overlying the fracture. Drill the screw holes for attachment of the plate or splint insertion in each fracture site of the rib. Secure the splint or plate to the rib with locking screws to fix the hardware in place over the fracture. Repeat this procedure at each rib and/or fracture site. Remove the thoracoscope, inflate the lung, and close the wounds in layers.

Clinical Example (21813)

A 24-year-old pedestrian is struck by a car and suffers multiple left-side rib fractures with obvious flail chest. A three-dimensional (3D) CT chest reconstruction confirms comminuted and displaced fractures of ribs 2 through 10, with flail segments of ribs 4 through 8 and significant chest wall collapse. Open reduction and internal fixation of the rib fractures is performed.

Description of Procedure (21813)

Make a small incision over the displaced rib, dividing the skin, subcutaneous tissue, and muscle and exposing the ribs. Deflate the lung with the dual lumen endotracheal tube. Place a thoracoscope through a small separate incision in the pleural cavity, and visualize the area of the fractured ribs. Make additional similar small skin incisions over the fracture sites as identified by thoracoscopic visualization. Identify and separate the intercostal nerve bundles. Using thoracoscopic visualization, fit the drill guide and plate or splint to the rib overlying the fracture. Drill the screw holes for attachment of the plate or splint insertion in each fracture site of the rib. Secure the splint or plate to the rib with locking screws to fix the hardware in place over the fracture. Repeat this procedure at each rib and/or fracture site. Remove the thoracoscope, inflate the lung, and close the wounds in layers.

Spine (Vertebral Column)

FRACTURE AND/OR DISLOCATION

22310   Closed treatment of vertebral body fracture(s), without manipulation, requiring and including casting or bracing

▶(Do not report 22310 in conjunction with 22510, 22511, 22512, 22513, 22514, 22515, when performed at the same level)◀

22315   Closed treatment of vertebral fracture(s) and/or dislocation(s) requiring casting or bracing, with and including casting and/or bracing by manipulation or traction

▶(Do not report 22315 in conjunction with 22510, 22511, 22512, 22513, 22514, 22515, when performed at the same level)◀

(For spinal subluxation, use 97140)

22325   Open treatment and/or reduction of vertebral fracture(s) and/or dislocation(s), posterior approach, 1 fractured vertebra or dislocated segment; lumbar

▶(Do not report 22325 in conjunction with 22511, 22512, 22514, 22515 when performed at the same level)◀

22326   cervical

▶(Do not report 22326 in conjunction with 22510, 22512, when performed at the same level)◀

22327   thoracic

▶(Do not report 22327 in conjunction with 22510, 22512, 22513, 22515 when performed at the same level)◀

🖎 Rationale

In support of the addition of the new percutaneous vertebroplasty and vertebral augmentation codes 22510-22515, exclusionary parenthetical notes have been added following several vertebral fracture codes restricting their use in addition to the new codes when performed at the same level.

▶PERCUTANEOUS VERTEBROPLASTY AND VERTEBRAL AUGMENTATION◀

▶Codes 22510, 22511, 22512, 22513, 22514, 22515 describe procedures for percutaneous vertebral augmentation that include vertebroplasty of the cervical, thoracic, lumbar, and sacral spine and vertebral augmentation of the thoracic and lumbar spine.

The procedure codes are inclusive of bone biopsy when performed, moderate sedation, and imaging guidance necessary to perform the procedure. Use one primary procedure code and an add-on code for additional levels. When treating the sacrum, sacral procedures are reported only once per encounter.◀

⊙●**22510**   Percutaneous vertebroplasty (bone biopsy included when performed), 1 vertebral body, unilateral or bilateral injection, inclusive of all imaging guidance; cervicothoracic

⊘=Modifier 51 Exempt   ⊙=Moderate Sedation   ✚=Add-on Code   𝑁=FDA approval pending

⊙●**22511**   lumbosacral

(For sacral augmentation, see 0200T, 0201T. For facet joint arthroplasty, use 0202T. For cervical augmentation, use 22899)

⊙+●**22512**   each additional cervicothoracic or lumbosacral vertebral body (List separately in addition to code for primary procedure)

▶(Use 22512 in conjunction with 22510, 22511)◀

▶(Do not report 22510, 22511, 22512 in conjunction with 20225, 22310, 22315, 22325, 22327, when performed at the same level as 22510, 22511, 22512)◀

⊙●**22513**   Percutaneous vertebral augmentation, including cavity creation (fracture reduction and bone biopsy included when performed) using mechanical device (eg, kyphoplasty), 1 vertebral body, unilateral or bilateral cannulation, inclusive of all imaging guidance; thoracic

⊙●**22514**   lumbar

⊙+●**22515**   each additional thoracic or lumbar vertebral body (List separately in addition to code for primary procedure)

▶(Use 22515 in conjunction with 22513, 22514)◀

▶(Do not report 22513, 22514, 22515 in conjunction with 20225, 22310, 22315, 22325, 22327, when performed at the same level as 22513, 22514, 22515)◀

Rationale

The American Medical Association/Specialty Society Relative Value Scale (RVS) Update Committee (RUC) identified codes 22520, 22521, 22522, 22523, 22524, 22525, and 72291 as being reported together 75% of the time or more. As a result, these codes have been deleted in order to add six new codes (22510-22515) to comprehensively describe services for vertebral vertebroplasty and augmentation and imaging. Parenthetical notes have been added to direct users to the new codes.

Guidelines have been added to instruct users on the use of these codes and to describe the included services of imaging, moderate sedation, and bone biopsy, when performed. The codes are listed in a new subsection under the heading, "Percutaneous Vertebroplasty and Vertebral Augmentation." Vertebroplasty procedures for the cervical, thoracic, lumbar, and sacral spine may be reported with new codes 22510-22512. As stated in the guidelines, one primary code should be reported along with add-on codes to describe additional levels, as appropriate. In addition, guidelines instruct that when treating the sacrum, the sacral procedures should be reported only once per encounter.

Percutaneous vertebral augmentation procedures may be reported with new codes 22513-22515. These codes are for the thoracic and lumbar areas only. Percutaneous augmentation of the sacral region should be reported with Category III codes 0200T and 0201T, as appropriate.

Clinical Example (22510)

A 73-year-old female develops sudden, severe midback pain after loading groceries into her car. A thoracic spine MRI shows an acute compression fracture involving

T9, and conservative medical management fails to relieve her pain. She is referred for thoracic vertebroplasty.

Description of Procedure (22510)

Place the patient in the prone position on the multiplanar fluoroscopy table. Prop and bolster the patient appropriately for comfort and positioning for the procedure. Perform a time out. Place the patient on physiologic monitors. Administer moderate conscious sedation. Perform preliminary fluoroscopy to localize the target vertebral body, which is marked. Prepare and drape the patient in the usual sterile fashion.

Infiltrate local anesthetic at the incision site and into the subcutaneous tissues and periosteum. Use a scalpel to incise the skin and subcutaneous tissue. Advance a bone biopsy trocar under multiplanar fluoroscopic imaging in a posterior-oblique approach, medial to the pleura, toward the base of the targeted pedicle, penetrating periosteum and targeting the ventral third of the vertebral body in the midline. Use additional imaging (CT, CT fluoroscopy, rotational fluoroscopic acquisition) to confirm trocar placement within the vertebral body in the desired position (imaging not separately reportable) as necessary. Mix bone cement with radio-opaque additives (eg, powdered barium or tungsten). Once the bone cement has cured to the desired consistency, incrementally inject the cement into the vertebral body in 1-ml aliquots under real-time multiplanar fluoroscopic imaging, making sure the cement does not migrate into the basilo-vertebral veins or into the ventral spinal canal. Inject the cement until the ventral two-thirds to three-quarters of the vertebral body has been opacified by cement. Remove the trocar. Obtain fluoroscopic spot images to assess adequacy of vertebral body cement filling and to verify that no venous migration of cement is observed. If only unilateral vertebral body filling with cement is demonstrated, repeat the procedure from the contralateral side with a bi-pedicular approach. Close the wound, and apply sterile dressings.

 ### Clinical Example (22511)

A 75-year-old female develops sudden, severe low back pain after bending over to retrieve a laundry item. A thoracic spine MRI shows an acute compression fracture involving L2. Despite a period of conservative medical management, the pain persists. Percutaneous lumbar vertebroplasty is performed.

Description of Procedure (22511)

Place the patient in the prone position on the multiplanar fluoroscopy table. Prop and bolster the patient appropriately for comfort and positioning for the procedure. Perform a time out. Place the patient on physiologic monitors. Administer moderate conscious sedation. Perform preliminary fluoroscopy to localize the target vertebral body, which is marked. Prepare and drape the patient in the usual sterile fashion.

Infiltrate local anesthetic at the incision site and into the subcutaneous tissues and periosteum. Use a scalpel to incise the skin and subcutaneous tissue. Advance a bone biopsy trocar under multiplanar fluoroscopic imaging in a posterior-oblique approach, medial to the pleura, toward the base of the targeted pedicle, penetrating periosteum and targeting the ventral third of the vertebral body in the midline. Use additional imaging (CT, CT fluoroscopy, rotational fluoroscopic acquisition) to confirm trocar placement within the vertebral body in the desired position (imaging not separately reportable), as necessary. Mix bone cement with radio-opaque additives (eg, powdered barium or tungsten). Once the bone cement has cured to the desired consistency, incrementally inject the cement into the vertebral body in 1-ml aliquots under real-time multiplanar fluoroscopic imaging, making sure that cement does not migrate into the basilo-vertebral veins or into the ventral spinal canal. Inject cement until the ventral two-thirds to three-quarters of the vertebral body has been opacified by cement. Remove the trocar. Obtain fluoroscopic spot images to assess adequacy of vertebral body cement filling and to verify that no venous migration of cement is observed. If only unilateral vertebral body filling with cement is demonstrated, repeat the procedure from the contralateral side with a bi-pedicular approach. Close the wound, and apply sterile dressings.

Clinical Example (22512)

A 75-year-old female develops sudden, severe mid- and low-back pain after bending over while working in her garden. A thoracolumbar spine MRI shows acute compression fractures involving T9 and L1. Despite appropriate conservative care, her pain persists. The patient is referred for thoracolumbar vertebroplasty. A percutaneous vertebroplasty (and bone biopsy, if indicated) has already been performed at T9. An additional percutaneous vertebroplasty of L1 is performed.

Description of Procedure (22512)

After completion of injections at the initial level, the work of the additional level vertebroplasty commences. Perform antiseptic skin preparation at the additional target level, and drape the skin.

Infiltrate local anesthetic at the incision site and into the subcutaneous tissues and periosteum. Use a scalpel to incise the skin and subcutaneous tissue. Advance a bone biopsy trocar under multiplanar fluoroscopic imaging in a posterior-oblique approach, medial to the pleura, toward the base of the targeted pedicle, penetrating periosteum and targeting the ventral third of the vertebral body in the midline. Use additional imaging (CT, CT fluoroscopy, rotational fluoroscopic acquisition) to confirm trocar placement within the vertebral body in the desired position (imaging not separately reportable) as necessary. Mix bone cement with radio-opaque additives (eg, powdered barium or tungsten). Once the bone cement has cured to the desired consistency, incrementally inject the cement into the vertebral body in 1-ml aliquots under real-time multiplanar fluoroscopic imaging, making sure the cement does not migrate into the basilo-vertebral veins or into the ventral spinal canal. Inject the cement until the ventral two-thirds to three-quarters of the vertebral body has been opacified by cement. Remove the trocar. Obtain fluoroscopic spot images to assess adequacy of vertebral body cement filling and to verify that no venous migration of cement is observed. If only unilateral vertebral body filling with cement is demonstrated, repeat the procedure from the contralateral side with a bi-pedicular approach. Close the wound, and apply sterile dressings.

Clinical Example (22513)

A 75-year-old female develops sudden, severe mid-back pain after lifting her grand-child. Plain radiographs reveal an acute compression fracture with severe anterior wedging involving T10 and consequent new kyphosis. Pain persists despite a period of conservative care. After referral, percutaneous thoracic vertebral aug-mentation (and bone biopsy, if indicated) is performed.

Description of Procedure (22513)

Place the patient in the prone position on the multiplanar fluoroscopy table. Prop and bolster the patient appropriately for comfort and positioning for the procedure. Perform a time out. Place the patient on physiologic monitors. Administer mod-erate conscious sedation. Perform preliminary fluoroscopy to localize the target vertebral body, which is marked. Prepare and drape the patient in the usual sterile fashion.

Infiltrate local anesthetic at the incision site and into the subcutaneous tissues and periosteum. Use a scalpel to incise the skin and subcutaneous tissue. Advance a bone biopsy trocar under multiplanar fluoroscopic imaging in a posterior-oblique approach via either a transpedicular or extrapedicular approach into the com-pressed vertebral body, medial to the pleura, penetrating periosteum and targeting the ventral third of the vertebral body in the midline. Use additional imaging (CT, CT fluoroscopy, rotational fluoroscopic acquisition) to confirm trocar place-ment within the vertebral body in the desired position (imaging bundled with procedure code) as necessary. Remove the metal cannula, and advance a drill through the needle. Repeat the entire process on the contralateral side. Gradually deploy a mechanical cavity creation fracture reduction device to create a cav-ity (eg, high-pressure balloon monitored by pressure gauge system). Remove the device, leaving behind the formed cavity. Mix bone cement with radio-opaque additives (eg, powdered barium or tungsten). Once the bone cement has cured to the desired consistency, incrementally inject the cement into the vertebral body in 1-ml aliquots under real-time multiplanar fluoroscopic imaging, making sure that cement does not migrate into the basilo-vertebral veins or into the ventral spinal canal. Inject the cement until the cavities are filled with bone cement. Remove the trocar needles. Obtain fluoroscopic spot images to assess adequacy of vertebral body cement filling, alignment, and to verify that no venous migration of cement is observed. Close the wound, and apply sterile dressings.

Clinical Example (22514)

A 75-year-old female presents with severe, persistent low-back pain and progressive spinal deformity secondary to osteoporotic vertebral collapse. Plain radiographs reveal an acute compression fracture of L3. Despite conservative medical manage-ment, pain persists. Percutaneous lumbar vertebral augmentation (and bone biopsy, if indicated) is performed.

Description of Procedure (22514)

Place the patient in the prone position on the multiplanar fluoroscopy table. Prop and bolster the patient appropriately for comfort and positioning for the proce-dure. Perform a time out. Place the patient on physiologic monitors. Administer moderate conscious sedation. Perform preliminary fluoroscopy to localize the target vertebral body, which is marked. Prepare and drape the patient in the usual sterile fashion.

Infiltrate local anesthetic at the incision site and into the subcutaneous tissues and periosteum. Use a scalpel to incise the skin and subcutaneous tissue. Advance a bone biopsy trocar under multiplanar fluoroscopic imaging in a posterior-oblique approach via either a transpedicular or extrapedicular approach into the compressed vertebral body, medial to the pleura, penetrating periosteum and targeting the ventral third of the vertebral body in the midline. Use additional imaging (CT, CT fluoroscopy, rotational fluoroscopic acquisition) to confirm trocar placement within the vertebral body in the desired position (imaging bundled with procedure code) as necessary. Remove the metal cannula, and advance a drill through the needle. Repeat the entire process on the contralateral side. Gradually deploy a mechanical cavity creation fracture reduction device to create a cavity (eg, high-pressure balloon monitored by pressure gauge system). Remove the device, leaving behind the formed cavity. Mix bone cement with radio-opaque additives (eg, powdered barium or tungsten). Once the bone cement has cured to the desired consistency, incrementally inject the cement into the vertebral body in 1-ml aliquots under real-time multiplanar fluoroscopic imaging, making sure the cement does not migrate into the basilo-vertebral veins or into the ventral spinal canal. Inject the cement until the cavities are filled with bone cement. Remove the trocar needles. Obtain fluoroscopic spot images to assess adequacy of vertebral body cement filling, alignment, and to verify that no venous migration of cement is observed. Close the wound, and apply sterile dressings.

Clinical Example (22515)

A 75-year-old female develops sudden, severe mid- and low-back pain after assisting her spouse getting out of bed. A thoracolumbar spine MRI demonstrates an acute compression fracture with severe anterior wedging involving T9, T10, and L1 and consequent new kyphosis. Pain persists despite bed rest and narcotic analgesics. Percutaneous thoracic vertebral augmentation (and bone biopsy, if indicated) is performed at T9. An additional percutaneous vertebral augmentation of T10 is performed.

Description of Procedure (22515)

After completion of injections at the initial level, the work of the additional level vertebral augmentation commences. Perform antiseptic skin preparation at the additional target level, and drape the skin.

Infiltrate local anesthetic at the incision site and into the subcutaneous tissues and periosteum. Use a scalpel to incise the skin and subcutaneous tissue. Advance a bone biopsy trocar under multiplanar fluoroscopic imaging in a posterior-oblique approach via either a transpedicular or extrapedicular approach into the compressed vertebral body, medial to the pleura, penetrating periosteum and targeting the ventral third of the vertebral body in the midline. Use additional imaging (CT, CT fluoroscopy, rotational fluoroscopic acquisition) to confirm trocar placement within the vertebral body in the desired position (imaging bundled with procedure code) as necessary. Remove the metal cannula, and advance a drill through the needle. Repeat the entire process on the contralateral side. Gradually deploy a mechanical cavity creation fracture reduction device to create a cavity (eg, high-pressure balloon monitored by pressure gauge system). Remove the device, leaving behind the formed cavity. Mix bone cement with radio-opaque additives (eg, powdered barium or tungsten). Once the bone cement has cured to the desired consistency, incrementally inject the cement in 1-ml aliquots into the vertebral body under real-time multiplanar fluoroscopic imaging, making sure that cement does not migrate into the basilo-vertebral veins or into the ventral spinal canal. Inject the cement until the cavities are filled with bone cement. Remove the trocar needles. Obtain fluoroscopic spot images to assess adequacy of vertebral body cement filling, alignment, and to verify that no venous migration of cement is observed. Close the wound, and apply sterile dressings.

▶PERCUTANEOUS AUGMENTATION AND ANNULOPLASTY◀

▶(22520, 22521, 22522, 22523, 22524, 22525 have been deleted. To report, see 22510, 22511, 22512, 22513, 22514, 22515)◀

⊙22526   Percutaneous intradiscal electrothermal annuloplasty, unilateral or bilateral including fluoroscopic guidance; single level

⊙+22527   1 or more additional levels (List separately in addition to code for primary procedure)

(Use 22527 in conjunction with 22526)

(Do not report codes 22526, 22527 in conjunction with 77002, 77003)

(For percutaneous intradiscal annuloplasty using method other than electrothermal, use 22899)

✐ **Rationale**

In correlation with the new percutaneous vertebroplasty and augmentation procedures, which are now listed in a new subsection, the heading of the previous subsection has been revised from "Vertebral Body, Embolization or Injection" to "Percutaneous Augmentation and Annuloplasty." The revised heading better reflects the procedures described by codes 22526 and 22527, which are encompassed under this heading.

Codes 22520, 22521, 22522, 22523, 22524, and 22525 have been deleted. A deletion parenthetical note directing users to new codes 22510, 22511, 22512, 22513, 22514, and 22515 has been added.

SPINAL INSTRUMENTATION

▲22856   Total disc arthroplasty (artificial disc), anterior approach, including discectomy with end plate preparation (includes osteophytectomy for nerve root or spinal cord decompression and microdissection); single interspace, cervical

▶(Do not report 22856 in conjunction with 22554, 22845, 22851, 63075, 0375T, when performed at the same level)◀

⊘=Modifier 51 Exempt   ⊙=Moderate Sedation   ✚=Add-on Code   ⚠=FDA approval pending

(Do not report 22856 in conjunction with 69990)

▶(For additional interspace cervical total disc arthroplasty, see 22858, 0375T)◀

#✛●22858   second level, cervical (List separately in addition to code for primary procedure)

▶(Use 22858 in conjunction with 22856)◀

▶(Do not report 22858 in conjunction with 0375T, when performed at the same level)◀

22857   Total disc arthroplasty (artificial disc), anterior approach, including discectomy to prepare interspace (other than for decompression), single interspace, lumbar

(Do not report 22857 in conjunction with 22558, 22845, 22851, 49010 when performed at the same level)

(For additional interspace, use Category III code 0163T)

Rationale

Category I code 22858 has been established to report the performance of total disc cervical arthroplasty at a second level. In correlation with this change, Category III code 0092T has been revised and renumbered to 0375T for reporting total disc cervical arthroplasty, specifically for three or more levels.

Total disc arthroplasty codes were added to the CPT 2006 code set as Category III codes. In the CPT 2009 code set, three of the Category III cervical disc arthroplasty, revision, and removal codes were converted to Category I status. However, the additional level code for cervical arthroplasty remained a Category III code. With the addition of new code 22858, the additional second level may now be reported as an add-on code in addition to code 22856. Code 22856 was revised with the addition of a semicolon as it is now considered a parent code to new add-on code 22858. A parenthetical note has been added following code 22858 instructing its use with code 22856. An exclusionary parenthetical note has also been added to preclude the use of code 22858 with code 0375T when performed at the same level. This is because the revised and renumbered Category III code is now used for total disc arthroplasty of three or more levels.

Clinical Example (22858)

A 37-year-old female presents with right-sided cervical radicular pain refractory to multimodality conservative therapy. Examination shows findings of nerve root compression with cervical motion, C6 and C7 radiculopathy on neurologic examination along with an MRI scan showing a C5-6 disc with focal right paracentral disc herniation and/or associated osteophyte formation with C6 foraminal and canal compromise and C6-7 para central or right-sided foraminal compression from either herniated disc or disc osteophyte causing compression of the C7 nerve root. After the first level (reported separately), a second level total disc arthroplasty is performed.

Description of Procedure (22858)

Identify the additional vertebral level using fluoroscopy. Dissect the edges of the longus coli muscles, and elevate them from the vertebral bodies. Reposition self-retaining retractors beneath the edge of the longus coli to expose the additional level. Incise the disc space, and remove the disc material with curettes and rongeurs to the posterior longitudinal ligament. Introduce disc space distractor pins into the C6 and C7 vertebral bodies, apply the distractors, and open up the space with end plates parallel to each other. Reposition the operating microscope in the field. Utilize standard microdissection techniques for the remainder of the procedure. Open and resect the posterior ligament. Identify the disc herniation, and remove it from the epidural space decompressing the nerve root. Use a micro-Kerrison punch and/or the high-speed air-powered drill to perform a foraminotomy on both sides to remove uncovertebral osteophytes. Achieve hemostasis; remove the cartilaginous end plate, sparing the bone. Introduce the implant trial into the disc space between the uncinate processes. Using anteroposterior (AP) and lateral plane fluoroscopy, confirm the trial is appropriately sized and located. Introduce a drill guide over the implant trial, create tracts in the inferior and superior end plates, and clean of bone debris. Remove the trial, and insert the final implant into the tracts previously cut and tapped into position. Use fluoroscopy to confirm position in AP and lateral projections; making adjustments as necessary. Achieve hemostasis; remove the retractors.

Pelvis and Hip Joint

FRACTURE AND/OR DISLOCATION

27216   Percutaneous skeletal fixation of posterior pelvic bone fracture and/or dislocation, for fracture patterns that disrupt the pelvic ring, unilateral (includes ipsilateral ilium, sacroiliac joint and/or sacrum)

(To report bilateral procedure, report 27216 with modifier 50)

▶(For percutaneous/minimally invasive arthrodesis of the sacroiliac joint without fracture and/or dislocation, use 27279)◀

27217   Open treatment of anterior pelvic bone fracture and/or dislocation for fracture patterns that disrupt the pelvic ring, unilateral, includes internal fixation, when performed (includes pubic symphysis and/or ipsilateral superior/inferior rami)

(To report bilateral procedure, report 27217 with modifier 50)

27218   Open treatment of posterior pelvic bone fracture and/or dislocation, for fracture patterns that disrupt the pelvic ring, unilateral, includes internal fixation, when performed (includes ipsilateral ilium, sacroiliac joint and/or sacrum)

(To report bilateral procedure, report 27218 with modifier 50)

▶(For percutaneous/minimally invasive arthrodesis of the sacroiliac joint without fracture and/or dislocation, use 27279)◀

✎ Rationale

In correlation with the conversion of Category III code 0334T to Category I code 27279, which describes minimally invasive sacroiliac joint arthrodesis, the parenthetical notes following codes 27216 and 27218 have been revised to include code 27279.

ARTHRODESIS

●**27279**   Arthrodesis, sacroiliac joint, percutaneous or minimally invasive (indirect visualization), with image guidance, includes obtaining bone graft when performed, and placement of transfixing device

►(For bilateral procedure, report 27279 with modifier 50)◄

▲**27280**   Arthrodesis, open, sacroiliac joint, including obtaining bone graft, including instrumentation, when performed

(To report bilateral procedure, report 27280 with modifier 50)

►(For percutaneous/minimally invasive arthrodesis of the sacroiliac joint without fracture and/or dislocation, use 27279)◄

 Rationale

Category III code 0334T has been deleted and replaced with Category I code 27279 to describe minimally invasive sacroiliac joint arthrodesis. The new Category I code descriptor also specifies placement of a transfixing device as part of the procedure performed. A parenthetical note has been added instructing users that bilateral procedures should be reported with modifier 50 appended. In addition to the conversion of code 0334T, code 27280 has also been revised to include the word "open" to distinguish it from code 27279 and to include instrumentation. A cross-reference parenthetical note following code 27280 has been added to provide additional instruction that code 27279 should be reported for percutaneous/minimally invasive arthrodesis of the sacroiliac joint without fracture and/or dislocation.

 Clinical Example (27279)

A 50-year-old female has chronic low-back and posterior, buttock, and thigh pain following a motor vehicle accident. She has been diagnosed with SI joint pain and has not responded to nonsurgical management. Physical examination provocation maneuvers have confirmed that the SI joint is the pain generator. A diagnostic injection has confirmed pain relief. She is scheduled for an SI joint fusion.

Description of Procedure (27279)

Incise the skin with a scalpel. Divide the subcutaneous tissues to the depth of the gluteus fascia with an electro cautery or with blunt dissection. Avoid dissection through the fascia or the fibers of the gluteus. Place a pin through the fascia of the gluteus muscle and dock into the lateral cortex of the ilium. Confirm the appropriate starting point for the pin. Start the pin caudal to the alar line and centered within the middle third of the sacral body (dorsal to ventral) as viewed on the lateral fluoroscopic image. Reposition the image intensifier to the inlet view, and adjust the trajectory of the pin so that the pin is headed toward the center of the S1 sacral body. Reposition the image intensifier to the outlet view, and adjust the pin so its trajectory is in a line parallel to the S1 vertebral endplate. Advance the pin in a medial direction, checking the fluoroscopic images often to confirm appropriate position and trajectory. Perform gentle blunt dissection around the pin, releasing a small amount of the gluteus fascia. Place the soft tissue protector over the pin, and advance it until it is firmly seated onto the lateral cortical wall of the sacrum. Remove the pin sleeve from the soft tissue protector assembly. Place the cannulated drill over the pin, and create a channel by drilling down through the ilium to the SI joint. Collect the bone removed during the drilling process for later grafting.

While leaving the soft tissue protector in place, remove the pin. Working through the soft tissue protector, remove the cartilage on the sacral and iliac sides of the SI joint using angled curettes. Employ direct and indirect visualization to confirm access to and debridement of the joint. After debridement of the joint, replace the pin and use the drill to create a channel into the lateral aspect of the sacral ala. Remove the drill, and collect bone fragments. Place the broach over the pin, and advance it to a point where the teeth of the broach are across the SI joint as visualized on the outlet view. This creates a triangular channel through the ilium and into the sacrum. Remove the broach, and place the 7-mm implant over the pin, and advance it across the ilium, across the SI joint, and into the sacrum. The trailing end of the implant should remain 2 mm to 3 mm proud, thus engaging the lateral cortical wall of the ilium. Confirm the final position of the implant with fluoroscopic imaging, direct and indirect visualization, tactile feedback from the inserter device, and digital palpation of the implant on the lateral surface of the ilium. Repeat identical steps for the placement of the second and third implants. Place subsequent pins and implants in a progressively caudal manner. Keep the pins (and implants) positioned within the osseous confines of the ilium and sacrum.

After the third implant is placed, remove all pins and soft tissue protectors from the surgical incision. Inspect the wound, and control any bleeding. Irrigate the incision, and close the wound in layers. Apply sterile dressing. Roll the patient supine, and reverse the anesthesia.

Clinical Example (27280)

A 32-year-old female has chronic posterior, buttock, and thigh pain following a motor vehicle accident with derangement of the sacroiliac joint. She has been diagnosed with SI joint pain and has not responded to nonsurgical management. Physical examination provocation maneuvers have confirmed that the SI joint is the pain generator. A diagnostic injection has confirmed pain relief. She is scheduled for an SI joint fusion.

Description of Procedure (27280)

Approach the sacroiliac joint anteriorly through an incision over the anterolateral iliac crest. The common insertion of the abdominal obliques joins the origins of the tensor fascia lata and gluteus medius at the lateral edge of the iliac crest. This tendinous structure is divided from anterior superior illiac spine (ASIS) to the gluteus medius pillar, leaving the abductor origin intact on the ilium. The gluteus medius pillar roughly marks the equator of the pelvic ring. Roughly at this landmark, the exposure may be either continued posteriorly along the iliac crest or extended cranially, splitting the fibers of the external oblique muscle. If the latter is performed, release the transversus abdominis and internal obliques from their insertion with electrocautery, working from the inner table of the iliac crest outward. Elevate the iliacus from iliac fossa, taking care to remain subperiosteal.

Significant bleeding is often encountered from the nutrient vessel that enters the ilium just lateral to the pelvic brim and anterior to the sacroiliac joint. Bone wax may help provide hemostasis for bleeding associated with this nutrient foramen. Continue blunt dissection posteriorly to identify the SI joint. To protect the traversing L5 nerve root, medially mobilize the soft tissues anterior to the sacral ala. Use a malleable retractor or Homan retractor to protect the L5 root, and retract it from the operative field. Expose the SI joint from its superior aspect at the top of the sacral ala. Remove the bridging osteophytes as needed to gain access to the joint. The SI joint is not freely mobile, therefore multiple different techniques can be utilized to gain access to the joint. One technique involves placing Schanz pins medial and lateral to the joint to forcefully distract and "open up" the joint. Laminar spreaders can also be used to hinge the joint open and provide access to the chondral surfaces. Once the joint surfaces are exposed, denude them of cartilage and soft tissue down to bare bone. Decorticate the bony surfaces with a burr down to bleeding bone to ensure osseous healing. Expect vigorous bleeding. Once the surfaces are prepared, harvest bone graft from the anterior iliac crest, usually in the region of the gluteus medius pillar. Open up the cortex with a bone cutting osteotome. Use curettes and gouges to harvest spongy cancellous bone. Collect the bone graft, and place it within the sacroiliac joint to promote bony fusion. Reduce and compress the joint. Apply a temporary reduction clamp to hold the surfaces together. Assure arthrodesis by the insertion of stable internal fixation, employing plates, iliosacral screws, or a combination of both. Avoid injury to the superior gluteal neurovascular bundle because the screw entry point is close to the neurovascular bundle as it exits the sciatic notch. Guide wire placement requires careful attention to avoid damage to important muscular and neurovascular structures. Use lateral X-ray projections as necessary to center the guide wire on the sacrum anterior to the spinal canal and to ensure that the guide wire is below the iliac cortical density and sacral alar slope to prevent injury to the L5 nerve root. Images taken in the pelvic outlet projection ensure that the guide wire passes above the S1 sacral foramen. In that view images are required to ensure that the guide wire is at the proper directory and coming to rest in the anterior aspect of the sacral promontory for maximal purchase. This ensures that the fixation screws will reside within the safe corridor in between the valley of the ala anteriorly (L5 nerve root), the sacral canal posteriorly, and the sacral foramen inferiorly (S1 nerve root). Use inlet radiographic views to confirm trajectory of screw path and that the screw does not extrude anterior to sacrum. Once the guide wire is satisfactorily placed, determine the length using the depth gauge. Over-drill the screw passage with a cannulated drill bit, and place a large (6.5 mm to 8.0 mm) cannulated screw over the guide between the ilium and the sacral ala. Place one or more additional screws to control rotation. Ensure that the bony surfaces of the sacrum and the ilium are well coapted and compressed to ensure fusion. Take final radiographic images to ensure coaptation of the bony surfaces and safe placement of the fixation hardware. Copiously irrigate the wound. Place a drain near the operative site. Re-attach the detached muscles to the iliac wing with sutures in multiple layers to promote reattachment of external obliques and prevent possible dehiscence. Close the superficial wound in layers.

Femur (Thigh Region) and Knee Joint

INTRODUCTION OR REMOVAL

▲**27370**   Injection of contrast for knee arthrography

(For radiological supervision and interpretation, use 73580. Do not report 77002 in conjunction with 73580)

▶(Do not report 27370 in conjunction with 20610, 20611, 29871)◀

▶(For arthrocentesis of the knee or injection other than contrast, see 20610, 20611)◀

▶(For arthroscopic lavage and drainage of the knee, use 29871)◀

 Rationale

The intent of code 27370 is specifically to identify the injection of a contrast agent into the knee. It is not intended to identify any other injection procedure for the knee. To exemplify this intent, the descriptor for code 27370 has been revised, adding the phrase "of contrast" to specify use for contrast agent injection only, and not for any type of injection and/or aspiration of the knee. If another type of injection procedure is performed for the knee, either code 20610 or 20611 should be reported to identify the major joint injection procedure performed. An exclusionary parenthetical note has also been placed following code 27370 to exclude use of this code with aspiration/injection of a major joint or bursa (20610, 20611) or with arthroscopy of the knee (29871). For more information regarding the intended use for codes 20610 and 20611, see the Rationale following those codes. In addition, two cross-references have been added in this section to provide additional instruction on the appropriate reporting of these codes.

Application of Casts and Strapping

BODY AND UPPER EXTREMITY

Casts

29010   Application of Risser jacket, localizer, body; only

29015   including head

▶(29020, 29025 have been deleted)◀

 Rationale

As part of an effort to ensure that the CPT code set reflects current clinical practice, codes 29020 and 29025 for application of turnbuckle jacket have been deleted due to low utilization.

REMOVAL OR REPAIR

29700   Removal or bivalving; gauntlet, boot or body cast

⊘=Modifier 51 Exempt   ⊙=Moderate Sedation   ✚=Add-on Code   ⋀=FDA approval pending

29705   full arm or full leg cast

29710   shoulder or hip spica, Minerva, or Risser jacket, etc.

▶(29715 has been deleted)◀

 Rationale

As part of an effort to ensure that the CPT code set reflects current clinical practice, code 29715 (removal of turnbuckle jacket) has been deleted due to low utilization.

Endoscopy/Arthroscopy

29871   Arthroscopy, knee, surgical; for infection, lavage and drainage

▶(Do not report 29871 in conjunction with 27370)◀

(For implantation of osteochondral graft for treatment of articular surface defect, see 27412, 27415, 29866, 29867)

 Rationale

A reciprocal parenthetical note has been added following code 29871. This parenthetical note restricts the use of code 29871 in conjunction with code 27370, which is used to identify the injection of contrast into the knee for arthrography. Additional parenthetical notes have been placed following code 27370. For more information regarding the parenthetical notes that follow this code, refer to the Rationale for code 27370.

Respiratory System

Larynx

ENDOSCOPY

31575   Laryngoscopy, flexible fiberoptic; diagnostic

▶(Do not report 31575 in conjunction with 43197, 43198)◀

 Rationale

A reciprocal exclusionary parenthetical note has been added instructing users not to report flexible fiberoptic laryngoscopy code 31575 in conjunction with flexible transnasal esophagoscopy codes 43197 and 43198. This parenthetical note complements the exclusionary note following codes 43197 and 43198, which includes code 31575.

Lungs and Pleura

INCISION

32100   Thoracotomy; with exploration

▶(Do not report 32100 in conjunction with 19260, 19271, 19272, 32503, 32504, 33955, 33956, 33957, 33963, 33964)◀

✐ Rationale

In support of the establishment of codes 33946-33989 for the reporting of extracorporeal membrane oxygenation (ECMO) and extracorporeal life support (ECLS) services, the exclusionary parenthetical note following code 32100 has been revised to include some of these services.

Cardiovascular System

Heart and Pericardium

▶PACEMAKER OR IMPLANTABLE DEFIBRILLATOR◀

A pacemaker system includes a pulse generator containing electronics, a battery, and one or more electrodes (leads). Pulse generators are placed in a subcutaneous "pocket" created in either a subclavicular site or underneath the abdominal muscles just below the ribcage. Electrodes may be inserted through a vein (transvenous) or they may be placed on the surface of the heart (epicardial). The epicardial location of electrodes requires a thoracotomy for electrode insertion.

A single chamber pacemaker system includes a pulse generator and one electrode inserted in either the atrium or ventricle. A dual chamber pacemaker system includes a pulse generator and one electrode inserted in the right atrium and one electrode inserted in the right ventricle. In certain circumstances, an additional electrode may be required to achieve pacing of the left ventricle (bi-ventricular pacing). In this event, transvenous (cardiac vein) placement of the electrode should be separately reported using code 33224 or 33225. Epicardial placement of the electrode should be separately reported using 33202-33203.

▶Like a pacemaker system, an implantable defibrillator system includes a pulse generator and electrodes. Two general categories of implantable defibrillators exist: transvenous implantable pacing cardioverter-defibrillator (ICD) and subcutaneous implantable defibrillator (S-ICD). Implantable pacing cardioverter-defibrillator devices use a combination of antitachycardia pacing, low-energy cardioversion or defibrillating shocks to treat ventricular tachycardia or ventricular fibrillation. The subcutaneous implantable defibrillator uses a single subcutaneous electrode to treat ventricular tachyarrhythmias. Subcutaneous implantable defibrillators differ from transvenous implantable pacing cardioverter-defibrillators in that subcutaneous defibrillators do not provide antitachycardia pacing or chronic pacing.

Implantable defibrillator pulse generators may be implanted in a subcutaneous infraclavicular, axillary, or abdominal pocket. Removal of an implantable defibrillator pulse generator requires opening of the existing subcutaneous pocket and disconnection of the pulse generator from its electrode(s).

A thoracotomy (or laparotomy in the case of abdominally placed pulse generators) is not required to remove the pulse generator.

The electrodes (leads) of an implantable defibrillator system may be positioned within the atrial and/or ventricular chambers of the heart via the venous system (transvenously), or placed on the surface of the heart (epicardial), or positioned under the skin overlying the heart (subcutaneous). Electrode positioning on the epicardial surface of the heart requires a thoracotomy or thoracoscopic placement of the leads. Epicardial placement of electrode(s) may be separately reported using 33202, 33203. The electrode (lead) of a subcutaneous implantable defibrillator system is tunneled under the skin to the left parasternal margin. Subcutaneous placement of electrode may be reported using 33270 or 33271. In certain circumstances, an additional electrode may be required to achieve pacing of the left ventricle (bi-ventricular pacing). In this event, transvenous (cardiac vein) placement of the electrode may be separately reported using 33224 or 33225.

Removal of a transvenous electrode(s) may first be attempted by transvenous extraction (33234, 33235, or 33244). However, if transvenous extraction is unsuccessful, a thoracotomy may be required to remove the electrodes (33238 or 33243). Use 33212, 33213, 33221, 33230, 33231, 33240 as appropriate, in addition to the thoracotomy or endoscopic epicardial lead placement codes (33202 or 33203) to report the insertion of the generator if done by the same physician during the same session. Removal of a subcutaneous implantable defibrillator electrode may be separately reported using 33272.

When the "battery" of a pacemaker or implantable defibrillator is changed, it is actually the pulse generator that is changed. Removal of only the pacemaker or implantable defibrillator pulse generator is reported with 33233 or 33241. If only a pulse generator is inserted or replaced without any right atrial and/or right ventricular lead(s) inserted or replaced, report the appropriate code for only pulse generator insertion or replacement based on the number of final existing lead(s) (33227, 33228, 33229 and 33262, 33263, 33264). Do not report removal of a pulse generator (33233 or 33241) separately for this service. Insertion of a new pulse generator, when existing lead(s) are already in place and when no prior pulse generator is removed, is reported with 33212, 33213, 33221, 33230, 33231, 33240. When a pulse generator insertion involves the insertion or replacement of one or more right atrial and/or right ventricular lead(s) or subcutaneous lead(s), use system codes 33206, 33207, 33208 for pacemaker, 33249 for implantable pacing cardioverter-defibrillator, or 33270 for subcutaneous implantable defibrillator. When reporting the system insertion or replacement codes, removal of a pulse generator (33233 or 33241) may be reported separately, when performed. In addition, extraction of leads 33234, 33235 or 33244 for transvenous or 33272 for subcutaneous may be reported separately, when performed. An exception involves a pacemaker upgrade from single to dual system that includes removal of pulse generator, replacement of new pulse generator, and insertion of new lead, reported with 33214.

Revision of a skin pocket is included in 33206-33249, 33262, 33263, 33264, 33270, 33271, 33272, 33273. When revision of a skin pocket involves incision and drainage of a hematoma or complex wound infection, see 10140, 10180, 11042, 11043, 11044, 11045, 11046, 11047, as appropriate.

Relocation of a skin pocket for a pacemaker (33222) or implantable defibrillator (33223) is necessary for various clinical situations such as infection or erosion. Relocation of an existing pulse generator may be performed as a stand-alone procedure or at the time of a pulse generator or electrode insertion, replacement, or repositioning. When skin pocket relocation is performed as part of an explant of an existing generator followed by replacement with a new generator, the pocket relocation is reported separately. Skin pocket relocation includes all work associated with the initial pocket (eg, opening the pocket, incision and drainage of hematoma or abscess if performed, and any closure performed), in addition to the creation of a new pocket for the new generator to be placed.

Repositioning of a pacemaker electrode, implantable defibrillator electrode(s), or a left ventricular pacing electrode is reported using 33215, 33226, or 33273, as appropriate.

Pacemaker and implantable defibrillator device evaluation codes 93261, 93260, 93279-93299 may not be reported in conjunction with pulse generator and lead insertion or revision codes 33206-33249, 33262, 33263, 33264, 33270, 33271, 33272, 33273. Defibrillator threshold testing (DFT) during transvenous implantable defibrillator insertion or replacement may be separately reported using 93640, 93641. DFT testing during subcutaneous implantable defibrillator system insertion is not separately reportable. DFT testing for transvenous or subcutaneous implantable defibrillator in follow-up or at the time of replacement may be separately reported using 93642 or 93644.

Radiological supervision and interpretation related to the pacemaker or implantable defibrillator procedure is included in 33206-33249, 33262, 33263, 33264, 33270, 33271, 33272, 33273. To report fluoroscopic guidance for diagnostic lead evaluation without lead insertion, replacement, or revision procedures, use 76000.

The following definitions apply to 33206-33249, 33262, 33263, 33264, 33270, 33271, 33272, 33273.

Single lead: a pacemaker or implantable defibrillator with pacing and sensing function in only one chamber of the heart or a subcutaneous electrode.

Dual lead: a pacemaker or implantable defibrillator with pacing and sensing function in only two chambers of the heart.

Multiple lead: a pacemaker or implantable defibrillator with pacing and sensing function in three or more chambers of the heart.◀

▶Procedure	System	
	Pacemaker	Implantable Defibrillator
Insert transvenous single lead only without pulse generator	33216	33216
Insert transvenous dual leads without pulse generator	33217	33217
Insert transvenous multiple leads without pulse generator	33217 + 33224	33217 + 33224
Insert subcutaneous defibrillator electrode only without pulse generator	N/A	33271
Initial pulse generator insertion only with existing single lead, includes transvenous or subcutaneous defibrillator lead	33212	33240
Initial pulse generator insertion only with existing dual leads	33213	33230
Initial pulse generator insertion only with existing multiple leads	33221	33231
Initial pulse generator insertion or replacement plus insertion of transvenous single lead	33206 (atrial) or 33207 (ventricular)	33249
Initial pulse generator insertion or replacement plus insertion of transvenous dual leads	33208	33249

⊘=Modifier 51 Exempt ⊙=Moderate Sedation ✚=Add-on Code ⨍=FDA approval pending

▶Procedure	System	
	Pacemaker	**Implantable Defibrillator**
Initial pulse generator insertion or replacement plus insertion of transvenous multiple leads	33208 + 33225	33249 + 33225
Initial pulse generator insertion or replacement plus insertion of subcutaneous defibrillator electrode	N/A	33270
Upgrade single chamber system to dual chamber system	33214 (includes removal of existing pulse generator)	33241 + 33249
Removal pulse generator only (without replacement)	33233	33241
Removal pulse generator with replacement pulse generator only single lead system, includes transvenous or subcutaneous defibrillator lead	33227	33262
Removal pulse generator with replacement pulse generator only dual lead system (transvenous)	33228	33263
Removal pulse generator with replacement pulse generator only multiple lead system (transvenous)	33229	33264
Removal transvenous electrode only single lead system	33234	33244
Removal transvenous electrode only dual lead system	33235	33244
Removal subcutaneous defibrillator lead only	N/A	33272
Removal and replacement of pulse generator and transvenous electrodes	33233 + (33234 or 33235) + (33206, 33207, or 33208) and 33225, when appropriate	33241 + 33244 + 33249 and 33225, when appropriate
Removal and replacement of implantable defibrillator pulse generator and subcutaneous electrode	N/A	33272 + 33241 +33270
Conversion of existing system to bi-ventricular system (addition of LV lead and removal of current pulse generator with insertion of new pulse generator with bi-ventricular pacing capabilities)	33225 + 33228 or 33229	33225 + 33263 or 33264◀

33202   Insertion of epicardial electrode(s); open incision (eg, thoracotomy, median sternotomy, subxiphoid approach)

33203   endoscopic approach (eg, thoracoscopy, pericardioscopy)

(When epicardial lead placement is performed with insertion of the generator, report 33202, 33203 in conjunction with 33212, 33213, 33221, 33230, 33231, 33240)

⊙**33206**   Insertion of new or replacement of permanent pacemaker with transvenous electrode(s); atrial

⊙**33207**   ventricular

⊙**33208**   atrial and ventricular

(Do not report 33206-33208 in conjunction with 33227-33229)

▶(Do not report 33206, 33207, 33208 in conjunction with 33216, 33217)◀

(Codes 33206-33208 include subcutaneous insertion of the pulse generator and transvenous placement of electrode[s])

(For removal and replacement of pacemaker pulse generator and transvenous electrode(s), use 33233 in conjunction with either 33234 or 33235 and 33206-33208)

⊙**33210**   Insertion or replacement of temporary transvenous single chamber cardiac electrode or pacemaker catheter (separate procedure)

⊙**33211**   Insertion or replacement of temporary transvenous dual chamber pacing electrodes (separate procedure)

⊙**33212**   Insertion of pacemaker pulse generator only; with existing single lead

⊙**33213**   with existing dual leads

#⊙**33221**   with existing multiple leads

►(Do not report 33212, 33213, 33221 in conjunction with 33216, 33217)◄

(Do not report 33212, 33213, 33221 in conjunction with 33233 for removal and replacement of the pacemaker pulse generator. Use 33227-33229, as appropriate, when pulse generator replacement is indicated)

(When epicardial lead placement is performed with insertion of generator, report 33202, 33203 in conjunction with 33212, 33213, 33221)

⊙**33214**   Upgrade of implanted pacemaker system, conversion of single chamber system to dual chamber system (includes removal of previously placed pulse generator, testing of existing lead, insertion of new lead, insertion of new pulse generator)

►(Do not report 33214 in conjunction with 33216, 33217, 33227, 33228, 33229)◄

▲**33215**   Repositioning of previously implanted transvenous pacemaker or implantable defibrillator (right atrial or right ventricular) electrode

⊙▲**33216**   Insertion of a single transvenous electrode, permanent pacemaker or implantable defibrillator

►(Do not report 33216 in conjunction with 33206, 33207, 33208, 33212, 33213, 33214, 33221, 33227, 33228, 33229, 33230, 33231, 33240, 33249, 33262, 33263, 33264)◄

⊙▲**33217**   Insertion of 2 transvenous electrodes, permanent pacemaker or implantable defibrillator

►(Do not report 33217 in conjunction with 33206, 33207, 33208, 33212, 33213, 33214, 33221, 33227, 33228, 33229, 33230, 33231, 33240, 33249, 33262, 33263, 33264)◄

(For insertion or replacement of a cardiac venous system lead, see 33224, 33225)

⊙▲**33218**   Repair of single transvenous electrode, permanent pacemaker or implantable defibrillator

►(For repair of single permanent pacemaker or implantable defibrillator electrode with replacement of pulse generator, see 33227, 33228, 33229 or 33262, 33263, 33264 and 33218)◄

⊙▲**33220**   Repair of 2 transvenous electrodes for permanent pacemaker or implantable defibrillator

►(For repair of 2 transvenous electrodes for permanent pacemaker or implantable defibrillator with replacement of pulse generator, use 33220 in conjunction with 33228, 33229, 33263, 33264)◄

⊙**33222**   Relocation of skin pocket for pacemaker

(Do not report 33222 in conjunction with 10140, 10180, 11042, 11043, 11044, 11045, 11046, 11047, 13100, 13101, 13102)

⊙▲**33223**   Relocation of skin pocket for implantable defibrillator

(Do not report 33223 in conjunction with 10140, 10180, 11042, 11043, 11044, 11045, 11046, 11047, 13100, 13101, 13102)

▲**33224**   Insertion of pacing electrode, cardiac venous system, for left ventricular pacing, with attachment to previously placed pacemaker or implantable defibrillator pulse generator (including revision of pocket, removal, insertion, and/or replacement of existing generator)

(When epicardial electrode placement is performed, report 33224 in conjunction with 33202, 33203)

+▲**33225**   Insertion of pacing electrode, cardiac venous system, for left ventricular pacing, at time of insertion of implantable defibrillator or pacemaker pulse generator (eg, for upgrade to dual chamber system) (List separately in addition to code for primary procedure)

(Use 33225 in conjunction with 33206, 33207, 33208, 33212, 33213, 33214, 33216, 33217, 33221, 33223, 33228, 33229, 33230, 33231, 33233, 33234, 33235, 33240, 33249, 33263, 33264)

▶(Use 33225 in conjunction with 33222 only with pacemaker pulse generator pocket relocation and with 33223 only with implantable defibrillator [ICD] pocket relocation)◀

33226   Repositioning of previously implanted cardiac venous system (left ventricular) electrode (including removal, insertion and/or replacement of existing generator)

⊙**33233**   Removal of permanent pacemaker pulse generator only

#⊙**33227**   Removal of permanent pacemaker pulse generator with replacement of pacemaker pulse generator; single lead system

#⊙**33228**   dual lead system

#⊙**33229**   multiple lead system

▶(Do not report 33227, 33228, 33229 in conjunction with 33214, 33216, 33217, 33233)◀

(For removal and replacement of pacemaker pulse generator and transvenous electrode[s], use 33233 in conjunction with either 33234 or 33235 and 33206-33208)

⊙▲**33240**   Insertion of implantable defibrillator pulse generator only; with existing single lead

▶(Do not report 33240 in conjunction with 33271, 93260, 93261)◀

(Use 33240, as appropriate, in addition to the epicardial lead placement codes to report the insertion of the generator when done by the same physician during the same session)

#⊙▲**33230**   with existing dual leads

#⊙▲**33231**   with existing multiple leads

▶(Do not report 33230, 33231, 33240 in conjunction with 33216, 33217)◀

▶(Do not report 33230, 33231, 33240 in conjunction with 33241 for removal and replacement of the implantable defibrillator pulse generator. Use 33262, 33263, 33264, as appropriate, when pulse generator replacement is indicated)◀

(When epicardial lead placement is performed with insertion of generator, report 33202, 33203 in conjunction with 33230, 33231, 33240)

⊙▲**33241** Removal of implantable defibrillator pulse generator only

▶(Do not report 33241 in conjunction with 93260, 93261)◀

▶(Do not report 33241 in conjunction with 33230, 33231, 33240 for removal and replacement of the implantable defibrillator pulse generator. Use 33262, 33263, 33264, as appropriate, when pulse generator replacement is indicated)◀

▶(For removal and replacement of an implantable defibrillator pulse generator and electrode[s], use 33241 in conjunction with either 33243 or 33244 and 33249 for transvenous electrode[s] or 33270 and 33272 for subcutaneous electrode)◀

⊙▲**33262** Removal of implantable defibrillator pulse generator with replacement of implantable defibrillator pulse generator; single lead system

▶(Do not report 33262 in conjunction with 33271, 93260, 93261)◀

⊙▲**33263**   dual lead system

⊙▲**33264**   multiple lead system

▶(Do not report 33262, 33263, 33264 in conjunction with 33216, 33217, 33241)◀

▶(For removal of electrode[s] by thoracotomy in conjunction with pulse generator removal or replacement, use 33243 in conjunction with 33241 or 33262, 33263, 33264)◀

▶(For removal of electrode[s] by transvenous extraction in conjunction with pulse generator removal or replacement, use 33244 in conjunction with 33241 or 33262, 33263, 33264)◀

▶(For repair of implantable defibrillator pulse generator and/or leads, see 33218, 33220)◀

▶(For removal of subcutaneous electrode in conjunction with implantable defibrillator pulse generator removal or replacement, use 33272 in conjunction with 33241 or 33262)◀

▲**33243** Removal of single or dual chamber implantable defibrillator electrode(s); by thoracotomy

⊙▲**33244**   by transvenous extraction

⊙▲**33249** Insertion or replacement of permanent implantable defibrillator system, with transvenous lead(s), single or dual chamber

▶(Do not report 33249 in conjunction with 33216, 33217)◀

▶(For removal and replacement of an implantable defibrillator pulse generator and transvenous electrode[s], use 33241 in conjunction with either 33243 or 33244 and 33249)◀

▶(For insertion of transvenous implantable defibrillator lead(s), without thoracotomy, use 33216 or 33217)◀

●**33270** Insertion or replacement of permanent subcutaneous implantable defibrillator system, with subcutaneous electrode, including defibrillation threshold evaluation, induction of arrhythmia, evaluation of sensing for arrhythmia termination, and programming or reprogramming of sensing or therapeutic parameters, when performed

▶(Do not report 33270 in conjunction with 33271, 93260, 93261, 93644)◀

▶(For removal and replacement of an implantable defibrillator pulse generator and subcutaneous electrode, use 33241 in conjunction with 33270 and 33272)◀

►(For insertion of subcutaneous implantable defibrillator lead[s], use 33271)◄

#●33271   Insertion of subcutaneous implantable defibrillator electrode

►(Do not report 33271 in conjunction with 33240, 33262, 33270, 93260, 93261)◄

►(For insertion or replacement of a cardiac venous system lead, see 33224, 33225)◄

#●33272   Removal of subcutaneous implantable defibrillator electrode

#●33273   Repositioning of previously implanted subcutaneous implantable defibrillator electrode

►(Do not report 33272, 33273 in conjunction with 93260, 93261)◄

Rationale

Category III codes 0319T-0328T related to subcutaneous implantable defibrillator procedures have been deleted and replaced with Category I codes 33270-33273, 93260, 93261, and 93644 to report the subcutaneous implantable defibrillator procedures. The subcutaneous implantable defibrillator system is an entirely subcutaneous system designed to avoid the need for the placement of sensing and therapy electrodes within or on the heart. Code 33270 describes the insertion or replacement of a subcutaneous implantable defibrillator system and includes any necessary defibrillation threshold evaluation, induction of arrhythmia, evaluation of sensing for arrhythmia termination, and programming or reprogramming of sensing or therapeutic parameters. Code 33271 is reported for insertion or placement of the electrode only. Code 33272 describes the removal of a subcutaneous implantable defibrillator electrode. Code 33273 is reported for the repositioning of a previously implanted electrode. In addition, codes 33215-33218, 33220, 33223-33225, 33240, 33241, 33243, 33249, 33262, and a table have been revised to allow the appropriate reporting of subcutaneous implantable defibrillator procedures. Guidelines have also been revised to address differences between subcutaneous implantable defibrillator (S-ICD) procedures versus a transvenous implantable cardioverter–defibrillator (ICD) procedure. Instructional and cross-reference parenthetical notes have been added throughout this section to provide additional instruction on the appropriate reporting of these codes.

Clinical Example (33270)

A 55-year-old asymptomatic patient presents with chronic ischemic heart disease and prior history of myocardial infarction two years ago. Echocardiography revealed 28% left ventricular ejection fraction (LVEF). Chronic cardiac pacing is not necessary, and patient is referred for subcutaneous implantable defibrillator system.

Description of Procedure (33270)

Perform the procedure under EKG, blood pressure, and pulse oximetry monitoring. Inject local anesthetic into the region (unless the patient is under general anesthesia), and make an incision over the sixth rib between the midaxillary line and the anterior axillary line where an appropriate size pocket is fashioned. The lead has an 8-cm shocking coil, flanked by two sensing electrodes. Guide its insertion by anatomical landmarks. Tunnel the lead medially from the pocket toward the sternum, and position the proximal electrode parallel to and 1 to 2 cm to the left of the sternal midline. Suture and secure the lead. From this point again tunnel the lead in a cephalic direction toward the manubriosternal junction; position and suture the distal sensing electrode. The final lead position is such that the distal electrode is adjacent to the manubriosternal junction and the proximal sensing electrode is positioned adjacent to the xiphoid process. Reposition the electrodes as necessary to ensure adequate sensing and defibrillation threshold. Upon final positioning, connect the lead to an electrically active pulse generator that is placed in the pocket which is then sutured to the underlying muscular tissue. Once the first layer of the pocket is closed, perform defibrillation testing by induction of ventricular fibrillation through the device (if the patient is under conscious sedation, deep sedation is now induced for defibrillation testing). Detect cardiac rhythm by the two sensing electrodes or by either of the sensing electrodes and the pulse generator. The subcutaneous implantable defibrillator system automatically selects an appropriate sense vector for rhythm detection for avoiding double QRS counting and T-wave oversensing. Once signals have been validated as free of noise and double detection, use discrimination feature analysis and rate detection to sort rhythm type and determine the need for therapy. As necessary, program a conditional discrimination zone incorporating a feature extraction technique between rates of 170 and 240 beats per minute to distinguish supraventricular tachycardia from ventricular tachycardia and avoid inappropriate treatment of the former. To avoid the delivery of shocks for nonsustained ventricular tachyarrhythmias, reconfirm ventricular tachyarrhythmia after capacitor charging. Defibrillator threshold testing of the device during implantation is done with the use of 65-J shocks to ensure an energy margin of safety. Close the incision, and dress the wound.

 ### Clinical Example (33271)

A 50-year-old patient developed a mild infection of a subcutaneous electrode. The subcutaneous electrode was removed previously and followed by treatment with antibiotics. The patient presents for insertion of a new subcutaneous electrode with connection to an existing functional subcutaneous pulse generator.

Description of Procedure (33271)

Perform the procedure under EKG, blood pressure, and pulse oximetry monitoring. Inject local anesthetic into the region over the existing device (unless the patient is under general anesthesia), and make an incision over the sixth rib between the midaxillary line and the anterior axillary. Perform subcutaneous dissection of the device (if present) followed by lead implantation. The lead has an 8-cm shocking coil, flanked by two sensing electrodes. Guide its insertion using anatomical landmarks. Tunnel the lead medially from the pocket toward the sternum, and position the proximal electrode parallel to and 1 to 2 cm to the left of the sternal midline, suturing and securing the lead. From this point tunnel the lead in a cephalic direction toward the manubriosternal junction, and position and suture the distal sensing electrode. The final lead position is such that the distal electrode is adjacent to the manubriosternal junction and the proximal sensing electrode is positioned adjacent to the xiphoid process. Reposition the electrodes as necessary to ensure adequate sensing and defibrillation threshold. Upon final positioning, connect the lead to an electrically active pulse generator placed in the pocket,

⊘=Modifier 51 Exempt ⊙=Moderate Sedation ✛=Add-on Code 𝑁=FDA approval pending which is then sutured to the underlying muscular tissue. Once the first layer of the pocket is closed, perform defibrillation testing by induction of ventricular fibrillation through the device. (If the patient is under conscious sedation, induce deep sedation for defibrillation testing at this point.) Detect cardiac rhythm by the two sensing electrodes or by either of the sensing electrodes and the pulse generator. The subcutaneous implantable defibrillator system automatically selects an appropriate sense vector for rhythm detection for avoiding double QRS counting and T-wave oversensing. Once signals have been validated as free of noise and double detection, use discrimination feature analysis and rate detection to sort rhythm type and determine the need for therapy. Program a conditional discrimination zone incorporating a feature extraction technique between rates of 170 and 240 beats per minute to distinguish supraventricular tachycardia from ventricular tachycardia and avoid inappropriate treatment of the former. Reconfirmation of ventricular tachyarrhythmia follows capacitor charging to avoid the delivery of shocks for nonsustained ventricular tachyarrhythmias. Perform defibrillator threshold testing of the device during implantation with the use of 65-J shocks to ensure an energy margin of safety. Close the incision, and dress the wound.

 ### Clinical Example (33272)

A 50-year-old patient with a subcutaneous implantable defibrillator system implanted six months previously develops a mild infection of the subcutaneous electrode site. Electrode removal is performed followed by antibiotic treatment. A new subcutaneous electrode will be placed after the infection has been resolved.

Description of Procedure (33272)

Make an incision over the sixth rib between the mid-axillary line and the anterior axillary line. If an existing generator is present, perform subcutaneous dissection of the pulse generator, and disconnect the lead from the generator. Make two incisions to gain access to the electrode at the xiphoid and another at the distal tip. Expose and cut the suture ties in these areas. Free the lead from adhesion and remove. Close the incisions, and dress the wounds.

Clinical Example (33273)

A subcutaneous implantable defibrillator system was placed yesterday. Interrogation of the device the day after surgery indicates the electrode has migrated and requires repositioning.

Description of Procedure (33273)

Make an incision over the sixth rib between the mid-axillary line and the anterior axillary line over an existing pulse generator. Perform subcutaneous dissection of the pulse generator. Disconnect the lead from the generator. Make two incisions to gain access to the electrode at the xiphoid and another at the distal tip. Expose and cut the suture ties in these areas. Free the lead from adhesions and then inspect, reposition, and reconnect it to ensure adequate sensing and defibrillation threshold. Upon final positioning, connect the electrode to an electrically active pulse generator and threshold dermination. Programming and follow-up is as described in the clinical example for code 33270.

ELECTROPHYSIOLOGIC OPERATIVE PROCEDURES

Incision

+ 33258 Operative tissue ablation and reconstruction of atria, performed at the time of other cardiac procedure(s), extensive (eg, maze procedure), without cardiopulmonary bypass (List separately in addition to code for primary procedure)

▶(Use 33258 in conjunction with 33130, 33250, 33300, 33310, 33320, 33321, 33330, 33401, 33414-33417, 33420, 33470, 33471, 33501-33503, 33510-33516, 33533-33536, 33690, 33735, 33737, 33800-33813, 33840-33852, 33915, 33925, when the procedure is performed without cardiopulmonary bypass)◀

✐ Rationale

In accordance with the deletion of codes 33332 and 33472, the parenthetical note following code 33258 has been revised with the removal of these codes.

HEART (INCLUDING VALVES) AND GREAT VESSELS

▶Patients receiving major cardiac procedures may require simultaneous cardiopulmonary bypass insertion of cannulae into the venous and arterial vasculatures with support of circulation and oxygenation by a heart-lung machine. Most services are described by codes in dyad arrangements to allow distinct reporting of procedures with or without cardiopulmonary bypass. Cardiopulmonary bypass is distinct from support of cardiac output using devices (eg, ventricular assist or intra-aortic balloon). For cardiac assist services, see 33946, 33947, 33948, 33949, 33967-33983, 33990, 33991, 33992, 33993.◀

33300 Repair of cardiac wound; without bypass

33330 Insertion of graft, aorta or great vessels; without shunt, or cardiopulmonary bypass

▶(33332 has been deleted)◀

✐ Rationale

The Heart (Including Valves) and Great Vessels guidelines have been revised to remove reference to the deleted cardiac assist code 33960 and to add new ECMO/ECLS codes 33946-33949.

As part of an effort to ensure that the CPT code set reflects current clinical practice, code 33332 (insertion of graft into the aorta or great vessels with shunt bypass) has been deleted due to low utilization.

CARDIAC VALVES

Aortic Valve

33361 Transcatheter aortic valve replacement (TAVR/TAVI) with prosthetic valve; percutaneous femoral artery approach

---

⊘=Modifier 51 Exempt   ⊙=Moderate Sedation   ✚=Add-on Code   𝒩=FDA approval pending

+ 33367   cardiopulmonary bypass support with percutaneous peripheral arterial and venous cannulation (eg, femoral vessels) (List separately in addition to code for primary procedure)

▶(Use 33367 in conjunction with 33361, 33362, 33363, 33364, 33365, 33366, 33418)◀

(Do not report 33367 in conjunction with 33368, 33369)

+ 33368   cardiopulmonary bypass support with open peripheral arterial and venous cannulation (eg, femoral, iliac, axillary vessels) (List separately in addition to code for primary procedure)

▶(Use 33368 in conjunction with 33361, 33362, 33363, 33364, 33365, 33366, 33418)◀

(Do not report 33368 in conjunction with 33367, 33369)

+ 33369   cardiopulmonary bypass support with central arterial and venous cannulation (eg, aorta, right atrium, pulmonary artery) (List separately in addition to code for primary procedure)

▶(Use 33369 in conjunction with 33361, 33362, 33363, 33364, 33365, 33366, 33418)◀

(Do not report 33369 in conjunction with 33367, 33368)

 Rationale

In support of the establishment of code 33418, the parenthetical notes following codes 33367-33369 have been revised to include code 33418.

Mitral Valve

▶Codes 33418 and 33419 are used to report transcatheter mitral valve repair (TMVR). Code 33419 should only be reported once per session.

Codes 33418 and 33419 include the work, when performed, of percutaneous access, placing the access sheath, transseptal puncture, advancing the repair device delivery system into position, repositioning the device as needed, and deploying the device(s).

Angiography, radiological supervision, and interpretation performed to guide TMVR (eg, guiding device placement and documenting completion of the intervention) are included in these codes.

Diagnostic right and left heart catheterization codes (93451, 93452, 93453, 93456, 93457, 93458, 93459, 93460, 93461, 93530, 93531, 93532, 93533) should **not** be used with 33418, 33419 to report:

1. Contrast injections, angiography, road-mapping, and/or fluoroscopic guidance for the transcatheter mitral valve repair (TMVR),

2. Left ventricular angiography to assess mitral regurgitation for guidance of TMVR, or

3. Right and left heart catheterization for hemodynamic measurements before, during, and after TMVR for guidance of TMVR.

Diagnostic right and left heart catheterization codes (93451, 93452, 93453, 93456, 93457, 93458, 93459, 93460, 93461, 93530, 93531, 93532, 93533) and diagnostic coronary angiography codes (93454, 93455, 93456, 93457, 93458, 93459, 93460, 93461, 93563, 93564) may be reported with 33418, 33419, representing separate and distinct services from TMVR, if:

1. No prior study is available and a full diagnostic study is performed, or

2. A prior study is available, but as documented in the medical record:

    a. There is inadequate visualization of the anatomy and/or pathology, or

    b. The patient's condition with respect to the clinical indication has changed since the prior study, or

    c. There is a clinical change during the procedure that requires new evaluation.

Other cardiac catheterization services may be reported separately when performed for diagnostic purposes not intrinsic to TMVR.

For same session/same day diagnostic cardiac catheterization services, report the appropriate diagnostic cardiac catheterization code(s) appended with modifier 59 indicating separate and distinct procedural service from TMVR.

Diagnostic coronary angiography performed at a separate session from an interventional procedure may be separately reportable.

Percutaneous coronary interventional procedures may be reported separately, when performed.

When transcatheter ventricular support is required in conjunction with TMVR, the appropriate code may be reported with the appropriate ventricular assist device (VAD) procedure code (33990, 33991, 33992, 33993) or balloon pump insertion code (33967, 33970, 33973).

When cardiopulmonary bypass is performed in conjunction with TMVR, 33418, 33419 may be reported with the appropriate add-on code for percutaneous peripheral bypass (33367), open peripheral bypass (33368), or central bypass (33369).◄

●**33418** Transcatheter mitral valve repair, percutaneous approach, including transseptal puncture when performed; initial prosthesis

    ►(Do not report 33418 in conjunction with 93462 unless transapical puncture is performed)◄

+●**33419**   additional prosthesis(es) during same session (List separately in addition to code for primary procedure)

    ►(Use 33419 in conjunction with 33418)◄

    ►(For transcatheter mitral valve percutaneous approach via the coronary sinus, use 0345T)◄

🖉 Rationale

Category III codes 0343T and 0344T have been deleted and replaced with Category I codes 33418 and 33419 to report transcatheter mitral valve repair (TMVR). In addition to the conversion of these codes to Category I status, new guidelines have been added to clarify the intended use of these codes and to provide clarification that these new codes include angiography, radiological supervision, and interpretation services to guide TMVR. Parenthetical notes have also been added to clarify the reporting of these services.

Clinical Example (33418)

A 75-year-old male presents with progressive shortness of breath and New York Heart Association Class III heart failure symptoms. He has established coronary

      ⊘=Modifier 51 Exempt   ⊙=Moderate Sedation   ✚=Add-on Code   𝒩=FDA approval pending

artery disease previously treated with coronary stenting and coronary artery bypass surgery and now has stable angina. He also has chronic atrial fibrillation and obstructive pulmonary disease requiring home oxygen. Echocardiography demonstrates severe functional mitral regurgitation (4+) with a single central jet, annular dilation, papillary muscle dysfunction, moderate pulmonary hypertension, and global hypokinesis of the left ventricle. An evaluation for ischemia shows no need for additional revascularization at this time. Due to multiple comorbities, he is considered high risk for mitral valve surgery.

Description of Procedure (33418)

Obtain bilateral venous access for right heart catheterization and evaluation of pulmonary pressures and transseptal puncture. Perform baseline right heart catheterization to assess intracardiac hemodynamics, including cardiac output, pulmonary arterial pressure, and pulmonary capillary wedge pressure. Advance a wire from the right femoral vein to the superior vena cava for placement of the transseptal sheath and needle. Insert the transseptal sheath and needle over the wire, and confirm entry into the right atrium using echocardiographic guidance. Perform transseptal puncture with echo verification of correct puncture location. (Often this requires several attempts.) Administer anticoagulant to patient, and check the activated clotting time (ACT) level at the appropriate time interval to obtain ACT > 250 seconds. Continue to check ACT every 30 minutes, and readminister anticoagulant during the procedure and check ACT to verify the patient is prophylactically anticoagulated. Place a stiff guide wire through the transseptal sheath into the left atrium and then the pulmonary vein.

Prepare the mitral valve repair device on the back table. Progressively dilate the femoral vein access site with a series of dilators. Advance the guide catheter over the wire into the left atrium, remove the wire, and de-air the guide catheter. Advance the mitral valve repair device and delivery system through the guide to the left atrium. Extreme care is required to prevent disruption of the interatrial septum and to avoid air embolus to the left heart. Position the prosthesis above the mitral valve using echocardiographic and angiographic guidance. Use multiple echocardiographic and angiographic views in a complex series of maneuvers to position the prosthesis at the proper position above the mitral valve, with careful avoidance of other structures. Deploy the device, grasping and coapting the anterior and mitral leaflets at that site, reducing mitral regurgitation. (Multiple grasps are often required.) Use echocardiographic and angiographic imaging to ensure proper device positioning and leaflet insertion into the device and adequate reduction in the mitral regurgitation. If the evaluation is favorable, release the device in a series of steps. After final release, again evaluate the patient by angiographic, hemodynamic, and echocardiographic criteria for suitability of the mitral valve repair and to ensure no complications. If there is no need for an additional device, withdraw the delivery system and remove it from the body.

Constantly monitor the patient's arterial pressure, EKG waveforms, and oxygen saturation throughout the procedure. Repeat right heart catheterization as needed to assess intracardiac hemodynamics, including cardiac output, pulmonary arterial pressure, and pulmonary capillary wedge pressure. Review images to ensure no additional views are required before leaving the procedure suite. Close the groin site, reverse anesthesia, and extubate the patient as appropriate. Treat potential complications, such as hypertension, hypotension, bleeding, and oxygen desaturation, accordingly with medications and/or oxygen as needed during the procedure.

Clinical Example (33419)

A transcatheter mitral valve repair has been performed. Evaluation of mitral regurgitation indicates there was some reduction from 4+ (severe) to 3+ (moderate to severe), and there is still a significant regurgitant jet present even with one prosthesis now securely in place on the leaflets. The interventional cardiologist and the echocardiographer determine that an additional device is needed in order to decrease the mitral regurgitation further.

Description of Procedure (33419)

Use hemodynamic parameters and echocardiographic interrogation to ensure that the first device placement has not narrowed the valve area enough to cause functional mitral stenosis.

Prepare a second device on the back table. Advance the mitral valve repair device and delivery system over the wire to the left atrium. Take extreme care to prevent disruption of the interatrial septum and to avoid air embolus to the left heart. Position the prosthesis above the mitral valve using echocardiographic and angiographic guidance. Use multiple echocardiographic and angiographic views in a complex series of maneuvers to position the prosthesis at the proper position above the mitral valve, with careful avoidance of other structures. Deploy the device, grasping and coapting the anterior and mitral leaflets at that site and reducing mitral regurgitation. (Multiple grasps are often required.) Use echocardiographic and angiographic imaging to ensure proper device positioning and leaflet insertion into the device and adequate reduction in the mitral regurgitation. If the evaluation is favorable, release the device in a series of steps. After final release, evaluate the patient by angiographic, hemodynamic, and echocardiographic criteria for suitability of the mitral valve repair and to ensure no complications. If there is no need for an additional device, withdraw and remove the delivery system.

Constantly monitor the patient's arterial pressure, EKG waveforms, and oxygen saturation throughout the procedure. Repeat right heart catheterization as needed to assess intracardiac hemodynamics, including cardiac output, pulmonary arterial pressure, and pulmonary capillary wedge pressure. Review images to ensure no additional views are required before leaving the procedure suite.

Pulmonary Valve

33470 Valvotomy, pulmonary valve, closed heart; transventricular

(Do not report modifier 63 in conjunction with 33470)

33471 via pulmonary artery

(To report percutaneous valvuloplasty of pulmonary valve, use 92990)

▶(33472 has been deleted)◀

⊘=Modifier 51 Exempt   ⊙=Moderate Sedation   ✚=Add-on Code   ⚕=FDA approval pending

Rationale

As part of an effort to ensure that the CPT code set reflects current clinical practice, code 33472 (an open heart pulmonary valve valvotomy with inflow occlusion) has been deleted due to low utilization.

PULMONARY ARTERY

+ 33924 Ligation and takedown of a systemic-to-pulmonary artery shunt, performed in conjunction with a congenital heart procedure (List separately in addition to code for primary procedure)

▶(Use 33924 in conjunction with 33470-33478, 33600-33617, 33622, 33684-33688, 33692-33697, 33735-33767, 33770-33783, 33786, 33917, 33920, 33922, 33925, 33926, 33935, 33945)◀

Rationale

The inclusionary parenthetical note following code 33924 has been revised with the addition of codes 33476, 33478, 33622, 33782, 33783, 33917, 33925, 33926, 33935, and 99345, and the removal of code 33619.

▶EXTRACORPOREAL MEMBRANE OXYGENATION OR EXTRACORPOREAL LIFE SUPPORT SERVICES◀

▶Prolonged extracorporeal membrane oxygenation (ECMO) or extracorporeal life support (ECLS) is a procedure that provides cardiac and/or respiratory support to the heart and/or lungs, which allows them to rest and recover when sick or injured. ECMO/ECLS supports the function of the heart and/or lungs by continuously pumping some of the patient's blood out of the body to an oxygenator (membrane lung) where oxygen is added to the blood, carbon dioxide (CO_2) is removed, and the blood is warmed before it is returned to the patient. There are two methods that can be used to accomplish ECMO/ECLS. One method is veno-arterial extracorporeal life support, which will support both the heart and lungs. Veno-arterial ECMO/ECLS requires that two cannula(e) are placed—one in a large vein and one in a large artery. The other method is veno-venous extracorporeal life support. Veno-venous ECMO/ECLS is used for lung support only and requires one or two cannula(e), which are placed in a vein.

Services directly related to the cannulation, initiation, management, and discontinuation of the ECMO/ECLS circuit and parameters (33946, 33947, 33948, 33949) are distinct from the daily overall management of the patient. The daily overall management of the patient is a factor that will vary greatly depending on the patient's age, disease process, and condition. Daily overall management of the patient may be separately reported using the relevant hospital observation services, hospital inpatient services, or critical care evaluation and management codes (99218, 99219, 99220, 99221, 99222, 99223, 99231, 99232, 99233, 99234, 99235, 99236, 99291, 99292, 99468, 99469, 99471, 99472, 99475, 99476, 99477, 99478, 99479, 99480).

Services directly related to the ECMO/ECLS involve the initial cannulation and repositioning, removing, or adding cannula(e) while the patient is being supported by the ECMO/ECLS. Initiation of the ECMO/ECLS circuit and setting parameters (33946, 33947) is performed by the physician and involves determining the necessary ECMO/ECLS device components, blood flow, gas exchange, and other necessary parameters to manage the circuit. The daily management of the ECMO/ECLS circuit and monitoring parameters (33948, 33949) requires physician oversight to ensure that specific features of the interaction of the circuit with the patient are met. Daily management of the circuit and parameters includes management of blood flow, oxygenation, CO_2 clearance by the membrane lung, systemic response, anticoagulation and treatment of bleeding, and cannula(e) positioning, alarms and safety. Once the patient's heart and/or lung function has sufficiently recovered, the physician will wean the patient from the ECMO/ECLS circuit and finally decannulate the patient. The basic management of the ECMO/ECLS circuit and parameters are similar, regardless of the patient's condition.

ECMO/ECLS commonly involves multiple physicians and supporting nonphysician personnel to manage each patient. Different physicians may insert the cannula(e) and initiate ECMO/ECLS, manage the ECMO/ECLS circuit, and decannulate the patient. In addition, it would be common for one physician to manage the ECMO/ECLS circuit and patient-related issues (eg, anticoagulation, complications related to the ECMO/ECLS devices), while another physician manages the overall patient medical condition and underlying disorders, all on a daily basis. The physicians involved in the patient's care are commonly of different specialties, and significant physician team interaction may be required. Depending on the type of circuit and the patient's condition, there is substantial nonphysician work by ECMO/ECLS specialists, cardiac perfusionists, respiratory therapists, and specially trained nurses who provide long periods of constant attention.

If the same physician provides any or all of the services for placing a patient on an ECMO/ECLS circuit, they may report the appropriate codes for the services they performed, which may include codes for the cannula(e) insertion (33951, 33952, 33953, 33954, 33955, 33956), ECMO/ECLS initiation (33946 or 33947), and overall patient management (99218, 99219, 99220, 99221, 99222, 99223, 99231, 99232, 99233, 99234, 99235, 99236, 99291, 99292, 99468, 99469, 99471, 99472, 99475, 99476, 99477, 99478, 99479, 99480).

ECMO/ECLS daily management (33948, 33949) and repositioning services (33957, 33958, 33959, 33962, 33963, 33964) may not be reported on the same day as initiation services (33946, 33947) by the same or different individuals.

If different physicians provide parts of the service, each physician may report the correct code(s) for the service(s) they provided, except as noted.

Repositioning of the ECMO/ECLS cannula(e) (33957, 33958, 33959, 33962, 33963, 33964) at the same session as insertion (33951, 33952, 33953, 33954, 33955, 33956) is not separately reportable. Replacement of ECMO/ECLS cannula(e) in the same vessel should only be reported using the insertion code (33951, 33952, 33953, 33954, 33955, 33956). If cannula(e) are removed from one vessel and new cannula(e) are placed in a different vessel, report the appropriate cannula(e) removal (33965, 33966, 33969, 33984, 33985, 33986) and insertion (33951, 33952, 33953, 33954, 33955, 33956) codes. Extensive repair or replacement of an artery may be additionally reported (eg, 35266, 35286, 35371, and 35665). Fluoroscopic guidance used for cannula(e) repositioning (33957, 33958, 33959, 33962, 33963, 33964) is included in the procedure when performed and should not be separately reported.

Daily management codes (33948 and 33949) should not be reported on the same day as initiation of ECMO (33946 or 33947).

Initiation codes (33946 or 33947) should not be reported on the same day as repositioning codes (33957, 33958, 33959, 33962, 33963, 33964).◄

⊘=Modifier 51 Exempt   ⊙=Moderate Sedation   ✚=Add-on Code   ⊮=FDA approval pending

●**33946** Extracorporeal membrane oxygenation (ECMO)/extracorporeal life support (ECLS) provided by physician; initiation, veno-venous

▶(Do not report modifier 63 in conjunction with 33946, 33947, 33948, 33949)◀

▶(For insertion of cannula[e] for extracorporeal circulation, see 33951, 33952, 33953, 33954, 33955, 33956)◀

●**33947** initiation, veno-arterial

▶(Do not report modifier 63 in conjunction with 33946, 33947, 33948, 33949)◀

▶(Do not report 33946, 33947 in conjunction with 33948, 33949, 33957, 33958, 33959, 33962, 33963, 33964)◀

●**33948** daily management, each day, veno-venous

▶(Do not report modifier 63 in conjunction with 33946, 33947, 33948, 33949)◀

●**33949** daily management, each day, veno-arterial

▶(Do not report modifier 63 in conjunction with 33946, 33947, 33948, 33949)◀

▶(Do not report 33948, 33949 in conjunction with 33946, 33947)◀

●**33951** insertion of peripheral (arterial and/or venous) cannula(e), percutaneous, birth through 5 years of age (includes fluoroscopic guidance, when performed)

▶(For initiation and daily management of extracorporeal circulation, see 33946, 33947, 33948, 33949)◀

●**33952** insertion of peripheral (arterial and/or venous) cannula(e), percutaneous, 6 years and older (includes fluoroscopic guidance, when performed)

▶(For maintenance of extracorporeal circulation, see 33946, 33947, 33948, 33949)◀

●**33953** insertion of peripheral (arterial and/or venous) cannula(e), open, birth through 5 years of age

▶(For maintenance of extracorporeal circulation, see 33946, 33947, 33948, 33949)◀

●**33954** insertion of peripheral (arterial and/or venous) cannula(e), open, 6 years and older

▶(Do not report 33953, 33954 in conjunction with 34812, 34820, 34834)◀

▶(For maintenance of extracorporeal circulation, see 33946, 33947, 33948, 33949)◀

●**33955** insertion of central cannula(e) by sternotomy or thoracotomy, birth through 5 years of age

▶(For maintenance of extracorporeal circulation, see 33946, 33947, 33948, 33949)◀

●**33956** insertion of central cannula(e) by sternotomy or thoracotomy, 6 years and older

▶(Do not report 33955, 33956 in conjunction with 32100, 39010)◀

▶(For maintenance of extracorporeal circulation, see 33946, 33947, 33948, 33949)◀

●**33957** reposition peripheral (arterial and/or venous) cannula(e), percutaneous, birth through 5 years of age (includes fluoroscopic guidance, when performed)

●33958   reposition peripheral (arterial and/or venous) cannula(e), percutaneous, 6 years and older (includes fluoroscopic guidance, when performed)

▶(Do not report 33957, 33958 in conjunction with 34812, 34820, 34834)◀

●33959   reposition peripheral (arterial and/or venous) cannula(e), open, birth through 5 years of age (includes fluoroscopic guidance, when performed)

#●33962   reposition peripheral (arterial and/or venous) cannula(e), open, 6 years and older (includes fluoroscopic guidance, when performed)

▶(Do not report 33959, 33962 in conjunction with 34812, 34820, 34834)◀

#●33963   reposition of central cannula(e) by sternotomy or thoracotomy, birth through 5 years of age (includes fluoroscopic guidance, when performed)

#●33964   reposition central cannula(e) by sternotomy or thoracotomy, 6 years and older (includes fluoroscopic guidance, when performed)

▶(Do not report 33963, 33964 in conjunction with 32100, 39010)◀

▶(Do not report 33957, 33958, 33959, 33962, 33963, 33964 in conjunction with 33946, 33947)◀

#●33965   removal of peripheral (arterial and/or venous) cannula(e), percutaneous, birth through 5 years of age

#●33966   removal of peripheral (arterial and/or venous) cannula(e), percutaneous, 6 years and older

#●33969   removal of peripheral (arterial and/or venous) cannula(e), open, birth through 5 years of age

▶(Do not report 33969 in conjunction with 34812, 34820, 34834, 35201, 35206, 35211, 35226)◀

#●33984   removal of peripheral (arterial and/or venous) cannula(e), open, 6 years and older

▶(Do not report 33984 in conjunction with 34812, 34820, 34834, 35201, 35206, 35211, 35226)◀

#●33985   removal of central cannula(e) by sternotomy or thoracotomy, birth through 5 years of age

▶(Do not report 33985 in conjunction with 35211)◀

#●33986   removal of central cannula(e) by sternotomy or thoracotomy, 6 years and older

▶(Do not report 33986 in conjunction with 35211)◀

#+●33987   Arterial exposure with creation of graft conduit (eg, chimney graft) to facilitate arterial perfusion for ECMO/ECLS (List separately in addition to code for primary procedure)

▶(Use 33987 in conjunction with 33953, 33954, 33955, 33956)◀

▶(Do not report 33987 in conjunction with 34833)◀

#●33988   Insertion of left heart vent by thoracic incision (eg, sternotomy, thoracotomy) for ECMO/ECLS

#●33989   Removal of left heart vent by thoracic incision (eg, sternotomy, thoracotomy) for ECMO/ECLS

⊘=Modifier 51 Exempt   ⊙=Moderate Sedation   ✚=Add-on Code   ⩘=FDA approval pending

CARDIAC ASSIST

The insertion of a ventricular assist device (VAD) can be performed via percutaneous (33990, 33991) or transthoracic (33975, 33976, 33979) approach. The location of the ventricular assist device may be intracorporeal or extracorporeal.

Open arterial exposure when necessary to facilitate percutaneous ventricular assist device insertion (33990, 33991), may be reported separately (34812). Extensive repair or replacement of an artery may be additionally reported (eg, 35226 or 35286).

Removal of a ventricular assist device (33977, 33978, 33980, 33992) includes removal of the entire device, including the cannulas. Removal of a percutaneous ventricular assist device at the same session as insertion is not separately reportable. For removal of a percutaneous ventricular assist device at a separate and distinct session, but on the same day as insertion, report 33992 appended with modifier 59 indicating a distinct procedural service.

Repositioning of a percutaneous ventricular assist device at the same session as insertion is not separately reportable. Repositioning of percutaneous ventricular assist device not necessitating imaging guidance is not a reportable service. For repositioning of a percutaneous ventricular assist device necessitating imaging guidance at a separate and distinct session, but on the same day as insertion, report 33993 with modifier 59 indicating a distinct procedural service.

Replacement of a ventricular assist device pump (ie, 33981-33983) includes the removal of the pump and insertion of a new pump, connection, de-airing, and initiation of the new pump.

Replacement of the entire implantable ventricular assist device system, ie, pump(s) and cannulas, is reported using the insertion codes (ie, 33975, 33976, 33979). Removal (ie, 33977, 33978, 33980) of the ventricular assist device system being replaced is not separately reported. Replacement of a percutaneous ventricular assist device is reported using implantation codes (ie, 33990, 33991). Removal (ie, 33992) is not reported separately.

▶(33960 has been deleted. To report, see 33946, 33947, 33948, 33949)◀

▶(33961 has been deleted. To report, see 33948, 33949)◀

Rationale

The American Medical Association/Specialty Society RUC identified prolonged extracorporeal circulation for cardiopulmonary insufficiency codes 33960 and 33961 as potentially misvalued codes. Codes 33960 and 33961 were originally developed for use in the neonatal population for severe postpartum respiratory insufficiency. However, this treatment has evolved and is now being provided to a variety of adults with severe influenza, pneumonia, and respiratory distress syndrome, as well as to pediatric patients.

As a result, codes 33960, 33961, and 36822 have been deleted, and the Cardiac Assist guidelines have been revised to remove reference to deleted code 36822. A new subsection entitled "Extracorporeal Membrane Oxygenation or Extracorporeal Life Support Services," introductory guidelines, and family of codes 33946-33989 in addition to instructional parenthetical notes have been established to report ECMO and/or ECLS procedures.

ECMO/ECLS is a procedure that provides cardiac and/or respiratory support to the heart and/or lungs, which allows them to rest and recover when sick or injured. ECMO/ECLS supports the function of the heart and/or lungs by continuously pumping some of the patient's blood out of the body to an oxygenator (membrane lung) where oxygen is added to the blood, carbon dioxide is removed, and the blood is warmed before it is returned to the patient. There are two methods that can be used to accomplish ECMO/ECLS. One method is veno-arterial extracorporeal life support, which supports both the heart and the lungs. Venoarterial ECMO/ECLS requires that two cannulae are placed: one in a large vein and one in a large artery. The other method is venovenous extracorporeal life support. Venovenous ECMO/ECLS is used for lung support only and requires one or two cannula(e), which are placed in a vein.

The insertion, repositioning, and removal of the cannula(e) are surgical procedures that can be performed percutaneously, open, or by sternotomy or thoracotomy approach and are done on different days. The initiation of ECMO and the daily management of the ECMO circuit and the ECMO parameters, as well as specific features of the interaction of the circuit with the patient, require intense physician management. Depending on the type of circuit and the patient's condition, there is substantial work and it requires constant attention. Codes 33946-33989 will facilitate proper reporting of physician work and allow the appropriate professionals who are involved in the treatment of these complex patients to report their services.

Codes 33946 and 33947 describe the initial insertion of the cannulation of the ECMO/ECLS circuit and setting of parameters performed by the physician, which involves determining the necessary ECMO/ECLS device components, blood flow, gas exchange, and other necessary parameters to manage the circuit. For insertion of a cannulation for extracorporeal circulation, report codes 33951-33956.

Codes 33948 and 33949 describe the daily management of the ECMO/ECLS circuit and monitoring parameters requiring physician oversight to ensure that specific features of the interaction of the circuit with the patient are met. ECMO therapy is very invasive and requires constant one-on-one monitoring, assessment, and adjustments. It would not be appropriate to append modifier 63 (Procedure Performed on Infants less than 4 kg) to codes 33946-33949. It would also not be appropriate to report the daily management codes 33948 and 33949 on the same day in conjunction with the initiation codes 33946 and 33947.

Codes 33951 and 33952 describe insertion of a peripheral arterial and/or venous cannulation by percutaneous approach, including fluoroscopic guidance, when performed, for neonates and adult patients. For initiation and daily management services, report codes 33946-33949.

Codes 33953 and 33954 describe insertion of a peripheral arterial and/or venous cannulation by open approach for neonate and adult patients. It would not be appropriate to report codes 33953 and 33954 with endovascular codes 34812, 34820, and 34834. For initiation and daily management services, report codes 33946-33949.

Codes 33955 and 33956 describe insertion of a central cannulation by sternotomy or thoracotomy approach for neonates and adult patients. For maintenance of extracorporeal circulation, report codes 33946-33949. It would not be appropriate to report codes 33955 and 33956 with thoracotomy and mediastinotomy codes 32100 and 39010.

Codes 33957 and 33958 describe repositioning of a peripheral arterial and/or venous cannulation by percutaneous approach for neonates and adult patients. It would not be appropriate to report codes 33957 and 33958 with endovascular codes 34812, 34820, and 34834.

Codes 33959 and 33962 describe repositioning of an arterial and/or venous cannulation by open approach including fluoroscopic guidance, when performed, for neonates and adult patients. It would not be appropriate to report codes 33959 and 33962 with endovascular codes 34812, 34820, and 34834.

Codes 33963 and 33964 describe repositioning of a central cannulation by sternotomy or thoracotomy approach for neonates and adult patients. It would not be appropriate to report codes 33963 and 33964 with thoracotomy and mediastinotomy codes 32100 and 39010.

It would also not be appropriate to report codes 33957-33964 on the same day in conjunction with the initiation codes 33946 and 33947.

Codes 33965 and 33966 describe removal of a peripheral arterial and/or venous cannulation by percutaneous approach for neonates and adult patients.

Codes 33969 and 33984 describe removal of peripheral arterial and/or venous cannula(e) by open approach for neonates and adult patients. It would not be appropriate to report codes 33969 and 33984 with codes 34812, 34820, 34834, 35201, 35206, 35211, and 35226.

Codes 33985 and 33986 describe removal of central cannula(e) by sternotomy or thoracotomy approach for neonates and adult patients. It would not be appropriate to report codes 33985 and 33986 with blood vessel repair code 35211.

Add-on code 33987 describes an arterial exposure with creation of a graft conduit to facilitate perfusion for an ECMO/ECLS procedure. Code 33987 can be reported with insertion codes 33953-33956. It would not be appropriate to report code 33987 with endovascular repair code 34833.

Code 33988 describes insertion of a left heart vent by thoracic incision and/or by sternotomy or thoracotomy approach for an ECMO/ECLS procedure.

Code 33989 has been established to describe removal of a left heart vent by thoracic incision and/or by sternotomy or thoracotomy approach for an ECMO/ECLS procedure.

Codes 33962-33989 appear with the hash tag (#) symbol to indicate that these codes are out of numerical sequence and follow code 33959. Parenthetical notes have been added to indicate that codes 33962-33989 are out of numerical sequence.

Clinical Example (33946)

A patient has overwhelming respiratory failure. Venovenous extracorporeal membrane oxygenation support (ECMO/ELSO) is initiated using age and body surface area–appropriate parameters, and the patient is stabilized. (Cannulation, patient management, and daily ECMO/ECLS circuit management are reported separately.)

Description of Procedure (33946)

Physician is present for entire procedure. Monitor cannula placement, initiation of anticoagulation, assessment of venous return to the ECMO circuit, and increase of ECMO flow; assess anticoagulation and necessary adjustments in anticoagulant dose; review images and discuss cannula placement and determination of when optimal flow is achieved with surgeon. Manage initial transition to ECMO support with adjustment of intravascular volume, mechanical ventilation, and vasopressor infusions.

Clinical Example (33947)

A patient has cardiac and respiratory failure. Venoarterial extracorporeal membrane oxygenation support (ECMO/ELSO) is initiated using age and body surface area–appropriate parameters, and the patient is stabilized. (Cannulation, patient management, and daily ECMO/ECLS circuit management are reported separately.)

Description of Procedure (33947)

Physician is present for entire procedure. Make assessment of cardiac and respiratory function to determine suitability of either venoarterial or venovenous bypass and whether the underlying pathophysiology is potentially reversible. Obtain brain and cardiac imaging studies for determining suitability for ECMO. Explain risks and benefits of prolonged ECMO to patient and/or family. Contact blood bank, and order appropriate volume of blood products. Contact the surgeon for cannula(e) placement, and discuss the case.

Clinical Example (33948)

Provide age-appropriate management of the extracorporeal membrane oxygenation support (ECMO/ECLS) circuit for a patient with a venovenous circuit for continued respiratory failure for a calendar day. (Cannulation, patient management, and circuit initiation are reported separately.)

Description of Procedure (33948)

Assess venous return to the ECMO circuit, discuss strategy for adjusting flows with ECMO specialists, assess anticoagulation and make necessary adjustments in anticoagulant dose, review images, and assess fluid balance, if necessary. Discuss strategy for balancing ECMO with mechanical ventilation and vasopressor infusions with care team.

Clinical Example (33949)

Age-appropriate management of the extracorporeal membrane oxygenation support (ECMO/ECLS) circuit provided by the physician for a patient with a venoarterial circuit for continued cardiac and respiratory failure for a calendar day. (Cannulation, patient management, and circuit initiation are reported separately.)

⃠=Modifier 51 Exempt   ⊙=Moderate Sedation   ✦=Add-on Code   𝑵=FDA approval pending

Description of Procedure (33949)

Assess venous return to the ECMO circuit, discuss with ECMO specialists strategy for adjusting flows, assess anticoagulation and make necessary adjustments in anticoagulant dose, review images, and assess fluid balance, if necessary. Discuss the strategy for balancing ECMO with mechanical ventilation and vasopressor infusions with the care team.

Clinical Example (33951)

An infant with persistent hypoxemia despite maximal ventilator support undergoes percutaneous placement of arterial and/or venous cannula(e) for ECMO support.

Description of Procedure (33951)

Position patient exposing the neck and possibly the groin. Prepare and drape cannulation site(s), and obtain percutaneous access to the neck and/or groin. After systemic antociagulation, place appropriate-sized single or double cannula(e). Suture cannula(e) into place, bring ECMO circuit up into field, and connect cannula(e), avoiding air in the cannula(e). If flow is inadequate, reposition cannula(e) or insert additional cannula(e). If there is no active bleeding, apply dressing.

Clinical Example (33952)

A critically ill patient with acute viral cardiomyopathy has persistent cardiac and respiratory failure despite all conventional methods of critical care management. The decision is made to place the patient on ECMO using a percutaneous method of cannula(e) insertion.

Description of Procedure (33952)

Position patient, exposing right neck and groin. Prepare and drape cannulation site(s) and obtain percutaneous access to the groin vessels. Place appropriate-sized single or double cannula(e) after systemic anticoagulation. Suture cannula(e) into place, bring ECMO circuit up into field, and connect cannula(e), avoiding air in the cannula(e). If flow is inadequate, may reposition cannula(e) or insert additional cannula(e). If there is no active bleeding, apply dressing.

Clinical Example (33953)

A newborn with persistent pulmonary hypertension, postductal hypoxemia, and hypotension requires open insertion of arterial and/or venous cannulation for ECMO due to patient's small size.

Description of Procedure (33953)

Position patient exposing the neck and possibly the groin. Prepare and drape cannulation site(s), and obtain open access to the neck and or groin. Place appropriate-sized single or double cannula(e) after systemic anticoagulation. Suture cannula(e) into place, bring ECMO circuit up into field, and connect cannula(e), avoiding air in the cannula(e). If flow is inadequate, may reposition cannula(e) or insert additional cannula. After hemostasis, close incisions, and apply dressing.

Clinical Example (33954)

A critically ill patient with acute viral cardiomyopathy has persistent cardiac and respiratory failure despite all conventional methods of critical care management. The decision is made to place the patient on ECMO using an open operative approach.

Description of Procedure (33954)

Position patient, exposing right neck and possible groin. Prepare and drape cannulation site(s), and obtain open exposure of appropriate vessels. Place appropriate-sized cannula(e) after systemic anticoagulation. Suture cannula(e) into place, bring ECMO circuit up into field, and connect cannula(e), avoiding air in the cannula(e). If flow is inadequate, may reposition cannula(e) or insert additional cannula. After hemostasis, close incisions, and apply dressing.

Clinical Example (33955)

A child, who is 12 hours status postreimplantation of his left coronary artery via a median sternotomy, develops low cardiac output syndrome and arrhythmias. The sternal incision is opened, and the central arterial and/or venous cannula(e) is placed for ECMO.

Description of Procedure (33955)

Position patient supine. Make a re-operative sternotomy incision, and expose the right atrium and aorta. Place purse-string sutures in the right atrium and aorta, and place appropriate-sized single or double cannula(e) after systemic anticoagulation. Suture cannula(e) into place, bring ECMO circuit up into field, and connect cannula(e), avoiding air in the cannula(e). If flow is inadequate, may reposition cannula(e) or insert additional cannula. After hemostasis, apply dressing.

Clinical Example (33956)

Following cardiac surgery earlier in the day, a patient is demonstrating deteriorating cardiac and respiratory function. The decision is made to place the patient on venoarterial ECMO via direct cannulation of the ascending aorta and right atrium after opening the sternotomy.

Description of Procedure (33956)

Position patient supine. Re-open the sternotomy incision, and expose the right atrium and aorta. Place purse-string sutures in the right atrium and aorta, and place appropriate-sized single or double cannula(e) after systemic anticoagulation. Suture cannula(e) into place, bring ECMO circuit up into field, and connect cannula(e), avoiding air in the cannula(e). If flow is inadequate, may reposition cannula(e) or insert additional cannula. After hemostasis, close incisions, and apply dressing.

Clinical Example (33957)

A child with submersion injury and acute respiratory distress syndrome (ARDS) has been on venovenous ECMO. The team has been unable to achieve adequate venous return despite repositioning of the patient and additional volume resuscitation. The chest radiograph shows the cannula position to be low. Surgical repositioning of the cannula is necessary.

Description of Procedure (33957)

Prepare and drape the cannula(e) with sterile technique. With or without fluoroscopy, advance or withdraw the cannula(e) until ECMO flows are adequate. Secure the cannula(e), and dress with sterile technique.

Clinical Example (33958)

A patient who was placed on ECMO one day earlier is noted to have decreased venous return requiring decreased ECMO flow with elevated central venous pressures. To improve venous drainage to the pump, repositioning of the existing venous cannula(e) is required.

Description of Procedure (33958)

Prepare and drape the cannula(e) with sterile technique. With or without fluoroscopy, advance or withdraw the cannula(e) until ECMO flows are adequate. Secure the cannula(e), and dress with sterile technique.

Clinical Example (33959)

A child is on venoarterial ECMO due to overwhelming pertussis with multisystem organ failure. The carotid artery cannula is found to be deep, resulting in left ventricular stress and maldistribution of oxygenated blood flow. Repositioning of the arterial cannula is necessary.

Description of Procedure (33959)

Prepare and drape the cannula(e) and incision with sterile technique. Re-open the incision. Advance or withdraw the venous cannula(e), and then secure it. Secure the cannula(e), close the incision, and reapply sterile dressings.

Clinical Example (33962)

A patient who was placed on ECMO one day earlier is noted to have decreased venous return requiring decreased ECMO flow with elevated central venous pressures. To improve venous drainage to the pump, repositioning of the existing venous cannula(e) is required.

Description of Procedure (33962)

Prepare and drape the cannula(e) and incision with sterile technique. Re-open the incision. Advance or withdraw the venous cannula(e), and secure it. Secure the cannula(e), close the incision, and reapply sterile dressings.

Clinical Example (33963)

A patient who was placed on ECMO one day earlier is noted to have decreased venous return requiring decreased ECMO flow with elevated central venous pressures. To improve venous drainage to the pump, repositioning of the existing venous cannula(e) is required.

Description of Procedure (33963)

Prepare and drape the cannula(e) and patient with sterile technique. Re-open the chest. Advance or withdraw the venous cannula(e), and secure it. After hemostasis, close the chest, and apply sterile dressings.

Clinical Example (33964)

A patient who was placed on ECMO one day earlier is noted to have decreased venous return requiring decreased ECMO flow with elevated central venous pressures. To improve venous drainage to the pump, repositioning of the existing venous cannula(e) is required.

Description of Procedure (33964)

Prepare and drape the cannula(e) and patient with sterile technique. Re-open the chest. Advance or withdraw the cannula(e), and secure it. After hemostasis, close the chest, and apply sterile dressings.

Clinical Example (33965)

A patient who was placed on ECMO using percutaneous cannulation has improved so that he or she can be weaned from ECMO. The percutaneous cannula(e) can now be removed.

Description of Procedure (33965)

Position patient exposing neck and/or groin. Prepare and drape cannulation site(s). Remove the cannula(e), and with pressure achieve hemostasis. Apply sterile dressing.

Clinical Example (33966)

A patient who was placed on ECMO using percutaneous cannulation has improved so that he or she can be weaned from ECMO. The percutaneous cannula(e) can now be removed.

Description of Procedure (33966)

Position patient, exposing neck and/or groin. Prepare and drape cannulation sitc(s). Remove the cannula(e), and with pressure achieve hemostasis. Apply sterile dressing.

Clinical Example (33969)

A patient who was placed on ECMO using open peripheral cannulation has improved so that he or she can be weaned from ECMO. The peripheral cannula(e) can now be removed.

Description of Procedure (33969)

Position patient, exposing neck and/or groin. Prepare and drape cannulation site(s). Wean the patient from the support device, and determine that it is safe to proceed with decannulation. Remove the cannula(e) with a cutdown and repair of the artery and vein. After hemostasis, close the wound, and apply sterile dressing.

Clinical Example (33984)

A patient who was placed on ECMO using open peripheral cannulation has improved so that he or she can be weaned from ECMO. The peripheral cannula(e) can now be removed.

Description of Procedure (33984)

Position patient, exposing neck and/or groin. Prepare and drape cannulation site(s). Wean the patient from the support device, and determine that it is safe to

⊘=Modifier 51 Exempt   ⊙=Moderate Sedation   ✚=Add-on Code   ✗=FDA approval pending

proceed with decannulation. Remove the cannula(e) with a cutdown and repair of the artery and vein. After hemostasis, close the wound, and apply sterile dressing.

Clinical Example (33985)

A patient who was placed on ECMO using open central cannulation has improved so that he or she can be weaned from ECMO. The central cannula(e) can now be removed.

Description of Procedure (33985)

Position patient supine exposing chest and possibly groin. Re-open the sternotomy incision. Wean the patient from the support device, and determine that it is safe to proceed with decannulation. Remove cannula(e), and re-enforce purse-string sutures. After hemostasis, position chest drains, close the sternotomy incision, and apply sterile dressing.

Clinical Example (33986)

A postcardiac surgery patient who was placed on ECMO using central cannulation has recovered cardiac and respiratory function to the degree that ECMO is no longer required. The decision is made to return the patient to the operating room for operative removal of the ascending aorta and right atrial cannula(e).

Description of Procedure (33986)

Position patient supine exposing chest and possibly groin. Re-open the sternotomy incision. Wean the patient from the support device, and determine that it is safe to proceed with decannulation. Remove the cannula(e), and re-enforce purse-string sutures. After hemostasis, position chest drains, close the sternotomy incision, and apply sterile dressing.

Clinical Example (33987)

Preparations are made to utilize an open arterial technique for a patient requiring peripheral cardiopulmonary bypass. However, upon direct exposure of the selected artery, it is apparent that direct anastomosis of a prosthetic graft to the artery sidewall is necessary to ensure simultaneous antegrade and retrograde perfusion.

Description of Procedure (33987)

Sew an appropriate-sized polyethelene terephthalate conduit end-to-side to the artery with a monofilament, permanent suture. Cannulate the graft with an arterial cannula for ECMO.

Clinical Example (33988)

Left ventricular (LV) distension remains problematic for a patient with a veno-arterial ECMO circuit. The decision is made to proceed with placement of a left ventricular vent.

Description of Procedure (33988)

Create the thoracotomy or sternotomy. Identify the left ventricular apex, and place two pledgetted purse-string sutures in the left ventricular apex. Cannulate the left ventricular apex with an appropriate-sized cannula, and de-air and splice this cannula into the venous return circuit of the ECMO. (Alternatively, cannulate the left atrium either through the left atrial wall or the left atrial appendage. In this case, cannulate the left atrium with an appropriate-sized cannula, and de-air and splice this cannula into the venous return circuit of the ECMO.) After hemostasis, position the chest drain, close the incision, and apply dressing.

Clinical Example (33989)

A patient who underwent left ventricular or left atrial venting for distention has improved, and it is determined that venting is no longer necessary.

Description of Procedure (33989)

Re-open the thoracotomy or sternotomy. Remove the left ventricular or left atrial vent, and tie the purse-string suture. After hemostasis, position the chest drain, close the incision, and apply sterile dressing.

Arteries and Veins

ENDOVASCULAR REPAIR OF ABDOMINAL AORTIC ANEURYSM

34812 Open femoral artery exposure for delivery of endovascular prosthesis, by groin incision, unilateral

▶(Do not report 34812 in conjunction with 33953, 33954, 33959, 33962, 33969, 33984)◀

(For bilateral procedure, use modifier 50)

34820 Open iliac artery exposure for delivery of endovascular prosthesis or iliac occlusion during endovascular therapy, by abdominal or retroperitoneal incision, unilateral

▶(Do not report 34820 in conjunction with 33953, 33954, 33959, 33962, 33969, 33984)◀

(For bilateral procedure, use modifier 50)

34833 Open iliac artery exposure with creation of conduit for delivery of aortic or iliac endovascular prosthesis, by abdominal or retroperitoneal incision, unilateral

▶(Do not report 34833 in conjunction with 33987, 34820)◀

(For bilateral procedure, use modifier 50)

34834 Open brachial artery exposure to assist in the deployment of aortic or iliac endovascular prosthesis by arm incision, unilateral

▶(Do not report 34834 in conjunction with 33953, 33954, 33959, 33962, 33969, 33984)◀

(For bilateral procedure, use modifier 50)

Rationale

In support of the establishment of codes 33946-33989 for reporting ECMO and ECLS services: (1) reciprocal exclusionary parenthetical notes following codes 34812, 34820, and 34834 have been added to preclude endovascular repair codes 34812, 34820, and 34834 from being reported in conjunction with ECMO codes 33953, 33954, 33959, 33962, 33969, and 33984; and (2) the exclusionary parenthetical note following code 34833 has been revised to preclude this code from being reported with codes 33987 and 34820.

○=Modifier 51 Exempt ⊙=Moderate Sedation ✚=Add-on Code 𝑵=FDA approval pending

FENESTRATED ENDOVASCULAR REPAIR OF THE VISCERAL AND INFRARENAL AORTA

►The upper abdominal aorta that contains the celiac, superior mesenteric, and renal arteries is termed the visceral aorta. For reporting purposes, the thoracic aorta extends from the aortic valve to the aortic segment just proximal to the celiac artery.

Code 34839 is used to report the physician planning and sizing for a patient-specific fenestrated visceral aortic endograft. The planning includes review of high-resolution cross-sectional images (eg, CT, CTA, MRI) and utilization of 3D software for iterative modeling of the aorta and device in multiplanar views and center line of flow analysis. Code 34839 may only be reported when the physician spends a minimum of 90 total minutes performing patient-specific fenestrated endograft planning. Physician planning time does not need to be continuous and should be clearly documented in the patient record. Code 34839 is reported on the date that planning work is complete and may not include time spent on the day before or the day of the fenestrated endovascular repair procedure (34841, 34842, 34843, 34844, 34845, 34846, 34847, 34848) nor be reported on the day before or the day of the fenestrated endovascular repair procedure.

Codes 34841, 34842, 34843, 34844, 34845, 34846, 34847, 34848 are used to report placement of a fenestrated endovascular graft in the visceral aorta, either alone or in combination with the infrarenal aorta for aneurysm, pseudoaneurysm, dissection, penetrating ulcer, intramural hematoma, or traumatic disruption. The fenestrated main body endoprosthesis is deployed within the visceral aorta. Fenestrations within the fabric allow for selective catheterization of the visceral and/or renal arteries and subsequent placement of an endoprosthesis (ie, bare metal or covered stent) to maintain flow to the visceral artery. Patient variation in the location and relative orientation of the renal and visceral artery origins requires use of a patient-specific fenestrated endograft for endovascular repair that preserves flow to essential visceral arteries and allows proximal seal and fixation to be achieved above the renal level as well as in the distal aorta or iliac vessel(s).◄

Fenestrated aortic repair is reported based on the extent of aorta treated. Codes 34841-34844 describe repair using proximal endoprostheses that span from the visceral aortic component to one, two, three, or four visceral artery origins and distal extent limited to the infrarenal aorta. These devices do not extend into the common iliac arteries. Codes 34845-34848 are used to report deployment of a fenestrated endoprosthesis that spans from the visceral aorta (including one, two, three, or four visceral artery origins) through the infrarenal aorta into the common iliac arteries. The infrarenal component may be a bifurcated unibody device, a modular bifurcated docking system with docking limb(s), or an aorto-uniiliac or aorta-unifemoral device. Codes 34845-34848 include placement of unilateral or bilateral docking limbs (depending on the device). Any additional stent graft extensions that terminate in the common iliac arteries are included in the work described by 34845-34848. Codes 34825 and 34826 may not be separately reported for proximal abdominal aortic extension prosthesis(es) or for distal extension prosthesis(es) that terminate in the aorta or the common iliac arteries. However, codes 34825 and 34826 may be reported for distal extension prosthesis(es) that terminate in the internal iliac, external iliac, or common femoral artery(s).

Codes 34841-34844 and 34845-34848 define the total number of visceral and/or renal arteries (ie, celiac, superior mesenteric, and/or unilateral or bilateral renal artery[s]) requiring placement of an endoprosthesis (ie, bare metal or covered stent) through an aortic endograft fenestration.

Introduction of guide wires and catheters in the aorta and visceral and/or renal arteries is included in the work of 34841-34848 and is not separately reportable. However, catheterization of the hypogastric artery(s) and/or arterial families outside the treatment zone of the graft may be separately reported. Balloon angioplasty within the target treatment zone of the endograft, either before or after endograft deployment, is not separately reportable. Fluoroscopic guidance and radiological supervision and interpretation in conjunction with fenestrated endovascular aortic repair is not separately reportable and includes angiographic diagnostic imaging of the aorta and its branches prior to deployment of the fenestrated endovascular device, fluoroscopic guidance in the delivery of the fenestrated endovascular components, and intraprocedural arterial angiography (eg, confirm position, detect endoleak, evaluate runoff) done at the time of the endovascular aortic repair.

Exposure of the access vessels (eg, 34812) may be reported separately. Extensive repair of an artery (eg, 35226, 35286) may be reported separately. For concomitant endovascular treatment of the descending thoracic aorta, report 33880-33886 and 75956-75959 with 34841-34848. For isolated endovascular infrarenal abdominal aortic aneurysm repair that does not require placement of a fenestrated graft to preserve flow to the visceral branch(es), see 34800-34805.

Other interventional procedures performed at the time of fenestrated endovascular abdominal aortic aneurysm repair may be reported separately (eg, arterial embolization, intravascular ultrasound, balloon angioplasty or stenting of native artery[s] outside the endoprosthesis target zone, when done before or after deployment of endoprosthesis).

●**34839** Physician planning of a patient-specific fenestrated visceral aortic endograft requiring a minimum of 90 minutes of physician time

▶(Do not report 34839 in conjunction with 76376, 76377)◀

▶(Do not report 34839 in conjunction with 34841, 34842, 34843, 34844, 34845, 34846, 34847, 34848, when performed on the day before or the day of the fenestrated endovascular repair procedure)◀

34841 Endovascular repair of visceral aorta (eg, aneurysm, pseudoaneurysm, dissection, penetrating ulcer, intramural hematoma, or traumatic disruption) by deployment of a fenestrated visceral aortic endograft and all associated radiological supervision and interpretation, including target zone angioplasty, when performed; including one visceral artery endoprosthesis (superior mesenteric, celiac or renal artery)

34842   including two visceral artery endoprostheses (superior mesenteric, celiac and/or renal artery[s])

34843   including three visceral artery endoprostheses (superior mesenteric, celiac and/or renal artery[s])

34844   including four or more visceral artery endoprostheses (superior mesenteric, celiac and/or renal artery[s])

▶(Do not report 34841, 34842, 34843, 34844 in conjunction with 34800, 34802, 34803, 34804, 34805, 34845, 34846, 34847, 34848, 35452, 35472, 75952)◀

▶(Do not report 34841, 34842, 34843, 34844 in conjunction with 34839, when planning services are performed on the day before or the day of the fenestrated endovascular repair procedure)◀

34845 Endovascular repair of visceral aorta and infrarenal abdominal aorta (eg, aneurysm, pseudoaneurysm, dissection, penetrating ulcer, intramural hematoma, or traumatic disruption) with a fenestrated visceral aortic endograft and concomitant unibody or modular infrarenal aortic endograft and all associated radiological supervision and interpretation, including target zone angioplasty, when performed; including one visceral artery endoprosthesis (superior mesenteric, celiac or renal artery)

34846   including two visceral artery endoprostheses (superior mesenteric, celiac and/or renal artery[s])

⊘=Modifier 51 Exempt   ⊙=Moderate Sedation   ✚=Add-on Code   𝑵=FDA approval pending

34847   including three visceral artery endoprostheses (superior mesenteric, celiac and/or renal artery[s])

34848   including four or more visceral artery endoprostheses (superior mesenteric, celiac and/or renal artery[s])

►(Do not report 34845, 34846, 34847, 34848 in conjunction with 34800, 34802, 34803, 34804, 34805, 34841, 34842, 34843, 34844, 35081, 35102, 35452, 35472, 75952)◄

►(Do not report 34845, 34846, 34847, 34848 in conjunction with 34839, when planning services are performed on the day before or the day of the fenestrated endovascular repair procedure)◄

(Do not report 34841-34848 in conjunction with 37236, 37237 for bare metal or covered stents placed into the visceral branches within the endoprosthesis target zone)

(For placement of distal extension prosthesis[es] terminating in the internal iliac, external iliac, or common femoral artery[s], see 34825-34826, 75953, 0254T, 0255T)

►(Use 34845, 34846, 34847, 34848 in conjunction with 37220, 37221, 37222, 37223, only when 37220, 37221, 37222, 37223 are performed outside the target treatment zone of the endoprosthesis)◄

🖉 Rationale

Code 34839 has been established to report the physician planning for a patient-specific manufactured fenestrated visceral aortic endograft. To clarify the intent of this code, new guidelines have been added to indicate that "planning" includes the review of high resolution cross-sectional images (eg, computed tomography [CT], computed tomography angiography [CTA], magnetic resonance imaging [MRI]) and the utilization of 3D software for iterative modeling of the aorta and device in multiplanar views and center line of flow analysis. Physician planning time does not need to be continuous, however, the physician must spend a minimum of 90 total minutes performing patient-specific endograft planning in order to report code 34839. To further clarify the intent of this code, the guidelines state that planning time may not include time spent on the day before or the day of the fenestrated endovascular repair procedure, and neither may this code be reported on the day of or the day before the day of the fenestrated endovascular repair procedure. Two exclusionary parenthetical notes have been added following code 34839 to provide additional instruction on the appropriate reporting of this code.

Codes 35081 and 35102 have been removed from the exclusionary parenthetical note following code 34844 because these codes may appropriately be reported in instances in which an open infrarenal aortic aneurysm repair (35081 or 35102) is done in conjunction with endovascular repair procedures (34841-34844).

An additional exclusionary parenthetical note has been added following code 34844 to preclude the reporting of codes 34841-34844 in conjunction with planning code 34839, when planning services are performed on the day before or the day of the fenestrated endovascular repair procedure.

An exclusionary parenthetical note has been added following code 34848 to preclude the reporting of codes 34845-34848 in conjunction with codes 34800-34805, 34839, 34841-34844, 35081, 35102, 35452, 35472, and 75952.

Endovascular repair of the visceral aorta and infrarenal abdominal aorta should only be reported in conjunction with endovascular revascularization codes 37220-37223 when endovascular revascularization is performed outside of the target treatment zone of the endoprosthesis. Previously, the 34845-34848 code series and the 37220-37223 code series in the parenthetical note following code 34848 that provides this instruction were erroneously transposed. The error has been corrected in the CPT 2015 code set.

Clinical Example (34839)

A 68-year-old male with coronary artery disease and chronic obstructive pulmonary disease (COPD) is found to have a 7-cm diameter aneurysm involving the visceral and infrarenal aorta. Imaging reveals that successful repair will require treatment of both aortic segments and inclusion of endoprostheses that extend from the visceral aortic endograft to visceral artery(ies). He has elected to undergo endovascular repair of the visceral and infrarenal aorta using a fenestrated branched endograft. The pre-operative imaging is analyzed to plan the endoprosthesis.

Description of Procedure (34839)

Review cross-sectional imaging from the aortic arch to femoral vessels with fine cuts and upload to a workstation in which 3D software is applied permitting iterative modeling of the aorta and device in multiplanar views and center line of flow analysis. (Although the center line of flow predicts the position of the fenestrated graft once deployed and the potential locations of the fenestrations for branch vessel cannulations, the physician needs to manually adjust modeling for altered anatomy, which is tortuous or thrombus laden.)

Use axial imaging to determine diameter measurements of the aorta, renal, and/or mesenteric vessels, iliac and femoral arteries for appropriate sizing of the fenestrated stent graft and branch stents. The iliac and femoral diameters also determine the success of the device delivery and any potential adjunctive manuevers that may be required to facilitate delivery. Additional bypasses or conduits may need to be planned based on the quantitative and qualitative characteristics of the access vessels. Tortuosity, calcification, thrombus presence, and stenoses require consideration as they may impact device delivery. In addition, evaluate the arch and brachiocephalic vessels for possible brachial or axillary access to facilitate graft deployment and or branch vessel origin cannulation from above. Axial imaging and center line of flow permit evaluation of the aorta at various levels. Document these measurements in the proximal seal and fixation zones, branch vessel origins, and distal aortic or iliac seal zones.

Evaluate the origins and path of the branch vessels for stenoses, thrombus, calcification, and tortuosity, which impact the size and location of the fenestration for each branch vessel, as well as the extent of bridging stent, which will be required based on the vessel length. Measure the proximity of the vessel origin to critical collaterals. Determine the bridging stent length to both maintain vessel patency and to prevent occlusion of essential branch collaterals. Map and measure the angle of the vessel origin with respect to the center line of flow. Annotate the origins of the visceral and/or renal arteries using clock positions and determine the location and sizes of these fenestrations by their proximity to the sealing stent. Identify the precise locations of the branch vessel origins using manipulation of the cross-sectional images on the workstation.

Map the distances between vessel origins on the fenestrated main body device using center line of flow measurements and with manual adjustments, where needed. A stretched/straightened view permits manual validation of the computer-generated lengths. Mandatory device requirements necessary to provide fixation and seal are also incorporated in the device design and may impact the location and sizes of the fenestrations.

Measure the remainder of the fenestrated main body based on the distal aortic seal zone length and diameter, permitting oversizing as needed for seal. (Different fenestrated platforms have specific overlap and oversizing requirements.)

REPAIR BLOOD VESSEL OTHER THAN FOR FISTULA, WITH OR WITHOUT PATCH ANGIOPLASTY

35201   Repair blood vessel, direct; neck

▶(Do not report 35201 in conjunction with 33969, 33984, 33985, 33986)◀

35206   upper extremity

▶(Do not report 35206 in conjunction with 33969, 33984, 33985, 33986)◀

35207   hand, finger

35211   intrathoracic, with bypass

▶(Do not report 35211 in conjunction with 33969, 33984, 33985, 33986)◀

35216   intrathoracic, without bypass

▶(Do not report 35216 in conjunction with 33969, 33984, 33985, 33986)◀

35221   intra-abdominal

35226   lower extremity

▶(Do not report 35226 in conjunction with 33969, 33984, 33985, 33986)◀

🖎 Rationale

In support of the establishment of the ECMO and ECLS codes 33946-33989, a reciprocal exclusionary parenthetical note has been added following codes 35201, 35206, 35211, 35216, and 35226 to preclude these codes from being reported in conjunction with codes 33969, 33984, 33985, and 33986.

VASCULAR INJECTION PROCEDURES

Intra-Arterial—Intra-Aortic

Diagnostic Studies of Cervicocerebral Arteries: Codes 36221-36228 describe non-selective and selective arterial catheter placement and diagnostic imaging of the aortic arch, carotid, and vertebral arteries. Codes 36221-36226 include the work of accessing the vessel, placement of catheter(s), contrast injection(s), fluoroscopy, radiological supervision and interpretation, and closure of the arteriotomy by pressure, or application of an arterial closure device. Codes 36221-36228 describe arterial contrast injections with arterial, capillary, and venous phase imaging, when performed.

Code 36227 is an add-on code to report unilateral selective arterial catheter placement and diagnostic imaging of the ipsilateral external carotid circulation and includes all the work of accessing the additional vessel, placement of catheter(s), contrast injection(s), fluoroscopy, radiological supervision and interpretation. Code 36227 is reported in conjunction with 36222, 36223, or 36224.

▶Code 36228 is an add-on code to report unilateral selective arterial catheter placement and diagnostic imaging of the initial and each additional intracranial branch of the internal carotid or vertebral arteries. Code 36228 is reported in conjunction with 36223, 36224, 36225 or 36226. This includes any additional second or third order catheter selective placement in the same primary branch of the internal carotid, vertebral, or basilar artery and includes all the work of accessing the additional vessel, placement of catheter(s), contrast injection(s), fluoroscopy, radiological supervision and interpretation. It is not reported more than twice per side, regardless of the number of additional branches selectively catheterized.◀

Codes 36221-36226 are built on progressive hierarchies with more intensive services inclusive of less intensive services. The code inclusive of all of the services provided for that vessel should be reported (ie, use the code inclusive of the most intensive services provided). Only one code in the range 36222-36224 may be reported for each ipsilateral carotid territory. Only one code in the range 36225-36226 may be reported for each ipsilateral vertebral territory.

Code 36221 is reported for non-selective arterial catheter placement in the thoracic aorta and diagnostic imaging of the aortic arch and great vessel origins. Codes 36222-36228 are reported for unilateral artery catheterization. Do not report 36221 in conjunction with 36222-36226 as these selective codes include the work of 36221 when performed.

Do not report 36222, 36223, or 36224 together for ipsilateral angiography. Instead, select the code that represents the most comprehensive service using the following hierarchy of complexity (listed in descending order of complexity): 36224>36223>36222.

Do not report 36225 and 36226 together for ipsilateral angiography. Select the code that represents the more comprehensive service using the following hierarchy of complexity (listed in descending order of complexity): 36226>36225.

When bilateral carotid and/or vertebral arterial catheterization and imaging is performed, add modifier 50 to codes 36222-36228 if the same procedure is performed on both sides. For example, bilateral extracranial carotid angiography with selective catheterization of each common carotid artery would be reported with 36222 and modifier 50. However, when different territory(ies) is studied in the same session on both sides of the body, modifiers may be required to report the imaging performed. Use modifier 59 to denote that different carotid and/or vertebral arteries are being studied. For example, when selective right internal carotid artery catheterization accompanied by right extracranial and intracranial carotid angiography is followed by selective left common carotid artery catheterization with left extracranial carotid angiography, use 36224 to report the right side and 36222-59 to report the left side.

Diagnostic angiography of the cervicocerebral vessels may be followed by an interventional procedure at the same session. Interventional procedures may be separately reportable using standard coding conventions.

▶Do not report 36218 or 75774 as part of diagnostic angiography of the extracranial and intracranial cervicocerebral vessels. It may be appropriate to report 36218 and 75774 for diagnostic angiography of upper extremities and other vascular beds of the neck and/or shoulder girdle performed in the same session as vertebral angiography (eg, workup of a neck tumor that requires catheterization and angiography of the vertebral artery as well as other brachiocephalic arteries).◀

Report 76376 or 76377 for 3D rendering when performed in conjunction with 36221-36228.

Report 76937 for ultrasound guidance for vascular access, when performed in conjunction with 36221-36228.

36215 Selective catheter placement, arterial system; each first order thoracic or brachiocephalic branch, within a vascular family

(For catheter placement for coronary angiography, see 93454-93461)

36216 initial second order thoracic or brachiocephalic branch, within a vascular family

36217 initial third order or more selective thoracic or brachiocephalic branch, within a vascular family

+36218 additional second order, third order, and beyond, thoracic or brachiocephalic branch, within a vascular family (List in addition to code for initial second or third order vessel as appropriate)

▶(Use 36218 in conjunction with 36216, 36217, 36225, 36226)◀

▶(For angiography, see 36222-36228, 75600-75774, 75791)◀

▶(For angioplasty, see 35472, 35475)◀

⊙36222 Selective catheter placement, common carotid or innominate artery, unilateral, any approach, with angiography of the ipsilateral extracranial carotid circulation and all associated radiological supervision and interpretation, includes angiography of the cervicocerebral arch, when performed

▶(Do not report 36222 in conjunction with 37215, 37216, 37218 for the treated carotid artery)◀

⊙36223 Selective catheter placement, common carotid or innominate artery, unilateral, any approach, with angiography of the ipsilateral intracranial carotid circulation and all associated radiological supervision and interpretation, includes angiography of the extracranial carotid and cervicocerebral arch, when performed

▶(Do not report 36223 in conjunction with 37215, 37216, 37218 for the treated carotid artery)◀

⊙36224 Selective catheter placement, internal carotid artery, unilateral, with angiography of the ipsilateral intracranial carotid circulation and all associated radiological supervision and interpretation, includes angiography of the extracranial carotid and cervicocerebral arch, when performed

▶(Do not report 36224 in conjunction with 37215, 37216, 37218 for the treated carotid artery)◀

⊙+36228 Selective catheter placement, each intracranial branch of the internal carotid or vertebral arteries, unilateral, with angiography of the selected vessel circulation and all associated radiological supervision and interpretation (eg, middle cerebral artery, posterior inferior cerebellar artery) (List separately in addition to code for primary procedure)

▶(Use 36228 in conjunction with 36223, 36224, 36225 or 36226)◀

(Do not report 36228 more than twice per side)

Rationale

The Diagnostic Studies of Cervicocerebral Arteries introductory guidelines have been editorially revised to clarify the appropriate reporting of codes 36218, 36223, and 36225. The editorial changes allow the reporting of code 36228 with codes 36223, 36224, 36225, or 36226. The editorial changes also clarify the appropriate reporting of codes 36218 and 75774 as part of the diagnostic angiography of the extracranial and intracranial cervicocerebral vessels and for diagnostic angiography of the upper extremities and other vascular beds of the neck and shoulder girdle performed in the same session as vertebral angiography.

Three related parenthetical notes following code 36218 have been revised to reflect these changes. The first inclusionary parenthetical note has been revised to include codes 36225 and 36226. Code 36147 has been removed from the second parenthetical note, and code 35471 has been removed from the third parenthetical note. The instructional parenthetical note following code 36228 has been revised to include codes 36223 and 36225 to correspond with the revisions to the introductory guidelines.

Reciprocal exclusionary instructions have been added following codes 36222, 36223, and 36224 to maintain consistency with the existing exclusionary parenthetical notes in the CPT code set.

Venous

36468 Single or multiple injections of sclerosing solutions, spider veins (telangiectasia), limb or trunk

(Do not report 36468 in conjunction with 37241 in the same surgical field)

▶(36469 has been deleted)◀

Rationale

As part of an effort to ensure that the CPT code set reflects current clinical practice, code 36469 (sclerosing solution injection of the face) has been deleted due to low utilization.

HEMODIALYSIS ACCESS, INTERVASCULAR CANNULATION FOR EXTRACORPOREAL CIRCULATION, OR SHUNT INSERTION

36818 Arteriovenous anastomosis, open; by upper arm cephalic vein transposition

36821   direct, any site (eg, Cimino type) (separate procedure)

▶(36822 has been deleted. To report, see 33951, 33952, 33953, 33954, 33955, 33956)◀

Rationale

In support of the new ECMO and ECLS codes 33946-33989, code 36822 (insertion of cannula for ECMO) has been deleted. A parenthetical note directing users to the new codes has been added following code 36821.

⊘=Modifier 51 Exempt   ⊙=Moderate Sedation   ✚=Add-on Code   ✗=FDA approval pending

TRANSCATHETER PROCEDURES

Other Procedures

⊙▲**37215** Transcatheter placement of intravascular stent(s), cervical carotid artery, open or percutaneous, including angioplasty, when performed, and radiological supervision and interpretation; with distal embolic protection

⊙▲**37216** without distal embolic protection

(37215 and 37216 include all ipsilateral selective carotid catheterization, all diagnostic imaging for ipsilateral, cervical and cerebral carotid arteriography, and all related radiological supervision and interpretation. When ipsilateral carotid arteriogram (including imaging and selective catheterization) confirms the need for carotid stenting, 37215 and 37216 are inclusive of these services. If carotid stenting is not indicated, then the appropriate codes for carotid catheterization and imaging should be reported in lieu of 37215 and 37216)

(Do not report 37215, 37216 in conjunction with 36222-36224 for the treated carotid artery)

▶(For open or percutaneous transcatheter placement of extracranial vertebral artery stent[s], see Category III codes 0075T, 0076T)◀

▲**37217** Transcatheter placement of intravascular stent(s), intrathoracic common carotid artery or innominate artery by retrograde treatment, open ipsilateral cervical carotid artery exposure, including angioplasty, when performed, and radiological supervision and interpretation

(37217 includes open vessel exposure and vascular access closure, all access and selective catheterization of the vessel, traversing the lesion, and any radiological supervision and interpretation directly related to the intervention when performed, standard closure of arteriotomy by suture, and imaging performed to document completion of the intervention in addition to the intervention[s] performed. Carotid artery revascularization services [eg, 33891, 35301, 35509, 35510, 35601, 35606] performed during the same session may be reported separately, when performed)

(Do not report 37217 in conjunction with 35201, 35458, 36221-36227, 75962 for ipsilateral services)

▶(For open or percutaneous transcatheter placement of intravascular cervical carotid artery stent[s], see 37215, 37216)◀

▶(For open or percutaneous antegrade transcatheter placement of innominate and/or intrathoracic carotid artery stent[s], use 37218)◀

▶(For open or percutaneous transcatheter placement of extracranial vertebral artery stent[s], see 0075T, 0076T)◀

(For transcatheter placement of intracranial stent[s], use 61635)

⊙●**37218** Transcatheter placement of intravascular stent(s), intrathoracic common carotid artery or innominate artery, open or percutaneous antegrade approach, including angioplasty, when performed, and radiological supervision and interpretation

▶(37218 includes all ipsilateral extracranial intrathoracic selective innominate and carotid catheterization, all diagnostic imaging for ipsilateral extracranial intrathoracic innominate and/or carotid artery stenting, and all related radiologic supervision and interpretation. Report 37218 when the ipsilateral extracranial intrathoracic carotid arteriogram (including imaging and selective catheterization) confirms the need for stenting. If stenting is not indicated, report the appropriate codes for selective catheterization and imaging)◀

▶(Do not report 37218 in conjunction with 36222, 36223, 36224 for the treated carotid artery)◄

▶(For open or percutaneous transcatheter placement of intravascular cervical carotid artery stent[s], see 37215, 37216)◄

▶(For open or percutaneous transcatheter placement of extracranial vertebral artery stent[s], see 0075T, 0076T)◄

▶(For transcatheter placement of intracranial stent[s], use 61635)◄

Rationale

Codes 37215 and 37216 have been editorially revised to clarify that they describe open or percutaneous procedures. This revision makes the language consistent with all other endovascular codes in the CPT code set. Both codes include all ipsilateral cervical and cerebral angiography, as well as carotid angioplasty, stent placement, deployment and removal of distal embolic protection systems, and all associated radiological supervision and interpretation services.

Code 37217 has been editorially revised by removing the terms "an" and "via" to make the language consistent with codes 37215 and 37216. Two cross-reference parenthetical notes have been revised, and one has been added following code 37217 directing users to the appropriate open or percutaneous transcatheter placement codes.

Code 37218 has been established to report transcatheter placement of intravascular stent or stents in the intrathoracic common carotid artery or innominate artery by antegrade approach. In this procedure, an endovascular stent or stents is inserted from the aortic arch into the common carotid artery, typically through femoral arterial vascular access. Code 37218 includes all ipsilateral extracranial intrathoracic selective innominate and carotid catheterization, diagnostic imaging for ipsilateral extracranial intrathoracic innominate and/or carotid artery stenting, and all related radiological supervision and interpretation. It would not be appropriate to report code 37218 with selective catheterization codes 36222, 36223, or 36224 for the treated carotid artery. New parenthetical notes have been added following code 37218 to provide instruction on the proper reporting of this code.

Clinical Example (37218)

A 70-year-old male with a history of left carotid endarterectomy presents with transient ischemic attacks. Diagnostic imaging demonstrates left common carotid ostial high grade stenosis without further distal disease in the carotid bulb or internal carotid artery. He undergoes intrathoracic left common carotid artery stent placement from a femoral approach.

Description of Procedure (37218)

Puncture the femoral artery, and place a sheath. Advance a long catheter and sheath over a guide wire to the thoracic aorta. Obtain roadmapping images for vessel sizing and to document anatomy. Cross the area of stenosis/occlusion with a guide wire, and advance a sheath to or through the stenosis/occlusion. Deploy

⊘=Modifier 51 Exempt   ⊙=Moderate Sedation   ✚=Add-on Code   𝒩=FDA approval pending

an embolic protection device. Initially treat the lesion with balloon angioplasty as predilatation to allow passage of the stent delivery system. Using fluoroscopic guidance and appropriate roadmapping, position a stent across the intended treatment zone, and deploy. Fully open the stent with additional balloon catheter. Remove the stent delivery system and balloon, and obtain follow-up images with contrast injection to determine if the stenosis has been treated adequately. Multiple balloon inflations may be required, or additional balloons with larger or smaller diameters may be used. Once a satisfactory result has been documented in the absence of extravasation or embolization, remove the embolic protection device, remove the sheath, and obtain hemostasis with closure device.

ENDOVASCULAR REVASCULARIZATION (OPEN OR PERCUTANEOUS, TRANSCATHETER)

⊙+ 37232   Revascularization, endovascular, open or percutaneous, tibial/peroneal artery, unilateral, each additional vessel; with transluminal angioplasty (List separately in addition to code for primary procedure)

⊙+ 37235   with transluminal stent placement(s) and atherectomy, includes angioplasty within the same vessel, when performed (List separately in addition to code for primary procedure)

(Use 37235 in conjunction with 37231)

▶Codes 37236-37239 are used to report endovascular revascularization for vessels other than lower extremity artery(s) for occlusive disease (ie, 37221, 37223, 37226, 37227, 37230, 37231, 37234, 37235), cervical carotid (ie, 37215, 37216), intracranial (ie, 61635), intracoronary (ie, 92928, 92929, 92933, 92934, 92937, 92938, 92941, 92943, 92944), innominate and/or intrathoracic carotid artery through an antegrade approach (37218), extracranial vertebral (ie, 0075T, 0076T) performed percutaneously and/or through an open surgical exposure, or open retrograde intrathoracic common carotid or innominate (37217).◀

Codes 37236, 37237 describe transluminal intravascular stent insertion in an artery while 37238, 37239 describe transluminal intravascular stent insertion in a vein. Multiple stents placed in a single vessel may only be reported with a single code. If a lesion extends across the margins of one vessel into another, but can be treated with a single therapy, the intervention should be reported only once. When additional, different vessels are treated in the same session, report 37237 and/or 37239 as appropriate. Each code in this family (37236-37239) includes any and all balloon angioplasty(s) performed in the treated vessel, including any pre-dilation (whether performed as a primary or secondary angioplasty), post-dilation following stent placement, treatment of a lesion outside the stented segment but in the same vessel, or use of larger/smaller balloon to achieve therapeutic result. Angioplasty in a separate and distinct vessel may be reported separately. Non-selective and/or selective catheterization(s) (eg, 36005, 36010-36015, 36200, 36215-36218, 36245-36248) is reported separately.

Codes 37236-37239 include radiological supervision and interpretation directly related to the intervention(s) performed, closure of the arteriotomy by pressure, application of an arterial closure device or standard closure of the puncture by suture, and imaging performed to document completion of the intervention in addition to the intervention(s) performed. Extensive repair or replacement of an artery may be reported separately (eg, 35226 or 35286). Report 76937 for ultrasound guidance for vascular access, when performed in conjunction with 37236-37239. Intravascular ultrasound may be reported separately (ie, 37250, 37251). For mechanical thrombectomy and/or thrombolytic therapy, when performed, see 37184-37188, 37211-37214.

Intravascular stents, both covered and uncovered, are a class of devices that may be used as part of an embolization procedure. As such, there is the potential for overlap among codes used for placement of vascular stents and those used for embolization. When a stent is placed for the purpose of providing a latticework for deployment of embolization coils, such as for embolization of an aneurysm, the embolization code is reported and not the stent code. If a covered stent is deployed as the sole management of an aneurysm, pseudoaneurysm, or vascular extravasation, then the stent deployment code should be reported and not the embolization code.

⊙▲37236   Transcatheter placement of an intravascular stent(s) (except lower extremity artery(s) for occlusive disease, cervical carotid, extracranial vertebral or intrathoracic carotid, intracranial, or coronary), open or percutaneous, including radiological supervision and interpretation and including all angioplasty within the same vessel, when performed; initial artery

⊙+▲37237   each additional artery (List separately in addition to code for primary procedure)

(Use 37237 in conjunction with 37236)

(Do not report 37236, 37237 in conjunction with 34841-34848 for bare metal or covered stents placed into the visceral branches within the endoprosthesis target zone)

▶(For stent placement(s) in iliac, femoral, popliteal, or tibial/peroneal artery(s) for occlusive disease, see 37221, 37223, 37226, 37227, 37230, 37231, 37234, 37235)◀

(For transcatheter placement of intravascular cervical carotid artery stent(s), see 37215, 37216)

(For transcatheter placement of intracranial stent(s), use 61635)

(For transcatheter placement of intracoronary stent(s), see 92928, 92929, 92933, 92934, 92937, 92938, 92941, 92943, 92944)

(For stenting of visceral arteries in conjunction with fenestrated endovascular repair, see 34841-34848)

▶(For open or percutaneous antegrade transcatheter placement of intrathoracic carotid/innominate artery stent(s), use 37218)◀

▶(For open or percutaneous transcatheter placement of extracranial vertebral artery stent(s), see Category III codes 0075T, 0076T)◀

(For open retrograde transcatheter placement of intrathoracic common carotid/innominate artery stent(s), use 37217)

✍ Rationale

Codes 37236 and 37237 have been editorially revised to clarify that they describe transcatheter stent placement in lower extremity artery(s), except when the procedure is performed for occlusive disease.

The guidelines for reporting codes 37236-37239 have been editorially revised to clarify that these codes are used to report endovascular revascularization for vessels other than lower extremity artery(s) when performed for occlusive disease, as well as for the innominate and/or intrathoracic carotid artery through an antegrade extracranial vertebral approach.

⊘=Modifier 51 Exempt   ⊙=Moderate Sedation   ✚=Add-on Code   ⊅=FDA approval pending

Stent placement in the iliac, femoral, popliteal, or tibial/peroneal arteries for occlusive disease should be reported with codes 37221, 37223, 37226, 37227, 37230, 37231, 37234, or 37235, as appropriate. Open or percutaneous antegrade transcatheter placement of intrathoracic carotid/innominate artery stents should be reported using new code 37218. Open or percutaneous transcatheter placement of extracranial vertebral artery stents should be reported using Category III codes 0075T and 0076T, as appropriate.

Parenthetical notes following code 37237 have been added and revised to instruct users on the proper reporting of transcatheter intravascular stent placement procedures.

VASCULAR EMBOLIZATION AND OCCLUSION

Codes 37241-37244 are used to describe the work of vascular embolization and occlusion procedures, excluding the central nervous system and the head and neck, which are reported using 61624, 61626, 61710, and 75894, and excluding the ablation/sclerotherapy procedures for venous insufficiency/telangiectasia of the extremities/skin, which are reported using 36468, 36470, and 36471. Embolization and occlusion procedures are performed for a wide variety of clinical indications and in a range of vascular territories. Arteries, veins, and lymphatics may all be the target of embolization.

▶The embolization codes include all associated radiological supervision and interpretation, intra-procedural guidance and road-mapping, and imaging necessary to document completion of the procedure. They do not include diagnostic angiography and all necessary catheter placement(s). Code(s) for catheter placement(s) may be separately reported using selective catheter placement code(s), if used consistent with guidelines. Code(s) for diagnostic angiography may also be separately reported, when performed according to guidelines for diagnostic angiography during endovascular procedures, using the appropriate diagnostic angiography codes. Report these services with an appropriate modifier (eg, modifier 59). Please see the guidelines on the reporting of diagnostic angiography preceding 75600 in the **Vascular Procedures, Aorta and Arteries** section.◀

Code 37241 is used to report vascular embolization or occlusion procedures performed for venous conditions other than hemorrhage. Examples include embolization of venous malformations, capillary hemangiomas, varicoceles, and visceral varices. Embolization of side branch(es) of an outflow vein from a hemodialysis access would be reported using 37241.

Code 37242 is used to report vascular embolization or occlusion performed for arterial conditions other than hemorrhage or tumor such as arteriovenous malformations and arteriovenous fistulas whether congenital or acquired. Embolizations of aneurysms and pseudoaneurysms are also reported with 37242. Tumor embolization is reported with 37243. Note that injection to treat an extremity pseudoaneurysm is correctly reported with 36002. Sometimes, embolization and occlusion of an artery are performed prior to another planned interventional procedure; an example is embolization of the left gastric artery prior to planned implantation of a hepatic artery chemotherapy port. The artery embolization is reported with 37242.

Code 37243 is used to report embolization for the purpose of tissue ablation and organ infarction or ischemia. This can be performed in many clinical circumstances, including embolization of benign or malignant tumors of the liver, kidney, uterus, or other organs. When chemotherapy is given as part of an embolization procedure, additional codes (eg, 96420) may be separately reported. When a radioisotope (eg, Yttrium-90) is injected as part of an embolization, then additional codes (eg, 79445) may be separately reported. Uterine fibroid embolization is reported with 37243.

Code 37244 is used to report embolization for treatment of hemorrhage or vascular or lymphatic extravasation. Examples include embolization for management of gastrointestinal bleed, trauma-induced hemorrhage of the viscera or pelvis, embolization of the thoracic duct for chylous effusion and bronchial artery embolization for hemoptysis. Embolization of the uterine arteries for management of hemorrhage (eg, postpartum hemorrhage) is also reported with 37244.

Intravascular stents, both covered and uncovered, are a class of devices that may be used as part of an embolization procedure. As such, there is the potential for overlap among codes used for placement of vascular stents and those used for embolization. When a stent is placed for the purpose of providing a latticework for deployment of embolization coils, such as for embolization of an aneurysm, the embolization code is reported and not the stent code. If a stent is deployed as the sole management of an aneurysm, pseudoaneurysm, or vascular extravasation, then the stent deployment code should be reported and not the embolization code.

Only one embolization code should be reported for each surgical field (ie, the area immediately surrounding and directly involved in a treatment/procedure). For example, embolization of one or more venous side branches in a single arm for a patient with a dialysis arteriovenous fistula is reported with 37241 only once per session. Embolization procedures performed at a single setting and including multiple surgical fields (eg, a patient with multiple trauma and bleeding from the pelvis and the spleen) may be reported with multiple embolization codes with the appropriate modifier (eg, modifier 59).

There may be overlapping indications for an embolization procedure. The code for the immediate indication for the embolization should be used. For instance, if the immediate cause for embolization is bleeding in a patient with an aneurysm, report 37244.

⊙37241 Vascular embolization or occlusion, inclusive of all radiological supervision and interpretation, intraprocedural roadmapping, and imaging guidance necessary to complete the intervention; venous, other than hemorrhage (eg, congenital or acquired venous malformations, venous and capillary hemangiomas, varices, varicoceles)

✒ Rationale

The guidelines in the Vascular Embolization and Occlusion subsection have been revised to clarify that codes that do not include angiography are separately reportable. Previous guidelines did not clearly instruct whether catheterization codes in the 36200-36254 code series that do not include angiography (eg, 36200-36218, 36245-36248) are separately reportable. The guidelines have now been revised to clearly state that catheter placement codes are separately reportable in addition to vascular embolization and occlusion codes.

⊘=Modifier 51 Exempt   ⊙=Moderate Sedation   ✚=Add-on Code   ⚡=FDA approval pending

Mediastinum and Diaphragm

Mediastinum

INCISION

39000 Mediastinotomy with exploration, drainage, removal of foreign body, or biopsy; cervical approach

39010 transthoracic approach, including either transthoracic or median sternotomy

 ►(Do not report 39010 in conjunction with 33955, 33956, 33963, 33964)◄

 (For VATS pericardial biopsy, use 32604)

✎ Rationale

In support of the new ECMO and ECLS codes 33946-33989, an exclusionary parenthetical note has been added following code 39010 to preclude this code from being reported in conjunction with ECMO codes 33955, 33956, 33963, and 33964.

Digestive System

Salivary Gland and Ducts

REPAIR

42507 Parotid duct diversion, bilateral (Wilke type procedure);

 ►(42508 has been deleted)◄

Esophagus

EXCISION

43130 Diverticulectomy of hypopharynx or esophagus, with or without myotomy; cervical approach

43135 thoracic approach

 ►(For endoscopic diverticulectomy of hypopharynx or cervical esophagus, use 43180)◄

ENDOSCOPY

When bleeding occurs as a result of an endoscopic procedure, control of bleeding is not reported separately during the same operative session.

►Esophagoscopy includes examination from the cricopharyngeus muscle (upper esophageal sphincter) to and including the gastroesophageal junction. It may also include examination of the proximal region of the stomach via retroflexion when performed.◄

Esophagoscopy

●**43180** Esophagoscopy, rigid, transoral with diverticulectomy of hypopharynx or cervical esophagus (eg, Zenker's diverticulum), with cricopharyngeal myotomy, includes use of telescope or operating microscope and repair, when performed

▶(Do not report 43180 in conjunction with 69990)◀

▶(For diverticulectomy of hypopharynx or esophagus [open], see 43130, 43135)◀

43191 Esophagoscopy, rigid, transoral; diagnostic, including collection of specimen(s) by brushing or washing when performed (separate procedure)

▶(Do not report 43191 in conjunction with 43192, 43193, 43194, 43195, 43196, 43197, 43198)◀

▶(For diagnostic transnasal esophagoscopy, see 43197, 43198)◀

(For diagnostic flexible transoral esophagoscopy, use 43200)

43192 with directed submucosal injection(s), any substance

▶(Do not report 43192 in conjunction with 43191, 43197, 43198)◀

(For flexible transoral esophagoscopy with directed submucosal injection(s), use 43201)

(For flexible transoral esophagoscopy with injection sclerosis of esophageal varices, use 43204)

(For rigid transoral esophagoscopy with injection sclerosis of esophageal varices, use 43499)

43193 with biopsy, single or multiple

▶(Do not report 43193 in conjunction with 43191, 43197, 43198)◀

▶(For flexible transoral esophagoscopy with biopsy, use 43202)◀

▲**43194** with removal of foreign body(s)

▶(Do not report 43194 in conjunction with 43191, 43197, 43198)◀

▶(If fluoroscopic guidance is performed, use 76000)◀

▶(For flexible transoral esophagoscopy with removal of foreign body(s), use 43215)◀

43195 with balloon dilation (less than 30 mm diameter)

▶(Do not report 43195 in conjunction with 43191, 43197, 43198)◀

▶(If fluoroscopic guidance is performed, use 74360)◀

(For esophageal dilation with balloon 30 mm diameter or larger, see 43214, 43233)

(For dilation without endoscopic visualization, see 43450, 43453)

(For flexible transoral esophagoscopy with balloon dilation [less than 30 mm diameter], use 43220)

43196 with insertion of guide wire followed by dilation over guide wire

▶(Do not report 43196 in conjunction with 43191, 43197, 43198)◀

▶(If fluoroscopic guidance is performed, use 74360)◀

(For flexible transoral esophagoscopy with insertion of guide wire followed by dilation over guide wire, use 43226)

▲**43197**   Esophagoscopy, flexible, transnasal; diagnostic, including collection of specimen(s) by brushing or washing, when performed (separate procedure)

▶(Do not report 43197 in conjunction with 31575, 43191, 43192, 43193, 43194, 43195, 43196, 43198, 43200-43232, 43235-43259, 43266, 43270, 92511)◀

(Do not report 43197 in conjunction with 31231 unless separate type of endoscope [eg, rigid endoscope] is used)

▶(For transoral esophagoscopy, see 43191, 43200)◀

43198   with biopsy, single or multiple

▶(Do not report 43198 in conjunction with 31575, 43191, 43192, 43193, 43194, 43195, 43196, 43197, 43200-43232, 43235-43259, 43266, 43270, 92511)◀

(Do not report 43198 in conjunction with 31231 unless separate type of endoscope [eg, rigid endoscope] is used)

▶(For transoral esophagoscopy with biopsy, see 43193, 43202)◀

⊙**43200**   Esophagoscopy, flexible, transoral; diagnostic, including collection of specimen(s) by brushing or washing, when performed (separate procedure)

▶(Do not report 43200 in conjunction with 43197, 43198, 43201-43232)◀

(For diagnostic rigid transoral esophagoscopy, use 43191)

(For diagnostic flexible transnasal esophagoscopy, use 43197)

▶(For diagnostic flexible esophagogastroduodenoscopy, use 43235)◀

⊙**43201**   with directed submucosal injection(s), any substance

▶(Do not report 43201 in conjunction with 43204, 43211, 43227 for the same lesion)◀

▶(Do not report 43201 in conjunction with 43197, 43198, 43200)◀

(For rigid transoral esophagoscopy with directed submucosal injection[s], use 43192)

(For flexible transoral esophagoscopy with injection sclerosis of esophageal varices, use 43204)

(For rigid transoral esophagoscopy with injection sclerosis of esophageal varices, use 43499)

⊙**43202**   with biopsy, single or multiple

▶(Do not report 43202 in conjunction with 43211 for the same lesion)◀

▶(Do not report 43202 in conjunction with 43197, 43198, 43200)◀

(For rigid transoral esophagoscopy with biopsy, use 43193)

(For flexible transnasal esophagoscopy with biopsy, use 43198)

⊙**43204**   with injection sclerosis of esophageal varices

▶(Do not report 43204 in conjunction with 43201, 43227 for the same lesion)◀

▶(Do not report 43204 in conjunction with 43197, 43198, 43200)◀

(For rigid transoral esophagoscopy with injection sclerosis of esophageal varices, use 43499)

⊙**43205**   with band ligation of esophageal varices

▶(Do not report 43205 in conjunction with 43227 for the same lesion)◀

▶(Do not report 43205 in conjunction with 43197, 43198, 43200)◀

▶(To report control of nonvariceal bleeding with band ligation, use 43227)◀

⊙**43206**   with optical endomicroscopy

(Report supply of contrast agent separately)

▶(Do not report 43206 in conjunction with 43197, 43198, 43200, 88375)◀

⊙▲**43215**   with removal of foreign body(s)

▶(Do not report 43215 in conjunction with 43197, 43198, 43200)◀

▶(If fluoroscopic guidance is performed, use 76000)◀

▶(For rigid transoral esophagoscopy with removal of foreign body(s), use 43194)◀

⊙▲**43216**   with removal of tumor(s), polyp(s), or other lesion(s) by hot biopsy forceps

▶(Do not report 43216 in conjunction with 43197, 43198, 43200)◀

⊙**43217**   with removal of tumor(s), polyp(s), or other lesion(s) by snare technique

▶(Do not report 43217 in conjunction with 43211 for the same lesion)◀

▶(Do not report 43217 in conjunction with 43197, 43198, 43200)◀

▶(For esophagogastroduodenoscopy with removal of tumor[s], polyp[s], or other lesion[s] by snare technique, use 43251)◀

▶(For endoscopic mucosal resection, use 43211)◀

⊙**43211**   with endoscopic mucosal resection

▶(Do not report 43211 in conjunction with 43201, 43202, 43217 for the same lesion)◀

▶(Do not report 43211 in conjunction with 43197, 43198, 43200)◀

⊙**43212**   with placement of endoscopic stent (includes pre- and post-dilation and guide wire passage, when performed)

▶(Do not report 43212 in conjunction with 43197, 43198, 43200, 43220, 43226, 43241)◀

▶(If fluoroscopic guidance is performed, use 74360)◀

⊙**43220**   with transendoscopic balloon dilation (less than 30 mm diameter)

▶(Do not report 43220 in conjunction with 43197, 43198, 43200, 43212, 43226, 43229)◀

▶(If fluoroscopic guidance is performed, use 74360)◀

⊘=Modifier 51 Exempt   ⊙=Moderate Sedation   ✚=Add-on Code   𝒩=FDA approval pending

(For rigid transoral esophagoscopy with balloon dilation [less than 30 mm diameter], use 43195)

(For esophageal dilation with balloon 30 mm diameter or larger, use 43214)

(For dilation without endoscopic visualization, see 43450, 43453)

\# ⊙**43213**   with dilation of esophagus, by balloon or dilator, retrograde (includes fluoroscopic guidance, when performed)

▶(Do not report 43213 in conjunction with 43197, 43198, 43200, 74360, 76000, 76001)◀

▶(For transendoscopic balloon dilation of multiple strictures during the same session, report 43213 with modifier 59 for each additional stricture dilated)◀

\# ⊙**43214**   with dilation of esophagus with balloon (30 mm diameter or larger) (includes fluoroscopic guidance, when performed)

▶(Do not report 43214 in conjunction with 43197, 43198, 43200, 74360, 76000, 76001)◀

⊙**43226**   with insertion of guide wire followed by passage of dilator(s) over guide wire

▶(Do not report 43226 in conjunction with 43229 for the same lesion)◀

▶(Do not report 43226 in conjunction with 43197, 43198, 43200, 43212, 43220)◀

▶(If fluoroscopic guidance is performed, use 74360)◀

(For rigid transoral esophagoscopy with insertion of guide wire followed by dilation over guide wire, use 43196)

⊙**43227**   with control of bleeding, any method

▶(Do not report 43227 in conjunction with 43201, 43204, 43205 for the same lesion)◀

▶(Do not report 43227 in conjunction with 43197, 43198, 43200)◀

⊙**43229**   with ablation of tumor(s), polyp(s), or other lesion(s) (includes pre- and post-dilation and guide wire passage, when performed)

▶(Do not report 43229 in conjunction with 43220, 43226 for the same lesion)◀

▶(Do not report 43229 in conjunction with 43197, 43198, 43200)◀

(For esophagoscopic photodynamic therapy, report 43229 in conjunction with 96570, 96571 as appropriate)

⊙**43231**   with endoscopic ultrasound examination

▶(Do not report 43231 in conjunction with 43197, 43198, 43200, 43232, 76975)◀

▶(Do not report 43231 more than once per session)◀

⊙**43232**   with transendoscopic ultrasound-guided intramural or transmural fine needle aspiration/biopsy(s)

▶(Do not report 43232 in conjunction with 43197, 43198, 43200, 43231, 76942, 76975)◀

▶(Do not report 43232 more than once per session)◀

Esophagogastroduodenoscopy

(For examination of the esophagus from the cricopharyngeus muscle [upper esophageal sphincter] to and including the gastroesophageal junction, including examination of the proximal region of the stomach via retroflexion when performed, see 43197, 43198, 43200, 43201, 43202, 43204, 43205, 43206, 43211, 43212, 43213, 43214, 43215, 43216, 43217, 43220, 43226, 43227, 43229, 43231, 43232)

(Use 43233, 43235-43259, 43266, 43270 for examination of a surgically altered stomach where the jejunum is examined distal to the anastomosis [eg, gastric bypass, gastroenterostomy {Billroth II}])

▶To report esophagogastroscopy where the duodenum is deliberately not examined (eg, judged clinically not pertinent), or because the clinical situation precludes such exam (eg, significant gastric retention precludes safe exam of duodenum), append modifier 52 if repeat examination is not planned, or modifier 53 if repeat examination is planned.◀

⊙**43235**　Esophagogastroduodenoscopy, flexible, transoral; diagnostic, including collection of specimen(s) by brushing or washing, when performed (separate procedure)

▶(Do not report 43235 in conjunction with 43197, 43198, 43236-43259, 43266, 43270, 44360, 44361, 44363, 44364, 44365, 44366, 44369, 44370, 44372, 44373, 44376, 44377, 44378, 44379)◀

⊙**43236**　　　with directed submucosal injection(s), any substance

▶(Do not report 43236 in conjunction with 43243, 43254, 43255 for the same lesion)◀

▶(Do not report 43236 in conjunction with 43197, 43198, 43235, 44360, 44361, 44363, 44364, 44365, 44366, 44369, 44370, 44372, 44373, 44376, 44377, 44378, 44379)◀

▶(For flexible, transoral esophagogastroduodenoscopy with injection sclerosis of esophageal and/or gastric varices, use 43243)◀

⊙**43237**　　　with endoscopic ultrasound examination limited to the esophagus, stomach or duodenum, and adjacent structures

▶(Do not report 43237 in conjunction with 43197, 43198, 43235, 43238, 43242, 43253, 43259, 44360, 44361, 44363, 44364, 44365, 44366, 44369, 44370, 44372, 44373, 44376, 44377, 44378, 44379, 76975)◀

▶(Do not report 43237 more than once per session)◀

⊙**43238**　　　with transendoscopic ultrasound-guided intramural or transmural fine needle aspiration/biopsy(s), (includes endoscopic ultrasound examination limited to the esophagus, stomach or duodenum, and adjacent structures)

▶(Do not report 43238 in conjunction with 43197, 43198, 43235, 43237, 43242, 44360, 44361, 44363, 44364, 44365, 44366, 44369, 44370, 44372, 44373, 44376, 44377, 44378, 44379, 76942, 76975)◀

▶(Do not report 43238 more than once per session)◀

⊙**43239**　　　with biopsy, single or multiple

▶(Do not report 43239 in conjunction with 43254 for the same lesion)◀

▶(Do not report 43239 in conjunction with 43197, 43198, 43235, 44360, 44361, 44363, 44364, 44365, 44366, 44369, 44370, 44372, 44373, 44376, 44377, 44378, 44379)◀

　　　⊘=Modifier 51 Exempt　⊙=Moderate Sedation　✛=Add-on Code　𝒩=FDA approval pending

⊙**43240**　　　with transmural drainage of pseudocyst (includes placement of transmural drainage catheter[s]/ stent[s], when performed, and endoscopic ultrasound, when performed)

▶(Do not report 43240 in conjunction with 43253 for the same lesion)◀

▶(Do not report 43240 in conjunction with 43197, 43198, 43235, 43242, 43259, 43266, 44360, 44361, 44363, 44364, 44365, 44366, 44369, 44370, 44372, 44373, 44376, 44377, 44378, 44379)◀

▶(Do not report 43240 more than once per session)◀

(For endoscopic pancreatic necrosectomy, use 48999)

⊙**43241**　　　with insertion of intraluminal tube or catheter

▶(Do not report 43241 in conjunction with 43197, 43198, 43212, 43235, 43266, 44360, 44361, 44363, 44364, 44365, 44366, 44369, 44370, 44372, 44373, 44376, 44377, 44378, 44379)◀

(For naso- or oro-gastric tube placement requiring physician's or other qualified health care professional's skill and fluoroscopic guidance, use 43752)

▶(For nonendoscopic enteric tube placement, see 44500, 74340)◀

⊙**43242**　　　with transendoscopic ultrasound-guided intramural or transmural fine needle aspiration/ biopsy(s) (includes endoscopic ultrasound examination of the esophagus, stomach, and either the duodenum or a surgically altered stomach where the jejunum is examined distal to the anastomosis)

▶(Do not report 43242 in conjunction with 43197, 43198, 43235, 43237, 43238, 43240, 43259, 44360, 44361, 44363, 44364, 44365, 44366, 44369, 44370, 44372, 44373, 44376, 44377, 44378, 44379, 76942, 76975)◀

▶(Do not report 43242 more than once per session)◀

▶(For transendoscopic ultrasound-guided transmural fine needle aspiration/biopsy limited to the esophagus, stomach, duodenum, or adjacent structure, use 43238)◀

⊙**43243**　　　with injection sclerosis of esophageal/gastric varices

▶(Do not report 43243 in conjunction with 43236, 43255 for the same lesion)◀

▶(Do not report 43243 in conjunction with 43197, 43198, 43235, 44360, 44361, 44363, 44364, 44365, 44366, 44369, 44370, 44372, 44373, 44376, 44377, 44378, 44379)◀

⊙**43244**　　　with band ligation of esophageal/gastric varices

▶(Do not report 43244 in conjunction with 43197, 43198, 43235, 43255, 44360, 44361, 44363, 44364, 44365, 44366, 44369, 44370, 44372, 44373, 44376, 44377, 44378, 44379)◀

▶(To report control of nonvariceal bleeding with band ligation, use 43255)◀

⊙**43245**　　　with dilation of gastric/duodenal stricture(s) (eg, balloon, bougie)

▶(Do not report 43245 in conjunction with 43197, 43198, 43235, 43266, 44360, 44361, 44363, 44364, 44365, 44366, 44369, 44370, 44372, 44373, 44376, 44377, 44378, 44379)◀

▶(If fluoroscopic guidance is performed, use 74360)◀

⊙**43246**   with directed placement of percutaneous gastrostomy tube

▶(Do not report 43246 in conjunction with 43197, 43198, 43235, 44360, 44361, 44363, 44364, 44365, 44366, 44369, 44370, 44372, 44376, 44377, 44378, 44379)◀

▶(For nonendoscopic percutaneous placement of gastrostomy tube, use 49440)◀

▶(For replacement of gastrostomy tube without imaging or endoscopy, use 43760)◀

⊙▲**43247**   with removal of foreign body(s)

▶(Do not report 43247 in conjunction with 43197, 43198, 43235, 44360, 44361, 44363, 44364, 44365, 44366, 44369, 44370, 44372, 44373, 44376, 44377, 44378, 44379)◀

▶(If fluoroscopic guidance is performed, use 76000)◀

⊙**43248**   with insertion of guide wire followed by passage of dilator(s) through esophagus over guide wire

▶(Do not report 43248 in conjunction with 43197, 43198, 43235, 43266, 43270, 44360, 44361, 44363, 44364, 44365, 44366, 44369, 44370, 44372, 44373, 44376, 44377, 44378, 44379)◀

▶(If fluoroscopic guidance is performed, use 74360)◀

⊙**43249**   with transendoscopic balloon dilation of esophagus (less than 30 mm diameter)

▶(Do not report 43249 in conjunction with 43197, 43198, 43235, 43266, 43270, 44360, 44361, 44363, 44364, 44365, 44366, 44369, 44370, 44372, 44373, 44376, 44377, 44378, 44379)◀

▶(If fluoroscopic guidance is performed, use 74360)◀

⊙**43233**   with dilation of esophagus with balloon (30 mm diameter or larger) (includes fluoroscopic guidance, when performed)

▶(Do not report 43233 in conjunction with 43197, 43198, 43235, 44360, 44361, 44363, 44364, 44365, 44366, 44369, 44370, 44372, 44373, 44376, 44377, 44378, 44379, 74360, 76000, 76001)◀

⊙▲**43250**   with removal of tumor(s), polyp(s), or other lesion(s) by hot biopsy forceps

▶(Do not report 43250 in conjunction with 43197, 43198, 43235, 44360, 44361, 44363, 44364, 44365, 44366, 44369, 44370, 44372, 44373, 44376, 44377, 44378, 44379)◀

⊙**43251**   with removal of tumor(s), polyp(s), or other lesion(s) by snare technique

▶(Do not report 43251 in conjunction with 43254 for the same lesion)◀

▶(Do not report 43251 in conjunction with 43197, 43198, 43235, 44360, 44361, 44363, 44364, 44365, 44366, 44369, 44370, 44372, 44373, 44376, 44377, 44378, 44379)◀

(For endoscopic mucosal resection, use 43254)

⊙**43252**   with optical endomicroscopy

(Report supply of contrast agent separately)

▶(Do not report 43252 in conjunction with 43197, 43198, 43235, 44360, 44361, 44363, 44364, 44365, 44366, 44369, 44370, 44372, 44373, 44376, 44377, 44378, 44379, 88375)◀

⊙**43253**   with transendoscopic ultrasound-guided transmural injection of diagnostic or therapeutic substance(s) (eg, anesthetic, neurolytic agent) or fiducial marker(s) (includes endoscopic ultrasound examination of the esophagus, stomach, and either the duodenum or a surgically altered stomach where the jejunum is examined distal to the anastomosis)

▶(Do not report 43253 in conjunction with 43240 for the same lesion)◀

▶(Do not report 43253 in conjunction with 43197, 43198, 43235, 43237, 43259, 44360, 44361, 44363, 44364, 44365, 44366, 44369, 44370, 44372, 44373, 44376, 44377, 44378, 44379, 76942, 76975)◀

▶(Do not report 43253 more than once per session)◀

▶(For transendoscopic ultrasound-guided transmural fine needle aspiration/biopsy, see 43238, 43242)◀

⊙**43254**   with endoscopic mucosal resection

▶(Do not report 43254 in conjunction with 43236, 43239, 43251 for the same lesion)◀

▶(Do not report 43254 in conjunction with 43197, 43198, 43235, 44360, 44361, 44363, 44364, 44365, 44366, 44369, 44370, 44372, 44373, 44376, 44377, 44378, 44379)◀

⊙**43255**   with control of bleeding, any method

▶(Do not report 43255 in conjunction with 43236, 43243, 43244 for the same lesion)◀

▶(Do not report 43255 in conjunction with 43197, 43198, 43235, 44360, 44361, 44363, 44364, 44365, 44366, 44369, 44370, 44372, 44373, 44376, 44377, 44378, 44379)◀

\# ⊙**43266**   with placement of endoscopic stent (includes pre- and post-dilation and guide wire passage, when performed)

▶(Do not report 43266 in conjunction with 43197, 43198, 43235, 43240, 43241, 43245, 43248, 43249, 44360, 44361, 44363, 44364, 44365, 44366, 44369, 44370, 44372, 44373, 44376, 44377, 44378, 44379)◀

▶(If fluoroscopic guidance is performed, use 74360)◀

⊙**43257**   with delivery of thermal energy to the muscle of lower esophageal sphincter and/or gastric cardia, for treatment of gastroesophageal reflux disease

▶(Do not report 43257 in conjunction with 43197, 43198, 43235, 44360, 44361, 44363, 44364, 44365, 44366, 44369, 44370, 44372, 44373, 44376, 44377, 44378, 44379)◀

▶(For ablation of metaplastic/dysplastic esophageal lesion [eg, Barrett's esophagus], see 43229, 43270)◀

\# ⊙**43270**   with ablation of tumor(s), polyp(s), or other lesion(s) (includes pre- and post-dilation and guide wire passage, when performed)

▶(Do not report 43270 in conjunction with 43248, 43249 for the same lesion)◀

▶(Do not report 43270 in conjunction with 43197, 43198, 43235, 44360, 44361, 44363, 44364, 44365, 44366, 44369, 44370, 44372, 44373, 44376, 44377, 44378, 44379)◀

▶(For esophagoscopic photodynamic therapy, use 43270 in conjunction with 96570, 96571 as appropriate)◀

⊙**43259** with endoscopic ultrasound examination, including the esophagus, stomach, and either the duodenum or a surgically altered stomach where the jejunum is examined distal to the anastomosis

▶(Do not report 43259 in conjunction with 43197, 43198, 43235, 43237, 43240, 43242, 43253, 44360, 44361, 44363, 44364, 44365, 44366, 44369, 44370, 44372, 44373, 44376, 44377, 44378, 44379, 76975)◀

▶(Do not report 43259 more than once per session)◀

Endoscopic Retrograde Cholangiopancreatography (ERCP)

▶Report the appropriate code(s) for each service performed. Therapeutic ERCP (43261, 43262, 43263, 43264, 43265, 43274, 43275, 43276, 43277, 43278) includes diagnostic ERCP (43260). ERCP includes guide wire passage when performed. An ERCP is considered complete if one or more of the ductal system(s), (pancreatic/biliary) is visualized. To report ERCP attempted but with unsuccessful cannulation of any ductal system, see 43235-43259, 43266, 43270.◀

Codes 43274, 43275, 43276, and 43277 describe ERCP with stent placement, removal or replacement (exchange) of stent(s), and balloon dilation within the pancreatico-biliary system. For reporting purposes, ducts that may be reported as stented or subject to stent replacement (exchange) or to balloon dilation include:

Pancreas: major and minor ducts

Biliary tree: common bile duct, right hepatic duct, left hepatic duct, cystic duct/gallbladder

ERCP with stent placement includes any balloon dilation performed in that duct. ERCP with more than one stent placement (eg, different ducts or side by side in the same duct) performed during the same day/session may be reported with 43274 more than once with modifier 59 appended to the subsequent procedure(s). For ERCP with more than one stent exchanged during the same day/session, 43276 may be reported for the initial stent exchange, and 43276 with modifier 59 for each additional stent exchange. ERCP with balloon dilation of more than one duct during the same day/session may be reported with modifier 59 appended to the subsequent procedure(s). Sphincteroplasty, which is balloon dilation of the ampulla (sphincter of Oddi), is reported with 43277, and includes sphincterotomy (43262) when performed.

To report ERCP via altered postoperative anatomy, see 43260, 43262, 43263, 43264, 43265, 43273, 43274, 43275, 43276, 43277, 43278, for Billroth II gastroenterostomy. See 47999 (Unlisted procedure, biliary tract) or 48999 (Unlisted procedure, pancreas) for ERCP via gastrostomy (laparoscopic or open) or via Roux-en-Y anatomy (eg, post-bariatric gastric bypass, post-total gastrectomy).

▶To report optical endomicroscopy of the biliary tract, use 47999. To report optical endomicroscopy of the pancreas, use 48999. Do not report optical endomicroscopy more than once per session.◀

Stone destruction includes any stone removal in the same ductal system (biliary/pancreatic). Code 43277 may be separately reported if sphincteroplasty or dilation of a ductal stricture is required before proceeding to remove stones/debris from the duct during the same session. Dilation that is incidental to the passage of an instrument to clear stones or debris is not separately reported.

(Do not report 43277 for use of a balloon catheter to clear stones/debris from a duct. Any dilation of the duct that may occur during this maneuver is considered inherent to the work of 43264 and 43265)

⊘=Modifier 51 Exempt   ⊙=Moderate Sedation   ✚=Add-on Code   ⟋=FDA approval pending

►(If imaging of the ductal systems is performed, including images saved to the permanent record and report of the imaging, see 74328, 74329, 74330)◄

⊙**43260**   Endoscopic retrograde cholangiopancreatography (ERCP); diagnostic, including collection of specimen(s) by brushing or washing, when performed (separate procedure)

►(Do not report 43260 in conjunction with 43261, 43262, 43263, 43264, 43265, 43274, 43275, 43276, 43277, 43278)◄

⊙**43261**   with biopsy, single or multiple

►(Do not report 43261 in conjunction with 43260)◄

⊙**43262**   with sphincterotomy/papillotomy

(43262 may be reported when sphincterotomy is performed in addition to 43261, 43263, 43264, 43265, 43275, 43278)

►(Do not report 43262 in conjunction with 43274 for stent placement or with 43276 for stent replacement [exchange] in the same location)◄

►(Do not report 43262 in conjunction with 43260, 43277)◄

⊙**43263**   with pressure measurement of sphincter of Oddi

►(Do not report 43263 in conjunction with 43260)◄

(Do not report 43263 more than once per session)

⊙**43264**   with removal of calculi/debris from biliary/pancreatic duct(s)

(Do not report 43264 if no calculi or debris are found, even if balloon catheter is deployed)

►(Do not report 43264 in conjunction with 43260, 43265)◄

⊙**43265**   with destruction of calculi, any method (eg, mechanical, electrohydraulic, lithotripsy)

►(Do not report 43265 in conjunction with 43260, 43264)◄

⊙**43274**   with placement of endoscopic stent into biliary or pancreatic duct, including pre- and post-dilation and guide wire passage, when performed, including sphincterotomy, when performed, each stent

(Do not report 43274 in conjunction with 43262, 43275, 43276, 43277 for stent placement or replacement [exchange] in the same duct)

(For stent placement in both the pancreatic duct and the common bile duct during the same operative session, placement of separate stents in both the right and left hepatic ducts, or placement of two side-by-side stents in the same duct, 43274 may be reported for each additional stent placed, using modifier 59 with the subsequent procedure[s])

(To report naso-biliary or naso-pancreatic drainage tube placement, use 43274)

⊙**43275**   with removal of foreign body(s) or stent(s) from biliary/pancreatic duct(s)

►(Do not report 43275 in conjunction with 43260, 43274, 43276)◄

(For removal of stent from biliary or pancreatic duct without ERCP, use 43247)

(Report 43275 only once for removal of one or more stents or foreign bodies from biliary/pancreatic duct[s] during the same session)

\# ⊙**43276**   with removal and exchange of stent(s), biliary or pancreatic duct, including pre- and post-dilation and guide wire passage, when performed, including sphincterotomy, when performed, each stent exchanged

(43276 includes removal and replacement [exchange] of one stent. For replacement [exchange] of additional stent[s] during the same session, report 43276 with modifier 59 for each additional replacement [exchange])

▶(Do not report 43276 in conjunction with 43260, 43275)◀

▶(Do not report 43276 in conjunction with 43262, 43274 for stent placement or exchange in the same duct)◀

\# ⊙**43277**   with trans-endoscopic balloon dilation of biliary/pancreatic duct(s) or of ampulla (sphincteroplasty), including sphincterotomy, when performed, each duct

▶(Do not report 43277 in conjunction with 43278 for the same lesion)◀

▶(Do not report 43277 in conjunction with 43260, 43262)◀

▶(Do not report 43277 for incidental dilation using balloon for stone/debris removal performed with 43264, 43265)◀

(If sphincterotomy without sphincteroplasty is performed on a separate pancreatic duct orifice during the same session [ie, pancreas divisum], report 43262 with modifier 59)

(Do not report 43277 in conjunction with 43274, 43276 for dilation and stent placement/replacement [exchange] in the same duct)

▶(For transendoscopic balloon dilation of multiple strictures during the same session, use 43277 with modifier 59 for each additional stricture dilated)◀

(For bilateral balloon dilation [both right and left hepatic ducts], 43277 may be reported twice with modifier 59 appended to the second procedure)

\# ⊙**43278**   with ablation of tumor(s), polyp(s), or other lesion(s), including pre- and post-dilation and guide wire passage, when performed

▶(Do not report 43278 in conjunction with 43277 for the same lesion)◀

▶(Do not report 43278 in conjunction with 43260)◀

(For ampullectomy, use 43254)

⊙✚**43273**   Endoscopic cannulation of papilla with direct visualization of pancreatic/common bile duct(s) (List separately in addition to code(s) for primary procedure)

(Report 43273 once per procedure)

(Use 43273 in conjunction with 43260, 43261, 43262, 43263, 43264, 43265, 43274, 43275, 43276, 43277, 43278)

⊘=Modifier 51 Exempt   ⊙=Moderate Sedation   ✚=Add-on Code   ⁄⁄=FDA approval pending

REPAIR

▶(43350 has been deleted)◄

43351   Esophagostomy, fistulization of esophagus, external; thoracic approach

43352   cervical approach

MANIPULATION

43460   Esophagogastric tamponade, with balloon (Sengstaken type)

▶(For removal of esophageal foreign body by balloon catheter, see 43499, 74235)◄

Stomach

EXCISION

43640   Vagotomy including pyloroplasty, with or without gastrostomy; truncal or selective

(For pyloroplasty, use 43800)

▶(For vagotomy, see 64755, 64760)◄

Intestines (Except Rectum)

ENDOSCOPY, SMALL INTESTINE

▶When bleeding occurs as the result of an endoscopic procedure, control of bleeding is not reported separately during the same operative session.

Antegrade transoral small intestinal endoscopy (enteroscopy) is defined by the most distal segment of small intestine that is examined. Codes 44360, 44361, 44363, 44364, 44365, 44366, 44369, 44370, 44372, 44373 are endoscopic procedures to visualize the esophagus through the jejunum using an antegrade approach. Codes 44376, 44377, 44378, 44379 are endoscopic procedures to visualize the esophagus through the ileum using an antegrade approach. If an endoscope cannot be advanced at least 50 cm beyond the pylorus, see 43233, 43235-43259, 43266, 43270; if an endoscope can be passed at least 50 cm beyond pylorus but only into jejunum, see 44360, 44361, 44363, 44364, 44365, 44366, 44369, 44370, 44372, 44373.

To report retrograde examination of small intestine via anus or colon stoma, use 44799, unlisted procedure, intestine.◄

▶(Do not report 44360, 44361, 44363, 44364, 44365, 44366, 44369, 44370, 44372, 44373 in conjunction with 43233, 43235-43259, 43266, 43270, 44376, 44377, 44378, 44379)◄

▶(Do not report 44376, 44377, 44378, 44379 in conjunction with 43233, 43235-43259, 43266, 43270, 44360, 44361, 44363, 44364, 44365, 44366, 44369, 44370, 44372, 44373)◄

▶(For esophagogastroduodenoscopy, see 43233, 43235-43259, 43266, 43270)◄

⊙▲**44360** Small intestinal endoscopy, enteroscopy beyond second portion of duodenum, not including ileum; diagnostic, including collection of specimen(s) by brushing or washing, when performed (separate procedure)

⊙**44361** with biopsy, single or multiple

⊙▲**44363** with removal of foreign body(s)

⊙**44376** Small intestinal endoscopy, enteroscopy beyond second portion of duodenum, including ileum; diagnostic, with or without collection of specimen(s) by brushing or washing (separate procedure)

▶(Do not report 44376 in conjunction with 44360, 44361, 44363, 44364, 44365, 44366, 44369, 44370, 44372, 44373)◀

⊙**44377** with biopsy, single or multiple

▶(Do not report 44377 in conjunction with 44360, 44361, 44363, 44364, 44365, 44366, 44369, 44370, 44372, 44373)◀

⊙**44378** with control of bleeding (eg, injection, bipolar cautery, unipolar cautery, laser, heater probe, stapler, plasma coagulator)

▶(Do not report 44378 in conjunction with 44360, 44361, 44363, 44364, 44365, 44366, 44369, 44370, 44372, 44373)◀

⊙**44379** with transendoscopic stent placement (includes predilation)

▶(Do not report 44379 in conjunction with 44360, 44361, 44363, 44364, 44365, 44366, 44369, 44370, 44372, 44373)◀

▶ENDOSCOPY, STOMAL◀

▶*Definitions*

Proctosigmoidoscopy is the examination of the rectum and may include examination of a portion of the sigmoid colon.

Sigmoidoscopy is the examination of the entire rectum, sigmoid colon and may include examination of a portion of the descending colon.

Colonoscopy is the examination of the entire colon, from the rectum to the cecum, and may include examination of the terminal ileum or small intestine proximal to an anastomosis.

Colonoscopy through stoma is the examination of the colon, from the colostomy stoma to the cecum or colon-small intestine anastomosis, and may include examination of the terminal ileum or small intestine proximal to an anastomosis.

When performing a diagnostic or screening endoscopic procedure on a patient who is scheduled and prepared for a total colonoscopy, if the physician is unable to advance the colonoscope to the cecum or colon-small intestine anastomosis due to unforeseen circumstances, report 45378 (colonoscopy) or 44388 (colonoscopy through stoma) with modifier 53 and provide appropriate documentation.

If a therapeutic colonoscopy (44389-44407, 45379, 45380, 45381, 45382, 45384, 45388, 45398) is performed and does not reach the cecum or colon-small intestine anastomosis, report the appropriate therapeutic colonoscopy code with modifier 52 and provide appropriate documentation.

⊘=Modifier 51 Exempt ⊙=Moderate Sedation ✚=Add-on Code ⩘=FDA approval pending

Report ileoscopy through stoma (44380, 44381, 44382, 44384) for endoscopic examination of a patient who has an ileostomy.

Report colonoscopy through stoma (44388-44408) for endoscopic examination of a patient who has undergone segmental resection of the colon (eg, hemicolectomy, sigmoid colectomy, low anterior resection) and has a colostomy.

For colonoscopy per rectum, see 45378, 45390, 45392, 45393, 45398.

Report proctosigmoidoscopy (45300-45327), flexible sigmoidoscopy (45330-45347), or anoscopy (46600, 46604, 46606, 46608, 46610, 46611, 46612, 46614, 46615), as appropriate for endoscopic examination of the defunctionalized rectum or distal colon in a patient who has undergone colectomy, in addition to colonoscopy through stoma (44388-44408) or ileoscopy through stoma (44380, 44381, 44382, 44384) if appropriate.

When bleeding occurs as the result of an endoscopic procedure, control of bleeding is not reported separately during the same operative session.

For computed tomographic colonography, see 74261, 74262, 74263. ◀

⊙▲**44380**   Ileoscopy, through stoma; diagnostic, including collection of specimen(s) by brushing or washing, when performed (separate procedure)

▶(Do not report 44380 in conjunction with 44381, 44382, 44384)◀

⊙**44382**   with biopsy, single or multiple

▶(Do not report 44382 in conjunction with 44380)◀

#⊙●**44381**   with transendoscopic balloon dilation

▶(Do not report 44381 in conjunction with 44380, 44384)◀

▶(If fluoroscopic guidance is performed, use 74360)◀

▶(For transendoscopic balloon dilation of multiple strictures during the same session, report 44381 with modifier 59 for each additional stricture dilated)◀

▶(44383 has been deleted. To report, use 44384)◀

⊙●**44384**   with placement of endoscopic stent (includes pre- and post-dilation and guide wire passage, when performed)

▶(Do not report 44384 in conjunction with 44380, 44381)◀

▶(If fluoroscopic guidance is performed, use 74360)◀

⊙▲**44385**   Endoscopic evaluation of small intestinal pouch (eg, Kock pouch, ileal reservoir [S or J]); diagnostic, including collection of specimen(s) by brushing or washing, when performed (separate procedure)

▶(Do not report 44385 in conjunction with 44386)◀

⊙▲**44386**   with biopsy, single or multiple

▶(Do not report 44386 in conjunction with 44385)◀

⊙▲**44388**   Colonoscopy through stoma; diagnostic, including collection of specimen(s) by brushing or washing, when performed (separate procedure)

▶(Do not report 44388 in conjunction with 44389-44408)◀

▲=Revised Code   ●=New Code   ▶◀=New or Revised Text   #=Resequenced Code

⊙**44389**   with biopsy, single or multiple

    ▶(Do not report 44389 in conjunction with 44403 for the same lesion)◀

    ▶(Do not report 44389 in conjunction with 44388)◀

⊙▲**44390**   with removal of foreign body(s)

    ▶(Do not report 44390 in conjunction with 44388)◀

    ▶(If fluoroscopic guidance is performed, use 76000)◀

⊙▲**44391**   with control of bleeding, any method

    ▶(Do not report 44391 in conjunction with 44404 for the same lesion)◀

    ▶(Do not report 44391 in conjunction with 44388)◀

⊙▲**44392**   with removal of tumor(s), polyp(s), or other lesion(s) by hot biopsy forceps

    ▶(Do not report 44392 in conjunction with 44388)◀

    ▶(44393 has been deleted. To report, use 44401)◀

#⊙●**44401**   with ablation of tumor(s), polyp(s), or other lesion(s) (includes pre-and post-dilation and guide wire passage, when performed)

    ▶(Do not report 44401 in conjunction with 44405 for the same lesion)◀

    ▶(Do not report 44401 in conjunction with 44388)◀

⊙**44394**   with removal of tumor(s), polyp(s), or other lesion(s) by snare technique

    ▶(Do not report 44394 in conjunction with 44403 for the same lesion)◀

    ▶(Do not report 44394 in conjunction with 44388)◀

    ▶(For endoscopic mucosal resection, use 44403)◀

    ▶(44397 has been deleted. To report, use 44402)◀

⊙●**44402**   with endoscopic stent placement (including pre- and post-dilation and guide wire passage, when performed)

    ▶(Do not report 44402 in conjunction with 44388, 44405)◀

    ▶(If fluoroscopic guidance is performed, use 74360)◀

⊙●**44403**   with endoscopic mucosal resection

    ▶(Do not report 44403 in conjunction with 44389, 44394, 44404 for the same lesion)◀

    ▶(Do not report 44403 in conjunction with 44388)◀

⊙●**44404**   with directed submucosal injection(s), any substance

    ▶(Do not report 44404 in conjunction with 44391, 44403 for the same lesion)◀

    ▶(Do not report 44404 in conjunction with 44388)◀

⊙●**44405**   with transendoscopic balloon dilation

    ▶(Do not report 44405 in conjunction with 44388, 44401, 44402)◀

        ⊘=Modifier 51 Exempt ⊙=Moderate Sedation ✚=Add-on Code ✅=FDA approval pending

▶(If fluoroscopic guidance is performed, use 74360)◀

▶(For transendoscopic balloon dilation of multiple strictures during the same session, report 44405 with modifier 59 for each additional stricture dilated)◀

⊙●**44406**   with endoscopic ultrasound examination, limited to the sigmoid, descending, transverse, or ascending colon and cecum and adjacent structures

▶(Do not report 44406 in conjunction with 44388, 44407, 76975)◀

▶(Do not report 44406 more than once per session)◀

⊙●**44407**   with transendoscopic ultrasound guided intramural or transmural fine needle aspiration/ biopsy(s), includes endoscopic ultrasound examination limited to the sigmoid, descending, transverse, or ascending colon and cecum and adjacent structures

▶(Do not report 44407 in conjunction with 44388, 44406, 76942, 76975)◀

▶(Do not report 44407 more than once per session)◀

⊙●**44408**   with decompression (for pathologic distention) (eg, volvulus, megacolon), including placement of decompression tube, when performed

▶(Do not report 44408 in conjunction with 44388)◀

▶(Do not report 44408 more than once per session)◀

OTHER PROCEDURES

▲**44799**   Unlisted procedure, small intestine

(For unlisted laparoscopic procedure, intestine except rectum, use 44238)

▶(For unlisted procedure, colon, use 45399)◀

▶Colon and Rectum◀

ENDOSCOPY

Definitions

▶*Proctosigmoidoscopy* is the examination of the rectum and may include examination of a portion of the sigmoid colon.◀

Sigmoidoscopy is the examination of the entire rectum, sigmoid colon and may include examination of a portion of the descending colon.

▶*Colonoscopy* is the examination of the entire colon, from the rectum to the cecum, and may include examination of the terminal ileum or small intestine proximal to an anastomosis.

Colonoscopy through stoma is the examination of the colon, from the colostomy stoma to the cecum, and may include examination of the terminal ileum or small intestine proximal to an anastomosis.

When performing a diagnostic or screening endoscopic procedure on a patient who is scheduled and prepared for a total colonoscopy, if the physician is unable to advance the colonoscope to the cecum or colon-small intestine anastomosis due to unforeseen circumstances, report 45378 (colonoscopy) or 44388 (colonoscopy through stoma) with modifier 53 and provide appropriate documentation.

If a therapeutic colonoscopy (44389-44407, 45379, 45380, 45381, 45382, 45384, 45388, 45398) is performed and does not reach the cecum or colon-small intestine anastomosis, report the appropriate therapeutic colonoscopy code with modifier 52 and provide appropriate documentation.

Report flexible sigmoidoscopy (45330-45347) for endoscopic examination during which the endoscope is not advanced beyond the splenic flexure.

Report flexible sigmoidoscopy (45330-45347) for endoscopic examination of a patient who has undergone resection of the colon proximal to the sigmoid (eg, subtotal colectomy) and has an ileo-sigmoid or ileo-rectal anastomosis. Report pouch endoscopy codes (44385, 44386) for endoscopic examination of a patient who has undergone resection of colon with ileo-anal anastomosis (eg, J-pouch).

Report colonoscopy (45378-45398) for endoscopic examination of a patient who has undergone segmental resection of the colon (eg, hemicolectomy, sigmoid colectomy, low anterior resection).

For colonoscopy through stoma, see 44388-44408.

Report proctosigmoidoscopy (45300-45327), flexible sigmoidoscopy (45330-45347), or anoscopy (46600, 46604, 46606, 46608, 46610, 46611, 46612, 46614, 46615), as appropriate for endoscopic examination of the defunctionalized rectum or distal colon in a patient who has undergone colectomy, in addition to colonoscopy through stoma (44388-44408) or ileoscopy through stoma (44380, 44381, 44382, 44384) if appropriate.

When bleeding occurs as a result of an endoscopic procedure, control of bleeding is not reported separately during the same operative session. ◄

For computed tomographic colonography, see 74261-74263.

Colonoscopy Decision Tree

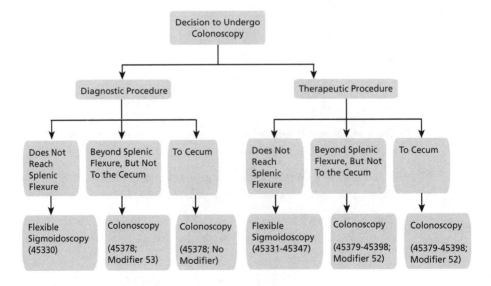

⊘=Modifier 51 Exempt   ⊙=Moderate Sedation   ✛=Add-on Code   𝒩=FDA approval pending

45300   Proctosigmoidoscopy, rigid; diagnostic, with or without collection of specimen(s) by brushing or washing (separate procedure)

▲**45330**   Sigmoidoscopy, flexible; diagnostic, including collection of specimen(s) by brushing or washing, when performed (separate procedure)

►(Do not report 45330 in conjunction with 45331-45342, 45346, 45347, 45349, 45350)◄

45331   with biopsy, single or multiple

►(Do not report 45331 in conjunction with 45349 for the same lesion)◄

⊙▲**45332**   with removal of foreign body(s)

►(Do not report 45332 in conjunction with 45330)◄

►(If fluoroscopic guidance is performed, use 76000)◄

⊙▲**45333**   with removal of tumor(s), polyp(s), or other lesion(s) by hot biopsy forceps

►(Do not report 45333 in conjunction with 45330)◄

⊙▲**45334**   with control of bleeding, any method

►(Do not report 45334 in conjunction with 45335, 45350 for the same lesion)◄

►(Do not report 45334 in conjunction with 45330)◄

⊙**45335**   with directed submucosal injection(s), any substance

►(Do not report 45335 in conjunction with 45334, 45349 for the same lesion)◄

►(Do not report 45335 in conjunction with 45330)◄

⊙▲**45337**   with decompression (for pathologic distention) (eg, volvulus, megacolon), including placement of decompression tube, when performed

►(Do not report 45337 in conjunction with 45330)◄

►(Do not report 45337 more than once per session)◄

⊙**45338**   with removal of tumor(s), polyp(s), or other lesion(s) by snare technique

►(Do not report 45338 in conjunction with 45349 for the same lesion)◄

►(Do not report 45338 in conjunction with 45330)◄

►(For endoscopic mucosal resection, use 45349)◄

►(45339 has been deleted. To report, use 45346)◄

⊙●**45346**   with ablation of tumor(s), polyp(s), or other lesion(s) (includes pre- and post-dilation and guide wire passage, when performed)

►(Do not report 45346 in conjunction with 45330)◄

►(Do not report 45346 in conjunction with 45340 for the same lesion)◄

⊙▲**45340**   with transendoscopic balloon dilation

▶(Do not report 45340 in conjunction with 45330, 45346, 45347)◀

▶(If fluoroscopic guidance is performed, use 74360)◀

▶(For transendoscopic balloon dilation of multiple strictures during the same session, use 45340 with modifier 59 for each additional stricture dilated)◀

⊙**45341**   with endoscopic ultrasound examination

▶(Do not report 45341 in conjunction with 45330, 45342, 76872, 76975)◀

▶(Do not report 45341 more than once per session)◀

⊙**45342**   with transendoscopic ultrasound guided intramural or transmural fine needle aspiration/biopsy(s)

▶(Do not report 45342 in conjunction with 45330, 45341, 76872, 76942, 76975)◀

▶(Do not report 45342 more than once per session)◀

▶(45345 has been deleted. To report, use 45347)◀

⊙●**45347**   with placement of endoscopic stent (includes pre- and post-dilation and guide wire passage, when performed)

▶(Do not report 45347 in conjunction with 45330, 45340)◀

▶(If fluoroscopic guidance is performed, use 74360)◀

⊙●**45349**   with endoscopic mucosal resection

▶(Do not report 45349 in conjunction with 45331, 45335, 45338, 45350 for the same lesion)◀

▶(Do not report 45349 in conjunction with 45330)◀

⊙●**45350**   with band ligation(s) (eg, hemorrhoids)

▶(Do not report 45350 in conjunction with 45334 for the same lesion)◀

▶(Do not report 45350 in conjunction with 45330, 45349, 46221)◀

▶(Do not report 45350 more than once per session)◀

▶(To report control of active bleeding with band ligation[s], use 45334)◀

▶(45355 has been deleted. To report, use 45399)◀

⊙▲**45378** Colonoscopy, flexible; diagnostic, including collection of specimen(s) by brushing or washing, when performed (separate procedure)

▶(Do not report 45378 in conjunction with 45379-45393, 45398)◀

▶(For colonoscopy with decompression [pathologic distention], use 45393)◀

⊙▲**45379**   with removal of foreign body(s)

▶(Do not report 45379 in conjunction with 45378)◀

▶(If fluoroscopic guidance is performed, use 76000)◀

⊘=Modifier 51 Exempt ⊙=Moderate Sedation ✚=Add-on Code 𝒩=FDA approval pending

⊙▲**45380**   with biopsy, single or multiple

▶(Do not report 45380 in conjunction with 45390 for the same lesion)◀

▶(Do not report 45380 in conjunction with 45378)◀

⊙▲**45381**   with directed submucosal injection(s), any substance

▶(Do not report 45381 in conjunction with 45382, 45390 for the same lesion)◀

▶(Do not report 45381 in conjunction with 45378)◀

⊙▲**45382**   with control of bleeding, any method

▶(Do not report 45382 in conjunction with 45381, 45398 for the same lesion)◀

▶(Do not report 45382 in conjunction with 45378)◀

▶(45383 has been deleted. To report, use 45388)◀

#⊙●**45388**   with ablation of tumor(s), polyp(s), or other lesion(s) (includes pre- and post-dilation and guide wire passage, when performed)

▶(Do not report 45388 in conjunction with 45386 for the same lesion)◀

▶(Do not report 45388 in conjunction with 45378)◀

⊙▲**45384**   with removal of tumor(s), polyp(s), or other lesion(s) by hot biopsy forceps

▶(Do not report 45384 in conjunction with 45378)◀

⊙▲**45385**   with removal of tumor(s), polyp(s), or other lesion(s) by snare technique

▶(Do not report 45385 in conjunction with 45390 for the same lesion)◀

▶(Do not report 45385 in conjunction with 45378)◀

▶(For endoscopic mucosal resection, use 45390)◀

⊙▲**45386**   with transendoscopic balloon dilation

▶(Do not report 45386 in conjunction with 45378, 45388, 45389)◀

▶(If fluoroscopic guidance is performed, use 74360)◀

▶(For transendoscopic balloon dilation of multiple strictures during the same session, report 45386 with modifier 59 for each additional stricture dilated)◀

▶(45387 has been deleted. To report, use 45389)◀

⊙●**45389**   with endoscopic stent placement (includes pre- and post-dilation and guide wire passage, when performed)

▶(Do not report 45389 in conjunction with 45378, 45386)◀

▶(If fluoroscopic guidance is performed, use 74360)◀

⊙▲**45391**   with endoscopic ultrasound examination limited to the rectum, sigmoid, descending, transverse, or ascending colon and cecum, and adjacent structures

▶(Do not report 45391 in conjunction with 45378, 45392, 76872, 76975)◀

▶(Do not report 45391 more than once per session)◀

⊙▲**45392**   with transendoscopic ultrasound guided intramural or transmural fine needle aspiration/biopsy(s), includes endoscopic ultrasound examination limited to the rectum, sigmoid, descending, transverse, or ascending colon and cecum, and adjacent structures

▶(Do not report 45392 in conjunction with 45378, 45391, 76872, 76942, 76975)◀

▶(Do not report 45392 more than once per session)◀

#⊙●**45390**   with endoscopic mucosal resection

▶(Do not report 45390 in conjunction with 45380, 45381, 45385, 45398 for the same lesion)◀

▶(Do not report 45390 in conjunction with 45378)◀

⊙●**45393**   with decompression (for pathologic distention) (eg, volvulus, megacolon), including placement of decompression tube, when performed

▶(Do not report 45393 in conjunction with 45378)◀

▶(Do not report 45393 more than once per session)◀

#⊙●**45398**   with band ligation(s) (eg, hemorrhoids)

▶(Do not report 45398 in conjunction with 45382 for the same lesion)◀

▶(Do not report 45398 in conjunction with 45378, 45390, 46221)◀

▶(Do not report 45398 more than once per session)◀

▶(To report control of active bleeding with band ligation[s], use 45382)◀

OTHER PROCEDURES

#⊙●**45399**   Unlisted procedure, colon

45990   Anorectal exam, surgical, requiring anesthesia (general, spinal, or epidural), diagnostic

(Do not report 45990 in conjunction with 45300-45327, 46600, 57410, 99170)

45999   Unlisted procedure, rectum

(For unlisted laparoscopic procedure, rectum, use 45499)

⊘=Modifier 51 Exempt   ⊙=Moderate Sedation   ✚=Add-on Code   ⊿=FDA approval pending

Anus

EXCISION

46221 Hemorrhoidectomy, internal, by rubber band ligation(s)

▶(Do not report 46221 in conjunction with 45350, 45398)◀

(For ligation, hemorrhoidal vascular bundle(s), including ultrasound guidance, use 0249T)

INTRODUCTION

46500 Injection of sclerosing solution, hemorrhoids

▶(For anoscopy with directed submucosal injection of bulking agent for fecal incontinence, use 0377T)◀

ENDOSCOPY

Surgical endoscopy always includes diagnostic endoscopy.

▶(For anoscopy with directed submucosal injection of bulking agent for fecal incontinence, use 0377T)◀

▲**46600** Anoscopy; diagnostic, including collection of specimen(s) by brushing or washing, when performed (separate procedure)

▶(Do not report 46600 in conjunction with 46020, 0249T, 0377T)◀

▶(For diagnostic high-resolution anoscopy [HRA], use 46601)◀

●**46601** diagnostic, with high-resolution magnification (HRA) (eg, colposcope, operating microscope) and chemical agent enhancement, including collection of specimen(s) by brushing or washing, when performed

▶(Do not report 46601 in conjunction with 69990)◀

46604 with dilation (eg, balloon, guide wire, bougie)

46606 with biopsy, single or multiple

▶(For high-resolution anoscopy [HRA] with biopsy, use 46607)◀

●**46607** with high-resolution magnification (HRA) (eg, colposcope, operating microscope) and chemical agent enhancement, with biopsy, single or multiple

▶(Do not report 46607 in conjunction with 69990)◀

46615 with ablation of tumor(s), polyp(s), or other lesion(s) not amenable to removal by hot biopsy forceps, bipolar cautery or snare technique

(For delivery of thermal energy to the muscle of the anal canal, use 0288T)

REPAIR

46760   Sphincteroplasty, anal, for incontinence, adult; muscle transplant

46761   levator muscle imbrication (Park posterior anal repair)

46762   implantation artificial sphincter

▶(For anoscopy with directed submucosal injection of bulking agent for fecal incontinence, use 0377T)◀

Liver

OTHER PROCEDURES

⊙**47382**   Ablation, 1 or more liver tumor(s), percutaneous, radiofrequency

(For imaging guidance and monitoring, see 76940, 77013, 77022)

⊙●**47383**   Ablation, 1 or more liver tumor(s), percutaneous, cryoablation

▶(For imaging guidance and monitoring, see 76940, 77013, 77022)◀

🖉 Rationale

As part of an effort to ensure that the CPT code set reflects current clinical practice, code 42508 (bilateral parotid duct diversion with excision of 1 submandibular gland) has been deleted due to low utilization.

A reciprocal parenthetical note has been added following code 43135 to direct users to code 43180 to identify endoscopic diverticulectomy of the hypopharynx or cervical esophagus.

Code 43180 has been established to report rigid transoral esophagoscopy performed for diverticulectomy of the hypopharynx or the cervical esophagus. A diverticulum of the hypopharynx is an abnormal formation of a pouch within the esophagus and hypopharynx. This procedure surgically treats the pouch formation by excising the pouch and conjoining the resultant defect within the throat. As is noted within the code descriptor, this procedure is performed endoscopically and includes cricopharyngeal myotomy, use of the telescope or operating microscope, and the repair procedure itself. Parenthetical notes have been placed to exclude the use of code 43180 in conjunction with code 69990 (operating microscope) and to direct users to the appropriate codes to report diverticulectomy of the hypopharynx esophagus. In addition, a guideline has been added following the Endoscopy heading to identify the specific anatomy that is included as part of the examination.

The Endoscopic Retrograde Cholangiopancreatography (ERCP) guidelines that direct users to codes 43235-43259 when an ERCP is attempted but with unsuccessful cannulation of any ductal system have been revised to include

⊘=Modifier 51 Exempt   ⊙=Moderate Sedation   ✚=Add-on Code   ⊮=FDA approval pending

esophagogastroduodenoscopy codes 43266 (stent placement) and 43270 (ablation of tumor[s], polyp[s], or other lesion[s]). Instructions stating not to report optical endomicroscopy more than once per session have also been added.

As part of an effort to ensure that the CPT code set is reflective of current clinical practice, code 43350 (esophagostomy, external fistulization of esophagus, abdominal approach) has been deleted due to low utilization. Code 43350 was a parent code to codes 43351 and 43352, and therefore, the parent language has been moved to code 43351. Note that this does not change the meaning or intent of codes 43351 or 43352.

In accordance with the gastroenterological changes in the Digestive System subsection, the cross-reference parenthetical note following code 43460 has been revised by removing foreign body removal codes 43215 and 43247 and adding unlisted procedure, esophagus code 43499.

In accordance with the deletion of code 64752, the cross-reference parenthetical note following code 43640 has been revised with the removal of this code.

In the CPT 2014 code set, the Esophagus/Endoscopy section was restructured into three subsections: Esophagoscopy, Esophagogastroduodenoscopy (EGD), and Endoscopic Retrograde Cholangiopancreatography (ERCP). In those subsections, the codes were revised, deleted, and added to bundle services that were commonly performed together and to describe current practice more accurately. Guidelines were also revised and added to define more clearly the various endoscopic procedures and to provide proper reporting instructions. In the CPT 2015 code set, changes have been made to the Intestines and Rectum Endoscopy subsections for the same purposes. A colonoscopy decision tree has been added to help users select the appropriate colonoscopy code. Please note that the last box in the last row of the Colonoscopy Decision Tree should state "Colonoscopy 45379-45398; No Modifier."

The Endoscopy, Small Intestine and Stomal subsection has been divided into two separate sections: one for small intestine endoscopy and one for stomal endoscopy. Codes 44360-44379 are listed under the Endoscopy, Small Intestine section and guidelines have been added to define the endoscopy procedures and to provide proper reporting instructions. Control of bleeding that occurs during the endoscopy is not reported separately. The guidelines include special instructions for when the endoscope cannot be advanced at least 50 cm beyond the pylorus, or when the endoscope can be passed at least 50 cm beyond the pylorus but only into the jejunum.

Codes 44380-44408 are listed under the Endoscopy, Stomal section and describe stomal ileoscopy and colonoscopy procedures. Definitions have been added for proctosigmoidoscopy, colonoscopy, and stomal colonoscopy procedures. Instructions have been added for specific scenarios, such as when the physician is unable to advance the scope to the cecum or colon-small intestine anastomosis due to unforeseen circumstances during a diagnostic or screening colonoscopy, or when a therapeutic colonoscopy does not reach the cecum or colon-small intestine anastomosis. These instructions have also been added to the Colon and Rectum/ Endoscopy guidelines.

Two new codes have been added to the ileoscopy through stoma code family. Code 44381 describes transendoscopic balloon dilation. Code 44384 describes endoscopic stent placement. Eight new codes have been added to the colonoscopy through stoma code family to describe endoscopic ablation (44401); stent placement (44402); mucosal resection (44403); directed submucosal injections (44404); transendoscopic balloon dilation (44405); endoscopic ultrasound examination (EUS) (44406); transendoscopic ultrasound-guided intramural or transmural fine needle aspiration (FNA) or biopsy(s) (44407); and decompression for pathologic distention (44408). Pathologic distention is an expansion of the abdomen from accumulated air caused by an underlying condition such as a volvulus or mega-colon. A volvulus is a winding or twisting of the colon, which causes a bowel obstruction. A megacolon is an enlargement or dilation of the colon. In the Other Procedures section, code 44799 has been revised to specify an unlisted procedure of the small intestine for clarity in distinguishing small intestine procedures from colon procedures.

Pouchoscopy base code 44385 has been revised to remove the reference to "abdominal or pelvic" and now lists "Kock pouch" and "ileal reservoir" as exam-ples. These revisions also apply to child code 44386.

The Rectum section heading has been revised to "Colon and Rectum" to clarify that the section includes procedures of the colon, as well as the rectum. The guidelines have also been revised. Previously, the guidelines stated that a procto-sigmoidoscopy included an examination of the rectum and sigmoid colon. In the CPT 2015 code set, the guidelines have been revised to clarify that proctosigmoid-oscopy may include examination of a portion of the sigmoid colon.

Transabdominal colonoscopy via colotomy code 45355 has been deleted. In rare instances when a colonoscopy cannot be performed through the anus or a stoma, it may be performed through one or more abdominal incisions. Because this pro-cedure is so rarely performed, code 45355 may potentially be misreported, and therefore, has been deleted. If this procedure is performed, it should be reported with the new unlisted colon procedure code, 45399.

Flexible colonoscopy base code 45378 has been revised to no longer indicate that the colonoscopy is performed proximal to the splenic flexure and to no longer include colon decompression. The inclusion of decompression has been removed from the descriptor because a new code (45393) has been established to report decompression. The revision to code 45378 extends to its child codes 45379-45398. In addition to code 45393, four more flexible colonoscopy codes have been estab-lished. Code 45388 describes ablation of tumors, polyps, or lesions; code 45389 describes flexible colonoscopy with endoscopic stent placement; code 45390 describes endoscopic mucosal resection; and code 45398 describes band ligation(s). Endoscopic ultrasound (EUS) codes 45391 and 45392 have been revised to specify

⊘=Modifier 51 Exempt   ⊙=Moderate Sedation   ✚=Add-on Code   ⅍=FDA approval pending

that the examination is limited to the rectum, sigmoid, descending, transverse, or ascending colon and cecum and adjacent structures.

Four new codes have been added to the flexible sigmoidoscopy code family (45330-45350): code 45346 describes ablation; code 45347 describes endoscopic stent placement; code 45349 describes endoscopic mucosal resection; and code 45350 describes band ligation.

In accordance with new Category III code 0377T, cross-reference parenthetical notes have been added following injection of sclerosing solution code 46500 and sphincteroplasty code 46762 to direct users to code 0377T for reporting the injection of a bulking agent. The exclusionary parenthetical note for anoscopy code 46600 has been revised with the addition of code 0377T.

Codes 46601 and 46607 have been established to report high-resolution anoscopy (HRA). These codes replace Category III codes 0226T and 0227T. HRA is often performed to anal intraepithelial neoplasia. HRA involves inserting a cotton swab with acetic acid and iodine into the anus using an anoscope. The acetic acid gives dysplastic tissue a white appearance. After a few minutes the cotton swab is removed, and a high-resolution colposcope is used to examine the anus. Code 46601 describes a diagnostic HRA and includes the collection of specimens by brushing or washing, when performed. Code 46607 describes HRA with single or multiple biopsies. Both codes include chemical agent enhancement (application of acetic acid). If an operating microscope is used in the procedure, code 69990 is not reported separately. The parenthetical notes following codes 46600 and 46606 directing users to codes 0226T and 0227T have been revised by replacing codes 0226T and 0227T with codes 46601 and 46607.

Code 47383 has been established to report percutaneous cryoablation of liver tumor(s). Percutaneous cryosurgical ablation of liver tumor(s) may be performed for patients with inoperable malignancy or who may be poor candidates for the open (47381) or laparoscopic (47371) procedures. Percutaneous cryoablation of liver tumor(s) is often performed with imaging guidance and monitoring using ultrasound (76940), computed tomography (CT) (77013), or magnetic resonance (77022) guidance. Imaging guidance and monitoring are reported separately.

In addition to the changes described above, editorial revisions have been made to guidelines, parenthetical notes, and code descriptors across all of the upper and lower endoscopy subsections in an effort to maintain language uniformity and clarity.

The following table is a listing of new, revised, and deleted codes in the Endoscopy, Small Intestinal, Stomal, Flexible Sigmoidscopy, and Colonoscopy sections for the CPT® 2015 code set. The table lists the CPT code, code descriptor, and, as appropriate, services included, terminology reconciliation with other codes in the code set, and other notable changes.

CPT Code	Code Descriptor	Change Detail
Ileoscopy		
⊙▲ 44380	Ileoscopy, through stoma; diagnostic, ~~with or without~~including collection of specimen(s) by brushing or washing, when performed (separate procedure)	Terminology reconciliation
~~44383~~	~~with ablation of tumor(s), polyp(s), or other lesion(s) not amenable to removal by hot biopsy forceps, bipolar cautery or snare technique~~	Use 44384
#⊙● 44381	with transendoscopic balloon dilation	Not separately reportable with stent placement described by 44384
		Use 74360 if fluoroscopic guidance is performed
		For transendoscopic balloon dilation of multiple strictures during the same session, report 44381 with modifier 59 for each additional stricture dilated
⊙●44384	with placement of endoscopic stent (includes pre- and post-dilation and guide wire passage, when performed)	Not separately reportable with codes 44380 and 44381
		Use 74360 if fluoroscopic guidance is performed
Endoscopy of Small Intestinal Pouch		
⊙▲44385	Endoscopic evaluation of small intestinal pouch (eg, Kock pouch, ileal reservoir [S or pelvicJ]) ~~pouch~~; diagnostic, ~~with or without~~ including collection of specimen(s) by brushing or washing, when performed (separate procedure)	Terminology reconciliation
⊙▲44386	with biopsy, single or multiple	Parent code revised
Colonoscopy through Stoma		
⊙▲44388	Colonoscopy through stoma; diagnostic, ~~with or without~~ including collection of specimen(s) by brushing or washing, when performed (separate procedure)	Terminology reconciliation/new definition
		Exam to cecum and/or small intestine anastomosis; if not complete, report screening exam with modifier 53
Guideline for codes 44389-44407	If a therapeutic colonoscopy (44389-44407, 45379, 45380, 45381, 45382, 45384, 45388, 45398) is performed and does not reach the cecum or colon-small intestine anastomosis, report the appropriate therapeutic colonoscopy code with modifier 52 and provide appropriate documentation.	Exam to cecum and/or small intestine anastomosis; if not complete, report diagnostic/therapeutic exam with modifier 52
⊙▲44390	with removal of foreign body(s)	"Foreign body(ies)" replaces "foreign body"
		Use 76000 if fluoroscopic guidance is performed
⊙▲44391	with control of bleeding, ~~(eg, injection, bipolar cautery, unipolar cautery, laser, heater probe, stapler, plasma coagulator)~~ any method	Includes injection described by 44404 for same lesion
⊙▲44392	with removal of tumor(s), polyp(s), or other lesion(s) by hot biopsy forceps ~~or bipolar cautery~~	Bipolar cautery was removed as an example of hot biopsy
~~44393~~	~~with ablation of tumor(s), polyp(s), or other lesion(s) not amenable to removal by hot biopsy forceps, bipolar cautery or snare technique~~	Use 44401
#⊙● 44401	with ablation of tumor(s), polyp(s), or other lesion(s) (includes pre-and post-dilation and guide wire passage, when performed)	Do not report in conjunction with 44405 for the same lesion

⊘=Modifier 51 Exempt　⊙=Moderate Sedation　✚=Add-on Code　⊿=FDA approval pending

CPT Code	Code Descriptor	Change Detail
44397	with transendoscopic stent placement (includes predilation)	Use 44402
⊙● 44402	with endoscopic stent placement (including pre- and post-dilation and guide wire passage, when performed)	Not separately reportable with codes 44388, 44405 Use 74360 if fluoroscopic guidance is performed
⊙● 44403	with endoscopic mucosal resection	Includes biopsy, snare, or submucosal injection described by 44389, 44394, 44404 for same lesion
⊙● 44404	with directed submucosal injection(s), any substance	Not separately reportable with control of bleeding or EMR described by 44391, 44403 for same lesion
⊙● 44405	with transendoscopic balloon dilation	Not separately reportable with ablation or stent placement described by 44401, 44402 Use 74360 if fluoroscopic guidance is performed For transendoscopic balloon dilation of multiple strictures during the same session, report 44405 with modifier 59 for each additional stricture dilated
⊙● 44406	with endoscopic ultrasound examination, limited to the sigmoid, descending, transverse, or ascending colon and cecum and adjacent structures	Report only once per session Not separately reportable with EUS FNA code 44407 or radiologic ultrasound codes described by 76975
⊙● 44407	with transendoscopic ultrasound guided intramural or transmural fine needle aspiration/biopsy(s), includes endoscopic ultrasound examination limited to the sigmoid, descending, transverse, or ascending colon and cecum and adjacent structures	Report only once per session Not separately reportable with EUS radiologic ultrasound codes described by 44406, 76942, 76975
⊙● 44408	with decompression (for pathologic distention) (eg, volvulus, megacolon), including placement of decompression tube, when performed	Report only once per session Includes decompression tube placement when performed
Flexible Sigmoidoscopy		
▲45330	Sigmoidoscopy, flexible; diagnostic, with or without including collection of specimen(s) by brushing or washing, when performed (separate procedure)	Terminology reconciliation
⊙▲45332	with removal of foreign body(s)	"Foreign body(ies)" replaces "foreign body" Use 76000 if fluoroscopic guidance is performed
⊙▲45333	with removal of tumor(s), polyp(s), or other lesion(s) by hot biopsy forceps or bipolar cautery	Bipolar cautery was removed as an example of hot biopsy
⊙▲45334	with control of bleeding, (eg, injection, bipolar cautery, unipolar cautery, laser, heater probe, stapler, plasma coagulator) any method	Includes injection or banding of hemorrhoids described by 45335, 45350 for same lesion
⊙▲45337	with decompression (for pathologic distention) (eg, volvulus, megacolon), including placement of volvulus decompression tube, any method when performed	Includes decompression tube placement when performed Report only once per session
45339	with ablation of tumor(s), polyp(s), or other lesion(s) not amenable to removal by hot biopsy forceps, bipolar cautery or snare technique	Use 45346

CPT Code	Code Descriptor	Change Detail
#⊙● 45346	with ablation of tumor(s), polyp(s), or other lesion(s) (includes pre- and post-dilation and guide wire passage, when performed)	Includes dilation described by code 45340 for same lesion
⊙▲45340	with ~~dilation by~~ transendoscopic balloon~~, 1 or more strictures~~ dilation	Report dilation of multiple strictures with modifier 59 for each additional stricture dilated
		Not reportable with ablation or stent placement described by 45346, 45347
		Use 74360 if fluoroscopic guidance is performed
~~45345~~	~~with transendoscopic stent placement (includes predilation)~~	Use 45347
⊙● 45347	with placement of endoscopic stent (includes pre- and post-dilation and guide wire passage, when performed)	Includes pre- and post-dilation and guide wire passage
		Not separately reportable with dilation code 45340
		Use 74360 if fluoroscopic guidance is performed
⊙● 45349	with endoscopic mucosal resection	Includes biopsy, submucosal injection, snare or band ligation(s) described by 45331, 45335, 45338, 45350 for the same lesion
⊙● 45350	with band ligation(s) (eg, hemorrhoids)	Not separately reportable with control of bleeding code 45334 for the same lesion
		Do not report in conjunction with EMR or hemorrhoidectomy described by 45349, 46221
~~45355~~	~~Colonoscopy, rigid or flexible, transabdominal via colotomy, single or multiple;~~	Use 45399
Colonoscopy		
⊙▲45378	Colonoscopy, flexible~~, proximal to splenic flexure~~; diagnostic, ~~with or without~~ including collection of specimen(s) by brushing or washing, ~~with or without colon decompression~~ when performed (separate procedure)	Terminology reconciliation/new definition
		Exam to cecum and may include terminal ileum or small intestine anastomosis; if not complete, report screening exam with modifier 53
Guideline for 45379-45398	If a therapeutic colonoscopy (44389-44407, 45379, 45380, 45381, 45382, 45384, 45388, 45398) is performed and does not reach the cecum or colon-small intestine anastomosis, report the appropriate therapeutic colonoscopy code with modifier 52 and provide appropriate documentation.	Exam to cecum and may include terminal ileum or small intestine anastomosis; if not complete, report therapeutic exam with modifier 52
⊙▲ 45379	with removal of foreign body(s)	Parent code revision
		"Foreign body(ies)" replaces "foreign body"
		Use 76000 if fluoroscopic guidance is performed
⊙▲ 45380	with biopsy, single or multiple	Parent code revision
		Do not report in conjunction with 45390 for the same lesion
⊙▲ 45381	with directed submucosal injection(s), any substance	Parent code revision
		Not separately reportable with control of bleeding or endoscopic mucosal resection described by 45382, 45390 for the same lesion
⊙▲45382	with control of bleeding~~, (eg, injection, bipolar cautery, unipolar cautery, laser, heater probe, stapler, plasma coagulator)~~ any method	Parent code revision
		Not separately reportable with injection or banding of hemorrhoids described by 45381, 45398 for the same lesion

⊘=Modifier 51 Exempt ⊙=Moderate Sedation ✚=Add-on Code 𝑵=FDA approval pending

CPT® 2015 Overview of GI Changes

CPT Code	Code Descriptor	Change Detail
~~45383~~	~~with ablation of tumor(s), polyp(s), or other lesion(s) not amenable to removal by hot biopsy forceps, bipolar cautery or snare technique~~	Use 45388
#⊙▲ 45388	with ablation of tumor(s), polyp(s), or other lesion(s) (includes pre- and post-dilation and guide wire passage, when performed)	Parent code revision Includes dilation described by code 45386 for the same lesion
⊙▲ 45384	with removal of tumor(s), polyp(s), or other lesion(s) by hot biopsy forceps ~~or bipolar cautery~~	Parent code revised Bipolar cautery was removed from descriptor
⊙▲ 45385	with removal of tumor(s), polyp(s), or other lesion(s) by snare technique	Parent code revised Do not report with endoscopic mucosal resection described by 45390 for same lesion
⊙▲ 45386	with ~~dilation by~~ transendoscopic balloon ~~, 1 or more strictures~~ dilation	Parent code revised Report dilation of multiple strictures with the modifier 59 for each additional stricture dilated Not reportable with ablation or stent placement described by 45388, 45389 Use 74360 if fluoroscopic guidance is performed
~~45387~~	~~with transendoscopic stent placement (includes predilation)~~	Use 45389
⊙● 45389	with endoscopic stent placement (includes pre- and post-dilation and guide wire passage, when performed)	Not separately reportable with dilation code 45386 Use 74360 if fluoroscopic guidance is performed
⊙▲ 45391	with endoscopic ultrasound examination limited to the rectum, sigmoid, descending, transverse, or ascending colon and cecum, and adjacent structures	Parent code revised Report only once per session Not separately reportable with EUS FNA code 45392 or radiologic ultrasound codes 76872, 76975
⊙▲ 45392	with transendoscopic ultrasound guided intramural or transmural fine needle aspiration/biopsy(s), includes endoscopic ultrasound examination limited to the rectum, sigmoid, descending, transverse, or ascending colon and cecum, and adjacent structures	Parent code revised Report only once per session Not separately reportable with EUS code 45391 or radiologic ultrasound codes 76872, 76942, 76975
#⊙● 45390	with endoscopic mucosal resection	Includes biopsy, snare, band ligation(s) or submucosal injection described by 45380, 45381, 45385, 45398 for same lesion
⊙● 45393	with decompression (for pathologic distention) (eg, volvulus, megacolon), including placement of decompression tube, when performed	Includes decompression tube placement when performed Report only once per session
#⊙● 45398	with band ligation(s) (eg, hemorrhoids)	Not separately reportable with control of bleeding code 45382 for the same lesion Do not report in conjunction with EMR or hemorrhoidectomy described by 45390, 46221
#● 45399	Unlisted procedure, colon	Includes unlisted procedures specific to the colon

Clinical Example (43180)

A 70-year-old female presents with difficulty swallowing and regurgitation and is at risk for developing aspiration pneumonia. A barium swallow radiograph (contrast esophagram) shows a hypopharyngeal (Zenker's) diverticulum.

Description of Procedure (43180)

Place tooth guard. Insert bivalve laryngoscope, and advance behind larynx into hypopharynx and then beyond into cervical esophagus. Perform endoscopy to identify the pouch, esophagus, and cricopharyngeal bar. Divide the bar using a stapler, laser, or other method. Expand jaws of telescoping laryngoscope to place diverticular bar on stretch. Suspend laryngoscope. Visualize bar using rigid telescope. Place sutures on both sides of the diverticular bar to maximally draw the bar up. Cut bar with stapler, laser, or other device. Examine cut with telescope. Repeat staple and laser procedure as needed to open diverticulum fully into esophageal lumen. Investigate base of pouch for signs of perforation. Suction blood and secretions. Relax and remove laryngoscope. Inspect teeth for signs of trauma. Return patient to anesthesia position.

Clinical Example (44380)

A 65-year-old patient with previous proctocolectomy and ileostomy for inflammatory bowel disease presents with diarrhea. Diagnostic ileoscopy and collection of specimens by brushings is performed.

Description of Procedure (44380)

Inspect the ileal stomal area. Lubricate a standard endoscope, insert it into the stoma, and advance it to the extent feasible. Slowly withdraw the endoscope to allow circumferential examination of the ileal mucosa. When indicated, obtain brushings or washings of suspicious abnormalities. Obtain photodocumentation of appropriate normal landmarks and abnormalities. Supervise the level of sedation and vital signs during the procedure, taking additional measures to maintain an appropriate level of sedation, vital signs, airway, and oxygenation as indicated. At the conclusion of the procedure, withdraw the endoscope.

Clinical Example (44381)

A 70-year-old patient with previous colectomy with ileostomy for colorectal cancer develops obstipation and abdominal discomfort. The patient is found to have a stricture in the ileum. The patient is referred for ileoscopy for evaluation of the ileum and transendoscopic balloon dilation.

Description of Procedure (44381)

Inspect the ileal stomal area. Lubricate a standard endoscope, insert it into the stoma, and advance it to the lesion to be dilated. Identify and assess the lesion to be dilated. Using endoscopic guidance, advance the dilating balloon, and position it at the lesion. Inflate the balloon to its recommended pressure, and hold it for approximately sixty seconds. Perform repeated incremental dilations until the lesion is satisfactorily dilated. Observe the area for bleeding. Advance the endoscope to the extent feasible. Slowly withdraw the endoscope to allow circumferential examination of the ileal mucosa. Obtain photodocumentation of appropriate normal landmarks and abnormalities. Supervise the level of sedation

⃠=Modifier 51 Exempt   ⊙=Moderate Sedation   ✚=Add-on Code   𝑵=FDA approval pending

and vital signs during the procedure, and take additional measures to maintain an appropriate level of sedation, vital signs, airway, and oxygenation as indicated. At the conclusion of the procedure, withdraw the endoscope.

Clinical Example (44384)

A 70-year-old patient with previous colectomy with ileostomy for colorectal cancer develops obstipation and abdominal discomfort. Imaging studies are consistent with a stricture in the ileum due to a mass lesion. The patient is not a candidate for surgical intervention. The patient is referred for a therapeutic ileoscopy with evaluation of the ileum and placement of a stent in the ileum for palliation.

Description of Procedure (44384)

Inspect the ileal stomal area. Lubricate a standard endoscope, insert it into the stoma, and advance it to the site of narrowing. Identify and assess the lesion to be stented. Insert a balloon dilating catheter through the endoscope, position it through the tumor under endoscopic guidance, and inflate it to allow passage of the endoscope through the tumor, confirming its extent. Withdraw the endoscope, allowing measurement of the tumor and marking the distal and proximal margins for stent placement. Insert a guidewire through the endoscope. Using fluoroscopic and endoscopic guidance, advance the expandable wire stent over the guidewire and position it across the tumor. If necessary, insert contrast under fluoroscopic guidance to confirm positioning of the stent. Obtain fluoroscopic imaging, and take spot digital images. Slowly deploy the stent across the tumor under fluoroscopic guidance, repositioning if necessary. Once the stent is placed, withdraw the guidewire and introducing device. Inject contrast through the endoscope to assess placement and patency. As needed, use deployment of balloon dilating catheter to expand the stent to sufficient lumen size. Observe the area to confirm absence of active bleeding. Advance the endoscope to the extent feasible. Slowly withdraw the endoscope to allow circumferential examination of the ileal mucosa. Obtain photodocumentation of appropriate normal landmarks and abnormalities. Supervise the level of sedation and vital signs during the procedure with additional measures taken to maintain an appropriate level of sedation, vital signs, airway, and oxygenation as indicated. At the conclusion of the procedure, withdraw the endoscope.

Clinical Example (44385)

A 40-year-old patient with previous colectomy and small intestinal pouch for ulcerative colitis disease presents with diarrhea. Diagnostic evaluation of the small intestinal pouch is performed.

Description of Procedure (44385)

Assess the level of sedation prior to inserting the endoscope. Perform endoscopic evaluation of small intestinal pouch (Kock or ileoanal J pouch) to assess mucosa and possible etiology of diarrhea. Perform brushings if indicated. Perform photodocumentation. Supervise the level of sedation and vital signs during the procedure with additional measures taken to maintain an appropriate level of sedation, vital signs, airway, and oxygenation as indicated. At the conclusion of the procedure, withdraw the endoscope.

Clinical Example (44386)

A 38-year-old patient with previous colectomy and small intestinal pouch for ulcerative colitis presents with diarrhea and abdominal discomfort. Endoscopic evaluation of the pouch is performed, and multiple biopsies are taken of abnormal tissue.

Description of Procedure (44386)

Assess the level of sedation prior to inserting the endoscope. Perform endoscopic evaluation of small intestinal pouch (Kock or ileoanal J pouch) to assess mucosa and etiology of diarrhea. Perform multiple biopsies. Perform photodocumentation. Supervise the level of sedation and vital signs during the procedure with additional measures taken to maintain an appropriate level of sedation, vital signs, airway, and oxygenation as indicated. At the conclusion of the procedure, withdraw the endoscope.

 Clinical Example (44388)

A 65-year-old patient with a history of abdominal perineal resection of a rectal cancer undergoes colonoscopy through stoma for surveillance.

Description of Procedure (44388)

Inspect the stomal area. Lubricate and insert a standard flexible colonoscope through the ostomy site. Advance the scope to the cecum using air insufflation, water flush, and suctioning as necessary to view the mucosa; identify the appendiceal orifice and ileocecal valve, and intubate the ileocecal valve, if indicated. Slowly withdraw the colonoscope through the ascending colon, hepatic flexure, transverse colon, splenic flexure, and sigmoid colon to allow circumferential examination of the colon mucosa. When indicated, obtain brushings or washings of suspicious abnormalities. Obtain photodocumentation of appropriate normal landmarks and abnormalities. Deflate the colon, and withdraw the scope.

Clinical Example (44390)

A 50-year-old patient with a permanent colostomy swallowed an object that became lodged at the ileocecal valve. Colonoscopy through stoma with removal of the foreign body is performed.

Description of Procedure (44390)

Inspect the stomal area. Lubricate and insert a standard flexible colonoscope through the ostomy site. Advance the scope to the foreign body using air insufflation, water flush, and suctioning as necessary to view the mucosa. Grasp the foreign body with an appropriate retrieval device. Withdraw the foreign body, retrieval device, and colonoscope. Re-insert the colonoscope to the cecum; identify the appendiceal orifice and ileocecal valve, and intubate the ileocecal valve, if indicated. Slowly withdraw the colonoscope through the ascending colon, hepatic flexure, transverse colon, splenic flexure, and sigmoid colon to allow circumferential examination of the colon mucosa. Obtain photodocumentation of appropriate normal landmarks and abnormalities. Deflate the colon, and withdraw the scope.

⊘=Modifier 51 Exempt   ⊙=Moderate Sedation   ✛=Add-on Code   ✎=FDA approval pending

Clinical Example (44391)

A 65-year-old patient with a history of abdominal perineal resection of a rectal cancer presents with active hemorrhage through the colostomy. Colonoscopy through stoma for control of bleeding is performed.

Description of Procedure (44391)

Inspect the stomal area. Lubricate and insert a standard flexible colonoscope through the ostomy site. Advance the scope using air insufflation, water flush, and suctioning as necessary to view the mucosa; identify the appendiceal orifice and the ileocecal valve, and intubate the ileocecal valve, if indicated. Slowly withdraw the colonoscope through the ascending colon, hepatic flexure, transverse colon, splenic flexure, and sigmoid colon to allow circumferential examination of the colon mucosa. Identify active bleeding from an angiodysplastic lesion in the colon. Insert a bipolar cautery probe through the colonoscope, and position on the bleeding lesion; apply therapy to control the bleeding. Obtain photodocumentation of appropriate normal landmarks and abnormalities. Deflate the colon, and withdraw the scope.

Clinical Example (44392)

A 66-year-old patient with a history of abdominal perineal resection of a rectal cancer undergoes colonoscopy through stoma. Diminutive polyps are identified in the proximal colon and removed.

Description of Procedure (44392)

Perform inspection of the stomal area. Lubricate and insert a standard flexible colonoscope through the ostomy site. Advance the scope to the cecum using air insufflation, water flush, and suctioning as necessary to view the mucosa; identify the appendiceal orifice and ileocecal valve, and intubate the ileocecal valve, if indicated. Withdraw the colonoscope to the ascending colon, and remove the identified lesions with successive applications of hot biopsy forceps until there is no residual. Slowly withdraw the colonoscope through the ascending colon, hepatic flexure, transverse colon, splenic flexure, and sigmoid colon to allow circumferential examination of the colon mucosa. Obtain photodocumentation of appropriate normal landmarks and abnormalities. Deflate the colon, and withdraw the scope.

Clinical Example (44401)

A 65-year-old patient with a history of abdominal perineal resection of a rectal cancer undergoes colonoscopy through stoma. A flat lesion is identified in the transverse colon and ablated.

Description of Procedure (44401)

Inspect the stomal area. Lubricate and insert a standard flexible colonoscope through the ostomy site. Advance the scope to the cecum using air insufflation, water flush, and suctioning as necessary to view the mucosa. Identify the appendiceal orifice and the ileocecal valve, and intubate the ileocecal valve, if indicated. Withdraw the colonoscope through the ascending colon and transverse colon. Identify a flat lesion in the transverse colon. Under endoscopic visualization, pass a guidewire through the colonoscope, and withdraw the scope. Re-insert the colonoscope, and place a sizing balloon catheter through the scope into the colon to straddle the region of abnormality to be ablated. Inflate the sizing balloon to ascertain the luminal diameter to be treated. Remove the sizing balloon, and pass an ablation catheter of appropriate caliber over the guidewire into the colon. Slowly withdraw the colonoscope through the descending and sigmoid colon, and examine the colonic mucosa. Obtain photodocumentation of appropriate normal landmarks and abnormalities. Deflate the colon, and withdraw the scope.

Clinical Example (44402)

A 68-year-old patient with a history of abdominal perineal resection of a rectal cancer presents with abdominal pain and imaging findings of an obstructing lesion in the mid-transverse colon. Colonoscopy through stoma with dilation of the colon and placement of a stent is performed.

Description of Procedure (44402)

Inspect the stomal area. Lubricate and insert a standard flexible colonoscope through the ostomy site. Advance the scope to the transverse colon using air insufflation, water flush, and suctioning as necessary to view the mucosa. Identify an obstructing, concentric tumor that prohibits passage of the standard colonoscope. Withdraw the colonoscope, and insert a thin caliber flexible colonoscope through the rectum, passing it through the colonic tumor to the cecum. Identify the appendiceal orifice and ileocecal valve, and intubate the ileocecal valve, if indicated. Withdraw the colonoscope, and examine the ascending colon and proximal transverse colon. Measure the tumor, and mark the distal and proximal margins of the tumor for stent placement. Re-insert the colonoscope to 2 cm past the distal end of the tumor, and insert a guidewire through the endoscope across the full length of the tumor. Withdraw the colonoscope. Under fluoroscopic guidance, advance the expandable wire mesh stent and introducing device over the guidewire into the colon and position across the tumor. If necessary, insert contrast under fluoroscopic guidance to confirm positioning of the stent. Obtain fluoroscopic imaging, and take spot digital images. Slowly deploy the stent across the tumor under fluoroscopic guidance, with repositioning if necessary. Once the stent is placed, withdraw the guidewire and introducing device, and re-insert the thin caliber colonoscope to confirm proper positioning of the stent. Balloon dilatation of the stent may be required. Slowly withdraw the colonoscope through the distal transverse colon and descending and sigmoid colon to allow circumferential examination of the colon mucosa. Obtain photodocumentation of appropriate normal landmarks and abnormalities. Deflate the colon, and withdraw the scope.

Clinical Example (44403)

A 65-year-old patient with a history of abdominal perineal resection of a rectal cancer undergoes colonoscopy through stoma. A large sessile polyp is identified, and endoscopic mucosal resection is performed.

Description of Procedure (44403)

Inspect the stomal area. Lubricate and insert a standard flexible colonoscope through the ostomy site. Advance the scope to the cecum using air insufflation, water flush, and suctioning as necessary to view the mucosa. Identify the

⊘=Modifier 51 Exempt   ⊙=Moderate Sedation   ✚=Add-on Code   ⯩=FDA approval pending

appendiceal orifice and ileocecal valve, and intubate the ileocecal valve, if indicated. Withdraw the colonoscope through the ascending colon, transverse colon, and descending and sigmoid colon to allow circumferential examination of the colonic mucosa. Identify the lesion in the sigmoid colon that cannot be removed by standard snare polypectomy technique. Withdraw the colonoscope, fit a friction cap onto the end of the scope, and insert the colonoscope through the rectum into the colon to the site where endoscopic mucosal resection is to be performed. Pass an injection needle through the colonoscope, and submucosally inject a solution of a topical contrast agent, such as methylene blue, saline, and epinephrine, to raise the lesion. Withdraw the injection needle. Suction the area of abnormality into the friction-fitted cap to create a pseudopolyp. Pass a snare through the colonoscope, and loop it around the lesion. As the snare is tightened, apply electrocautery in a controlled manner, and remove the identified lesion. Repeat snare removal until all visually identified portions of the lesion are resected. Withdraw the snare, and insert a retrieval device through the colonoscope to capture the lesion. Withdraw the retrieval device with the lesion to the tip of the colonoscope, which is withdrawn through the stoma. Re-insert the colonoscope through the stoma to the area of the lesion. Examine the base of the lesion; if there is residual tissue, apply the snare or other appropriate technique until there is no residual. Control bleeding, as necessary. Obtain photodocumentation of appropriate normal landmarks and abnormalities. Deflate the colon, and withdraw the scope.

Clinical Example (44404)

A 68-year-old patient with a history of abdominal perineal resection of a rectal cancer is found to have a colonic cancer that cannot be resected endoscopically. Colonoscopy through stoma with injection of India ink to tattoo the lesion is performed prior to surgical referral.

Description of Procedure (44404)

Inspect stomal area. Lubricate and insert a standard flexible colonoscope through the ostomy site. Advance the scope to the cecum using air insufflation, water flush, and suctioning as necessary to view the mucosa. Identify the lesion in the proximal transverse colon that is highly suspect as being a malignancy not suitable for endoscopic resection. Advance a 23-gauge sclerotherapy needle through the instrument channel, and inject multiple small boluses of India ink into submucosa at sites around the lesion to facilitate surgical identification of the lesion. Advance the scope to the cecum using air insufflation as necessary; identify the appendiceal orifice and ileocecal valve, and intubate the ileocecal valve, if indicated. Slowly withdraw the colonoscope through the ascending colon, hepatic flexure, transverse colon, splenic flexure, and sigmoid colon to allow circumferential examination of the colon mucosa. Obtain photodocumentation of appropriate normal landmarks and abnormalities. Deflate the colon, and withdraw the scope.

Clinical Example (44405)

A 65-year-old patient with a history of abdominal perineal resection of a rectal cancer presents with an anastomotic stricture. Therapeutic colonoscopy through stoma with dilation of the stricture is performed.

Description of Procedure (44405)

Inspect the stomal area. Lubricate and insert a standard flexible colonoscope through the ostomy site. Advance the scope to the descending colon using air insufflation, water flush, and suctioning as necessary to view the mucosa. Identify the stricture that prohibits passage of the colonoscope. Position the colonoscope. Advance a through-the-scope fixed wire balloon catheter through the colonoscope, position it across the stricture, and inflate it to a diameter of approximately 15 mm. Deflate the balloon catheter, and observe the stricture. If necessary, remove the balloon dilator, insert subsequent balloon catheters of larger diameter through the colonoscope, position them across the stricture, and inflate. Deflate the balloon catheter, and observe the stricture to confirm adequate dilation of the stricture. When dilation is adequate, remove the balloon catheter. Following dilation, observe the area for bleeding. Advance the colonoscope to the cecum using air insufflation as necessary; identify the appendiceal orifice and ileocecal valve, and intubate the ileocecal valve, if indicated. Slowly withdraw the colonoscope through the ascending colon, hepatic flexure, transverse colon, splenic flexure, and sigmoid colon to allow circumferential examination of the colon mucosa. Obtain photodocumentation of appropriate normal landmarks and abnormalities. Deflate the colon, and withdraw the scope.

 Clinical Example (44406)

A 58-year-old patient with history of abdominal perineal resection of a rectal cancer presents with abdominal discomfort and weight loss. Diagnostic colonoscopy through stoma with endoscopic ultrasound is performed.

Description of Procedure (44406)

Inspect the stomal area. Lubricate and insert a standard flexible colonoscope through the ostomy site. Advance the scope to the cecum using air insufflation, water flush, and suctioning as necessary to view the mucosa. Identify the appendiceal orifice and the ileocecal valve, and intubate the ileocecal valve, if indicated. Slowly withdraw the colonoscope through the ascending colon, hepatic flexure, transverse colon, splenic flexure, and sigmoid colon to allow circumferential examination of the colon mucosa. Identify the lesion in the sigmoid colon. Obtain photodocumentation of appropriate normal landmarks and abnormalities. Deflate the colon, and withdraw the scope. Prepare a dedicated echoendoscope with a balloon placed over the transducer housing. Introduce the echoendoscope through the ostomy site, and advance it to the level of the identified abnormality under direct endoscopic visualization. While slowly withdrawing the echoendoscope, obtain ultrasound imaging. Take ultrasound spot digital images, and have them reviewed by the endoscopist. At the conclusion of the procedure, remove the echoendoscope.

 Clinical Example (44407)

A 72-year-old patient with history of abdominal perineal resection of a rectal cancer presents with abdominal discomfort and weight loss. Enlarged regional lymph nodes are found on imaging studies. Diagnostic colonoscopy through stoma with endoscopic ultrasound staging of the tumor and fine needle aspiration biopsy of the lymph nodes are performed to plan therapy.

⊘=Modifier 51 Exempt   ⊙=Moderate Sedation   ✚=Add-on Code   𝒩=FDA approval pending

Description of Procedure (44407)

Inspect the stomal area. Insert a standard flexible colonoscope into the ostomy site. Advance the scope to the cecum using air insufflation, water flush, and suctioning as necessary to view the mucosa. Identify the appendiceal orifice and the ileocecal valve, and intubate the ileocecal valve, if indicated. Slowly withdraw the colonoscope through the ascending colon, hepatic flexure, transverse colon, splenic flexure, and sigmoid colon to allow circumferential examination of the colon mucosa. Identify the lesion in the sigmoid colon. Perform photodocumentation. Deflate the colon, and withdraw the scope. Prepare a dedicated echoendoscope with a balloon placed over the transducer housing. Introduce the echoendoscope through the ostomy site, and advance it to the level of the identified abnormality under direct endoscopic visualization. While slowly withdrawing the echoendoscope, perform ultrasound imaging. Take ultrasound spot digital images, and have them reviewed by the endoscopist. Determine the risks and benefits of biopsying the lesion. Advance the needle biopsy device through the biopsy channel of the echoendoscope. Perform Doppler imaging to ensure that any vascular structures or areas within the lesion are recognized prior to biopsy. Under direct ultrasound visualization, advance the needle through the colon wall into the lesion. Remove the central stylet from the needle, apply negative pressure to the hub of the device, and make to and fro movements with the needle in the lesion. After multiple passes of the needle, withdraw the needle from the echoendoscope, and spray the aspirated material onto glass slides for examination. At the conclusion of procedure, remove the echoendoscope.

Clinical Example (44408)

A 76-year-old patient with altered mental status and a permanent colostomy presents with abdominal distension and a megacolon on imaging studies. Colonoscopy through stoma with decompression of the colon and placement of tube is performed.

Description of Procedure (44408)

Inspect the stomal area. Insert a standard flexible colonoscope into the ostomy site. Advance the scope to the cecum using minimal air insufflation across grossly patulous regions of colon containing gas, stool, and fluid, performing continuous suctioning of the colonic contents to decompress the colon. Identify the appendiceal orifice and ileocecal valve, and intubate the ileocecal valve, if indicated. Withdraw the colonoscope through the ascending colon, transverse colon, and descending and sigmoid colon, and examine the colon mucosa, with continuous suctioning to decompress the colon. Insert a 10-Fr tube through the rectum into the colon. Identify the tip of the tube, position the tube and colonoscope, insert a grasping device through the colonoscope, and grasp the tube. Advance the tube endoscopically into the transverse colon. Release the grasping device from the tube, and withdraw the colonoscope maintaining the position of the tube. Perform photodocumentation. Deflate the colon, and withdraw the scope.

Clinical Example (45330)

A 73-year-old patient presents with diarrhea without evidence of bleeding. Laboratory evaluation of stool was unrevealing for the presence of infectious pathogens. Diagnostic flexible sigmoidoscopy with examination of the rectum and sigmoid colon and collection of specimens by brushings is performed.

Description of Procedure (45330)

Inspect the perianal area, and perform a digital rectal examination. Lubricate a standard flexible sigmoidoscope, insert it into the rectum, and advance it to the splenic flexure using air insufflation as necessary. Slowly withdraw the sigmoidoscope to allow circumferential examination of the colon mucosa. When indicated, obtain brushings or washings of suspicious abnormalities. Obtain photodocumentation of appropriate normal landmarks and abnormalities. In the rectum, retroflex the sigmoidoscope to allow examination of the rectal mucosa. Straighten the sigmoidoscope, deflate the colon, and withdraw the scope.

Clinical Example (45332)

A 35-year-old patient presents after inserting an object into the rectum that cannot be manually removed. Therapeutic flexible sigmoidoscopy with examination of the rectum and sigmoid colon and removal of the foreign body is performed.

Description of Procedure (45332)

Inspect the perianal area, and perform a digital rectal examination. Lubricate a standard flexible sigmoidoscope, insert it into the rectum, and advance it to the foreign body using air insufflation as necessary. Identify and assess the foreign body to be removed. Using a retrieval device advanced through the biopsy channel of the sigmoidoscope, grasp the foreign body and pull it to the tip of the sigmoidoscope. Withdraw the sigmoidoscope and foreign body. Re-insert the sigmoidoscope to the region of the splenic flexure, and slowly withdraw it to allow circumferential examination of the colon mucosa. Obtain photodocumentation of appropriate normal landmarks and abnormalities. In the rectum, retroflex the sigmoidoscope to allow examination of the rectal mucosa. Straighten the sigmoidoscope, deflate the colon, and withdraw the scope.

Clinical Example (45333)

A 66-year-old patient with a history of subtotal colectomy for colon cancer presents with diarrhea. Flexible sigmoidoscopy with examination of the rectum and sigmoid colon and removal of a polyp with hot biopsy forceps is performed.

Description of Procedure (45333)

Inspect the perianal area, and perform a digital rectal examination. Lubricate a standard flexible sigmoidoscope, insert it into the rectum, and advance it to the splenic flexure using air insufflation, as necessary. Slowly withdraw the sigmoidoscope to allow circumferential examination of the colon mucosa. Identify and assess the lesion to be removed. Remove the identified lesion with hot biopsy forceps until there is no residual. Assess the area for bleeding. Obtain photodocumentation of appropriate normal landmarks and abnormalities. In the rectum, retroflex the sigmoidoscope to allow examination of the rectal mucosa. Straighten the sigmoidoscope, deflate the colon, and withdraw the scope.

Clinical Example (45334)

A 73-year-old patient with a history of cancer who has previously received radiation therapy to the pelvic region presents with hematochezia. Flexible sigmoidoscopy with examination of the rectum and sigmoid colon and control of bleeding from a rectal ulcer is performed.

Description of Procedure (45334)

Inspect the perianal area, and perform a digital rectal examination. Lubricate a standard flexible sigmoidoscope, insert it into the rectum, and advance it to the splenic flexure using air insufflation as necessary. Slowly withdraw the sigmoidoscope to allow circumferential examination of the colon mucosa. Identify and assess the bleeding lesion. Insert a bipolar cautery probe through the endoscope, and position it on the bleeding lesion; apply therapy to control the bleeding. When indicated, inject epinephrine submucosally and/or place endoclips. Once the bleeding is controlled, assess the area, and observe it for further bleeding. Obtain photodocumentation of appropriate normal landmarks and abnormalities. In the rectum, retroflex the sigmoidoscope to allow examination of the rectal mucosa. Straighten the sigmoidoscope, deflate the colon, and withdraw the scope.

Clinical Example (45337)

An 80-year-old patient with a past history of pelvic surgery presents with abdominal distension, obstipation, and pain. Imaging studies reveal the presence of a sigmoid volvulus. The patient is not a candidate for surgical intervention. The patient undergoes therapeutic flexible sigmoidoscopy with examination of the rectum and sigmoid colon and decompression of the volvulus.

Description of Procedure (45337)

Inspect the perianal area, and perform a digital rectal examination. Lubricate an endoscope, and insert it into the rectum using air insufflation as necessary. In the rectum, retroflex the sigmoidoscope to allow examination of the rectal mucosa. Straighten the sigmoidoscope, and advance it to the splenic flexure. Insert a guidewire through the biopsy channel into the colon. Withdraw the sigmoidoscope maintaining the position of the guidewire while decompressing the colon with suction during withdrawal and allowing circumferential examination of the colon mucosa. Obtain photodocumentation of appropriate normal landmarks and abnormalities. Advance a decompression tube over the guidewire after the sigmoidoscope is withdrawn, and secure it to a drainage bag.

Clinical Example (45340)

A 72-year-old patient with a history of a previous low anterior resection for cancer now presents with abdominal discomfort. Imaging studies reveal a stricture at the anastomotic site. Therapeutic flexible sigmoidoscopy with examination of the rectum and sigmoid colon and dilation of the stricture is performed.

Description of Procedure (45340)

Inspect the perianal area, and perform a digital rectal examination. Lubricate a standard flexible sigmoidoscope, insert it into the rectum, and advance it to the lesion to be dilated using air insufflation as necessary. Identify and assess the lesion to be dilated. Advance the dilating balloon, and position it at the lesion using sigmoidoscopic guidance. Inflate the balloon to its recommended pressure, and hold it for approximately sixty seconds. Perform repeated incremental dilations until the lesion is satisfactorily dilated. Observe the area for bleeding. Advance the sigmoidoscope to the splenic flexure. Slowly withdraw the sigmoidoscope to allow circumferential examination of the colon mucosa. Obtain photodocumentation of appropriate normal landmarks and abnormalities. In the rectum, retroflex the sigmoidoscope to allow examination of the rectal mucosa. Straighten the sigmoidoscope, deflate the colon, and withdraw the scope.

 ## Clinical Example (45346)

A 68-year-old patient previously underwent a screening colonoscopy and removal of a large flat polyp in the distal sigmoid colon that was confirmed by pathology as a serrated adenoma. The patient undergoes therapeutic flexible sigmoidoscopy for ablation of the remaining polyp tissue.

Description of Procedure (45346)

Inspect the perianal area, and perform a digital rectal examination. Lubricate a standard flexible sigmoidoscope, insert it into the rectum, and advance it to the splenic flexure using air insufflation as necessary. Slowly withdraw the sigmoidoscope to allow circumferential examination of the colon mucosa. Identify and assess the lesion to be ablated. Advance the ablation catheter, and position it at the lesion using sigmoidoscopic guidance. Repeatedly ablate the lesion until there is no residual. Observe the area for bleeding. Obtain photodocumentation of appropriate normal landmarks and abnormalities. In the rectum, retroflex the sigmoidoscope to allow examination of the rectal mucosa. Straighten the sigmoidoscope, deflate the colon, and withdraw the scope.

 ## Clinical Example (45347)

A 79-year-old patient presents with abdominal pain and distension. Imaging studies are consistent with a distal obstruction of the large bowel due to a mass lesion. The patient is not a candidate for surgical intervention. The patient is referred for a therapeutic flexible sigmoidoscopy with evaluation of the rectum and sigmoid colon and placement of a stent in the sigmoid colon for palliation.

Description of Procedure (45347)

Inspect the perianal area, and perform a digital rectal examination. Lubricate a standard flexible sigmoidoscope, insert it into the rectum, and advance it to the lesion to be stented using air insufflation as necessary. Identify and assess the lesion to be stented. When necessary, position a balloon dilating catheter through the tumor using sigmoidoscopic and fluoroscopic guidance, and inflate it to allow passage of the sigmoidoscope through the tumor, confirming its extent. Withdraw the sigmoidoscope, allowing measurement of the tumor and marking the distal and proximal margins for stent placement. Insert a guidewire through the sigmoidoscope. Using fluoroscopic and sigmoidoscopic guidance, advance the expandable wire stent over the guidewire, and position it across the tumor. If necessary, insert contrast under fluoroscopic guidance to confirm positioning of the stent. Obtain fluoroscopic imaging, and take spot digital images. Slowly deploy the stent across the tumor under fluoroscopic guidance, with repositioning if necessary. Once the

⊘=Modifier 51 Exempt   ⊙=Moderate Sedation   ✛=Add-on Code   ✚=FDA approval pending

stent is placed, withdraw the guidewire and introduce the device. Inject contrast through the sigmoidoscope to assess placement and patency. As needed, deploy the balloon dilating catheter to expand the stent to sufficient lumen size. Observe the area to confirm absence of active bleeding. Slowly withdraw the sigmoidoscope to allow circumferential examination of the colon mucosa. Obtain photodocumentation of appropriate normal landmarks and abnormalities. In the rectum, retroflex the sigmoidoscope to allow examination of the rectal mucosa. Straighten the sigmoidoscope, deflate the colon, and withdraw the scope.

Clinical Example (45349)

A 49-year-old patient with abdominal discomfort is referred for flexible sigmoidoscopy. A large sessile polyp is identified, and endoscopic mucosal resection is performed.

Description of Procedure (45349)

Inspect the perianal area, and perform a digital rectal examination. Lubricate the flexible sigmoidoscope, insert it into the rectum, and advance it to the sigmoid colon. In the rectum, retroflex the sigmoidoscope to allow examination of the rectal mucosa, and then straighten it. Identify a sessile polyp in the sigmoid colon, and perform an endoscopic mucosal resection involving submucosal injection of a solution of saline methylene blue and epinephrine to raise the lesion. Use a specific cap and snare to create a pseudopolyp of the nodule, and resect by snare cautery technique. Accomplish hemostasis with electrocautery, clips, or other devices as appropriate. Close mucosal defects with endoscopically placed clips. Grasp the lesion with a retrieval device, and place it in a specimen container. Re-insert the endoscope to the point of mucosal resection, observe the area for bleeding, and assess it for perforation. Obtain photodocumentation. Straighten the sigmoidoscope, deflate the colon, and withdraw the scope.

Clinical Example (45350)

A 42-year-old patient with frequent hematochezia is evaluated with flexible sigmoidoscopy. Banding of hemorrhoids is performed.

Description of Procedure (45350)

Inspect the perianal area, and perform a digital rectal examination. Lubricate the flexible sigmoidoscope, insert it into the rectum, and advance it to the sigmoid colon. In the rectum, retroflex the sigmoidoscope to allow examination of the rectal mucosa, and then straighten it. Identify hemorrhoids with stigmata of recent bleeding. Withdraw the sigmoidoscope, and install the multiband device on the endoscope. Re-insert the sigmoidoscope through the rectum and retroflex, angulate, and advance it to the suspected bleeding site. With suction applied to the hemorrhoid, deploy a band, and inspect the site. Apply additional bands proximally on the same hemorrhoid and onto the other most prominent hemorrhoids. Obtain photodocumentation. Straighten the sigmoidoscope, deflate the colon, and withdraw the scope.

Clinical Example (45378)

A 64-year-old patient is referred for colorectal cancer screening.

Description of Procedure (45378)

Inspect the perianal area, and perform a digital rectal examination. Lubricate a standard flexible colonoscope, and insert it into the rectum. Advance the scope to the cecum using air insufflation, water flush, and suctioning as necessary to view the mucosa; identify the appendiceal orifice and ileocecal valve, and intubate the ileocecal valve, if indicated. Slowly withdraw the colonoscope through the ascending colon, hepatic flexure, transverse colon, splenic flexure, and sigmoid colon to allow circumferential examination of the colon mucosa. When indicated, obtain brushings or washings of suspicious abnormalities. Obtain photodocumentation of appropriate normal landmarks and abnormalities. In the rectum, retroflex the colonoscope to allow examination of the rectal mucosa. Straighten the colonoscope, deflate the colon, and withdraw the scope.

Clinical Example (45379)

A 50-year-old patient with abdominal pain and constipation swallowed a diagnostic capsule, which became lodged at the ileocecal valve. Colonoscopy with removal of the foreign body is performed.

Description of Procedure (45379)

Inspect the perianal area, and perform a digital rectal examination. Lubricate a standard flexible colonoscope, insert it into the rectum, and advance it to the foreign body using air insufflation, water flush, and suctioning as necessary to view the mucosa. Grasp the foreign body with an appropriate retrieval device. Withdraw the foreign body, retrieval device, and colonoscope. Re-insert the colonoscope into the cecum; identify the appendiceal orifice and ileocecal valve, and intubate the ileocecal valve, if indicated. Slowly withdraw the colonoscope through the ascending colon, hepatic flexure, transverse colon, splenic flexure, and sigmoid colon to allow circumferential examination of the colon mucosa. Obtain photodocumentation of appropriate normal landmarks and abnormalities. In the rectum, retroflex the colonoscope to allow examination of the rectal mucosa. Straighten the colonoscope, deflate the colon, and withdraw the scope.

Clinical Example (45382)

A 70-year-old patient presents with painless, active lower gastrointestinal (GI) hemorrhage. Colonoscopy for control of bleeding is performed.

Description of Procedure (45382)

Inspect the perianal area, and perform a digital rectal examination. Lubricate a standard flexible colonoscope, insert it into the rectum, and advance it to the cecum using air insufflation, water flush, and suctioning as necessary to view the mucosa; identify the appendiceal orifice and the ileocecal valve, and intubate the ileocecal valve, if indicated. Slowly withdraw the colonoscope through the ascending colon, hepatic flexure, transverse colon, splenic flexure, and sigmoid colon to allow circumferential examination of the colon mucosa. Identify active bleeding from an angiodysplastic lesion in the colon. Insert a bipolar cautery probe through the colonoscope, and position it on the bleeding lesion; apply therapy to control

⊘=Modifier 51 Exempt ⊙=Moderate Sedation ✚=Add-on Code ✗=FDA approval pending

the bleeding. Obtain photodocumentation of appropriate normal landmarks and abnormalities. In the rectum, retroflex the colonoscope to allow examination of the rectal mucosa. Straighten the colonoscope, deflate the colon, and withdraw the scope.

Clinical Example (45384)

A 66-year-old patient undergoes colonoscopy for colorectal cancer screening. Diminutive polyps are identified in the proximal colon and removed.

Description of Procedure (45384)

Inspect the perianal area, and perform a digital rectal examination. Lubricate a standard flexible colonoscope and insert it into the rectum. Advance the scope to the cecum using air insufflation, water flush, and suctioning as necessary to view the mucosa; identify the appendiceal orifice and ileocecal valve, and intubate the ileocecal valve, if indicated. Withdraw the colonoscope to the ascending colon where the identified lesions are removed with successive applications of hot biopsy forceps until there is no residual. Slowly withdraw the colonoscope through the ascending colon, hepatic flexure, transverse colon, splenic flexure, and sigmoid colon to allow circumferential examination of the colon mucosa. Obtain photo-documentation of appropriate normal landmarks and abnormalities. In the rectum, retroflex the colonoscope to allow examination of the rectal mucosa. Straighten the colonoscope, deflate the colon, and withdraw the scope.

Clinical Example (45386)

A 65-year-old patient with history of resection of a sigmoid colon cancer presents with abdominal pain. Therapeutic colonoscopy with dilation of the anastomotic stricture is performed.

Description of Procedure (45386)

Inspect the perianal area, and perform a digital rectal examination. Insert a standard flexible colonoscope through the rectum, and advance it to the descending colon using air insufflation, water flush, and suctioning as necessary to view the mucosa. Identify a stricture that prohibits passage of the colonoscope. Position the colonoscope. Advance a through-the-scope fixed wire balloon catheter through the colonoscope, position it across the stricture, and inflate it to a diameter of approximately 15 mm. Deflate the balloon catheter, and observe the stricture. If necessary, remove the balloon dilator, and insert subsequent balloon catheters of larger diameter through the colonoscope, position them across the stricture, and inflate them. Deflate the balloon catheter, and observe the stricture to confirm adequate dilation of the stricture. When dilation is adequate, remove the balloon catheter. Following dilation, observe the area for bleeding. Advance the colonoscope to the cecum using air insufflation as necessary; identify the appendiceal orifice and ileocecal valve, and intubate the ileocecal valve, if indicated. Slowly withdraw the colonoscope through the ascending colon, hepatic flexure, transverse colon, splenic flexure, and sigmoid colon to allow circumferential examination of the colon mucosa. Obtain photodocumentation of appropriate normal landmarks and abnormalities. In the rectum, retroflex the colonoscope to allow examination of the rectal mucosa. Straighten the colonoscope, deflate the colon, and withdraw the scope.

 **Clinical Example (45388)**

A 65-year-old patient undergoes colonoscopy for evaluation of anemia and GI blood loss. A flat lesion is identified in the transverse colon and ablated.

Description of Procedure (45388)

Inspect the perianal area, and perform a digital rectal examination. Lubricate a standard flexible colonoscope, insert it into the rectum, and advance it to the cecum using air insufflation, water flush, and suctioning as necessary to view the mucosa. Identify the appendiceal orifice and the ileocecal valve, and intubate the ileocecal valve, if indicated. Withdraw the colonoscope through the ascending colon and transverse colon. Slowly withdraw the colonoscope through the descending and sigmoid colon, and examine the colonic mucosa. Obtain photo-documentation of appropriate normal landmarks and abnormalities. Identify a flat lesion in the transverse colon. Under endoscopic visualization, pass a guidewire through the colonoscope, and withdraw the scope. Re-insert the colonoscope, and place a sizing balloon catheter through the scope into the colon to straddle the region of abnormality to be ablated. Inflate the sizing balloon to ascertain the luminal diameter to be treated. Remove the sizing balloon, and pass an ablation catheter of appropriate caliber over the guidewire into the colon. In the rectum, retroflex the colonoscope to allow examination of the rectal mucosa. Straighten the colonoscope, deflate the colon, and withdraw the scope.

 Clinical Example (45389)

A 68-year-old patient with history of resection of a sigmoid cancer presents with abdominal pain and imaging findings of an obstructing lesion in the mid-transverse colon. Colonoscopy with dilation of the colon and placement of a stent is performed.

Description of Procedure (45389)

Inspect the perianal area, and perform a digital rectal examination. Insert a standard flexible colonoscope through the rectum, and advance it to the transverse colon using air insufflation, water flush, and suctioning as necessary to view the mucosa. Identify the obstructing, concentric tumor that prohibits passage of the standard colonoscope. Withdraw the colonoscope, insert a thin caliber flexible colonoscope through the rectum, and pass it through the colonic tumor to the cecum. Identify the appendiceal orifice and ileocecal valve, and intubate the ileocecal valve, if indicated. Withdraw the colonoscope, and examine the ascending colon and proximal transverse colon. Measure the tumor, and mark the distal and proximal margins of the tumor for stent placement. Re-insert the colonoscope to 2 cm past the distal end of the tumor, and insert a guidewire through the endoscope across the full length of the tumor. Withdraw the colonoscope. Under fluoroscopic guidance, advance the expandable wire mesh stent and introducing device over the guidewire into the colon, and position it across the tumor. If necessary, insert contrast under fluoroscopic guidance to confirm positioning of the stent. Obtain fluoroscopic imaging, and take spot digital images. Slowly deploy the stent across the tumor under fluoroscopic guidance, repositioning if necessary. Once the stent is placed, withdraw the guidewire and introducing device, and re-insert the thin caliber colonoscope to confirm proper positioning of the stent. Balloon dilatation

---

⊘=Modifier 51 Exempt ⊙=Moderate Sedation ✛=Add-on Code 𝘕=FDA approval pending

of the stent may be required. Slowly withdraw the colonoscope through the distal transverse colon and descending and sigmoid colon to allow circumferential examination of the colon mucosa. Obtain photodocumentation of appropriate normal landmarks and abnormalities. In the rectum, retroflex the colonoscope to allow examination of the rectal mucosa. Straighten the colonoscop, deflate the colon, and withdraw the scope.

Clinical Example (45390)

A 70-year-old patient with abdominal discomfort and occult GI bleeding is referred for colonoscopy. A large sessile polyp is identified, and endoscopic mucosal resection is performed.

Description of Procedure (45390)

Inspect the perianal area, and perform a digital rectal examination. Lubricate a standard flexible colonoscope, insert it into the rectum, and advance it to the cecum using air insufflation, water flush, and suctioning as necessary to view the mucosa. Identify the appendiceal orifice and ileocecal valve, and intubate ileocecal valve, if indicated. Withdraw the colonoscope through the ascending colon, transverse colon, and descending and sigmoid colon to allow circumferential examination of the colon mucosa. In the rectum, retroflex the colonoscope to allow examination of the rectal mucosa, and then straighten it. Identify a lesion in the sigmoid colon that cannot be removed by standard snare polypectomy technique. Withdraw the colonoscope, fit a friction cap onto the end of the scope, and insert the colonoscope through the rectum into the colon to the site where endoscopic mucosal resection is to be performed. Pass an injection needle through the colonoscope, and inject a solution of a topical contrast agent such as methylene blue, saline, and epinephrine submucosally to raise the lesion. Withdraw the injection needle. Suction the area of abnormality into the friction fitted cap to create a pseudopolyp. Pass a snare through the colonoscope, and loop it around the lesion. As the snare is tightened, apply electrocautery in a controlled manner, and remove the identified lesion. Repeat snare removal until all visually identified portions of the lesion are resected. Withdraw the snare, and insert a retrieval device through the colonoscope to capture the lesion. Withdraw the retrieval device with the lesion to the tip of the colonoscope, and withdraw it through the rectum. Re-insert the colonoscope through the rectum to the area of the lesion. Examine the base of the lesion; if there is residual tissue, apply the snare or other appropriate technique until there is no residual. Control bleeding, if any. Obtain photodocumentation of appropriate normal landmarks and abnormalities. Straighten the colonoscope, deflate the colon, and withdraw the scope.

Clinical Example (45391)

A 52-year-old patient with abdominal discomfort and weight loss is found to have a sigmoid colon mass with adenopathy on imaging studies. Diagnostic colonoscopy with endoscopic ultrasound is performed to evaluate and stage the tumor.

Description of Procedure (45391)

Inspect the perianal area, and perform a digital rectal examination. Lubricate a standard flexible colonoscope, insert it into the rectum, and advance it to the cecum using air insufflation, water flush, and suctioning as necessary to view the mucosa. Identify the appendiceal orifice and the ileocecal valve, and intubate ileocecal valve, if indicated. Slowly withdraw the colonoscope through the ascending colon, hepatic flexure, transverse colon, splenic flexure, and sigmoid colon to allow circumferential examination of the colon mucosa. Identify a lesion in the sigmoid colon. Obtain photodocumentation of appropriate normal landmarks and abnormalities. In the rectum, retroflex the colonoscope to allow examination of the rectal mucosa. Straighten the colonoscope, deflate the colon, and withdraw the scope. Prepare a dedicated echoendoscope with a balloon placed over the transducer housing. Introduce the echoendoscope through the rectum, and advance it to the level of the identified abnormality under direct endoscopic visualization. While slowly withdrawing the echoendoscope, obtain ultrasound imaging. Take ultrasound spot digital images, and have endoscopist review them. At the conclusion of the procedure, remove the echoendoscope.

Clinical Example (45392)

A 72-year-old patient with history of resection of gastric cancer presents with abdominal discomfort and weight loss. Enlarged regional lymph nodes are found on imaging studies. Diagnostic colonoscopy with endoscopic ultrasound staging of the tumor and fine needle aspiration biopsy are performed to plan therapy.

Description of Procedure (45392)

Inspect the perianal area, and perform a digital rectal examination. Lubricate a standard flexible colonoscope, insert it into the rectum, and advance it to the cecum using air insufflation, water flush, and suctioning as necessary to view the mucosa. Identify the appendiceal orifice and the ileocecal valve, and intubate ileocecal valve, if indicated. Slowly withdraw the colonoscope through the ascending colon, hepatic flexure, transverse colon, splenic flexure, and sigmoid colon to allow circumferential examination of the colon mucosa. Identify a lesion in the sigmoid colon. In the rectum, retroflex the colonoscope to allow examination of the rectal mucosa, and then straighten it. Perform photodocumentation. Withdraw the colonoscope. Prepare a dedicated echoendoscope with a balloon placed over the transducer housing. Introduce the echoendoscope through the rectum, and advance it to the level of the identified abnormality under direct endoscopic visualization. While slowly withdrawing the echoendoscope, perform ultrasound imaging. Take ultrasound spot digital images, and have the endoscopist review them. Make a determination of the risks and benefits of biopsying the lesion. Advance the needle biopsy device through the biopsy channel of the echoendoscope. Perform Doppler imaging to ensure that any vascular structures or areas within the lesion are recognized prior to biopsy. Under direct ultrasound visualization, advance the needle through the colon wall into the lesion. Remove the central stylet from the needle, apply negative pressure to the hub of the device, and make to and fro movements with the needle in the lesion. After multiple passes of the needle, withdraw the needle from the echoendoscope, and spray the aspirated material onto glass slides for examination. At the conclusion of procedure, deflate the colon, and remove the echoendoscope.

◎=Modifier 51 Exempt   ⊙=Moderate Sedation   ✚=Add-on Code   𝒩=FDA approval pending

Clinical Example (45393)

A 76-year-old patient with history of altered mental status presents with abdominal distension and a megacolon on imaging studies. Colonoscopy with decompression of the colon and placement of a tube is performed.

Description of Procedure (45393)

Inspect the perianal area, and perform a digital rectal examination. Insert a standard flexible into the rectum and advance to the cecum using minimal air insufflation across grossly patulous regions of colon containing gas, stool, and fluid, performing continuous suctioning of the colonic contents to decompress the colon. Identify the appendiceal orifice and ileocecal valve, and intubate the ileocecal valve, if indicated. Withdraw the colonoscope through the ascending colon, transverse colon, and descending and sigmoid colon, and examine the colon mucosa, with continuous suctioning to decompress the colon. In the rectum, retroflex the colonoscope to allow examination of the rectal mucosa, and then straighten it. Insert a 10-Fr tube through the rectum into the colon. Identify the tip of the tube, position the tube and colonoscope, insert a grasping device through the colonoscope, and grasp the tube. Advance the tube endoscopically into the transverse colon. Release the grasping device from the tube, and withdraw the colonoscope maintaining the position of the tube. Perform photodocumentation. Straighten the colonoscope, deflate the colon, and withdraw the scope.

Clinical Example (45398)

A 58-year-old patient with frequent hematochezia is referred for evaluation. Colonoscopy with banding of rectal varices is performed.

Description of Procedure (45398)

Inspect the perianal area, and perform a digital rectal examination. Insert a standard flexible colonoscope into the rectum, and advance it to the cecum using air insufflation, water flush, and suctioning as necessary to view the mucosa. Identify the appendiceal orifice and the ileocecal valve, and intubate ileocecal valve, if indicated. Withdraw the colonoscope through the ascending colon, transverse colon, descending and sigmoid colon, and examine the colonic mucosa. In the rectum, retroflex the colonoscope to allow examination of the rectal mucosa, and then straighten it. Identify rectal varices with stigmata of recent bleeding. Withdraw the colonoscope, and install the multiband device on the colonoscope. Re-insert the colonoscope through the rectum, retroflex it, angulate it, and advance it to the suspected bleeding site. With suction applied to the varix, deploy a band, and inspect the site. Apply additional bands proximally on the same varix. Repeat the process with bands deployed on additional varices. Straighten the colonoscope, deflate the colon, and withdraw the scope.

Clinical Example (46601)

A 40-year-old male presents with an abnormal anal cytology. He is HIV positive and engages in sex with men. Anoscopy with high-resolution magnification (HRA) and chemical agent enhancement for evaluation of anal dysplasia is performed.

Description of Procedure (46601)

As indicated, swab the anus to obtain a cytology sample. Visually inspect the perineum. Perform digital anorectal examination, assessing sphincter tone as well as the presence or absence of any anal canal masses. Also palpate the perianal tissue for masses. Place an anoscope coated with lubricant and anesthetic jelly in the anal canal, and remove the obturator. Insert a swab with acetic acid through the anoscope. Remove the anoscope, leaving the swab behind. After a few minutes, remove the swab. Re-insert the anoscope, and examine the interior of the anus using a high-resolution colposcope. Visually inspect the area. Remove fecal matter with suction as needed. Insert additional acetic acid–soaked swabs throughout the examination as necessary. Also insert swabs as needed to stretch the mucosa to assist with visualization. After the first pass examination, remove the anoscope. Apply acetic acid to the perianal tissue, and inspect the perianal area for neoplastic or preneoplastic changes. Repeat the HRA examination at least once (ie, acetic acid swabs, insert anoscope, high-resolution exam). The examination shows no evidence of neoplastic or preneoplastic changes. Accordingly, biopsies are not performed. Remove the anoscope.

Clinical Example (46607)

A 40-year-old male presents with an abnormal anal cytology. He is HIV positive and engages in sex with men. HRA examination and chemical agent enhancement with biopsy(ies) is performed.

Description of Procedure (46607)

As indicated, swab the anus to obtain a cytology sample. Visually inspect the perineum. Perform digital anorectal examination, assessing sphincter tone, as well as the presence or absence of any anal canal masses. Also palpate the perianal tissue for masses. Place an anoscope coated with lubricant and anesthetic jelly in the anal canal, and remove the obturator. Insert a swab with acetic acid through the anoscope. Remove the anoscope, leaving the swab behind. After a few minutes, remove the swab. Re-insert the anoscope, and examine the interior of the anus using a high-resolution colposcope. Visually inspect the area. Remove fecal matter with suction as needed. Insert additional acetic acid–soaked swabs throughout the examination as necessary. Also insert swabs as needed to stretch the mucosa to assist with visualization. Stain abnormal areas with Lugol's solution. Topical anesthetic cream is applied to those areas that require local anesthesia for biopsy, followed by an anesthetic injection. Take biopsy(ies), and control bleeding with silver nitrate as needed. After the first pass examination, remove the anoscope. The HRA examination may be repeated several times, including between biopsies. Swab acetic acid on the perineum, and examine the perineum with the colposcope. Take additional biopsy(ies) as needed. At the end of the examination, remove the anoscope.

Clinical Example (47383)

A 50-year-old female with metastatic colon cancer and previous partial hepatectomy for liver metastases was referred by her oncologist due to a 3.8-cm liver metastasis that was seen on imaging to be growing despite chemotherapy. The

⃠=Modifier 51 Exempt ⊙=Moderate Sedation ✚=Add-on Code ⊮=FDA approval pending patient was deemed inoperable and was referred to the interventional radiology department for percutaneous cryoablation.

Description of Procedure (47383)

Place the patient in the supine position on the computerized tomography (CT) gantry table. Place the patient on physiologic monitors. Perform a time out. Administer moderate conscious sedation. Prepare the right upper quadrant of the patient's abdomen, and drape it in sterile fashion. Give the local anesthetic. Use prior CT imaging to plan probe placement for cryoablation. Assess the patient, sterile field, and cryoablation probes for safe transit in and out of the scanner to ensure that the leads, lines, and probe cables will not be tethered.

Position the patient in the CT scanner, and scan the liver. (CT guidance is separately reported.) Perform imaging for localization/targeting purposes for selection of the site for initial cryoablation probe placement and for avoidance of critical structures. Based on the imaging, make a plan for four 17-gauge cryoablation probes to be placed percutaneously into the tumor. Mark each site on the skin. Use local anesthetic at each site, including skin, subcutaneous structures, and the liver capsule. Place each probe according to the CT parameters. Perform follow-up imaging scans to guide and confirm correct placement. Apply cycles of 15-minute freeze, 10-minute thaw, and 15-minute freeze with periodic CT monitoring of the iceball. After a 10-minute active thaw, remove the cryoablation probes. End-of-procedure CT shows a small perihepatic hematoma. Clean the needle sites, and cover with sterile adhesive dressings. Send the patient to the recovery room in stable condition.

Urinary System

Bladder

INTRODUCTION

51715   Endoscopic injection of implant material into the submucosal tissues of the urethra and/or bladder neck

▶(For anoscopy with directed submucosal injection of bulking agent for fecal incontinence, use 0377T)◀

🖎 Rationale

In accordance with new Category III code 0377T, a cross-reference parenthetical note has been added following urethral endoscopic injection code 51715 directing users to code 0377T to report injection of a bulking agent.

URODYNAMICS

51784   Electromyography studies (EMG) of anal or urethral sphincter, other than needle, any technique

▶(Do not report 51784 in conjunction with 51792)◀

51785 Needle electromyography studies (EMG) of anal or urethral sphincter, any technique

51792 Stimulus evoked response (eg, measurement of bulbocavernosus reflex latency time)

▶(Do not report 51792 in conjunction with 51784)◀

Rationale

The American Medical Association/Specialty Society RUC identified codes 51784 and 51792 as being reported together 75% of the time or more. However, it was determined that these codes should not be reported together and exclusionary parenthetical notes following codes 51784 and 51792 have been added to preclude the reporting of anal/urethral sphincter electromyography (EMG) studies in conjunction with stimulus-evoked response procedures.

VESICAL NECK AND PROSTATE

52402 Cystourethroscopy with transurethral resection or incision of ejaculatory ducts

●52441 Cystourethroscopy, with insertion of permanent adjustable transprostatic implant; single implant

✚●52442 each additional permanent adjustable transprostatic implant (List separately in addition to code for primary procedure)

▶(Use 52442 in conjunction with 52441)◀

▶(To report removal of implant[s], use 52310)◀

▶(For insertion of a permanent urethral stent, use 52282. For insertion of a temporary prostatic urethral stent, use 53855)◀

Rationale

Codes 52441 and 52442 have been established to report cystourethroscopic insertion of adjustable transprostatic implants. Code 52441 is reported for insertion of the initial implant and code 52442 is reported for insertion of each additional implantation procedures. Because code 52442 is an add-on procedure, parenthetical notes have been included to instruct users regarding the appropriate use of this code. Instructional parenthetical notes have also been included to direct users to the correct codes to report removal of the implant(s) (52310) and insertion of a stent—both permanent (52282) and temporary (53855).

Cystourethroscopic implantation of transprostatic implants involves the insertion of permanent adjustable transprostatic devices that reshape and expand the prostatic channel. This reduces obstruction associated with benign prostatic hyperplasia (BPH) and it is an alternative to debulking vaporization, resection, incision, or laser enucleation of prostate tissue. In addition, the procedure is minimally invasive and does not involve placement of a urethral stent.

Clinical Example (52441)

A 67-year-old male has benign prostatic hyperplasia and bothersome voiding symptoms. The patient has an elevated international prostate symptom score (IPSS), a low peak urinary flow rate, and elevated postvoid residual volume. His symptoms have failed to improve on medical therapy. Cystoscopy excludes a significant median lobe component, and ultrasound shows the patient's prostate is 20 grams. After discussion of treatment options, the patient elects a permanent adjustable transprostatic implant procedure with a single implant.

Description of Procedure (52441)

Once adequate anesthesia is achieved, insert a 20-Fr cystoscope sheath into the meatus. Advance the cystoscope toward the bladder to assess the precise location of the prostatic obstruction, the intended location for implants, and the amount of compression required to apply to the obstructing lateral lobes so as to achieve the intended result. Press the cystoscope against the prostate lobe to determine the level of opening that should be created. Once the locations of the implantation sites are confirmed, proceed with placement of the first implant. With the sheath in the bladder, replace the telescope bridge with the implant delivery device, and re-introduce the telescope lens into the device. Determine the first treatment site by orienting the delivery device tip in an anterolateral direction (typically 2 to 3 o'clock position) in the bladder and slowly moving the device distally within the prostatic fossa approximately 1.5 cm from the bladder neck. Angle the distal tip of the delivery device laterally at least 20° at this position so as to compress the lateral lobe and assure proper needle trajectory. Prior to deploying the implant, confirm cystoscopically that adequate tissue is captured both anterior and posterior to the implant. Pull the trigger, thereby deploying a needle containing the implant through the prostate. Retract the needle, allowing one end of the implant to be delivered to the capsular surface of the prostate. Tension the implant to assure capsular seating and removal of slack monofilament. Angle the device back toward midline, and slowly advance it proximally (typically 3 mm to 4 mm) until cystoscopic verification of the monofilament being centered in the delivery bay. Affix the urethral end piece to the monofilament, thereby tailoring the size and tension of the implant. Sever excess filament.

After each implant is deployed, readvance the device into the bladder, and replace the delivery device with cystoscope and bridge, allowing the bladder to drain between attachments. Inspect the degree of prostatic compression achieved at the site so as to ultimately shape an anterior channel through the prostatic fossa.

If additional implants are necessary, those implants are then placed in the prostate (see intraservice time for code 52442.)

Conduct a final cystoscopy first to inspect the location and state of the implant(s) to assure proper seating and location. Finally, conduct cystoscopy with irrigation turned off to assure that the prostatic channel remains patent without irrigation pressure. Fill the bladder with 100 to 200 ml of saline to assist the patient in a postprocedure trial to void, conducted before he is discharged. Place an indwelling urinary catheter with drainage bag.

Clinical Example (52442)

The initial implant has been placed (reported with code 52441) and the patient now undergoes additional placement.

Description of Procedure (52442)

Determine the additional treatment site by pressing the cystoscope against the prostate lobe to determine the level of opening that should be created. Advance the cystoscope into the bladder. With the sheath in the bladder, replace the telescope bridge with a new implant delivery device, and re-introduce the telescope lens into the device. Orient the distal tip of the delivery device to either the 2 to 3 o'clock or 9 to 10 o'clock position, and retract it into the prostatic fossa to the intended delivery site. Laterally angle the device at least 20° at this position so as to compress the lateral lobe and assure proper needle trajectory. Prior to deploying the implant, confirm cystoscopically that adequate tissue is captured both anterior and posterior to the implant. Pull the trigger, thereby deploying a needle containing the implant through the prostate. Retract the needle, allowing one end of the implant to be delivered to the capsular surface of the prostate. Tension the implant to assure capsular seating and removal of slack monofilament. Angle the device back toward midline, and slowly advance it proximally (typically 3 mm to 4 mm) until cystoscopic verification of the monofilament being centered in the delivery bay. Affix the urethral end piece to the monofilament, thereby tailoring the size and tension of the implant. Sever excess filament. Advance the delivery device into the bladder. Replace the delivery device with cystoscope and bridge. Inspect the degree of prostatic compression achieved at the site, and determine where the next implant should be delivered so as to ultimately shape an anterior channel through the prostatic fossa.

(For additional implant, repeat the above sequence, installing the cystoscope and reinspecting successful placement of each implant and degree of lateral lobe obstruction remaining. If there is persistent obstruction distally, repeat the above sequence with additional implants delivered and inspected until a satisfactory result is obtained, namely a reshaping of the prostate that offers a continuous channel through the anterior aspect of the prostatic fossa.)

Maternity Care and Delivery

▶The services normally provided in uncomplicated maternity cases include antepartum care, delivery, and postpartum care. Pregnancy confirmation during a problem oriented or preventive visit is not considered a part of antepartum care and should be reported using the appropriate E/M service codes 99201, 99202, 99203, 99204, 99205, 99211, 99212, 99213, 99214, 99215, 99241, 99242, 99243, 99244, 99245, 99281, 99282, 99283, 99284, 99285, 99384, 99385, 99386, 99394, 99395, 99396 for that visit.

Antepartum care includes the initial prenatal history and physical examination; subsequent prenatal history and physical examinations; recording of weight, blood pressures, fetal heart tones, routine chemical urinalysis, and monthly visits up to 28 weeks gestation; biweekly visits to 36 weeks gestation; and weekly visits until delivery. Any other visits or services within this time period should be coded separately.◀

Delivery services include admission to the hospital, the admission history and physical examination, management of uncomplicated labor, vaginal delivery (with or without episiotomy, with or without forceps), or cesarean delivery. When reporting delivery only services (59409, 59514, 59612, 59620), report inpatient postdelivery management and discharge services using Evaluation and Management Services codes (99217-99239). Delivery and postpartum services (59410, 59515, 59614, 59622) include delivery services and all inpatient and outpatient postpartum services. Medical complications of pregnancy (eg, cardiac problems, neurological problems, diabetes, hypertension, toxemia, hyperemesis, preterm labor, premature rupture of membranes, trauma) and medical problems complicating labor and delivery management may require additional resources and may be reported separately.

▶Postpartum care only services (59430) include office or other outpatient visits following vaginal or cesarean section delivery.◀

For surgical complications of pregnancy (eg, appendectomy, hernia, ovarian cyst, Bartholin cyst), see services in the **Surgery** section.

If all or part of the antepartum and/or postpartum patient care is provided except delivery due to termination of pregnancy by abortion or referral to another physician or other qualified health care professional for delivery, see the antepartum and postpartum care codes 59425, 59426, and 59430.

(For circumcision of newborn, see 54150, 54160)

✍ Rationale

The Maternity Care and Delivery guidelines have been editorially revised to clarify that pregnancy confirmation during a problem-oriented or preventive visit is not considered a part of antepartum care and should be reported using the appropriate Evaluation and Management (E/M) code for that visit. Guidelines further describe that antepartum care also includes the initial prenatal history and physical examination. In addition, the Postpartum Care guidelines have been moved to reflect a chronological sequence of events.

Nervous System

Skull, Meninges, and Brain

INJECTION, DRAINAGE, OR ASPIRATION

61050 Cisternal or lateral cervical (C1-C2) puncture; without injection (separate procedure)

▲61055   with injection of medication or other substance for diagnosis or treatment

▶(Do not report 61055 in conjunction with 62302, 62303, 62304, 62305)◀

▶(For radiological supervision and interpretation by a different physician or qualified health care professional, see **Radiology**)◀

✍ Rationale

In support of the addition of four new bundled codes for myelography procedures for cervical (62302), thoracic (62303), lumbosacral (62304), and two or more regions (eg, lumbar/thoracic, cervical/thoracic, lumbar/cervical, lumbar/thoracic/cervical) (62305), a new exclusionary parenthetical note has been added following code 61055 to restrict the reporting of code 61055 in conjunction with these procedures. The existing cross-reference note following code 61055 has also been clarified by the addition and specification of "physician or other qualified health care professional" for radiological supervision and interpretation services. Finally, the descriptor for code 61055 has been editorially revised to remove "(eg, C1-C2)," as this reference to C1-C2 was redundant.

CRANIECTOMY OR CRANIOTOMY

61332 Exploration of orbit (transcranial approach); with biopsy

61333   with removal of lesion

▶(61334 has been deleted)◀

61343 Craniectomy, suboccipital with cervical laminectomy for decompression of medulla and spinal cord, with or without dural graft (eg, Arnold-Chiari malformation)

61345 Other cranial decompression, posterior fossa

(For orbital decompression by lateral wall approach, Kroenlein type, use 67445)

▶(61440 has been deleted)◀

61458 Craniectomy, suboccipital; for exploration or decompression of cranial nerves

61460   for section of 1 or more cranial nerves

▶(61470 has been deleted)◀

61480   for mesencephalic tractotomy or pedunculotomy

▶(61490 has been deleted)◀

61533 Craniotomy with elevation of bone flap; for subdural implantation of an electrode array, for long-term seizure monitoring

(For continuous EEG monitoring, see 95950-95954)

61534   for excision of epileptogenic focus without electrocorticography during surgery

61535   for removal of epidural or subdural electrode array, without excision of cerebral tissue (separate procedure)

61536   for excision of cerebral epileptogenic focus, with electrocorticography during surgery (includes removal of electrode array)

61537   for lobectomy, temporal lobe, without electrocorticography during surgery

61538   for lobectomy, temporal lobe, with electrocorticography during surgery

61539   for lobectomy, other than temporal lobe, partial or total, with electrocorticography during surgery

61540   for lobectomy, other than temporal lobe, partial or total, without electrocorticography during surgery

61541   for transection of corpus callosum

▶(61542 has been deleted)◀

⊘=Modifier 51 Exempt ⊙=Moderate Sedation ✚=Add-on Code ⩐=FDA approval pending

Rationale

As part of an effort to ensure that the CPT code set reflects current clinical practice, codes 61334, 61440, 61470, 61490, and 61542, which represent various craniotomy and craniectomy procedures, have been deleted due to low utilization.

SURGERY OF SKULL BASE

Definitive Procedures

Base of Middle Cranial Fossa

61607 Resection or excision of neoplastic, vascular or infectious lesion of parasellar area, cavernous sinus, clivus or midline skull base; extradural

61608 intradural, including dural repair, with or without graft

▶Codes 61610, 61611, 61612 are reported in addition to code(s) for primary procedure(s) 61605-61608. Report only one transection or ligation of carotid artery code per operative session.◀

▶(61609 has been deleted)◀

+61610 Transection or ligation, carotid artery in cavernous sinus, with repair by anastomosis or graft (List separately in addition to code for primary procedure)

 Rationale

As part of an effort to ensure that the CPT code set reflects current clinical practice, add-on code 61609 (carotid artery transection or ligation without repair) has been deleted due to low utilization. In accordance with this deletion, the guideline following code 61608 has been revised with the removal of code 61609.

STEREOTACTIC RADIOSURGERY (CRANIAL)

Cranial stereotactic radiosurgery is a distinct procedure that utilizes externally generated ionizing radiation to inactivate or eradicate defined target(s) in the head without the need to make an incision. The target is defined by and the treatment is delivered using high-resolution stereotactic imaging. Stereotactic radiosurgery codes and headframe application procedures are reported by the neurosurgeon. The radiation oncologist reports the appropriate code(s) for clinical treatment planning, physics and dosimetry, treatment delivery, and management from the **Radiation Oncology** section (77261-77790). Any necessary planning, dosimetry, targeting, positioning, or blocking by the neurosurgeon is included in the stereotactic radiation surgery services. The same individual should not report stereotactic radiosurgery services with radiation treatment management codes (77427-77435).

Cranial stereotactic radiosurgery is typically performed in a single planning and treatment session, using a rigidly attached stereotactic guiding device, other immobilization technology and/or a stereotactic image-guidance system, but can be performed with more than one planning session and in a limited number of treatment sessions, up to a maximum of five sessions. Do not report stereotactic radiosurgery more than once per lesion per course of treatment when the treatment requires more than one session.

Codes 61796 and 61797 involve stereotactic radiosurgery for simple cranial lesions. Simple cranial lesions are lesions less than 3.5 cm in maximum dimension that do not meet the definition of a complex lesion provided below. Report code 61796 when all lesions are simple.

Codes 61798 and 61799 involve stereotactic radiosurgery for complex cranial lesions and procedures that create therapeutic lesions (eg, thalamotomy or pallidotomy). All lesions 3.5 cm in maximum dimension or greater are complex. When performing therapeutic lesion creation procedures, report code 61798 only once regardless of the number of lesions created. Schwannomas, arterio-venous malformations, pituitary tumors, glomus tumors, pineal region tumors and cavernous sinus/parasellar/petroclival tumors are complex. Any lesion that is adjacent (5mm or less) to the optic nerve/optic chasm/optic tract or within the brainstem is complex. If treating multiple lesions, and any single lesion treated is complex, use 61798.

Do not report codes 61796-61800 in conjunction with code 20660.

Codes 61796-61799 include computer-assisted planning. Do not report codes 61796-61799 in conjunction with 61781-61783.

▶(For intensity modulated beam delivery plan and treatment, see 77301, 77385, 77386. For stereotactic body radiation therapy, see 77373, 77435)◀

61796   Stereotactic radiosurgery (particle beam, gamma ray, or linear accelerator); 1 simple cranial lesion

 Rationale

A cross-reference parenthetical note following the Stereotactic Radiosurgery (Cranial) guidelines has been revised to reflect the establishment of new intensity-modulated radiation therapy (IMRT) treatment delivery codes 77385 and 77386.

NEUROSTIMULATORS (INTRACRANIAL)

61870   Craniectomy for implantation of neurostimulator electrodes, cerebellar, cortical

▶(61875 has been deleted)◀

 Rationale

As part of an effort to ensure that the CPT code set reflects current clinical practice, code 61875 (craniectomy for implantation of cerebellar subcortical neurostimulator electrodes) has been deleted due to low utilization.

REPAIR

62115   Reduction of craniomegalic skull (eg, treated hydrocephalus); not requiring bone grafts or cranioplasty

▶(62116 has been deleted)◀

62117   requiring craniotomy and reconstruction with or without bone graft (includes obtaining grafts)

 Rationale

As part of an effort to ensure that the CPT code set reflects current clinical practice, code 62116 (reduction of craniomegalic skull with simple cranioplasty) has been deleted due to low utilization.

Spine and Spinal Cord

INJECTION, DRAINAGE, OR ASPIRATION

▶Injection of contrast during fluoroscopic guidance and localization is an inclusive component of 62263, 62264, 62267, 62270, 62272, 62273, 62280, 62281, 62282, 62302, 62303, 62304, 62305, 62310-62319. Fluoroscopic guidance and localization is reported with 77003, unless a formal contrast study (myelography, epidurography, or arthrography) is performed, in which case the use of fluoroscopy is included in the supervision and interpretation codes or the myelography via lumbar injection code. Image guidance and the injection of contrast are inclusive components and are required for the performance of myelography, as described by codes 62302, 62303, 62304, 62305.◀

For radiologic supervision and interpretation of epidurography, use 72275. Code 72275 is only to be used when an epidurogram is performed, images documented, and a formal radiologic report is issued.

Code 62263 describes a catheter-based treatment involving targeted injection of various substances (eg, hypertonic saline, steroid, anesthetic) via an indwelling epidural catheter. Code 62263 includes percutaneous insertion and removal of an epidural catheter (remaining in place over a several-day period), for the administration of multiple injections of a neurolytic agent(s) performed during serial treatment sessions (ie, spanning two or more treatment days). If required, adhesions or scarring may also be lysed by mechanical means. Code 62263 is **not** reported for each adhesiolysis treatment, but should be reported **once** to describe the entire series of injections/infusions spanning two or more treatment days.

Code 62264 describes multiple adhesiolysis treatment sessions performed on the same day. Adhesions or scarring may be lysed by injections of neurolytic agent(s). If required, adhesions or scarring may also be lysed mechanically using a percutaneously-deployed catheter.

Codes 62263 and 62264 include the procedure of injections of contrast for epidurography (72275) and fluoroscopic guidance and localization (77003) during initial or subsequent sessions.

Fluoroscopy (for localization) may be used in the placement of injections reported with 62310-62319, but is not required. If used, fluoroscopy should be reported with 77003. For epidurography, use 72275.

The placement and use of a catheter to administer one or more epidural or subarachnoid injections on a single calendar day should be reported in the same manner as if a needle had been used, ie, as a single injection using either 62310 or 62311. Such injections should not be reported with 62318 or 62319.

Threading a catheter into the epidural space, injecting substances at one or more levels and then removing the catheter should be treated as a single injection (62310, 62311). If the catheter is left in place to deliver substance(s) over a prolonged period (ie, more than a single calendar day) either continuously or via intermittent bolus, use 62318, 62319 as appropriate.

When reporting 62310-62319, code choice is based on the region at which the needle or catheter entered the body (eg, lumbar). Codes 62310-62319 should be reported only once, when the substance injected spreads or catheter tip insertion moves into another spinal region (eg, 62311 is reported only once for injection or catheter insertion at L3-4 with spread of the substance or placement of the catheter tip to the thoracic region).

Percutaneous spinal procedures are done with indirect visualization (eg, image guidance or endoscopic approaches) and without direct visualization (including through a microscope). Endoscopic assistance during an open procedure with direct visualization is reported using excision codes (eg, 63020-63035).

(Report 01996 for daily hospital management of continuous epidural or subarachnoid drug administration performed in conjunction with 62318-62319)

62263   Percutaneous lysis of epidural adhesions using solution injection (eg, hypertonic saline, enzyme) or mechanical means (eg, catheter) including radiologic localization (includes contrast when administered), multiple adhesiolysis sessions; 2 or more days

▲**62284**   Injection procedure for myelography and/or computed tomography, lumbar (other than C1-C2 and posterior fossa)

▶(Do not report 62284 in conjunction with 62302, 62303, 62304, 62305, 72240, 72255, 72265, 72270)◀

▶(When both 62284 and 72240, 72255, 72265, 72270 are performed by the same physician or other qualified health care professional for myelography, see 62302, 62303, 62304, 62305)◀

(For injection procedure at C1-C2, use 61055)

(For radiological supervision and interpretation, see **Radiology**)

●**62302**   Myelography via lumbar injection, including radiological supervision and interpretation; cervical

▶(Do not report 62302 in conjunction with 62284, 62303, 62304, 62305, 72240, 72255, 72265, 72270)◀

●**62303**   thoracic

▶(Do not report 62303 in conjunction with 62284, 62302, 62304, 62305, 72240, 72255, 72265, 72270)◀

●**62304**   lumbosacral

▶(Do not report 62304 in conjunction with 62284, 62302, 62303, 62305, 72240, 72255, 72265, 72270)◀

●**62305**   2 or more regions (eg, lumbar/thoracic, cervical/thoracic, lumbar/cervical, lumbar/thoracic/cervical)

▶(Do not report 62305 in conjunction with 62284, 62302, 62303, 62304, 72240, 72255, 72265, 72270)◀

▶(For myelography lumbar injection and imaging performed by different physicians or other qualified health care professionals, see 62284 or 72240, 72255, 72265, 72270)◀

▶(For injection procedure at C1-C2, use 61055)◀

✍ Rationale

In the CPT 2015 code set, four new bundled codes have been added for myelography procedures for cervical (62302), thoracic (62303), lumbosacral (62304), and two or more regions (eg, lumbar/thoracic, cervical/thoracic, lumbar/cervical, lumbar/thoracic/cervical) (62305). The existing injection and radiological supervision and interpretation codes for myelography (72240, 72255, 72265, and 72270) have been

⊘=Modifier 51 Exempt   ⊙=Moderate Sedation   ✚=Add-on Code   ✗=FDA approval pending

retained as these procedures are occasionally performed by two physicians; one performs the contrast injection and the second provides the radiological supervision and interpretation.

Exclusionary parenthetical notes have been added following codes 62302, 62303, 62304, and 62305 to restrict the use of codes 62284, 62302, 62303, 62304, 62305, 72240, 72255, 72265, 72270, as appropriate. A cross-reference parenthetical note has been added following code 62305 to direct users to report code 62284 or codes 72240, 72255, 72265, and 72270 for myelography lumbar injection and imaging performed by different physicians or other qualified health care professionals. In addition, a third instructional parenthetical note has been added following code 62305 to direct users to report code 61055 for an injection procedure at C1-C2.

Code 62284 has been revised to specify an injection procedure for myelography and/or computed tomography (CT) of the lumbar region.

Further revisions have been made to the Radiology subsection to parallel the establishment of new myelography procedures, including the addition and revision of exclusionary parenthetical notes and cross-reference parenthetical notes following codes 72240, 72255, 72265, and 72270.

Finally, the Injection, Drainage, or Aspiration guidelines have been updated in response to the establishment of myelography codes 62302, 62303, 62304, and 62305. The guidelines now reference myelography codes 62302, 62303, 62304, and 62305 and provide appropriate reporting instructions for the use of these codes.

Clinical Example (62284)

A 68-year-old patient with sciatica and neurogenic claudication symptoms who has multilevel degenerative disc disease and facet osteoarthritis on radiography presents having failed conservative therapy. Patient has a permanent pacemaker, precluding MRI examination.

Description of Procedure (62284)

Advance a spinal needle under fluoroscopic guidance into the spinal canal and sequentially into the thecal sac. Avoid damage to the nerve roots, conus medullaris, and cauda equina. Remove the stylet from the needle. Confirm egress of cerebrospinal fluid (CSF) from the needle hub, and evaluate fluid quality. Draw up iodinated contrast media. Attach the syringe-tubing combination, and then slowly (over several minutes) instill intrathecal contrast using intermittent fluoroscopy. During contrast injection, question the patient for symptoms. Carefully review the fluoroscopic images in real time to assure optimal intrathecal opacification and differentiation of nerve roots, spinal cord, and surrounding soft tissue structures and to confirm that there is no epidural, intramedullary, or intravascular contrast opacification. Evaluate the flow of contrast media from the needle tip during real time fluoroscopy. Replace the stylet, slowly remove the needle, and apply a bandage.

Clinical Example (62302)

A 47-year-old patient status post prior anterior cervical discectomy and fusion (ACDF) presents with new left upper extremity radiculopathy. A cervical myelogram is ordered.

Description of Procedure (62302)

Advance a spinal needle under fluoroscopic guidance into the spinal canal and sequentially into the thecal sac. Avoid damage to the nerve roots, conus medullaris, and cauda equina. Remove the stylet from the needle. Confirm egress of CSF from the needle hub, and evaluate fluid quality. Draw up iodinated contrast media. Attach the syringe-tubing combination, and then slowly (over several minutes) instill intrathecal contrast using intermittent fluoroscopy. During contrast injection, question the patient for symptoms. Perform real-time assessment of flow of contrast media from the needle and mixture with cerebrospinal fluid. Carefully review the fluoroscopic images in real time to assure optimal intrathecal opacification and differentiation of nerve roots, spinal cord, and surrounding soft tissue structures and to confirm that there is no epidural, intramedullary, or intravascular contrast opacification. Replace the stylet, slowly remove the needle, and apply a bandage.

Tilt the table into the Trendelenburg position, and use intermittent fluoroscopy to confirm the flow of contrast into the cervical region. Return the table to the horizontal position. Carefully review fluoroscopic images in real time to assure optimal intrathecal opacification and differentiation of nerve roots, spinal cord, and surrounding soft tissue structures and to confirm that there is no epidural, intramedullary, or intravascular contrast opacification. Take prone images in anteroposterior (AP), lateral, and both oblique projections. Obtain additional images with patient's head turned or with lateral flexion as necessary. Obtain additional AP and/or lateral images with the patient supine as necessary. Immediately review images for adequate positioning, contrast opacification, and pathology.

Evaluate the vertebral bodies for fractures, lesions, and misalignment. Evaluate for uneven contrast filling of thecal sac, which can suggest adhesions. Assess spinal canal for stenoses or blocks. Evaluate contrast outline of nerve roots and visible spinal cord. Assess vertebral hardware for loosening, fracture, or misalignment. Consider tilt table and oblique views to assess for dynamic lateral recess nerve root compression.

Clinical Example (62303)

A 36-year-old patient status post motor vehicle accident with lower thoracic vertebral compression, treated by spinal instrumentation, presents with increasing spastic gait and urinary incontinence. A thoracic myelogram is ordered.

Description of Procedure (62303)

Advance a spinal needle under fluoroscopic guidance into the spinal canal and sequentially into the thecal sac. Avoid damage to the nerve roots, conus medullaris, and cauda equina. Remove the stylet from the needle. Confirm egress of CSF from the needle hub, and evaluate fluid quality. Draw up iodinated contrast media. Attach the syringe-tubing combination, and then slowly (over several minutes) instill intrathecal contrast using intermittent fluoroscopy. During contrast injection, question the patient for symptoms. Carefully review the fluoroscopic images in real time to assure optimal intrathecal opacification and differentiation of nerve roots, spinal cord, and surrounding soft tissue structures and to confirm that there is no epidural, intramedullary, or intravascular contrast opacification. Assess in real time the flow of contrast media from the needle and mixture with cerebrospinal fluid. Replace the stylet, slowly remove the needle, and apply a bandage.

Tilt the table into the Trendelenburg position, and use intermittent fluoroscopy to confirm the flow of contrast into the thoracic region. Return the table to the horizontal position. Carefully review fluoroscopic images in real time to assure optimal intrathecal opacification and differentiation of nerve roots, spinal cord, and surrounding soft tissue structures and to confirm that there is no epidural, intramedullary, or intravascular contrast opacification. Take prone images in AP, lateral, and both oblique projections. Obtain additional images with patient's head turned or with lateral flexion as necessary. Obtain additional AP and/or lateral images with the patient supine as necessary. Immediately review images for adequate positioning, contrast opacification, and pathology.

Evaluate the vertebral bodies for fractures, lesions, and misalignment. Evaluate for uneven contrast filling of thecal sac, which can suggest adhesions. Assess spinal canal for stenoses or blocks. Evaluate contrast outline of nerve roots and visible spinal cord. Assess vertebral hardware for loosening, fracture, or misalignment. Consider tilt table and oblique views to assess for dynamic lateral recess nerve root compression.

 ### Clinical Example (62304)
A 68-year-old patient with progressive sciatica and neurogenic claudication has multilevel degenerative disc and facet osteoarthritis. Patient has failed conservative therapy. A lumbosacral myelogram is ordered.

Description of Procedure (62304)
Advance a spinal needle under fluoroscopic guidance into the spinal canal and sequentially into the thecal sac. Avoid damage to the nerve roots, conus medullaris, and cauda equina. Remove the stylet from the needle. Confirm egress of CSF from the needle hub, and evaluate fluid quality. Draw up iodinated contrast media. Attach the syringe-tubing combination, and slowly (over several minutes) instill intrathecal contrast using intermittent fluoroscopy. During contrast injection, question the patient for symptoms. Carefully review fluoroscopic images in real time to assure optimal intrathecal opacification and differentiation of nerve roots, spinal cord, and surrounding soft tissue structures and to confirm that there is no epidural, intramedullary, or intravascular contrast opacification. Assess in real time the flow of contrast media from the needle and mixture with cerebrospinal fluid. Replace the stylet, slowly remove the needle, and apply a bandage.

Tilt the table into the Trendelenburg position, and use intermittent fluoroscopy to confirm the flow of contrast into the lumbar region. Return the table to the horizontal position. Carefully review in real time the fluoroscopic images to assure optimal intrathecal opacification and differentiation of nerve roots, spinal cord, and surrounding soft tissue structures and to confirm that there is no epidural, intramedullary, or intravascular contrast opacification. Take prone images in AP, lateral, and both oblique projections. Obtain additional images with patient's head turned or with lateral flexion as necessary. Obtain additional AP and/or lateral images with the patient supine as necessary. Immediately review the images for adequate positioning, contrast opacification, and pathology.

Evaluate the vertebral bodies for fractures, lesions, and misalignment. Evaluate for uneven contrast filling of thecal sac, which can suggest adhesions. Assess spinal canal for stenoses or blocks. Evaluate contrast outline of nerve roots and visible spinal cord. Assess vertebral hardware for loosening, fracture, or misalignment. Consider tilt table and oblique views to assess for dynamic lateral recess nerve root compression.

Clinical Example (62305)

A 77-year-old patient has a spinal stimulator implanted for failed back surgery. Patient presents with progressive paraparesis and lower extremity pain. Thoracic and lumbosacral myelography are ordered.

Description of Procedure (62305)

Advance a spinal needle under fluoroscopic guidance into the spinal canal and sequentially into the thecal sac. Avoid damage to the nerve roots, conus medullaris, and cauda equina. Remove the stylet from the needle. Confirm egress of CSF from the needle hub, and evaluate fluid quality. Draw up iodinated contrast media. Attach the syringe-tubing combination, and then slowly instill (over several minutes) intrathecal contrast using intermittent fluoroscopy. During contrast injection, question the patient for symptoms. Carefully review fluoroscopic images in real time to assure optimal intrathecal opacification and differentiation of nerve roots, spinal cord, and surrounding soft tissue structures and to confirm that there is no epidural, intramedullary, or intravascular contrast opacification. Replace the stylet, slowly remove the needle, and apply a bandage.

Tilt the table into the Trendelenburg position, and use intermittent fluoroscopy to confirm the flow of contrast into the thoracic and/or cervical region. Return the table to the horizontal position. Carefully review fluoroscopic images in real time to assure optimal intrathecal opacification and differentiation of nerve roots, spinal cord, and surrounding soft tissue structures and to confirm that there is no epidural, intramedullary, or intravascular contrast opacification. Assess in real time the flow of contrast media from the needle and mixture with cerebrospinal fluid. Take prone images in AP, lateral, and both oblique projections. Obtain additional images with patient's head turned or with lateral flexion as necessary. Obtain additional AP and/or lateral images with the patient supine as necessary. Immediately review the images for adequate positioning, contrast opacification, and pathology.

Evaluate the vertebral bodies for fractures, lesions, and misalignment. Evaluate for uneven contrast filling of thecal sac, which can suggest adhesions. Assess spinal canal for stenoses or blocks. Evaluate contrast outline of nerve roots and visible spinal cord. Assess vertebral hardware for loosening, fracture, or misalignment. Consider tilt table and oblique views to assess for dynamic lateral recess nerve root compression.

STEREOTACTIC RADIOSURGERY (SPINAL)

Spinal stereotactic radiosurgery is a distinct procedure that utilizes externally generated ionizing radiation to inactivate or eradicate defined target(s) in the spine without the need to make an incision. The target is defined by and the treatment is delivered using high-resolution stereotactic imaging. These codes are reported by the surgeon. The radiation oncologist reports the appropriate code(s) for clinical treatment planning, physics and dosimetry, treatment delivery and management from the **Radiation Oncology** section (77261-77790). Any necessary planning, dosimetry, targeting, positioning, or blocking by the neurosurgeon is included in the stereotactic radiation surgery services. The same individual should not report stereotactic radiosurgery services with radiation treatment management codes (77427-77432).

Spinal stereotactic radiosurgery is typically performed in a single planning and treatment session using a stereotactic image-guidance system, but can be performed with a planning session and in a limited number of treatment sessions, up to a maximum of five sessions. Do not report stereotactic radiosurgery more than once per lesion per course of treatment when the treatment requires greater than one session.

Stereotactic spinal surgery is only used when the tumor being treated affects spinal neural tissue or abuts the dura mater. Arteriovenous malformations must be subdural. For other radiation services of the spine, see **Radiation Oncology** services.

Codes 63620, 63621 include computer-assisted planning. Do not report 63620, 63621 in conjunction with 61781-61783.

▶(For intensity modulated beam delivery plan and treatment, see 77301, 77385, 77386. For stereotactic body radiation therapy, see 77373, 77435)◀

63620 Stereotactic radiosurgery (particle beam, gamma ray, or linear accelerator); 1 spinal lesion

Rationale

A cross-reference parenthetical note following the Stereotactic Radiosurgery (Spinal) guidelines has been revised to reflect the establishment of new IMRT treatment delivery codes 77385 and 77386.

Extracranial Nerves, Peripheral Nerves, and Autonomic Nervous System

INTRODUCTION/INJECTION OF ANESTHETIC AGENT (NERVE BLOCK), DIAGNOSTIC OR THERAPEUTIC

Somatic Nerves

●**64486** Transversus abdominis plane (TAP) block (abdominal plane block, rectus sheath block) unilateral; by injection(s) (includes imaging guidance, when performed)

●**64487** by continuous infusion(s) (includes imaging guidance, when performed)

●**64488** Transversus abdominis plane (TAP) block (abdominal plane block, rectus sheath block) bilateral; by injections (includes imaging guidance, when performed)

●**64489** by continuous infusions (includes imaging guidance, when performed)

 Rationale

Four codes (64486-64489) have been established to report administration of local anesthetic for postoperative pain control and abdominal wall analgesia, including imaging guidance when performed. Because more than 50% of the time these services are typically performed bilaterally, codes 64486 and 64487 are intended to report the transversus abdominis plane (TAP) block performed unilaterally, and codes 64488 and 64489 are intended to report bilateral services.

 Clinical Example (64486)

A 25-year-old male undergoes open appendectomy under general anesthesia. He is at risk for postoperative pain. In order to provide postoperative pain control, a TAP block is placed at the request of the surgeon.

Description of Procedure (64486)

Place a linear, high-frequency ultrasound transducer in an axial (transverse) plane, above the iliac crest within the region of the anterior axillary line. Using continuous ultrasound guidance, identify the layers of the abdominal wall: the external oblique (superficial), the internal oblique, and the transversus abdominis muscles. Anesthetize the skin at the proposed entry site with a small amount of local anesthetic via a small-gauge needle (27-gauge). Insert a 100-mm, 22-gauge short-beveled ultrasound needle inplane with the transducer. While advancing under live ultrasound guidance, feel two distinct "pops" as the needle passes through the external oblique fascia and then the internal oblique fascia. Now, the needle is in the TAP plane between the internal oblique and the transversus abdominis muscles. Once correct needle position is obtained, aspirate the needle to confirm the absence of blood. Following negative aspiration, administer a small test dose of local anesthetic, monitor the patient's vital signs, and question the patient for symptoms of intravascular local anesthetic injection. If there are no signs or symptoms of intravascular injection, then incrementally inject 20 ml of local anesthetic with verification of a hypoechoic fluid pocket immediately deep to the hyperechoic fascial plane between the internal oblique and the transversus abdominis. After completion of the injection, remove the needle. Observe the patient for any signs or symptoms of local anesthetic toxicity. After several minutes have passed, evaluate the initial effects of the TAP block by physical examination to determine if the patient is developing numbness and relief of pain in the expected nerve distribution.

 Clinical Example (64487)

A 58-year-old male undergoes partial nephrectomy under general anesthesia for renal cell carcinoma. In order to provide postoperative pain control, a TAP block with catheter placement for continuous infusion is placed at the request of the surgeon.

◯=Modifier 51 Exempt   ◉=Moderate Sedation   ✚=Add-on Code   𝒩=FDA approval pending

Description of Procedure (64487)

Place a linear, high-frequency ultrasound transducer in an axial (transverse) plane, above the iliac crest within the region of the anterior axillary line. Using continuous ultrasound guidance, identify the layers of the abdominal wall: the external oblique (superficial), the internal oblique, and the transversus abdominis muscles. Anesthetize the skin at the proposed entry site with a small amount of local anesthetic via a small-gauge needle (27-gauge). Insert an 18-gauge needle inplane with the transducer. While advancing under live ultrasound guidance, feel two distinct "pops" as the needle passes through the external oblique fascia and then the internal oblique fascia. Now, the needle is in the TAP plane between the internal oblique and the transversus abdominis muscles. Once correct needle position is obtained, perform aspiration of the needle to confirm the absence of blood. Next, thread a 20-gauge catheter through the cannula, and remove the cannula. Following negative aspiration, administer a small test dose of local anesthetic, monitor the patient's vital signs, and question the patient for symptoms of intravascular local anesthetic injection. If there are no signs or symptoms of intravascular injection, then incrementally inject 20 ml of local anesthetic with verification of a hypoechoic fluid pocket immediately deep to the hyperechoic fascial plane between the internal oblique and the transversus abdominis. Secure the catheter with a sterile liquid adhesive, and apply a sterile occlusive dressing. Deliver ropivacaine 0.2% via an infusion pump at 8 ml-10 ml/hr. Observe the patient for any signs or symptoms of local anesthetic toxicity. After several minutes have passed, evaluate the initial effects of the TAP block by physical examination to determine if the patient is developing numbness and relief of pain in the expected nerve distribution.

 Clinical Example (64488)

A 45-year-old female undergoes laparoscopy cholecystectomy under general anesthesia. She is at risk for postoperative pain. In order to provide postoperative pain control, bilateral TAP blocks are placed at the request of the surgeon.

Description of Procedure (64488)

Place a linear, high-frequency ultrasound transducer in an axial (transverse) plane, above the iliac crest within the region of the anterior axillary line. Using continuous ultrasound guidance, identify the layers of the abdominal wall: the external oblique (superficial), the internal oblique, and the transversus abdominis muscles. Anesthetize the skin at the proposed entry site with a small amount of local anesthetic via a small-gauge needle (27-gauge). Insert a 100-mm, 22-gauge short-beveled block needle in plane with the transducer. While advancing under live ultrasound guidance, feel two distinct "pops" as the needle passes through the external oblique fascia and then the internal oblique fascia. Now, the needle is in the TAP plane between the internal oblique and the transversus abdominis muscles. Once correct needle position is obtained, perform aspiration of the needle to confirm the absence of blood. Following negative aspiration, administer a small test dose of local anesthetic, monitor the patient's vital signs, and question the patient for symptoms of intravascular local anesthetic injection. If there are no signs or symptoms of intravascular then incrementally inject 20 ml of local anesthetic with verification of a hypoechoic fluid pocket immediately deep to the hyperechoic fascial plane between the internal oblique and the transversus abdominis. After completion of the injection, remove the needle.

Next, repeat the procedure in an identical fashion on the opposite side. The skin has already been prepped and draped in a sterile fashion.

Observe the patient for any signs or symptoms of local anesthetic toxicity. After several minutes have passed, evaluate the initial effects of the TAP block by physical examination to determine if the patient is developing numbness and relief of pain in the expected nerve distribution.

Clinical Example (64489)

A 64-year-old female undergoes hysterectomy under general anestheisa for uterine cancer. In order to provide postoperative pain control, bilateral TAP blocks with catheter placement for continuous infusion are placed at the request of the surgeon.

Description of Procedure (64489)

Place a linear, high-frequency ultrasound transducer in an axial (transverse) plane, above the iliac crest within the region of the anterior axillary line. Using continuous ultrasound guidance, identify the layers of the abdominal wall: the external oblique (superficial), the internal oblique, and the transversus abdominis muscles. Anesthetize the skin at the proposed entry site with a small amount of local anesthetic via a small-gauge needle (27-gauge). Insert an 18-gauge needle inplane with the transducer. While advancing under live ultrasound guidance, feel two distinct "pops" as the needle passes through the external oblique fascia and then the internal oblique fascia. Now, the needle is in the TAP plane between the internal oblique and the transversus abdominis muscles. Once correct needle position is obtained, perform aspiration of the needle to confirm the absence of blood. Next, thread a 20-gauge catheter through the cannula, and remove the cannula. Following negative aspiration, administer a small test dose of local anesthetic, monitor the patient's vital signs, and question the patient for symptoms of intravascular local anesthetic injection. If there are no signs or symptoms of intravascular injection, then incrementally inject 20 ml of local anesthetic with verification of a hypoechoic fluid pocket immediately deep to the hyperechoic fascial plane between the internal oblique and the transversus abdominis. Secure the catheter with a sterile liquid adhesive, and apply a sterile occlusive dressing. Deliver ropivacaine 0.2% via an infusion pump at 8 ml to 10 ml/hr.

Next, repeat the procedure in an identical fashion on the opposite side. The skin has already been prepped and draped in a sterile fashion.

Observe the patient for any signs or symptoms of local anesthetic toxicity. After several minutes have passed, evaluate the initial effects of the TAP block by physical examination to determine if the patient is developing numbness and relief of pain in the expected nerve distribution.

Paravertebral Spinal Nerves and Branches

64490   Injection(s), diagnostic or therapeutic agent, paravertebral facet (zygapophyseal) joint (or nerves innervating that joint) with image guidance (fluoroscopy or CT), cervical or thoracic; single level

+64491   second level (List separately in addition to code for primary procedure)

        ▶(Use 64491 in conjunction with 64490)◀

+64492   third and any additional level(s) (List separately in addition to code for primary procedure)

    (Do not report 64492 more than once per day)

        ▶(Use 64492 in conjunction with 64490, 64491)◀

64493   Injection(s), diagnostic or therapeutic agent, paravertebral facet (zygapophyseal) joint (or nerves innervating that joint) with image guidance (fluoroscopy or CT), lumbar or sacral; single level

+64494   second level (List separately in addition to code for primary procedure)

        ▶(Use 64494 in conjunction with 64493)◀

+64495   third and any additional level(s) (List separately in addition to code for primary procedure)

    (Do not report 64495 more than once per day)

        ▶(Use 64495 in conjunction with 64493, 64494)◀

✒ Rationale

Parenthetical notes following the paravertebral spinal nerve injection codes in the Surgery section (64490-64495) have been added and revised to clarify the intended use of these codes. The inclusionary parenthetical notes are editorial and have been added to direct users on the appropriate use of the add-on codes included for these services. The add-on code families listed in this section are intended to be used together in a "progressive" fashion to denote the appropriate service(s) performed (ie, the codes are "additive" and build on each other to note the number of levels of injections provided).

TRANSECTION OR AVULSION

64732   Transection or avulsion of; supraorbital nerve

64734   infraorbital nerve

64736   mental nerve

64738   inferior alveolar nerve by osteotomy

64740   lingual nerve

64742   facial nerve, differential or complete

64744   greater occipital nerve

    (For section of recurrent laryngeal nerve, use 31595)

64746   phrenic nerve

▶(64752 has been deleted)◀

64755   vagus nerves limited to proximal stomach (selective proximal vagotomy, proximal gastric vagotomy, parietal cell vagotomy, supra- or highly selective vagotomy)

(For laparoscopic approach, use 43652)

64760   vagus nerve (vagotomy), abdominal

(For laparoscopic approach, use 43651)

▶(64761 has been deleted)◀

 Rationale

As part of an effort to ensure that the CPT code set reflects current clinical practice, codes 64752 and 64761 (transection or avulsion procedures of the vagus (transthoracic) and pudendal nerves) have been deleted due to low utilization.

NEURORRHAPHY

64866   Anastomosis; facial-spinal accessory

64868   facial-hypoglossal

▶(64870 has been deleted)◀

 Rationale

As part of an effort to ensure that the CPT code set reflects current clinical practice, code 64870 (anastomosis of the facial-phrenic nerve) has been deleted due to low utilization.

Eye and Ocular Adnexa

Eyeball

REMOVAL OF FOREIGN BODY

▶(For removal of foreign body from orbit: frontal approach, use 67413; lateral approach, use 67430)◀

(For removal of foreign body from eyelid, embedded, use 67938)

(For removal of foreign body from lacrimal system, use 68530)

65205   Removal of foreign body, external eye; conjunctival superficial

 Rationale

In accordance with the deletion of code 61334, the cross-reference parenthetical note above code 65205 has been revised with the deletion of the instruction to report code 61334 for the removal of a foreign body by transcranial approach.

⊘=Modifier 51 Exempt   ⊙=Moderate Sedation   ✚=Add-on Code   ✔=FDA approval pending

Anterior Segment

ANTERIOR SCLERA

Excision

66150   Fistulization of sclera for glaucoma; trephination with iridectomy

66155   thermocauterization with iridectomy

66160   sclerectomy with punch or scissors, with iridectomy

►(66165 has been deleted)◄

Rationale

As part of an effort to ensure that the CPT code set reflects current clinical practice, code 66165 (iridenclesis or iridotasis) has been deleted due to low utilization.

Aqueous Shunt

●66179   Aqueous shunt to extraocular equatorial plate reservoir, external approach; without graft

▲66180   with graft

►(Do not report 66180 in conjunction with 67255)◄

66183   Insertion of anterior segment aqueous drainage device, without extraocular reservoir, external approach

●66184   Revision of aqueous shunt to extraocular equatorial plate reservoir; without graft

▲66185   with graft

►(Do not report 66185 in conjunction with 67255)◄

(For removal of implanted shunt, use 67120)

Rationale

The American Medical Association/Specialty Society RUC identified codes 66180 and 67255 as being reported together 73% of the time due to the frequency of the erosion of the aqueous shunt into the overlying conjunctiva necessitating reinforcement with a scleral patch graft to seal leakage from the open conjunctiva. It was determined that the frequency of the utilization of grafts in the family of aqueous shunt procedures warranted a new code structure to reflect actual practice ie, by revising codes 66180 and 66185 to include the graft, and establish new codes 66179 and 66184 for the non-graft procedures. In addition, exclusionary parenthetical notes following codes 66180 and 66185 have been added to direct users not to report code 66180 in conjunction with code 67255.

Clinical Example (66179)

A 35-year-old female with open angle glaucoma and a previous trabeculectomy presents with worsening intraocular pressure control on maximal tolerated medical therapy. Surgical treatment is suggested.

Description of Procedure (66179)

Place a lid speculum. Place a silk traction suture through partial-thickness clear cornea, and rotate the eye inferiorly to expose the superior limbus and conjunctiva. Perform a conjunctival peritomy for approximately 120° at the superior and temporal limbus. Perform cautery to control bleeding as needed. Extensive deep subconjunctival dissection is accomplished in the superotemporal quadrant, encountering scar tissue and areas of scleral thinning from prior surgery, taking care to prevent damage to the delicate conjunctiva.

Identify the superior rectus, superior oblique, and lateral rectus muscles and muscle hooks placed to position the globe for optimal insertion of the device. Use scissors to spread Tenon's capsule and other episcleral tissue in the superotemporal quadrant for implantation of the external reservoir. Inspect, flush, or prime the glaucoma reservoir implant as required while the assistant maintains positioning on the eye with the muscle hooks. Maneuver the large-diameter plate into position on the sclera beneath the conjunctival flap, again taking care not to damage the overlying conjunctiva or distort Tenon's capsule. Position the proximal edge of the plate 8 mm to 10 mm posterior to the limbus, placing the wings of the implant beneath the adjacent superior and lateral rectus muscles. Place two 8-0 nylon sutures through the proximal positioning holes of the plate, and secure them to the sclera. Rotate the surgical knots beneath the implant to avoid conjunctival erosion. Place a polyglactin ligature around the drainage tubing near the connection with the plate. Irrigate the tube to confirm that the ligature allows no fluid movement past the ligature. Create a corneal paracentesis. Use a 23-gauge needle to tunnel through the sclera adjacent to the limbus and enter the anterior chamber, taking care to avoid trauma to the iris or corneal endothelium. Measure and cut the end of the glaucoma implant tubing to the desired length, and carefully introduce it into the anterior chamber. Re-expand the anterior chamber with balanced salt solution. Position the external portion of the tubing to lie flush against the sclera, and secure it to the sclera with a 10-0 nylon mattress suture. Puncture the external tube three times with a surgical needle to allow for limited flow out of the tubing in the early postoperative period. Pull the conjunctiva forward to cover the plate and tubing, and re-approximate it to the limbus using a combination of interrupted and running sutures. Fill the anterior chamber with balanced salt solution, and inspect the wound for leaks. Remove the traction suture and lid speculum. Apply subconjunctival antibiotics, and perform steroid injections.

Clinical Example (66180)

A 70-year-old female with open angle glaucoma and a previous trabeculectomy presents with worsening intraocular pressure control on maximal tolerated medical therapy. Surgical management is indicated.

Description of Procedure (66180)

Administer a local anesthetic block while the patient is monitored with pulse oximetry and electrocardiography. Prepare and drape the eye and periocular area. Place a lid speculum. Place a silk traction suture through partial-thickness clear cornea, and rotate the eye inferiorly to expose the superior limbus and conjunctiva. Perform a conjunctival peritomy for approximately 120 degrees at the superior and temporal limbus. Perform cautery to control bleeding as needed.

Perform extensive deep subconjunctival dissection in the superotemporal quadrant, encountering scar tissue and areas of scleral thinning from prior glaucoma surgery and taking care to prevent damage to the delicate conjunctiva. Identify the superior rectus, superior oblique, and lateral rectus muscles, and place muscle hooks to position the globe for optimal insertion of the device. Use scissors to spread Tenon's capsule and other episcleral tissue in the superotemporal quadrant for implantation of the external reservoir. Inspect the glaucoma reservoir implant and flush or prime as required while the assistant maintains positioning on the eye with the muscle hooks. Maneuver the large-diameter plate into position on the sclera beneath the conjunctival flap, again taking care not to damage the overlying conjunctiva or distort Tenon's capsule. Position the proximal edge of the plate 8 mm to 10 mm posterior to the limbus, placing the wings of the implant beneath the adjacent superior and lateral rectus muscles. Place two 8-0 nylon sutures through the proximal positioning holes of the plate, and secure them to the sclera. Rotate the surgical knots beneath the implant to avoid conjunctival erosion. Place a polyglactin ligature around the drainage tubing near the connection with the plate. Irrigate the tube to confirm that the ligature allows no fluid movement past the ligature. Create a corneal paracentesis. Use a 23-gauge needle to tunnel through the sclera adjacent to the limbus and enter the anterior chamber, taking care to avoid trauma to the iris or corneal endothelium. Measure and cut the end of the glaucoma implant tubing to the desired length, and carefully introduce it into the anterior chamber. Re-expand the anterior chamber with balanced salt solution. Position the external portion of the tubing to lie flush against the sclera, and secure it to the sclera with a 10-0 nylon mattress suture. Puncure the external tube three times with a surgical needle to allow for limited flow from the tubing in the early postoperative period.

Measure the area for the patch graft with calipers. Prepare the donor sclera by freehand dissection, and anchor it with interrupted sutures to cover the tube. Trim the donor material as needed, and place additional interrupted sutures. Pull the conjunctiva forward to cover the graft, plate, and tubing, and re-approximate it to the limbus using a combination of interrupted and running sutures. Fill the anterior chamber with balanced salt solution, and inspect the wound for leaks. Remove the traction suture and lid speculum. Apply subconjunctival antibiotics, and perform steroid injections. Dress the eye with topical ophthalmic ointment, apply a patch, and place a shield.

Clinical Example (66184)

A 72-year-old female, who had a glaucoma implant device surgery four years ago, presents with blurred vision and a foreign-body sensation is found to have exposure of the shunt tube with erosion of the overlying conjunctiva and low intraocular pressure due to leakage from the open conjunctiva. Urgent surgical management is required to prevent further complications.

Description of Procedure (66184)

Administer the local anesthetic block while the patient is monitored with pulse oximetry and electrocardiography. Prepare and drape the operative eye and periocular area. Place a lid speculum. Make a corneal paracentesis, and pressurize the eye with balanced salt solution and viscoelastic material. Place a silk traction suture through partial-thickness clear cornea, and rotate the eye inferiorly to expose the superior limbus and conjunctiva over the implant. Perform a conjunctival peritomy at the superior limbus. Explore the area of surface exposure over the external shunt tubing. Perform cautery to control bleeding. Accomplish subconjunctival dissection to mobilize surrounding conjunctiva, encountering scar tissue and scleral thinning from the prior surgery, while taking care to prevent damage to the remaining conjunctiva. Clean, scrape, cauterize, and treat the exposed bare sclera with dehydrated alcohol to remove any epithelial cells that hinder healing.

Locate the tube entry site into the anterior chamber, and confirm it to be stable. Identify the posterior external plate, and confirm it to be in stable position. Close the conjunctival wound with interrupted and running sutures to ensure a traction-free closure. Evacuate viscoelastic from the anterior chamber, which is refilled with balanced salt solution. Inspect the incisions for leaks. Remove the traction suture and lid speculum. Apply subconjunctival antibiotic, and perform steroid injections. Dress the eye with topical ointment, apply a patch, and place a shield.

Clinical Example (66185)

A 72-year-old female who had a glaucoma implant device surgery four years ago presents with blurred vision and a foreign-body sensation and is found to have exposure of the shunt tube with erosion of the overlying conjunctiva and low intraocular pressure due to leakage from the open conjunctiva. Urgent surgical management with a tissue graft is required to prevent further complications.

Description of Procedure (66185)

Administer the local anesthetic block while the patient is monitored with pulse oximetry and electrocardiography. Prepare and drape the operative eye and periocular area. Place a lid speculum. Make a corneal paracentesis, and pressurize the eye with balanced salt solution and viscoelastic material. Place a silk traction suture through partial-thickness clear cornea, and rotate the eye inferiorly to expose the superior limbus and conjunctiva over the implant. Perform a conjunctival peritomy at the superior limbus. Explore the area of surface exposure over the external shunt tubing. Perform cautery to control bleeding. Accomplish subconjunctival dissection to mobilize surrounding conjunctiva, encountering scar tissue and scleral thinning from the prior surgery, while taking care to prevent damage to the remaining conjunctiva. Clean, scrape, cauterize, and treat the exposed bare sclera with dehydrated alcohol to remove any epithelial cells that hinder healing. Locate the tube entry site into the anterior chamber, and confirm it to be stable. Identify the posterior external plate, and confirm it to be in stable position. Measure the area for the patch graft with calipers. Prepare the donor sclera by freehand dissection, and anchor it with interrupted sutures to cover the tube. Trim the donor material as needed, and place additional interrupted sutures. Pull conjunctiva to cover the graft, expose the tubing, and suture it to the surrounding conjunctiva with interrupted and running sutures to ensure a traction-free closure. Evacuate viscoelastic from the anterior chamber, which is refilled with balanced salt solution. Inspect the incisions for leaks. Remove the traction suture and lid speculum. Apply subconjunctival antibiotic, and perform steroid injections. Dress the eye with topical ointment, apply a patch, and place a shield.

Posterior Segment

POSTERIOR SCLERA

Repair

67250 Scleral reinforcement (separate procedure); without graft

67255   with graft

▶(Do not report 67255 in conjunction with 66180, 66185)◀

(For repair scleral staphyloma, see 66220, 66225)

 Rationale

A reciprocal exclusionary parenthetical note following code 67255 has been added to restrict the use of codes 66180 and 66185 with code 67255. For more information, see the Rationale for code 66179.

Ocular Adnexa

ORBIT

Exploration, Excision, Decompression

67420 Orbitotomy with bone flap or window, lateral approach (eg, Kroenlein); with removal of lesion

67450   for exploration, with or without biopsy

▶(For orbitotomy, transcranial approach, see 61330, 61332, 61333)◀

 Rationale

In accordance with the deletion of code 61334, the cross-reference parenthetical note following code 67450 has been revised to remove the reference to this code.

Conjunctiva

LACRIMAL SYSTEM

Repair

68760   Closure of the lacrimal punctum; by thermocauterization, ligation, or laser surgery

68761   by plug, each

▶(For insertion and removal of drug-eluting implant into lacrimal canaliculus for intra-ocular pressure, use 0356T)◀

🖎 Rationale

A parenthetical note has been created following code 68761 to direct the use of new code 0356T for reporting the insertion and removal of drug-eluting implants into the lacrimal canaliculus for intra-ocular pressure. For more information, see the Rationale for code 0356T.

Probing and/or Related Procedures

68801   Dilation of lacrimal punctum, with or without irrigation

(To report a bilateral procedure, use 68801 with modifier 50)

68810   Probing of nasolacrimal duct, with or without irrigation;

(For bilateral procedure, report 68810 with modifier 50)

68811   requiring general anesthesia

(For bilateral procedure, report 68811 with modifier 50)

68815   with insertion of tube or stent

(See also 92018)

(For bilateral procedure, report 68815 with modifier 50)

▶(For insertion and removal of drug-eluting implant into lacrimal canaliculus for intra-ocular pressure, use 0356T)◀

🖎 Rationale

A parenthetical note has been added following code 68815 to direct the use of new code 0356T for reporting the insertion and removal of drug-eluting implants into the lacrimal canaliculus for intra-ocular pressure. For more information, see the Rationale for code 0356T.

⃠=Modifier 51 Exempt   ⊙=Moderate Sedation   ✚=Add-on Code   𝒩=FDA approval pending

Auditory System

Middle Ear

INTRODUCTION

▶(69400 has been deleted. To report, use 69799)◀

▶(69401 has been deleted. To report, see the appropriate Evaluation and Management code 99201, 99202, 99203, 99204, 99205, 99211, 99212, 99213, 99214, 99215)◀

▶(69405 has been deleted. To report, use 69799)◀

✎ Rationale

Eustachian tube procedure codes 69400, 69401, and 69405 have been deleted as they describe outdated procedures. Cross-reference parenthetical notes have been added to direct users to the appropriate codes when these procedures are performed: code 69799 for transnasal Eustachian tube inflation with catheterization (69400) or Eustachian tube catheterization (69405), or an appropriate level of Evaluation and Management (E/M) code (99201-99215) for Eustachian tube inflation without catheterization (69401).

Code 69400 was originally intended to identify the placement of a catheter up to the nasopharyngeal orifice of the Eustachian tube to insufflate it and aerate the middle ear. However, the technique is rarely used today and most consider it obsolete. If performed, this procedure should be reported using middle ear unlisted procedure code 69799. The procedure previously reported with code 69401 may now be reported with the appropriate level of E/M code according to the key components and type of E/M service that is being provided. Code 69405 describes a procedure that has been identified as clinically unnecessary. (No case exists in which this service should be reported.)

Operating Microscope

▶The surgical microscope is employed when the surgical services are performed using the techniques of microsurgery. Code 69990 should be reported (without modifier 51 appended) in addition to the code for the primary procedure performed. Do not use 69990 for visualization with magnifying loupes or corrected vision. Do not report 69990 in addition to procedures where use of the operating microscope is an inclusive component (15756-15758, 15842, 19364, 19368, 20955-20962, 20969-20973, 22551, 22552, 22856-22861, 26551-26554, 26556, 31526, 31531, 31536, 31541, 31545, 31546, 31561, 31571, 43116, 43180, 43496, 46601, 46607, 49906, 61548, 63075-63078, 64727, 64820-64823, 65091-68850, 0184T, 0308T).◀

+ 69990   Microsurgical techniques, requiring use of operating microscope (List separately in addition to code for primary procedure)

🔖 Rationale

In accordance with the establishment of code 43180 (rigid, transoral diverticu-lectomy) and Category III codes 0226T and 0227T (transition of high-resolution anoscopy) to Category I codes 46601 and 46607, the exclusionary parenthetical note that precedes code 69990 (operating microscope) has been revised with the addition of codes 46601, 46607, and 43180 and the removal of codes 0226T and 0227T.

⊘=Modifier 51 Exempt   ⊙=Moderate Sedation   ✛=Add-on Code   ⅣＮ=FDA approval pending

Radiology

The most substantial changes to the Radiology section are the revisions to the exclusionary parenthetical notes and cross-references to include appropriate reporting instructions for these codes. In addition, a few other changes have been made, which include: (1) deletion of code 76645 (breast ultrasound) and addition of two new codes, 76641 and 76642, to report limited (focused) and complete breast ultrasound procedures; (2) addition of three new codes, 77061, 77062, and 77063, to report diagnostic and screening breast tomosynthesis; (3) deletion of code 77082 (vertebral fracture assessment) and addition of new code 77085 to report the bone density study and vertebral fracture assessment and new code 77086 to report vertebral fracture assessment via dual-energy X-ray absorptiometry (DXA); (4) deletion of codes 77305, 77310, 77315, 77326, 77327 and 77328 (radiation oncology) and addition of five new codes, 77306, 77307, 77316, 77317, and 77318, to report combined teletherapy brachytherapy isodose planning with basic dosimetry calculations.

Numerous revisions have been made to the Radiation Treatment Delivery section, which include: (1) deletion of codes 77403, 77404, 77406, 77408, 77409, 77411, 77413, 77414, 77416, 77418, and 77421, and addition of new guidelines, definitions, and codes 77385, 77386, and 77387.

Radiology

Diagnostic Radiology (Diagnostic Imaging)

Spine and Pelvis

72240　Myelography, cervical, radiological supervision and interpretation

　▶(Do not report 72240 in conjunction with 62284, 62302, 62303, 62304, 62305)◀

　▶(When both 62284 and 72240 are performed by the same physician or other qualified health care professional for cervical myelography, use 62302)◀

　▶(For complete cervical myelography via injection procedure at C1-C2, see 61055, 72240)◀

72255　Myelography, thoracic, radiological supervision and interpretation

　▶(Do not report 72255 in conjunction with 62284, 62302, 62303, 62304, 62305)◀

　▶(When both 62284 and 72255 are performed by the same physician or other qualified health care professional for thoracic myelography, use 62303)◀

　▶(For complete thoracic myelography via injection procedure at C1-C2, see 61055, 72255)◀

72265　Myelography, lumbosacral, radiological supervision and interpretation

　▶(Do not report 72265 in conjunction with 62284, 62302, 62303, 62304, 62305)◀

　▶(When both 62284 and 72265 are performed by the same physician or other qualified health care professional for lumbosacral myelography, use 62304)◀

　▶(For complete lumbosacral myelography via injection procedure at C1-C2, see 61055, 72265)◀

72270　Myelography, 2 or more regions (eg, lumbar/thoracic, cervical/thoracic, lumbar/cervical, lumbar/thoracic/cervical), radiological supervision and interpretation

　▶(Do not report 72270 in conjunction with 62284, 62302, 62303, 62304, 62305)◀

　▶(When both 62284 and 72270 are performed by the same physician or other qualified health care professional for myelography of 2 or more regions, use 62305)◀

　▶(For complete myelography of 2 or more regions via injection procedure at C1-C2, see 61055, 72270)◀

　▶(72291 and 72292 have been deleted. To report, see 22510, 22511, 22512, 22513, 22514, 22515, 0200T, 0201T)◀

✍ Rationale

In correlation with the establishment of four new bundled myelography codes in the Surgery section for cervical (62302), thoracic (62303), lumbosacral (62304), and two or more regions (eg, lumbar/thoracic, cervical/thoracic, lumbar/cervical, lumbar/thoracic/cervical) (62305), the exclusionary parenthetical notes and cross-reference notes following codes 72240, 72255, 72265, and 72270 have been revised and updated to include appropriate reporting instructions for these codes.

In addition, instructional parentheticals have been added following each imaging code to identify the codes to select for these procedures (imaging and vertebroplasty) when they are performed by the same physician (or other qualified health care professional). These instructions direct users to new codes 62302 (cervical), 62303 (thoracic), 62304 (lumbar), or 62305 (multiple regions), when the same physician or other qualified health care professional performs the service.

To correlate with the addition of the new comprehensive codes for percutaneous vertebroplasty and augmentation that include imaging, codes 72291 and 72292 have been deleted. These codes were specific to the radiologic supervision and interpretation of percutaneous vertebroplasty and augmentation procedures, which are no longer reported separately. A cross-reference note has been added to indicate that these services should be reported with the new comprehensive codes 22510-22515 and revised codes 0200T and 0201T.

Gastrointestinal Tract

74235   Removal of foreign body(s), esophageal, with use of balloon catheter, radiological supervision and interpretation

►(For procedure, use 43499)◄

 Rationale

In accordance with the gastroenterological changes in the Digestive System section, the cross-reference parenthetical note following code 74235 has been revised with the removal of codes 43194, 43215, and 43247 (foreign body) and the addition of code 43499 (unlisted procedure, esophagus).

74290   Cholecystography, oral contrast

►(74291 has been deleted)◄

 Rationale

As part of an effort to ensure that the CPT code set reflects current clinical practice, code 74291 (additional or repeat examination or multiple day cholecystography services) has been deleted due to low utilization.

Other Procedures

76000   Fluoroscopy (separate procedure), up to 1 hour physician or other qualified health care professional time, other than 71023 or 71034 (eg, cardiac fluoroscopy)

►(Do not report 76000 in conjunction with 33957, 33958, 33959, 33962, 33963, 33964)◄

76001   Fluoroscopy, physician or other qualified health care professional time more than 1 hour, assisting a nonradiologic physician or other qualified health care professional (eg, nephrostolithotomy, ERCP, bronchoscopy, transbronchial biopsy)

►(Do not report 76001 in conjunction with 33957, 33958, 33959, 33962, 33963, 33964)◄

⊘=Modifier 51 Exempt   ⊙=Moderate Sedation   ✛=Add-on Code   𝒩=FDA approval pending

Rationale

In support of the establishment of codes 33946-33989 to report extracorporeal membrane oxygenation (ECMO) and extracorporeal life support (ECLS) services, a reciprocal exclusionary parenthetical note has been added following codes 76000, 76001 to preclude these codes from being reported in conjunction with codes 33957-33964. Fluoroscopic guidance is considered an inclusive component to ECMO/ECLS services, and therefore, should not be reported separately.

76376   3D rendering with interpretation and reporting of computed tomography, magnetic resonance imaging, ultrasound, or other tomographic modality with image postprocessing under concurrent supervision; not requiring image postprocessing on an independent workstation

(Use 76376 in conjunction with code[s] for base imaging procedure[s])

►(Do not report 76376 in conjunction with 31627, 34839, 70496, 70498, 70544, 70545, 70546, 70547, 70548, 70549, 71275, 71555, 72159, 72191, 72198, 73206, 73225, 73706, 73725, 74174, 74175, 74185, 74261, 74262, 74263, 75557, 75559, 75561, 75563, 75565, 75571, 75572, 75573, 75574, 75635, 76377, 77061, 77062, 77063, 78012-78999, 93355, 0159T)◄

76377   requiring image postprocessing on an independent workstation

(Use 76377 in conjunction with code[s] for base imaging procedure[s])

►(Do not report 76377 in conjunction with 34839, 70496, 70498, 70544, 70545, 70546, 70547, 70548, 70549, 71275, 71555, 72159, 72191, 72198, 73206, 73225, 73706, 73725, 74174, 74175, 74185, 74261, 74262, 74263, 75557, 75559, 75561, 75563, 75565, 75571, 75572, 75573, 75574, 75635, 76376, 77061, 77062, 77063, 78012-78999, 93355, 0159T)◄

(To report computer-aided detection, including computer algorithm analysis of MRI data for lesion detection/characterization, pharmacokinetic analysis, breast MRI, use Category III code 0159T)

(76376, 76377 require concurrent supervision of image postprocessing 3D manipulation of volumetric data set and image rendering)

Rationale

In support of the establishment of code 34839 to report physician planning and sizing for a patient-specific fenestrated visceral aortic endograft, codes to report diagnostic and screening breast tomosynthesis (77061, 77062, 77063) and echocardiography, transesophageal (93355) were added to the exclusionary parenthetical note following codes 76376, 76377 to ensure appropriate reporting of these procedures.

Diagnostic Ultrasound

Chest

►Code 76641 represents a complete ultrasound examination of the breast. Code 76641 consists of an ultrasound examination of all four quadrants of the breast and the retroareolar region. It also includes ultrasound examination of the axilla, if performed.

Code 76642 consists of a focused ultrasound examination of the breast limited to the assessment of one or more, but not all of the elements listed in code 76641. It also includes ultrasound examination of the axilla, if performed.

Use of ultrasound, without thorough evaluation of organ(s) or anatomic region, image documentation, and final written report, is not separately reportable.◄

76604   Ultrasound, chest (includes mediastinum), real time with image documentation

●**76641**   Ultrasound, breast, unilateral, real time with image documentation, including axilla when performed; complete

●**76642**   limited

▶(Report 76641, 76642 only once per breast, per session)◄

▶(For axillary ultrasound only, use 76882)◄

▶(76645 has been deleted. To report, see 76641, 76642)◄

 ### Rationale

The ultrasound breast, unilateral or bilateral, code 76645 was identified by the AMA/Specialty Society Relative Value Scale (RVS) Update Committee (RUC) Relative Assessment Workgroup's screen of Centers of Medicare and Medicaid Services/Other codes with Medicare utilization of 500,000 or more. As a result, code 76645 has been deleted and two codes 76641, 76642 have been established to split the complexity of these services to report limited (focused) and complete breast ultrasound procedures. New instructional guidelines and parenthetical notes have been added to clarify the reporting of these services.

Code 76641 is intended to describe a complete ultrasound examination of all four quadrants of the breast, the retroareolar region, and the axilla when performed. Code 76642 is intended to describe a focused ultrasound examination of the breast, with a limited assessment of one or more of the elements included in code 76641, but not all, and of the axilla when performed. Codes 76641, 76642 should be reported only once per breast per session. An instructional parenthetical note has been added to direct the user to report code 76882 only for the axillary ultrasound procedure.

Clinical Example (76641)

A 37-year-old female presents with diffuse left breast pain of two months' duration.

Description of Procedure (76641)

Supervise the sonographer performing the examination. Scan with ultrasound throughout all four quadrants and the retroareolar region of the affected breast in both transverse and longitudinal planes (or in radial and antiradial planes), including image documentation of normal structures in each quadrant and in the retroareolar region. Document any visualized pathology in each quadrant and in the retroareolar region. Scan with ultrasound through the ipsilateral axilla in transverse and longitudinal planes. Document any significant pathology as well as

    ⊘=Modifier 51 Exempt   ⊙=Moderate Sedation ✚=Add-on Code ℕ=FDA approval pending

any visualized normal axillary lymph nodes. Compare the examination, and correlate the findings to previous studies. Dictate a report for the medical record.

Clinical Example (76642)

A 25-year-old female presents with newly palpable lump in the left breast upper outer quadrant.

Description of Procedure (76642)

Supervise the sonographer performing the examination. Scan with ultrasound throughout the area of concern within the affected breast in both transverse and longitudinal planes (or in radial and antiradial planes), including image documentation of normal structures. Document any visualized pathology. Compare the examination, and correlate the findings to previous studies. Dictate a report for the medical record.

Genitalia

76872 Ultrasound, transrectal;

▶(Do not report 76872 in conjunction with 45341, 45342, 45391, 45392, 0249T)◀

Rationale

In accordance with the changes to the Digestive System endoscopy codes, the exclusionary parenthetical note following code 76872 (transrectal ultrasound) was revised with the addition of codes 45341, 45342, 45391, and 45392 (lower gastrointestinal endoscopic ultrasound).

Ultrasonic Guidance Procedures

76940 Ultrasound guidance for, and monitoring of, parenchymal tissue ablation

▶(Do not report 76940 in conjunction with 20982, 20983, 50250, 50542, 76942, 76998, 0340T)◀

▶(For ablation, see 32998, 47370-47382, 47383, 50592, 50593)◀

76942 Ultrasonic guidance for needle placement (eg, biopsy, aspiration, injection, localization device), imaging supervision and interpretation

▶(Do not report 76942 in conjunction with 10030, 19083, 19285, 20604, 20606, 20611, 27096, 32554, 32555, 32556, 32557, 37760, 37761, 43232, 43237, 43242, 45341, 45342, 64479-64484, 64490-64495, 76975, 0213T-0218T, 0228T-0231T, 0232T, 0249T, 0301T)◀

▶(76950 has been deleted. To report, use 77387)◀

Rationale

In accordance with instructions to separately report ultrasound guidance and monitoring for new percutaneous cryoablation of liver tumor(s) (47383), the cross-reference parenthetical note following code 76940 (ultrasound guidance), which directs users to ablation codes, has been revised to include code 47383.

In addition, a reciprocating exclusionary parenthetical has been updated following code 76940 to exclude the use of this code in conjunction with codes 20983 and 0340T. For more information regarding the intended use of codes 20983 and 0340T, see the Rationales for these codes.

To support the establishment of three new codes for reporting ultrasound guidance for arthrocentesis procedures (20604, 20606, 20611), the exclusionary parenthetical note following code 76942 has been updated to include these procedures.

Code 76950 has been deleted and a deletion parenthetical note directs users to new code 77387 that has been added.

Other Procedures

76975 Gastrointestinal endoscopic ultrasound, supervision and interpretation

▶(Do not report 76975 in conjunction with 43231, 43232, 43237, 43238, 43240, 43242, 43259, 44406, 44407, 45341, 45342, 45391, 45392, 76942)◀

 Rationale

In accordance with the gastroenterological changes in the Digestive System section, the cross-reference parenthetical note following code 76975 has been updated to include codes 43240, 44406, 44407, 45391, 45392.

Radiologic Guidance

Fluoroscopic Guidance

+ 77001 Fluoroscopic guidance for central venous access device placement, replacement (catheter only or complete), or removal (includes fluoroscopic guidance for vascular access and catheter manipulation, any necessary contrast injections through access site or catheter with related venography radiologic supervision and interpretation, and radiographic documentation of final catheter position) (List separately in addition to code for primary procedure)

▶(Do not report 77001 in conjunction with 33957, 33958, 33959, 33962, 33963, 33964, 77002)◀

Rationale

In support of the establishment of codes 33946-33989 for the reporting of extracorporeal membrane oxygenation (ECMO) and extracorporeal life support (ECLS) services, the parenthetical note following code 77001 has been revised to include these services (33957-33964).

⃠=Modifier 51 Exempt   ⊙=Moderate Sedation   ✚=Add-on Code   𝗡=FDA approval pending

77002 Fluoroscopic guidance for needle placement (eg, biopsy, aspiration, injection, localization device)

(See appropriate surgical code for procedure and anatomic location)

(77002 is included in all arthrography radiological supervision and interpretation codes. See **Administration of Contrast Material[s]** introductory guidelines for reporting of arthrography procedures)

▶(Do not report 77002 in conjunction with 10030, 19081-19086, 19281-19288, 20982, 20983, 32554, 32555, 32556, 32557, 70332, 73040, 73085, 73115, 73525, 73580, 73615, 0232T)◀

🖊 Rationale

The reciprocal exclusionary parenthetical note following code 77002 has been updated to exclude the use of this code in conjunction with code 20983. For more information regarding the intended use of code 20983, see the Rationale for this code.

Computed Tomography Guidance

77013 Computed tomography guidance for, and monitoring of, parenchymal tissue ablation

▶(Do not report 77013 in conjunction with 20982, 20983, 0340T)◀

▶(For percutaneous ablation, see 32998, 47382, 47383, 50592, 50593)◀

🖊 Rationale

The reciprocal exclusionary parenthetical note following code 77013 has been updated to exclude the use of this code in conjunction with codes 20983 and 0340T. For more information regarding the intended use of codes 20983 and 0340T, see the Rationales for these codes.

In accordance with instructions to separately report computed tomography guidance and monitoring for new percutaneous cryoablation of liver tumor(s) (code 47383), the cross-reference parenthetical note following code 77013 (computed tomography guidance), which directs users to ablation codes, has been revised to include code 47383.

Magnetic Resonance Guidance

77022 Magnetic resonance guidance for, and monitoring of, parenchymal tissue ablation

▶(Do not report 77022 in conjunction with 0071T, 0072T, 20982, 20983, 0340T)◀

▶(For percutaneous ablation, see 32998, 47382, 47383, 50592, 50593)◀

(For focused ultrasound ablation treatment of uterine leiomyomata, see Category III codes 0071T, 0072T)

(To report stereotactic localization guidance for breast biopsy or for placement of breast localization device[s], see 19081, 19283)

(To report mammographic guidance for placement of breast localization device[s], use 19281)

Rationale

The reciprocal exclusionary parenthetical note following code 77022 has been updated to exclude the use of this code in conjunction with codes 20983 and 0340T. For more information regarding the intended use of codes 20983 and 0340T, see the Rationales for these codes.

In accordance with instructions to separately report computed tomography guidance and monitoring for the new percutaneous cryoablation of liver tumor(s) (code 47383), the cross-reference parenthetical note following code 77022 has been revised to include code 47383.

Breast, Mammography

77055   Mammography; unilateral

77056   bilateral

▶(Do not report 77055, 77056 in conjunction with 77063)◀

(Use 77055, 77056 in conjunction with 77051 for computer-aided detection applied to a diagnostic mammogram)

77057   Screening mammography, bilateral (2-view film study of each breast)

▶(Do not report 77057 in conjunction with 77061, 77062)◀

(Use 77057 in conjunction with 77052 for computer-aided detection applied to a screening mammogram)

(For electrical impedance breast scan, use 76499)

77058   Magnetic resonance imaging, breast, without and/or with contrast material(s); unilateral

77059   bilateral

●**77061**   Digital breast tomosynthesis; unilateral

●**77062**   bilateral

▶(Do not report 77061, 77062 in conjunction with 76376, 76377, 77057)◀

+●**77063**   Screening digital breast tomosynthesis, bilateral (List separately in addition to code for primary procedure)

▶(Do not report 77063 in conjunction with 76376, 76377, 77055, 77056)◀

▶(Use 77063 in conjunction with 77057)◀

Rationale

Codes 77061, 77062, and 77063 have been established to report diagnostic and screening breast tomosynthesis, unilateral and bilateral procedure. Breast tomosynthesis is a digital tomographic technique performed using multiple low-dose X-ray exposures, which are obtained as the X-ray tube swings in an arc around the compressed breast. The resulting image-data are reconstructed using standard

---

⊘=Modifier 51 Exempt   ⊙=Moderate Sedation   ✚=Add-on Code   ⚡=FDA approval pending

computer algorithms to produce a series of sequential stacked slices through the breast. This type of tomographic imaging allows the physician to view the breast as thin discrete image slices on a computer workstation. The digital breast tomosynthesis images, and if acquired, the conventional mammography images, are utilized for interpretation for screening and diagnostic mammograms. The addition of digital breast tomosynthesis to conventional mammography has been shown to be more sensitive and specific for breast-cancer screening. Note that there are distinctions between digital breast tomosynthesis and conventional mammography. Typically, conventional screening mammography looks at four views; while digital tomosynthesis looks at approximately 200 views and requires a long period of sustained concentration.

Instructional parenthetical notes have been added to ensure appropriate reporting of breast tomosynthesis imaging procedures. It is appropriate to report codes 77061 and 77062 (diagnostic breast tomosynthesis) in conjunction with codes 77055 and 77056 (conventional diagnostic mammography). It is appropriate to report code 77063 (bilateral screening breast tomosynthesis) in conjunction with code 77057 (conventional bilateral screening mammography).

Exclusionary parenthetical notes have been added to further clarify the reporting of breast tomosynthesis imaging procedures. It would not be appropriate to report code 77063 (screening breast tomosynthesis) in conjunction with codes 77055 and 77056 (conventional diagnostic mammography), or codes 76376 or 76377 (three-dimensional reconstruction). It would not be appropriate to report codes 77061 and 77062 (diagnostic breast tomosynthesisa) in conjunction with code 77057 (conventional screening mammography) or codes 76376 or 76377 (three-dimensional reconstruction).

Clinical Example (77061)

A 68-year-old asymptomatic female recalled from a screening mammogram for a unilateral focal asymmetry presents for further evaluation with digital breast tomosynthesis.

Description of Procedure (77061)

Determine whether the DBT images of that side are of adequate quality for interpretation or whether any of the data sets require repeating due to motion, inadequate positioning, or artifacts. View the DBT images of that side to determine if the DBT resolves the focal asymmetry seen previously as overlapping breast tissue or if an abnormality persists that requires further attention. Evaluate the remainder of the DBT image data set to determine if there are any additional suspicious findings. Perform annotation of DBT images, and perform secondary screen capture of selected images to indicate findings of concern for future reference. Formulate recommendations.

Clinical Example (77062)

A 53-year-old asymptomatic female recalled from a screening mammogram for bilateral focal asymmetries presents for further evaluation with bilateral digital breast tomosynthesis.

Description of Procedure (77062)

Determine whether the DBT images of both sides are of adequate quality for interpretation or whether any of the data sets require repeating due to motion, inadequate positioning, or artifacts. View the DBT images of both sides to determine if the DBT resolves the focal asymmetries seen bilaterally as overlapping breast tissue or if an abnormality persists on either side that requires further attention. Evaluate the remainder of the DBT image data sets to determine if there are any additional suspicious findings. Perform annotation of DBT images, and perform secondary screen capture of selected images to indicate findings of concern for future reference. Formulate recommendations.

 #### Clinical Example (77063)

A 47-year-old asymptomatic female with heterogeneously dense breasts seen on prior mammograms presents for her regular screening mammogram.

Description of Procedure (77063)

Determine whether the DBT images on both sides are of adequate quality for interpretation or whether any of the data sets require repeating due to motion, inadequate positioning, or artifacts. View the DBT images on both sides to determine if there are any additional suspicious findings. Compare to the conventional mammogram. If the conventional mammographic images showed an abnormality for which recall is contemplated, determine if the DBT images can obviate the need for this recall. Determine the significance of abnormal findings, and formulate recommendations. Perform annotation of DBT images, and perform secondary screen capture of selected images to indicate findings of concern for future reference.

Bone/Joint Studies

77080   Dual-energy X-ray absorptiometry (DXA), bone density study, 1 or more sites; axial skeleton (eg, hips, pelvis, spine)

▶(Do not report 77080 in conjunction with 77085, 77086)◀

77081   appendicular skeleton (peripheral) (eg, radius, wrist, heel)

▶(77082 has been deleted. To report, use 77086)◀

(For dual energy x-ray absorptiometry [DXA] body composition study, use 76499)

#●77085   axial skeleton (eg, hips, pelvis, spine), including vertebral fracture assessment

▶(Do not report 77085 in conjunction with 77080, 77086)◀

#●77086   Vertebral fracture assessment via dual-energy X-ray absorptiometry (DXA)

▶(Do not report 77086 in conjunction with 77080, 77085)◀

77084   Magnetic resonance (eg, proton) imaging, bone marrow blood supply

⊘=Modifier 51 Exempt   ⊙=Moderate Sedation   ✚=Add-on Code   �ⁿ=FDA approval pending

✎ Rationale

The AMA/Specialty Society RUC has identified codes 77080 (dual-energy X-ray absorptiometry [DXA], bone density study) and 77082 (vertebral fracture assessment) as being reported together 75% of the time or more. As a result, code 77082 has been deleted and new code 77085, which bundles the bone density study and vertebral fracture assessment, was created. In addition, code 77086 was created to report vertebral fracture assessment via DXA. Exclusionary parenthetical notes to provide additional instructions on the appropriate reporting of these two codes have been added in this section as well.

🩺 Clinical Example (77085)

A 70-year-old female presents with a two-year history of intermittent acute sharp back pain along with a one-inch loss in height. Evaluation for osteoporosis and vertebral fracture assessment is ordered.

Description of Procedure (77085)

Supervise the technologist in acquiring images. Review images to determine levels to be included in bone density calculations. Interpret the DXA scan data, and compare to established norms. Compare the results of the DXA scan to previous studies. Compare the reported bone density values to standards based on World Health Organization's (WHO) fracture risk assessment tool (FRAX) or other criteria. Obtain computerized FRAX score for possible treatment. Review the vertebral fracture assessment (VFA) images obtained and the postprocessed measurements to assure that the measurements were done accurately and that scanning technique was satisfactory. Interpret the VFA thoracic and lumbar images (lateral views) using accepted fracture assessment methodology, the Semiquantitative Analysis of Genant and Quantitative Morphometry, to determine the number and severity of fractures present. Compare the results of the VFA interpretation to previous radiographic or VFA images to determine whether a significant change in vertebral anatomy has occurred in the interim. Dictate report.

🩺 Clinical Example (77086)

A 70-year-old female presents with osteopenia diagnosed on screening bone density test done one month ago. Treatment was deferred at that time based on FRAX score and lack of symptoms. Patient now returns for follow-up with a history of several days of severe acute localized back pain, and physical examination shows tenderness in the L2 area. VFA by DXA is done because the presence of a vertebral fracture would influence the decision about treatment.

Description of Procedure (77086)

Supervise the technologist in acquiring images. Review the obtained VFA images and the postprocessed measurements to assure that the measurements were accurately done and that scanning technique was satisfactory. Interpret the VFA thoracic and lumbar images (lateral views) using accepted fracture assessment methodology to determine the number and severity of fractures present. Compare the results of the VFA interpretation to previous radiographic or VFA images to determine whether a significant change in vertebral anatomy has occurred in the interim. Dictate report.

Medical Radiation Physics, Dosimetry, Treatment Devices, and Special Services

77300   Basic radiation dosimetry calculation, central axis depth dose calculation, TDF, NSD, gap calculation, off axis factor, tissue inhomogeneity factors, calculation of non-ionizing radiation surface and depth dose, as required during course of treatment, only when prescribed by the treating physician

▶(Do not report 77300 in conjunction with 77306, 77307, 77316, 77317, 77318, 77321)◀

77301   Intensity modulated radiotherapy plan, including dose-volume histograms for target and critical structure partial tolerance specifications

(Dose plan is optimized using inverse or forward planning technique for modulated beam delivery [eg, binary, dynamic MLC] to create highly conformal dose distribution. Computer plan distribution must be verified for positional accuracy based on dosimetric verification of the intensity map with verification of treatment set-up and interpretation of verification methodology)

▶(77305 has been deleted. To report, use 77306)◀

●**77306**   Teletherapy isodose plan; simple (1 or 2 unmodified ports directed to a single area of interest), includes basic dosimetry calculation(s)

●**77307**   complex (multiple treatment areas, tangential ports, the use of wedges, blocking, rotational beam, or special beam considerations), includes basic dosimetry calculation(s)

(Only 1 teletherapy isodose plan may be reported for a given course of therapy to a specific treatment area)

▶(Do not report 77306, 77307 in conjunction with 77300)◀

▶(77310 has been deleted. To report, see 77306, 77307)◀

▶(77315 has been deleted. To report, use 77307)◀

●**77316**   Brachytherapy isodose plan; simple (calculation[s] made from 1 to 4 sources, or remote afterloading brachytherapy, 1 channel), includes basic dosimetry calculation(s)

▶(For definition of source, see clinical brachytherapy introductory guidelines)◀

●**77317**   intermediate (calculation[s] made from 5 to 10 sources, or remote afterloading brachytherapy, 2-12 channels), includes basic dosimetry calculation(s)

●**77318**   complex (calculation[s] made from over 10 sources, or remote afterloading brachytherapy, over 12 channels), includes basic dosimetry calculation(s)

▶(Do not report 77316, 77317, 77318 in conjunction with 77300)◀

77321   Special teletherapy port plan, particles, hemibody, total body

▶(77326 has been deleted. To report, use 77316)◀

▶(77327 has been deleted. To report, use 77317)◀

▶(77328 has been deleted. To report, use 77318)◀

77338   Multi-leaf collimator (MLC) device(s) for intensity modulated radiation therapy (IMRT), design and construction per IMRT plan

> ▶(Do not report 77338 in conjunction with 77385 for compensator based IMRT)◀

> (Do not report 77338 more than once per IMRT plan)

> (For immobilization in IMRT treatment, see 77332-77334)

✎ Rationale

In response to the AMA/Specialty Society RUC's Five-Year Review Identification Workgroup's analysis of combined codes that are frequently reported together, RUC has identified that codes 77305, 77310, 77315 (teletherapy isodose planning) and codes 77326, 77327, 77328 (brachytherapy isodose planning) are frequently reported with code 77300 (basic radiation dosimetry calculation).

In response to these analyses and changes in clinical practice, the family of teletherapy and brachytherapy isodose planning codes has been updated to reflect the current practice. Firstly, new codes (77306, 77307) have been established to report combined teletherapy isodose with basic dosimetry calculation(s). Secondly, new codes (77316, 77317, 77318) have been established to report combined brachytherapy isodose planning with basic dosimetry calculation(s).

Codes 77305, 77310, 77315, 77326, 77327, and 77328 have been deleted, and parenthetical notes have been added to direct users to the appropriate codes to report. In addition, exclusionary parenthetical notes to restrict the use of codes 77306 and 77307 (teletherapy isodose planning services) with code 77300 (basic radiation dosimetry calculation) have been added following codes 77306 and 77307. An exclusionary parenthetical note to restrict the use of code 77300 (basic radiation dosimetry calculation) has also been added following codes 77316, 77317, and 77318 (brachytherapy isodose planning services.)

Finally, an exclusionary parenthetical note to restrict the use of code 77300 with teletherapy and brachytherapy isodose services (77306, 77307, 77316, 77317, 77318, 77321) has been added following basic radiation dosimetry calculation (77300). The exclusionary parenthetical note following code 77338 has been revised by removing deleted code 0073T and replacing it with new code 77385.

🩺 Clinical Example (77306)

A 65-year-old male with advanced lung cancer presents with a painful metastasis to the lumbar spine. Following simulation, a teletherapy isodose plan and monitor unit calculation is performed.

Description of Procedure (77306)

The radiation oncologist defines treatment borders for each field, ensuring that the fields cover the intended treatment area. The physician determines beam energy, beam configuration, tissue homogeneity factor, prescription point, and dose/fractionation, and discusses this information with the medical dosimetrist. The dosimetrist then initiates the planning process by placing megavoltage beams on the treatment planning system, using the fields defined by the physician. Calculate dose from each beam to be delivered to the isocenter (prescription point). The radiation oncologist and dosimetrist examine and review the isodose curves to determine dose coverage, hot spots, and cold spots, and evaluate the effect of tissue inhomogeneity. The physician and dosimetrist evaluate multiple beam weightings from the anterior and posterior beams to provide optimal coverage of the treatment area, with the fewest hot or cold spots. Evaluate the dose to the spinal cord throughout the length of the field to keep this within tolerance dose. The radiation oncologist selects and approves the optimal coverage. Perform basic dosimetry monitor unit calculations (which take into account the source axis distance, time dose factors, inhomogeneity, beam energy, machine characteristics, and other parameters) to deliver the prescribed dose. Perform independent calculations to check the monitor unit calculations and verify critical point doses. The radiation oncologist finalizes and approves the plan. The dosimetrist downloads all treatment planning parameters into the record and verifies the system in preparation for treatment.

Clinical Example (77307)

A 65-year-old female with an infiltrating cancer in the upper outer quadrant (UOQ) of the right breast presents for radiation therapy. Following lumpectomy and simulation, a teletherapy isodose plan and monitor unit calculation is performed.

Description of Procedure (77307)

The radiation oncologist reviews all images to make sure that the six surgical clips placed at the lumpectomy site and external markers placed at time of simulation are identified and transferred accurately (marker at anteroposterior (AP) set-up point; four wire markers for clinical estimate of cranial, caudal, medial, and lateral extent of anticipated tangents; wire extending around the infra-mammary fold; and wire over lumpectomy scar). In addition, review breast, chest wall, axilla, and supraclavicular areas for inclusion on the images as follows:

Cranial: clinical reference plus second rib insertion;

Caudal: clinical reference plus loss of computerized tomographic (CT) apparent breast;

Anterior: skin;

Posterior: excludes pectoralis muscles, chest wall muscles, and ribs;

Lateral: clinical reference plus mid axillary line; and

Medial: sternal rib junction.

After verification of all borders, the physician contours the breast tissue and the chest wall on the superior and inferior slices, the central axis slices, and multiple off-axis slices; and contours the lumpectomy site. In addition, depending on stage of disease, contour the axilla (level 1, 2, or 3) supraclavicular and internal mammary nodes. The physician may modify the borders and expansion margin to exclude heart and lung tissue. As necessary, include lymph node chains based on stage and risk criteria.

The radiation oncologist determines beam energy, beam configuration, tissue homogeneity factor, prescription point, and dose/fractionation and discusses with the medical dosimetrist. The dosimetrist then generates a treatment plan based on parameters determined by the physician to ensure necessary coverage. Each plan typically utilizes tangential beams with matched nondivergent posterior borders and with collimator rotation to match the chest wall slope. As the beams pass through the lung and as there is tissue inhomogeneity throughout the treatment area, correct at multiple axes throughout the field starting with the central axis. Minimize dose inhomogeneity within the central plane by modifying the beam energies, weighting, angles, shapes, wedges, and compensators to ensure adequate dose distribution. Repeat the process at other off-axis planes. Normalize the dose at the breast and pectoralis major interface at mid-separation in the central plane. Plot dose distributions for each 1-cm slice, and calculate the area of each isodose curve within the breast on each CT slice. The physician reviews the entire process and the final treatment plan. Evaluate plan by reviewing dose homogeneity, as well as the hot/cold areas within the plan. The physician edits the plan based on target volume coverage. Approve the final plan if overall prescribed dose and dose constraints are met. Perform basic dosimetry monitor unit calculations (which take into account the source axis distance, time dose factors, inhomogeneity, beam energy, machine characteristics, and other parameters) to deliver the prescribed dose. Perform independent calculations to check these monitor unit calculations and verify critical point doses.

Once the radiation oncologist finalizes and approves the plan, the dosimetrist downloads all treatment planning parameters into the record and verifies the system in preparation for treatment.

 ### Clinical Example (77316)

A 68-year-old female with high grade stage II endometrial cancer undergoes post-operative pelvic radiotherapy. Following placement of a single-channel vaginal after-loading applicator and simulation, a brachytherapy isodose plan is performed including calculation of dwell times, source decay, and point doses.

Description of Procedure (77316)

After simulation, send the images to the treatment planning work station. The physician reviews all the images, identifies the anatomy, rotates the anatomy in each view box so the vertical axis runs parallel to the cylinder, and identifies the gold seed placed at the vaginal apex. Starting at the apex, contour the entire vaginal surface. The physician identifies the treatment length and depth based on review of the final pathology, stage, and grade; in this case it is determined to be a half-cm around the mucosa and a 4-cm length of vagina. The physician outlines the treatment area. The dosimetrist identifies and contours the vaginal cylinder and the central source channel. The physician enters the fractional dose and the number of fractions in the computer plan prescription. The dosimetrist plans source positions in the central channel, starting at the apex and using multiple positions through the single central channel. The physician and the dosimetrist evaluate and review multiple combinations of dwell times and source positions. Perform manual adjustment of the isodose lines to meet the objectives, and manually enter the dwell times and position to achieve an acceptable plan that covers the target volume with the prescribed dose. The medical physicist reviews and approves the plan. Evaluate the plan and the dose distribution before the plan is made deliverable. Perform independent dose calculations by creating three reference points in the plan and exporting those points to an independent calculation system. Calculate the dose to these three points, and compare to the dose calculated by the treatment planning system. Approve the final treatment times.

Clinical Example (77317)

A 70-year-old male presents with a squamous cancer of the scalp. Radiation is prescribed using surface brachytherapy to this curved surface. A brachytherapy flap apparatus is applied and simulation performed. Brachytherapy isodose planning is performed including calculation of dwell times, source decay, and point doses.

Description of Procedure (77317)

After simulation, send the image data set to the treatment planning workstation. The radiation oncologist reviews all images to identify both the depth of the target volume and the critical avoidance structures, in this case notably eyes, bone, and brain tissue underlying the skull. Carefully review the notes and skin photos, and as necessary discuss with the provider who performed the original biopsies. Evaluate in all directions the initial target volume, with contours drawn to determine the superior, inferior, medial, lateral, anterior, and posterior borders. The target volume may require expansion to encompass an anatomic area that would be at risk of microscopic or subclinical spread. For curved planes, the reference isodose projects further at the concave than at the convex side. The arrangement of implanted or applied sources must take into account this geometry that will result in isodose line shifts.

Once the final target volume has been established and the plan treatment goals have been defined by the radiation oncologist, the dosimetrist will develop a treatment plan. Each of the 10 catheters is identified on each CT slice and recreated in the planning system. Dummy sources (previously placed) within each channel are used to demarcate the dwell positions within the region of the target volume. An initial plan is generated that encompasses the entire tumor and the plan modified in an iterative fashion to reduce normal tissue dosing and hot spots, which create alternatives for review. The different plans will involve stepwise modification of the dwell positions and dwell times for the radiation source as the radiation oncologist considers the risk-benefit ratio of achieving maximum target volume coverage with minimal radiation exposure to non-target critical structures, in this case, different parts of the brain. It is ultimately the radiation oncologist's responsibility to approve the plan that offers the best combination of tumor coverage and critical structure avoidance. The radiation oncologist works side-by-side with the dosimetrist to adjust both dwell positions and dwell times to best optimize the radiation therapy plan. Review differences between areas of maximum and minimum dose at depth so that values are within tolerance of the prescribed dose. Perform review at the edges of the implant to optimize a sharp dose gradient, so that the detected dose at 5 mm beyond the planning target volume is acceptable. The medical physicist reviews and approves the plan.

⊘=Modifier 51 Exempt   ⊙=Moderate Sedation   ✚=Add-on Code   ✗=FDA approval pending

Evaluate the approved plan generated by the treatment planning system by using an independent dose calculation method to perform point dose calculations at multiple points within and/or adjacent to the treatment volume. Perform a separate calculation to account for the decay of the radioactive source between the time of plan calculation and ultimate treatment time. The radiation oncologist signs the approved plan, including isodose distribution and calculated dwell positions and times for each of the 10 channels.

Clinical Example (77318)

A 60-year-old male presents with localized prostate cancer and a low dose rate (LDR) brachytherapy implant is recommended. A prostate volume ultrasound study is performed in preparation for brachytherapy isodose planning including calculation(s) and point doses.

Description of Procedure (77318)

These transrectal ultrasonography (TRUS) images have the necessary grid coordinates showing the location of possible needle placement. The radiation oncologist co-registers and scales these images using the electronic prostate template in the planning software. The physician then contours the prostate, urethra, rectum, seminal vesicles, and periprostatic soft tissue margin on each of the axial slices. Planning target volumes includes the entire prostate and typically extends 0.3 cm to include the base of the seminal vesicles and periprostatic soft tissues. The physician may modify the expansion margin to exclude the rectal muscularis posteriorly and bladder base superiorly. The physician then determines the isotope to be used based on the procedure date, source strengths available by the source manufacturer, and prescribed dose.

Stereotactic Radiation Treatment Delivery

77373   Stereotactic body radiation therapy, treatment delivery, per fraction to 1 or more lesions, including image guidance, entire course not to exceed 5 fractions

▶(Do not report 77373 in conjunction with 77385, 77386, 77401, 77402, 77407, 77412)◀

(For single fraction cranial lesion[s], see 77371, 77372)

Rationale

An exclusionary parenthetical note following code 77373 has been revised to reflect the establishment of new intensity modulated radiation therapy (IMRT) treatment delivery codes 77385 and 77386.

Radiation Treatment Delivery

▶Following dosimetry calculations, there are a number of alternative methods to deliver external radiation treatments, which are described with specific CPT codes:

- X-ray (photon), including conventional and intensity modulated radiation therapy (IMRT) beams;

- Electron beams;

- Neutron beams;

- Proton beams.

All treatment delivery codes are reported once per treatment session. The treatment delivery codes recognize technical-only services and contain no physician work (the professional component). In contrast, the treatment management codes contain only the professional component.

Radiation treatment delivery with conventional X-ray or electron beams is assigned levels of complexity based on the number of treatment sites and complexity of the treatment fields, blocking, wedges, and physical or virtual tissue compensators. A simple block is straight-edged or an approximation of a straight edge created by a multileaf collimator (MLC). Energy of the megavoltage (≥ 1 MeV) beam does not contribute to complexity. Techniques such as treating a field-in-field to ensure dose homogeneity reflect added complexity.

Energies below the megavoltage range may be used in the treatment of skin lesions. Superficial radiation energies (up to 200 kV) may be generated by a variety of technologies and should not be reported with megavoltage (77402, 77407, 77412) for surface application. Do not report clinical treatment planning (77261, 77262, 77263), treatment devices (77332, 77333, 77334), isodose planning (77306, 77307, 77316, 77317, 77318), physics consultation (77336), or radiation treatment management (77427, 77431, 77432, 77435, 77469, 77470, 77499) with 77401. When reporting 77401 alone, physician evaluation and management, when performed, may be reported with the appropriate E/M codes.

Intensity modulated radiation therapy (IMRT) uses computer-based optimization techniques with non-uniform radiation beam intensities to create highly conformal dose distributions that can be delivered by a radiotherapy treatment machine. A number of technologies, including spatially and temporally modulated beams, cylindrical beamlets, dynamic MLC, single or multiple fields or arcs, or compensators, may be used to generate IMRT. The complexity of IMRT may vary depending on the area being treated or the technique being used.

Image guided radiation therapy (IGRT) may be used to direct the radiation beam and to reflect motion during treatment. A variety of techniques may be used to perform this guidance including imaging (eg, ultrasound, CT, MRI, stereoscopic imaging) and non-imaging (eg, electromagnetic or infrared) techniques. Guidance may be used with any radiation treatment delivery technique and is typically used with IMRT delivery. IMRT delivery codes include the technical component of guidance or tracking, if performed. Because only the technical portion of IGRT is bundled into IMRT, the physician involvement in guidance or tracking may be reported separately. When guidance is required with conventional radiation treatment delivery, both the professional and technical components are reported because neither component of guidance is bundled into conventional radiation treatment delivery services.

The technical and professional components of guidance are handled differently with each radiation delivery code depending on the type of radiation being administered. The **Radiation Management and Treatment Table** (see page [189]) is provided for clarity.

⊘=Modifier 51 Exempt   ⊙=Moderate Sedation   ✚=Add-on Code   ✗=FDA approval pending

Definitions

Radiation Treatment Delivery, megavoltage (≥ 1 MeV), any energy

Simple: All of the following criteria are met (and none of the complex or intermediate criteria are met): single treatment area, one or two ports, and two or fewer simple blocks.

Intermediate: Any of the following criteria are met (and none of the complex criteria are met): 2 separate treatment areas, 3 or more ports on a single treatment area, or 3 or more simple blocks.

Complex: Any of the following criteria are met: 3 or more separate treatment areas, custom blocking, tangential ports, wedges, rotational beam, field-in-field or other tissue compensation that does not meet IMRT guidelines, or electron beam.

Intensity Modulated Radiation Therapy (IMRT), any energy, includes the technical services for guidance

Simple: Any of the following: prostate, breast, and all sites using physical compensator based IMRT.

Complex: Includes all other sites if not using physical compensator based IMRT.◄

▲**77401**   Radiation treatment delivery, superficial and/or ortho voltage, per day

►(Do not report 77401 in conjunction with 77373)◄

▲**77402**   Radiation treatment delivery, ≥1 MeV; simple

►(Do not report 77402 in conjunction with 77373)◄

►(77403, 77404, 77406 have been deleted. To report, use 77402)◄

▲**77407**   intermediate

►(Do not report 77407 in conjunction with 77373)◄

►(77408, 77409, 77411 have been deleted. To report, use 77407)◄

▲**77412**   complex

►(Do not report 77412 in conjunction with 77373)◄

►(77413, 77414, 77416 have been deleted. To report, use 77412)◄

77417   Therapeutic radiology port film(s)

►(77418 has been deleted)◄

(For intensity modulated treatment planning, use 77301)

#●**77385**   Intensity modulated radiation treatment delivery (IMRT), includes guidance and tracking, when performed; simple

►(To report professional component [PC] of guidance and tracking, use 77387 with modifier 26)◄

#●**77386**   complex

►(To report professional component [PC] of guidance and tracking, use 77387 with modifier 26)◄

►(Do not report 77385, 77386 in conjunction with 77371, 77372, 77373)◄

#●77387   Guidance for localization of target volume for delivery of radiation treatment delivery, includes intrafraction tracking, when performed

▶(Do not report technical component [TC] with 77385, 77386, 77371, 77372, 77373)◀

▶(77421 has been deleted. To report, use 77387)◀

(For placement of interstitial device[s] for radiation therapy guidance, see 31627, 32553, 49411, 55876)

✍ Rationale

There have been significant changes in the entire treatment delivery family of codes. Radiation treatment is delivered using various methods, therefore, energy level and complexity of treatment determine the appropriate treatment delivery codes used and reported for the procedure. However, since the development of these codes, clinical practice has significantly evolved and there was no longer any justification for the levels of complexity. As a result, codes 77403, 77404, 77406, 77408, 77409, 77411, 77413, 77414, 77416, 77418, and 77421 have been deleted.

New introductory guidelines have been established to help determine which services fall into the conventional treatment delivery vs IMRT. A table has been added (see the Radiation Management Treatment Table) to reflect which codes contain only the technical component (TC) or professional component (PC) to help clarify which code(s) image guided radiation therapy (IGRT) is bundled into, for both the treatment and management work. To further clarify the intent of these services, new definitions have also been added for radiation treatment delivery and IMRT treatments to differentiate the levels of complexity with clear language and to identify the levels.

Codes 77402, 77407, and 77412 have been revised to reflect three levels of complexity with no differentiation based on energy. In addition, three new codes 77385, 77386, and 77387 have been established: codes 77385 and 77386 should be reported for simple and complex levels and include guidance when performed, and code 77387 should be reported for guidance and tracking. Several parenthetical notes have been added in this section to assist in the use of these codes.

In addition to the revision of codes 77401 and 77402, guideline instruction has been provided to direct the appropriate reporting of superficial radiation therapy. Because this level of radiation treatment delivery uses energies below the megavoltage range for the treatment of skin lesions, the instructional guidelines regarding appropriate reporting when superficial radiation therapy is provided includes restrictions for reporting this service when other more intensive services are also provided on the same day. These restrictions pertain to the reporting of the following services with code 77401: (1) Megavoltage services (codes 77402, 77407, 77412); (2) clinical treatment planning (77261, 77262, 77263); (3) treatment device design and construction (77332, 77333, 77334); (4) isodose planning (77306, 77307, 77316, 77317, 77318); (5) physics consultation (77336); or (6) radiation treatment management (77427, 77431, 77432, 77435, 77469, 77470, 77499). The guidelines also direct users to separately report evaluation and management services, if only superficial radiation therapy (77401) services are provided.

Clinical Example (77387)

A 67-year-old male who presents with stage III lung cancer will undergo concurrent chemotherapy and 3D conformal radiation. Before daily radiation therapy, cone-beam CT image guidance scan is performed and reviewed, and the patient's position is adjusted to localize the primary tumor and the mediastinal nodes accurately before treatment. Surface tracking is performed during treatment delivery to ensure no movement exceeds safe thresholds.

Description of Procedure (77387)

The physician oversees patient preparation, including placement of external markers used for alignment and camera system used for surface tracking. Under physician supervision, the therapist aligns the patient using the four directional alignment room lasers via external skin marks and markers.

Immediately prior to treatment acquire a CT scan in the treatment position, and while this data is loaded on the treatment console, align, register, and fuse it using various manual or automatic tools to visualize the target volume or implanted markers and critical normal structures. The physician then ensures that the fusion is accurate, and evaluates the images. Calculate the translation errors of the patient set-up and the table movement necessary to optimally align the patient's target volume at the isocenter in longitudinal, lateral, and vertical directions. Identify and correct any rotational errors. If present, determine and correct deviations by adjusting the patient's treatment position to the treatment target volume isocenter. Under physician supervision, the therapist performs the adjustments by applying the required translational shifts to the treatment couch. Achieve accurate positioning, then start the treatment delivery, tracking and observing patient motion during radiation therapy using surface rendering to calculate precisely any patient movement in all six degrees of freedom, and monitor respiratory motion to confirm that it is within the planning parameters.

The physician reviews the images, evaluates target volume changes and normal tissue variation, and compares with previous shifts. The physician provides feedback to the therapists about the adequacy of registrations and about the steps necessary to take to improve registrations as well as for required treatment modifications for the subsequent day. Convey to staff in an ongoing process throughout treatments any patient-specific preferences regarding the relative importance of targets vs normal tissues.

Radiation Treatment Management

Radiation treatment management is reported in units of five fractions or treatment sessions, regardless of the actual time period in which the services are furnished. The services need not be furnished on consecutive days. Multiple fractions representing two or more treatment sessions furnished on the same day may be counted separately as long as there has been a distinct break in therapy sessions, and the fractions are of the character usually furnished on different days. Code 77427 is also reported if there are three or four fractions beyond a multiple of five at the end of a course of treatment; one or two fractions beyond a multiple of five at the end of a course of treatment are not reported separately.

Radiation treatment management requires **and includes** a minimum of one examination of the patient by the physician for medical evaluation and management (eg, assessment of the patient's response to treatment, coordination of care and treatment, review of imaging and/or lab test results with documentation) for each reporting of the radiation treatment management service. Code 77469 represents only the intraoperative session management and does not include medical evaluation and management outside of that session. The professional services furnished during treatment management typically include:

■ Review of port films;

■ Review of dosimetry, dose delivery, and treatment parameters;

■ Review of patient treatment set-up.

▶Stereotactic radiosurgery (SRS) and stereotactic body radiation treatment (SBRT) also include the professional component of guidance for localization of target volume for the delivery of radiation therapy (77387). *See also the Radiation Management and Treatment Table.*◀

🖎 Rationale

In support of the establishment of code 77387, new language has been added to the guidelines clarifying that stereotactic radiosurgery (SRS) and stereotactic body radiation treatment (SBRT) also include professional components.

77427   Radiation treatment management, 5 treatments

77431   Radiation therapy management with complete course of therapy consisting of 1 or 2 fractions only

(77431 is not to be used to fill in the last week of a long course of therapy)

77432   Stereotactic radiation treatment management of cranial lesion(s) (complete course of treatment consisting of 1 session)

(The same physician should not report both stereotactic radiosurgery services [61796-61800] and radiation treatment management [77432 or 77435] for cranial lesions)

(For stereotactic body radiation therapy treatment, use 77435)

▶(To report the technical component of guidance for localization of target volume, use 77387 with a technical component modifier [TC])◀

77435   Stereotactic body radiation therapy, treatment management, per treatment course, to 1 or more lesions, including image guidance, entire course not to exceed 5 fractions

(Do not report 77435 in conjunction with 77427-77432)

(The same physician should not report both stereotactic radiosurgery services [32701, 63620, 63621] and radiation treatment management [77435])

▶(To report the technical component of guidance for localization of target volume, use 77387 with a technical component modifier [TC])◀

🖎 Rationale

In support of the establishment of code 77387, parenthetical cross-references have been added following codes 77432 and 77435 to direct the use of a technical component modifier when reporting the technical component of guidance for the localization of target volume.

⊘=Modifier 51 Exempt   ⊙=Moderate Sedation   ✚=Add-on Code   ⅄=FDA approval pending

Radiation Management and Treatment Table

Category	Code	Descriptor	IGRT TC (77387-TC) Bundled into Code?	IGRT PC (77387-PC) Bundled into Code?	Code Type (Technical / Professional)
		SRS: Stereotactic radiosurgery IMRT: Intensity modulated radiation therapy TC :Technical component	SBRT: Stereotactic body radiation therapy IGRT: Image guided radiation therapy PC: Professional component (modifier 26)		
Radiation Treatment Management	77427	Treatment Management, 1-5 Treatments	N	N	Professional
	77431	Treatment Management, 1-2 Fractions	N	N	Professional
	77432	SRS Management, Cranial Lesion(s)	N	Y	Professional
	77435	SBRT Management	N	Y	Professional
SRS Treatment Delivery	77371	SRS Multisource 60 Based	Y	N	Technical
	77372	SRS Linear Based	Y	N	Technical
SBRT Treatment Delivery	77373	SBRT, 1 or More Lesions, 1-5 Fractions	Y	N	Technical
Radiation Treatment Delivery	77401	Superficial and/or Ortho Voltage	N	N	Technical
	77402	Radiation Treatment Delivery, Simple	N	N	Technical
	77407	Radiation Treatment Delivery, Intermediate	N	N	Technical
	77412	Radiation Treatment Delivery, Complex	N	N	Technical
IMRT Treatment Delivery	77385	IMRT Treatment Delivery, Simple	Y	N	Technical
	77386	IMRT Treatment Delivery, Complex	Y	N	Technical
Neutron Beam Treatment Delivery	77422	Neutron Beam Treatment, Simple	N	N	Technical
	77423	Neutron Beam Treatment, Complex	N	N	Technical
Proton Treatment Delivery	77520	Proton Treatment, Simple	N	N	Technical
	77522	Proton Treatment, Simple	N	N	Technical
	77523	Proton Treatment, Intermediate	N	N	Technical
	77525	Proton Treatment, Complex	N	N	Technical

▶Radioimmunoassay tests are found in the **Clinical Pathology** section (codes 82009-84999). These codes can be appropriately used by any specialist performing such tests in a laboratory licensed and/or certified for radioimmunoassays. The reporting of these tests is not confined to clinical pathology laboratories alone.◀

🖉 Rationale

A paragraph has been added within the guidelines for Nuclear Medicine. These guidelines direct users to the Clinical Pathology section for radioimmunoassay reporting. In addition, the guidelines also provide instructions to identify the clinicians who are qualified to report these services, as well as to provide information about situations in which these services may be reported.

⊘=Modifier 51 Exempt ⊙=Moderate Sedation ✦=Add-on Code ⚡=FDA approval pending

Pathology and Laboratory

Numerous changes have been made to the Pathology and Laboratory section. A substantial change to this section is the deletion of the Drug Testing subsection. In support of this deletion, a new Drug Assay subsection has been added. The new subsection includes introductory guidelines and is further divided into two subsections (Presumptive Drug Class Screening and Definitive Drug Testing) with accompanying guidelines and examples that provide instructions regarding the intended use of the codes. Within the Drug Assay subsection, several listings have been included to provide additional instruction and guidance for the use of these codes. These include the addition of: (1) a Definitions and Acronyms Conversion Listing; (2) Drug Class List A and Drug Class List B (identification of drugs and classes of drugs commonly assayed by presumptive procedures); and (3) a Definitive Drug Classes Listing.

In concert with the addition of the new Drug Assay subsection, changes have also been made to the Therapeutic Drug Assay (TDA) and Chemistry subsections. These changes include code additions, deletions, and revisions as well as guideline changes to the TDA subsection.

New definitions for exome, genome, heteroplasmy, mitochondrial DNA, and nuclear DNA have been added to the introduction of the Molecular Pathology section. In Tier 1, three new codes have been added and one code has been revised. The Tier 2 code series (81400-81408) has been revised to include the addition and deletion of several analytes.

A new Genomic Sequencing Procedures (GSPs) and Other Molecular Multianalyte Assays subsection has been added to provide a reporting mechanism for next generation sequencing or massively parallel sequencing (MPS) procedures. The new subsection includes introductory guidelines to clarify the use of the 21 new codes that have been added.

The Multianalyte Assays with Algorithmic Analyses (MAAA) introductory guidelines have been revised to support the addition of the new GSPs and Other Molecular Multianalyte Assays subsection. One new Category I MAAA code has been added. Three new Administrative MAAA codes have been added to Appendix O and the introductory guidelines in Appendix O have been revised.

Pathology and Laboratory

Organ or Disease-Oriented Panels

▶(80100, 80101, 80102, 80103, 80104 have been deleted. To report presumptive and/or definitive drug testing, see 80300, 80301, 80302, 80303, 80304)◀

🖎 Rationale

The Drug Testing subsection has been removed as this section primarily instructed users to report according to qualitative methods, such as chromatographic methods that focused on the number of phases done to accomplish the screening procedure. In place of this reporting method, a new section, Drug Assay, has been added. For more instruction, see the Drug Assay section.

▶Drug Assay◀

🖎 Rationale

To alleviate ambiguity regarding the reporting of drug procedures, a number of significant changes have been made within the Pathology and Laboratory section. The revisions allow for additional specificity in differentiating the materials being tested.

The previous mechanism for identifying drug testing relied on the use of qualitative and quantitative criteria, which included use of codes in the Drug Testing, Therapeutic Drug Assays, and Chemistry subsections within the Pathology and Laboratory section. Existing codes in the Drug Testing subsection were inherently qualitative, ie, if a qualitative drug screen did not sufficiently identify the drug or drug class, it could be followed by a quantitative procedure. And for quantitation of drugs screened, code(s) in the Therapeutic Drug Assays or Chemistry subsections were reported. In general, existing codes in these subsections were used to identify individual analytes.

With technological advances in drug testing, many updated testing procedures that allow for quantitative testing of multiple analytes within a single procedure have now become available. As a result, the methods for reporting these procedure(s) and analyte(s) have been updated.

Instead of differentiating testing procedures based on qualitative or quantitative methodology, the new reporting mechanism differentiates procedures according to whether they are: (1) presumptive (used to identify possible use or non-use of a drug or drug class); (2) definitive (qualitative or quantitative methods that identify possible drug use or non-use and can also identify specific drugs and associated metabolites); or (3) therapeutic drug assays (quantitative procedures performed to monitor clinical response to a known, prescribed medication). The updated reporting mechanism has been designed to address the following: (1) the ability to be easily modified for future changes and technological advances; (2) the identification of updated clinical settings; and (3) the identification of "sources" for specimen(s).

Many changes have been made to accommodate the addition of Presumptive and Definitive Drug Class procedures in the Drug Assay subsection and to accommodate the revisions to the Therapeutic Drug Assays subsection.

First, the Drug Testing subsection has been deleted to accommodate new codes and sections that will be used to identify current practice for drug testing procedures. The associated changes to the Drug Testing section consist of:

1. Deletion of the section heading and guidelines for the Drug Testing section;

2. Deletion of codes 80100-80104 and all associated parenthetical notes;

3. Inclusion of a deletion parenthetical note that directs users to the appropriate codes to use to report the Drug Testing services (Presumptive Drug Class Screening codes 80300-80304 for both Drug Classes A and B).

Second, a new heading and section titled "Drug Assay" has been added. This new section includes the addition of guidelines, parenthetical notes, and tables that should be used to direct reporting within the two new subsections, Presumptive Drug Class Screening and Definitive Drug Testing. The codes included within these subsections identify drug procedures according to the purpose of the procedure and type of patient results obtained. Specifically, the Drug Assay section includes:

1. Addition of a Definitions and Acronyms Conversion Listing to define terms used within the changed sections for users;

2. Addition of guidelines explaining the two new sections listed under the Drug Assay listing;

3. Addition of two new subsections: Presumptive Drug Class Screening and Definitive Drug Testing.

The Definitive Drug Testing subsection is further divided into the following two subsections:

1. Presumptive Drug Class Screening (new), which includes:

   a. Guidelines for the Presumptive Drug Class Screening section;

   b. Drug Class List A, which itemizes commonly assayed drugs within the listing. It also includes guidelines that explain the listing and intended use of the codes;

   c. Drug Class List B, which itemizes assays that require more resources than Class A. This section also includes guidelines that explain the intended use for the listing and the codes;

   d. Five new codes to identify presumptive testing (80300-80304) with introductory guidelines explaining the intent for use of these codes;

   e. A list of examples that provides samples of coding for the section.

2. Definitive Drug Testing, which includes:

    a. Fifty-nine new definitive drug testing codes (80320-80377). The codes are arranged by drug classes. Refer to the Definitive Drug Classes Listing for drugs and metabolites included in each definitive drug class. If applicable, the number of analytes tested has been included in the code descriptor.

    b. Guidelines and parenthetical notes for intended use of these codes. The guidelines include: (1) the purpose of definitive drug identification methods to identify individual drugs and distinguish between structural isomers (not necessarily stereoisomers); (2) examples of the types of methodologies that are used for testing; (3) a statement that these procedures may include qualitative, quantitative, or a combination of both analyses; (4) instruction regarding the number of codes that may be reported for multiple analytes; and (5) how to report definitive drug procedures that are not specified in this subsection.

    c. A listing of examples for use of these codes (80320-80349);

    d. A Definitive Drug Classes Listing table and guidelines to direct users to the appropriate codes.

The Therapeutic Drug Assays (TDA) subsection has been revised to include the addition of two new codes (80163 and 80165) to identify "Digoxin; free" and "Valproic acid; free." In addition, revisions have been made to three existing codes: code 80162 has been revised to allow separate reporting for total (80162) versus free (80163) digoxin testing; code 80164 has been revised to allow separate reporting for total (80164) versus free (80165) valproic acid testing; and code 80171 has been revised to reflect the specimen for the testing.

Finally, eight codes (80152, 80154, 80160, 80166, 80172, 80174, 80182, and 80196) have been deleted from this section to support the addition of the new presumptive and definitive testing codes. Deletion parenthetical notes have been added that direct users to appropriate replacement codes.

Revisions have also been made to the Chemistry section to accommodate the changes made for drug procedures and these revisions include:

1. Deletion of 21 codes to accommodate new methods for reporting within the presumptive and definitive subsections (82000, 82003, 82055, 82101, 82145, 82205, 82520, 82646, 82649, 82651, 82654, 82666, 82690, 82742, 82980, 83840, 83858, 83887, 83925, 84022, and 84228);

2. Revision of five codes (82541-82544, and 84600) as the drug testing procedures (82541, 82544) and the metabolites (listed within code 84600) have been included within the Definitive Drug Testing section;

3. Inclusion of 19 deletion parenthetical notes for the deleted codes;

4. Deletion of 15 instructional parenthetical notes;

5. Revisions to existing parenthetical notes.

Rationales for each of the changes itemized in the preceding have been included to further explain the changes.

DEFINITIONS AND ACRONYM CONVERSION LISTING

Drug Testing Term/Acronym	Definition
6-MAM	Acronym for the heroin drug metabolite 6-monacetylmorphine
Acid	Descriptor for classifying drug/drug metabolite molecules based upon chemical ionization properties. Laboratory procedures for drug isolation and identification may include acid, base, or neutral groupings.
AM	A category of synthetic marijuana drugs discovered by and named after Alexandros Makriyannis at Northeastern University
Analog	A structural derivative of a parent chemical compound that often differs from it by a single element
Analyte	The substance or chemical constituent that is of interest in an analytical procedure
Base	Descriptor for classifying drug/drug metabolite molecules based upon chemical ionization properties. Laboratory procedures for drug isolation and identification may include acid, base, or neutral groupings.
Card(s)	Multiplexed presumptive drug class(es) immunoassay product that is read by visual observation, including instrumented when performed
Cassette(s)	Multiplexed presumptive drug class immunoassay product(s) that is read by visual observation, including instrumented when performed
CEDIA	Acronym for Cloned-Enzyme-Donor-Immuno-Assay. CEDIA immunoassay is a competitive antibody binding procedure that utilizes enzyme donor fragment-labeled antigens (drugs) to compete for antigens (drugs) contained in the patient sample. Recombination of enzyme donor fragment and enzyme acceptor fragment produces a functional enzyme. CEDIA immunoassay enzyme activity is proportional to concentration of drug(s) detected.
Chromatography	An analytical technique used to separate components of a mixture. See thin layer chromatography, gas chromatography, and high performance chromatography.
Confirmatory	Term used to describe definitive identification/quantitation procedures that are secondary to presumptive screening methods
DART	Acronym for Direct-Analysis-in-Real-Time. DART is an atmospheric pressure ionization method for mass spectrometry analysis
Definitive Drug Procedure	A procedure that provides specific identification of individual drugs and drug metabolites
DESI	Acronym for Desorption-ElectroSpray-Ionization. DESI is a combination of electrospray ionization and desorption ionization methods for mass spectrometry analysis.
Dipstick	A multiplexed presumptive drug class immunoassay product that is read by visual observation, including instrumented when performed
Drug test cup	A multiplexed presumptive drug class immunoassay product that is read by visual observation, including instrumented when performed
EDDP	Acronym for the methadone drug metabolite 2-ethylidene-1,5-dimethyl-3,3-diphenylpyrrolidine
EIA	Acronym for Enzyme-Immuno-Assay. Enzyme immunoassay is a competitive antibody binding procedure that utilizes enzyme-labeled antigens (drugs) to compete for antigens (drugs) contained in the patient sample. Enzyme immunoassay enzyme activity is proportional to concentration of drug(s) detected.
ELISA	Acronym for Enzyme-Linked Immunosorbent Assay. ELISA is a competitive binding immunoassay that is design to measure antigens (drugs) or antibodies. ELISA immunoassay results are proportional to concentration of drug(s) detected.

⊘=Modifier 51 Exempt ⊙=Moderate Sedation ✚=Add-on Code 𝑵=FDA approval pending

Drug Testing Term/Acronym	Definition
EMIT	Acronym for Enzyme-Multiplied-Immunoassay-Test. EMIT is a trade name for a type of enzyme immunoassay (EIA).
FPIA	Acronym for Fluorescence-Polarization-Immuno-Assay. FPIA is a competitive binding immunoassay that utilizes fluorescein-labeled antigens (drugs) to compete for antigens (drugs) contained in the patient sample. The measure of polarized light emission is inversely proportional to the concentration of drug(s) detected.
Gas chromatography	Gas chromatography is a chromatography technique in which patient sample preparations are vaporized into a gas (mobile phase) which flows through a tubular column (containing a stationary phase) and into a detector. The retention time of a drug on the column is determined by partitioning characteristics of the drug into the mobile and stationary phases. Chromatography column detectors may be non-specific (eg, flame ionization) or specific (eg, mass spectrometry). The combination of column retention time and specific detector response provides a definitive identification of the drug or drug metabolite.
GC	Acronym for gas chromatography
GC-MS	Acronym for gas chromatography mass spectrometry
GC-MS/MS	Acronym for gas chromatography mass spectrometry/mass spectrometry
High performance liquid chromatography	High performance liquid chromatography is a chromatography technique in which patient sample preparations are injected into a liquid (mobile phase) which flows through a tubular column (containing a stationary phase) and into a detector. The retention time of a drug on the column is determined by partitioning characteristics of the drug into the mobile and stationary phases. Chromatography column detectors may be non-specific (eg, ultra-violet spectrophotometry) or specific (eg, mass spectrometry). The combination of column retention time and specific detector response provides a definitive identification of the drug or drug metabolite. High performance liquid chromatography is also called high pressure liquid chromatography.
HPLC	Acronym for high performance liquid chromatography
HU	A category of synthetic marijuana drugs discovered by and named after Raphael Mechoulam at Hebrew University
IA	Acronym for immunoassay
Immunoassay	Antigen-antibody binding procedures utilized to detect antigens (eg, drugs and/or drug metabolites) in patient samples. Immunoassay designs include competitive or non-competitive with various mechanisms for detection.
Isobaric	In mass spectrometry, ions with the same mass
Isomers	Compounds that have the same molecular formula but differ in structural formula
JWH	A category of synthetic marijuana drugs discovered by and named after John W. Huffman at Clemson University.
KIMS	Acronym for kinetic interaction of microparticles in solution. KIMS immunoassay is a competitive antibody binding procedure that utilizes microparticle-labeled antigens (drugs) to compete for antigens (drugs) contained in the patient sample. Microparticle immunoassay absorbance increase is inversely proportional to concentration of drug(s) detected.
LC-MS	Acronym for liquid chromatography mass spectrometry
LC-MS/MS	Acronym for liquid chromatography mass spectrometry/mass spectrometry
LDTD	Acronym for laser diode thermal desorption. LDTD is a combination of atmospheric pressure chemical ionization and laser diode thermal desorption methods for mass spectrometry analysis.
MALDI	Acronym for matrix assisted laser desorption/Ionization mass spectrometry. MALDI is a soft ionization technique that reduces molecular fragmentation.

Drug Testing Term/Acronym	Definition
MDA	Acronym for the drug 3,4-methylenedioxyamphetamine. MDA is also a drug metabolite of MDMA.
MDEA	Acronym for the drug 3,4-methylenedioxy-N-ethylamphetamine
MDMA	Acronym for the drug 3,4-methylenedioxy-N-methylamphetamine
MDPV	Acronym for the drug methylenedioxypyrovalerone
MS	Acronym for mass spectrometry. MS is an identification technique that measures the charge-to-mass ratio of charged particles. There are several types of mass spectrometry instruments, such as magnetic sectoring, time of flight, quadrapole mass filter, ion traps, and Fourier transformation. Mass spectrometry is used as part of the process to assign definitive identification of drugs and drug metabolites.
MS/MS	Acronym for mass spectrometry/mass spectrometry. MS/MS instruments combine multiple units of mass spectrometry filters into a single instrument. MS/MS is also called tandem mass spectrometry.
MS-TOF	Acronym for mass spectrometry time of flight. Time of flight is a mass spectrometry identification technique that utilizes ion velocity to determine the mass-to-charge ratio.
Multiplexed	Descriptor for a multiple component test device that simultaneously measures multiple analytes (drug classes) in a single analysis.
Neutral	Descriptor for classifying drug/drug metabolite molecules based upon chemical ionization properties. Laboratory procedures for drug isolation and identification may include acid, base, or neutral groupings.
ng/mL	Unit of measure for weight per volume calculated as nanograms per milliliter. The ng/mL unit of measure is equivalent to the ug/L unit of measure.
Optical observation	Optical observation refers to procedure results that are interpreted visually with or without instrumentation assistance.
Opiate	Medicinal category of narcotic alkaloid drugs that are natural products in the opium poppy plant *Papaver somniferum*. This immunoassay class of drugs typically includes detection of codeine, dihydrocodeine, hydrocodone, hydromorphone, and morphine.
Opioids	A category of medicinal synthetic or semi-synthetic narcotic alkaloid opioid receptor stimulating drugs including butorphanol, desomorphine, dextromethorphan, dextrorphan, levorphanol, meperidine, naloxone, naltrexone, normeperidine, and pentazocine.
Presumptive	Drug test results that indicate possible, but not definitive, presence of drugs and or drug metabolites
QTOF	Acronym for quadrapole-time of flight mass spectrometry. QTOF is a hybrid mass spectrometry identification technique that combines ion velocity with tandem quadrapole mass spectrometry (MS or MS/MS) to determine the mass-to-charge ratio.
RCS	A category of synthetic marijuana drugs that are analogs of JHW compounds. *See* JWH.
RIA	Acronym for radio-immuno-assay. Radioimmunoassay is a competitive antibody binding procedure that utilizes radioactive-labeled antigens (drugs) to compete for antigens (drugs) contained in the patient sample. The measure of radioactivity is inversely proportional to concentration of drug(s) detected.
Stereoisomers	Isomeric molecules that have the same molecular formula and sequence of bonded atoms (constitution), but that differ only in the three-dimensional orientations of their atoms in space
Substance	A substance is a drug that does not have an established therapeutic use as distinguished from other analytes listed in the Chemistry section (82000-84999).
TDM	Acronym for therapeutic drug monitoring
THC	Acronym for marijuana active drug ingredient tetrahydrocannabinol

⊘=Modifier 51 Exempt   ⊙=Moderate Sedation   ✚=Add-on Code   ⊿=FDA approval pending

Drug Testing Term/Acronym	Definition
Therapeutic Drug Monitoring	Analysis of blood (serum, plasma) drug concentration to monitor clinical response to therapy
Time of flight	Time of flight is a mass spectrometry technique that utilizes ion velocity to determine the mass-to-charge ratio
TLC	Acronym for thin layer chromatography
TOF	Acronym for time of flight
ug/L	Unit of measure for mass per volume calculated as micrograms per liter. The ug/L unit of measure is equivalent to the ng/mL unit of measure.

✎ Rationale

A Definitions and Acronyms Conversion Listing has been added to define terms used within the new and revised sections. The list is not comprehensive but defines some of the more common terms for users.

▶Drug procedures are divided into three subsections:

Therapeutic Drug Assay, **Drug Assay**, and **Chemistry**—with code selection dependent on the purpose and type of patient results obtained. Therapeutic Drug Assays are performed to monitor clinical response to a known, prescribed medication. The two major categories for drug testing in the Drug Assay subsection are:

1. **Presumptive Drug Class** procedures are used to identify possible use or non-use of a drug or drug class. A presumptive test may be followed by a definitive test in order to specifically identify drugs or metabolites.

2. **Definitive Drug Class** procedures are qualitative or quantitative test to identify possible use or non-use of a drug. These test identify specific drugs and associated metabolites, if performed. A presumptive test is not required prior to a definitive drug test.

The material for drug class procedures may be any specimen type unless otherwise specified in the code descriptor (eg, urine, blood, oral fluid, meconium, hair). Procedures can be qualitative (eg, positive/negative or present/absent), semi-quantitative, or quantitative (measured) depending on the purpose of the testing. Therapeutic drug assay (TDA) procedures are typically quantitative tests and the specimen type is whole blood, serum, plasma, or cerebrospinal fluid.

When the same procedure(s) is performed on more than one specimen type (eg, blood and urine), the appropriate code is reported separately for each specimen type using modifier 59.

Drugs or classes of drugs may be commonly assayed first by a presumptive screening method followed by a definitive drug identification method. Presumptive methods include, but are not limited to, immunoassays (IA, EIA, ELISA, RIA, EMIT, FPIA, etc), enzymatic methods (alcohol dehydrogenase, etc), chromatographic methods without mass spectrometry (TLC, HPLC, GC, etc), or mass spectrometry without adequate drug resolution by chromatography (MS-TOF, DART, DESI, LDTD, MALDI). LC-MS, LCMS/MS, or mass spectrometry without adequate drug resolution by chromatography may also be used for presumptive testing if the chromatographic phase is not adequate to identify individual drugs and distinguish between structural isomers or isobaric compounds. All drug class immunoassays are considered presumptive, whether qualitative, semi-quantitative, or quantitative. Methods that cannot distinguish between structural isomers (such as morphine and hydromorphone or methamphetamine and phentermine) are also considered presumptive.

Definitive drug identification methods are able to identify individual drugs and distinguish between structural isomers but not necessarily stereoisomers. Definitive methods include, but are not limited to, gas chromatography with mass spectrometry (any type, single or tandem) and liquid chromatography mass spectrometry (any type, single or tandem) and excludes immunoassays (eg, IA, EIA, ELISA, RIA, EMIT, FPIA), and enzymatic methods (eg, alcohol dehydrogenase).

For chromatography, each combination of stationary and mobile phase is to be counted as one procedure.◄

►Presumptive Drug Class Screening◄

►Drugs or classes of drugs may be commonly assayed first by a presumptive screening method followed by a definitive drug identification method. The list of drug classes and the methodology are considered when coding presumptive procedures. If a drug class is not listed in List A or List B and it is not performed by TLC, use 80304 unless the specific analyte is listed in the Chemistry Section (82009-84830).◄

🖎 Rationale

The guidelines included for Presumptive Drug Class Screening provide specific instructions regarding the intended use for these codes. These include: (1) identification of the three sections in which drug testing codes may be found (Drug Assay, Therapeutic Drug Assay [TDA], and Chemistry); (2) identification of the two subsections included within the Drug Assay section (Presumptive Drug Class Screening and Definitive Drug Testing); (3) addition of specific instruction regarding the source of the sample for each type of procedure (blood or blood components for TDA versus any specimen for Drug Assay and Chemistry listings); (4) instruction regarding how to report services for multiple specimen types; (5) identification of methods that are typically performed for presumptive and definitive procedures; and (6) how to report stationary and mobile phases performed for chromatography.

Presumptive procedures identify use or non-use of a drug or drug class. A presumptive test may be followed by a definitive test to specifically identify drugs or metabolites.

►DRUG CLASS LIST A◄

►The following list contains drugs or classes of drugs that are commonly assayed by presumptive procedures. The methodology is typically one in which the results are capable of being read by direct optical observation, including instrument-assisted when performed (eg, dipsticks, cups, cards, cartridges), or by instrumented test systems (eg, discrete multichannel chemistry analyzers utilizing immunoassay or enzyme assay). These procedures may also be followed by a definitive procedure.

⃠=Modifier 51 Exempt   ⊙=Moderate Sedation   ✚=Add-on Code   ⋌=FDA approval pending

- Alcohol (Ethanol)

- Amphetamines

- Barbiturates

- Benzodiazepines

- Buprenorphine

- Cocaine metabolite

- Heroin metabolite (6-monoacetylmorphine)

- Methadone

- Methadone metabolite (EDDP)

- Methamphetamine

- Methaqualone

- Methylenedioxymethamphetamine (MDMA)

- Opiates

- Oxycodone

- Phencyclidine

- Propoxyphene

- Tetrahydrocannabinol (THC) metabolites (marijuana)

- Tricyclic Antidepressants◄

►DRUG CLASS LIST B◄

►The following list contains drugs or classes of drugs that may be assayed by presumptive procedures. The methodology typically requires more resources than the drugs listed in Drug Class List A. The procedure may include drug class specific preanalytical sample preparation. It may be a manual process such as ELISA.

- Acetaminophen

- Carisoprodol/Meprobamate

- Ethyl Glucuronide

- Fentanyl

- Ketamine

- Meperidine

- Methylphenidate

- Nicotine/Cotinine

- Salicylate

- Synthetic Cannabinoids

- Tapentadol

- Tramadol

- Zolpidem

- Not otherwise specified◄

✍ Rationale

The guidelines and tables listed for Drug Class List A and Drug Class List B have been included to direct users to the different drugs and methodologies that may be assayed by presumptive procedures. Because there are two different levels of presumptive testing, Drug Class List A and Drug Class List B, separate tables and guidelines provide users with instructions for differentiating the two levels. Procedures typically read by direct optical observation are identified within Drug Class List A. This includes instrument-assisted procedures, when performed (eg, dipstick methods and procedures that utilize cups, cards, or cartridges) as well as instrumented test systems, such as discrete multichannel chemistry analyzers utilizing immunoassay or enzyme assay. Drug Class List B may include drug class–specific preanalytical sample preparation and may include manual processes such as enzyme-linked immunosorbent assay (ELISA). Definitive procedures may be necessary after completion of presumptive procedures.

►Use code 80300 to report single or multiple drug class procedures, other than TLC, using direct optical observation (eg, dipsticks, drug test cups, cassettes, and cards that are interpreted visually, with or without instrument assistance) for Class List A drug classes. Report 80300 once, irrespective of the number of direct observation drug class procedures or results on any date of service.

Use code 80301 to report single drug classes included in Drug Class List A, performed by methods other than direct optical observation or TLC, using discrete multichannel chemistry analyzers utilizing immunoassay or enzyme assay (eg, EIA, KIMS, CEDIA immunoassays) once per date of service. Use 80301 once to report single or multiple procedures performed, irrespective of the number of procedures, classes, or results on any date of service.

Use code 80302 to report presumptive, single drug classes other than those in Drug Class List A (ie, Drug Class List B), other than direct optical observation or TLC, using immunoassays or chromatography without mass spectrometry, each drug class/procedure.

Use 80303 to report single or multiple drug procedures using thin layer chromatography (TLC), per day of service.

Use 80304 to report single or multiple drug screenings not specified elsewhere (eg, TOF, MALDI, LDTD, DESI, DART), per testing site, per date of service, each procedure.◄

\#●80300   Drug screen, any number of drug classes from Drug Class List A; any number of non-TLC devices or procedures, (eg, immunoassay) capable of being read by direct optical observation, including instrumented-assisted when performed (eg, dipsticks, cups, cards, cartridges), per date of service

►(Use 80303 for Drug Class List A analyte(s) performed by thin layer chromatography)◄

#●80301   single drug class method, by instrumented test systems (eg, discrete multichannel chemistry analyzers utilizing immunoassay or enzyme assay), per date of service

#●80302   Drug screen, presumptive, single drug class from Drug Class List B, by immunoassay (eg, ELISA) or non-TLC chromatography without mass spectrometry (eg, GC, HPLC), each procedure

►(Use 80303 for Drug Class List A and List B analyte(s) performed by thin layer chromatography)◄

#●80303   Drug screen, any number of drug classes, presumptive, single or multiple drug class method; thin layer chromatography procedure(s) (TLC) (eg, acid, neutral, alkaloid plate), per date of service

#●80304   not otherwise specified presumptive procedure (eg, TOF, MALDI, LDTD, DESI, DART), each procedure

►**For example:**

■ To report five (5) presumptive drug classes performed using a direct optical observation device procedure (drug test cup or 5 separate dipsticks), report 80300 once per date of service.

■ To report three (3) presumptive drug classes (Drug Class List A) performed using an automated chemistry analyzer, report 80301 once per facility, per date of service.

■ To report thirteen (13) presumptive drug classes (Drug Class List A) performed using an automated chemistry analyzer, report 80301 once per facility, per date of service.

■ To report two (2) presumptive drug classes (Drug Class List B) performed using a semi-automated analyzer, report 80302 X 2.

■ To report two (2) multiple drug TLC procedures (one acid/neutral analysis for 10 drugs; one base analysis for 45 drugs), report 80303 X 1, per date of service.

■ To report one (1) single drug procedure performed using TLC, report 80303 X 1, per date of service.

■ To report three (3) multiple drug class procedures (one acid/neutral drug analysis; one base drug analysis; one ultra-sensitive base drug analysis) performed using time of flight (TOF) mass spectrometry (chromatography insufficient to provide definitive drug identification), report 80304 X 3.◄

Rationale

Guidelines that include samples of procedures have been included to instruct users on the appropriate reporting of codes in the Presumptive Drug Class Screening section. In addition, an Examples section has been added for further guidance. The samples and examples model circumstances in which these codes may be reported.

Clinical Example (80300)

A 55-year-old male, a new patient, with post-accident severe low back pain requests a continuation of morphine treatment and has enough medication for three more days. Patient scores negative on an opioid risk evaluation, and there is no evidence of intravenous drug abuse. The state guidelines require a drug test and prescription drug monitoring program (PDMP) review prior to writing a new prescription for controlled pain medications.

Description of Procedure (80300)

Qualitative direct optical observation drug screen (dipstick) for five drug classes is performed. CPT code(s): 1 count of 80300.

Clinical Example (80301)

A 43-year-old male, a new patient, with post-accident severe low back pain requests a continuation of morphine treatment and has enough medication for three more days. Patient scores positive on an opioid risk evaluation and admits to past drug abuse (marijuana and cocaine). State guidelines require a drug test and PDMP review prior to writing a new prescription for controlled pain medications.

Description of Procedure (80301)

Discrete multichannel instrument qualitative analysis for three immunoassay drug classes (opiates, marijuana metabolite, and cocaine metabolite) is performed. CPT code(s): 1 count of 80301.

Clinical Example (80302)

A 35-year-old male with post-accident severe burn pain requests continuation of buprenorphine transdermal treatment. The patient scores positive on an opioid risk evaluation and admits to past drug abuse with carisoprodol. State guidelines require a drug test and PDMP review prior to writing a new prescription for controlled pain medications.

Description of Procedure (80302)

Single qualitative analysis for one immunoassay drug class (carisoprodol/meprobamate) is performed. CPT code(s): 1 count of 80302.

Clinical Example (80303)

A 41-year-old male, a new patient, with failed back syndrome pain requests continuation of buprenorphine transdermal treatment. The patient scores positive on an opioid risk evaluation and admits to past drug abuse with multiple designer drugs. State guidelines require a drug test and PDMP review prior to writing a new prescription for controlled pain medications.

Description of Procedure (80303)

Two qualitative multiple drug thin layer chromatography analyses (one for acid neutral drugs, one for base drugs) are performed. CPT code(s): 1 count of 80303.

Clinical Example (80304)

A 57-year-old male, a new patient, with severe diabetic neuropathic pain requests a continuation of buprenorphine transdermal treatment. The patient scores positive on an opioid risk evaluation and admits to past drug abuse with multiple designer drugs. State guidelines require a drug test and PDMP review prior to writing a new prescription for controlled pain medications.

Description of Procedure (80304)

One qualitative multiple drug time-of-flight mass spectrometry analysis for 65 designer drugs is performed. CPT code(s): 1 count of 80304.

►Definitive Drug Testing◄

►Definitive drug identification methods are able to identify individual drugs and distinguish between structural isomers but not necessarily stereoisomers. Definitive methods include, but are not limited to, gas chromatography with mass spectrometry (any type, single or tandem) and liquid chromatography mass spectrometry (any type, single or tandem) and exclude immunoassays (eg, IA, EIA, ELISA, RIA, EMIT, FPIA) and enzymatic methods (eg, alcohol dehydrogenase).

Use 80320-80377 to report definitive drug class procedures. Definitive testing may be qualitative, quantitative, or a combination of qualitative and quantitative for the same patient on the same date of service.

The **Definitive Drug Classes Listing** provides the drug classes, their associated CPT codes, and the drugs included in each class. Each category of a drug class, including metabolite(s) if performed (except stereoisomers), is reported once per date of service. Metabolites not listed in the table may be reported using the code for the parent drug. Drug class metabolite(s) is not reported separately unless the metabolite(s) is listed as a separate category in **Definitive Drug Classes Listing** (eg, heroin metabolite).

Drug classes may contain one or more codes based on the number of analytes. For example, an analysis in which five or more amphetamines and/or amphetamine metabolites would be reported with 80326. The code is based on the number of reported analytes and not the capacity of the analysis.

Definitive drug procedures that are not specified in 80320-80373 should be reported using the unlisted definitive procedure codes 80375, 80376, 80377, unless the specific analyte is listed in the **Therapeutic Drug Assays** (80150-80203) or **Chemistry** (82009-84830) sections.

See the **Definitive Drug Classes Listing** on pages [232-234] for a listing of the more common analytes within each drug class.◄

🖉 Rationale

Procedures to identify specific drugs and associated metabolites by a variety of methods have been included in the Definitive Drug Testing section. Definitive drug class procedures can be qualitative, quantitative, or a combination of qualitative and quantitative.

Guidelines in this section direct users to the Definitive Drug Classes Listing to identify drugs and metabolites included in each definitive drug class. In addition, instructional cross-reference parenthetical notes have been included to direct users to the appropriate codes to report.

#●**80320** Alcohols

#●**80321** Alcohol biomarkers; 1 or 2

#●**80322**   3 or more

#●**80323** Alkaloids, not otherwise specified

#●**80324** Amphetamines; 1 or 2

#●**80325**   3 or 4

# ● 80326	5 or more
# ● 80327	Anabolic steroids; 1 or 2
# ● 80328	3 or more
# ● 80329	Analgesics, non-opioid; 1 or 2
# ● 80330	3-5
# ● 80331	6 or more
# ● 80332	Antidepressants, serotonergic class; 1 or 2
# ● 80333	3-5
# ● 80334	6 or more
# ● 80335	Antidepressants, tricyclic and other cyclicals; 1 or 2
# ● 80336	3-5
# ● 80337	6 or more
# ● 80338	Antidepressants, not otherwise specified
# ● 80339	Antiepileptics, not otherwise specified; 1-3
# ● 80340	4-6
# ● 80341	7 or more

▶(To report definitive drug testing for antihistamines, see 80375, 80376, 80377)◀

# ● 80342	Antipsychotics, not otherwise specified; 1-3
# ● 80343	4-6
# ● 80344	7 or more
# ● 80345	Barbiturates
# ● 80346	Benzodiazepines; 1-12
# ● 80347	13 or more
# ● 80348	Buprenorphine
# ● 80349	Cannabinoids, natural
# ● 80350	Cannabinoids, synthetic; 1-3
# ● 80351	4-6
# ● 80352	7 or more
# ● 80353	Cocaine
# ● 80354	Fentanyl
# ● 80355	Gabapentin, non-blood

▶(For therapeutic drug assay, use 80171)◀

⊘=Modifier 51 Exempt   ⊙=Moderate Sedation   ✚=Add-on Code   ⟋=FDA approval pending

#●**80356**	Heroin metabolite
#●**80357**	Ketamine and norketamine
#●**80358**	Methadone
#●**80359**	Methylenedioxyamphetamines (MDA, MDEA, MDMA)
#●**80360**	Methylphenidate
#●**80361**	Opiates, 1 or more
#●**80362**	Opioids and opiate analogs; 1 or 2
#●**80363**	3 or 4
#●**80364**	5 or more
#●**80365**	Oxycodone
#**83992**	Phencyclidine (PCP)
	▶(Phenobarbital, use 80345)◀
#●**80366**	Pregabalin
#●**80367**	Propoxyphene
#●**80368**	Sedative hypnotics (non-benzodiazepines)
#●**80369**	Skeletal muscle relaxants; 1 or 2
#●**80370**	3 or more
#●**80371**	Stimulants, synthetic
#●**80372**	Tapentadol
#●**80373**	Tramadol
#●**80374**	Stereoisomer (enantiomer) analysis, single drug class
	▶(Use 80374 in conjunction with an index drug analysis, when performed)◀
#●**80375**	Drug(s) or substance(s), definitive, qualitative or quantitative, not otherwise specified; 1-3
#●**80376**	4-6
#●**80377**	7 or more
	▶(To report definitive drug testing for antihistamines, see 80375, 80376, 80377)

✒ Rationale

Fifty-eight new definitive drug testing codes (80320-80377, which includes the resequencing of code 83992) arranged by drug classes have been added. Refer to the Definitive Drug Classes Listing table for drugs and metabolites included in each definitive drug class. If applicable, the number of analytes tested has been included in the code descriptor.

For an overview of the changes made regarding drug testing, see the Rationale for the Drug Assay subsection.

For Example:

To report amphetamine and methamphetamine using any number of definitive procedures, report 80324 once per facility per date of service.

To report codeine, hydrocodone, hydromorphone, morphine using any number of definitive procedures, report 80361 once per facility per date of service.

To report codeine, hydrocodone, hydromorphone, morphine, oxycodone, oxymorphone, naloxone, naltrexone performed using any number of definitive procedures report 80361 X1, 80362 X1, and 80365 X 1 per facility per date of service.

To report benzoylecgonine, cocaine, carboxy-THC, meperidine, normeperidine using any number of definitive procedures, report 80349 X 1, 80353 X 1, and 80362 X 1 per facility per date of service. ◀

Rationale

An Example section has been added to further instruct users regarding the intended use of the definitive drug testing codes. The examples provided are not meant to be a comprehensive listing of all procedures that may be performed.

The first example instructs users to report code 80324 once per facility per date of service for two metabolites in the amphetamine family (amphetamine and methamphetamine).

In the second example, four opiate metabolites are listed for identification. Because any number of opiates may be identified by a single procedure, report code 80361 once per facility per date of service.

The third example lists metabolites from several different drug families. For opiate metabolites (hydrocodone, hydromorphone, and morphine), report code 80361 once per facility per date of service. For oxycodone metabolites (oxycodone and oxymorphone), report code 80365 once per facility per date of service. For opioids and opiate analogs (naloxone and naltrexone), report code 80362 once per facility per date of service.

In the fourth example, report code 80353 once per facility per date of service for cocaine metabolites (benzoylecgonine and cocaine). Carboxy-tetrahydrocannabinol (THC) is a natural cannabinoid that is reported with code 80349 once per facility per date of service. For opioids and opiate analogs (meperidine and normeperidine), report code 80362 once per facility per date of service.

Clinical Example (80320)

A 52-year-old male is admitted to the emergency department unconscious after ingesting a one-liter bottle of spirits. Patient is pulseless, apneic with a rectal temperature of 98.6°F. The patient is intubated, mechanically ventilated, and resuscitated with epinephrine. Blood volatiles are ordered to determine blood levels for alcohols, including ethanol and methanol.

⊘=Modifier 51 Exempt   ⊙=Moderate Sedation   ✚=Add-on Code   ⟋=FDA approval pending

Description of Procedure (80320)

A quantitative analysis for alcohols (including ethanol, isopropanol, and methanol) is performed. Analytical techniques must be capable of specifically identifying the type of compound present and not as a general category. Independent identification of each compound is necessary for adequate treatment. Results indicate the presence of methanol. The use of this definitive test was necessary for the proper treatment, such as the administration of ethanol. (The use of ethanol in the treatment of the patient would be contraindicated if the patient were suffering from ethanol intoxication.)

Clinical Example (80321)

A 32-year-old female with back pain is prescribed 10 mg morphine twice per day for pain management. She has a history of alcohol use, and there is reason to believe she is consuming alcohol at night. However, test results for ethanol are negative because it is rapidly metabolized and not detectable the day after alcohol use. Testing for persistent biomarkers is necessary to confirm alcohol use, which is contraindicated with the prescribed morphine and violates patient's practice agreement. Before the prescription refill is issued, a urine specimen is sent to the laboratory to verify the possible use of ethanol.

Description of Procedure (80321)

One quantitative analysis for alcohol biomarkers, in this case, ethylglucuronide and ethylsulfate, is performed. Quantitative analysis is necessary to separate casual contact of alcohol due to products containing ethanol, such as hand sanitizers and mouthwashes, and actual ethanol consumption. Any of the instrumental techniques that are defined as definitive may be used. These are high-complexity tests, such as liquid chromatography mass spectrometry/mass spectrometry (LC-MS/MS). Exact methodology varies by testing facility, but all are instrumental techniques with the ability to specifically identify individual drugs and metabolites, if tested, within a class and rule out interfering drugs and other substances. See descriptions of definitive tests in the Definitive Drug Testing introductory guidelines. Results indicate the presence of ethylglucuronide (>10,000 ng/ml) and ethylsulfate (5221 ng/ml). The use of this definitive test was necessary to diagnose alcohol use. This high level is consistent with the consumption of ethanol and not with casual contact. From these results, the clinician must take necessary precaution prior to refilling the prescription.

Clinical Example (80322)

A 32-year-old female with back pain is prescribed 10 mg morphine twice per day for pain management. She has a history of alcohol use, and there is reason to believe she is consuming alcohol at night. However, test results for ethanol are negative because it is rapidly metabolized and not detectable the day after alcohol use. Testing for persistent biomarkers is necessary to confirm alcohol use, which is contraindicated with the prescribed morphine and violates patient's practice agreement. Before the prescription refill is issued, a urine specimen is sent to the laboratory to verify the possible use of ethanol.

Description of Procedure (80322)

One quantitative analysis for alcohol biomarkers, in this case, ethylglucuronide and ethylsulfate, is performed. Quantitative analysis is necessary to separate casual contact of alcohol due to products containing ethanol, such as hand sanitizers and mouthwashes, and actual ethanol consumption. Any of the instrumental techniques that are defined as definitive may be used. These are high-complexity tests, such as liquid chromatography mass spectrometry/mass spectrometry (LC-MS/MS). Exact methodology varies by testing facility, but all are instrumental techniques with the ability to specifically identify individual drugs and metabolites, if tested, within a class and rule out interfering drugs and other substances. See descriptions of definitive tests in the Definitive Drug Testing introductory guidelines. Results indicate the presence of ethylglucuronide (>10,000 ng/ml) and ethylsulfate (5221 ng/ml). The use of this definitive test was necessary to diagnose alcohol use. This high level is consistent with the consumption of ethanol and not with casual contact. From these results, the clinician must take necessary precaution prior to refilling the prescription.

Clinical Example (80323)

An 18-year-old male is admitted to the emergency department after ingesting an unknown herbal remedy obtained on the Internet. The patient was sedated and delirious. Routine point-of-care tests performed by the hospital were negative. A urine specimen is sent to the laboratory to rule out presence of Kratom (mitragynine) and other illicit substances.

Description of Procedure (80323)

A definitive, quantitative LC-MS/MS analysis is ordered for the plant alkaloid mitragynine and other common illicit drugs. Any of the instrumental techniques that are defined as definitive may be used. These are high-complexity tests, such as LC-MS/MS or gas chromatography/mass spectrometry (GC/MS). Exact methodology varies by testing facility, but all are instrumental techniques with the ability to specifically identify individual drugs and metabolites, if tested, within a class and rule out interfering drugs and other substances. See descriptions of definitive tests in the Definitive Drug Testing introductory guidelines.

Results indicate use of the mitragynine, a plant alkyoid that acts as a stimulant at low doses and a sedative and opiate agonist as the dose is increased.

Clinical Example (80324)

A 42-year-old female with post-amputation severe phantom limb pain, who is prescribed 20 mg twice per day controlled-release oxycodone, tests amphetamine qualitative presumptive positive using a direct observation dipstick device. The patient is not prescribed any amphetamines but does admit to recent use of a nonprescription decongestant. Before the prescription refill is issued, a urine specimen is sent to the laboratory to confirm amphetamine(s) present or if presumptive results are false positive.

Description of Procedure (80324)

A qualitative definitive GC/MS analysis for amphetamine and methamphetamine is performed. Any of the instrumental techniques that are defined as definitive

⊘=Modifier 51 Exempt ⊙=Moderate Sedation ✚=Add-on Code 𝒩=FDA approval pending

may be used. These are high-complexity tests, such as LC-MS/MS or GC/MS. Exact methodology varies by testing facility, but all are instrumental techniques with the ability to specifically identify individual drugs and metabolites, if tested, within a class and rule out interfering drugs and other substances. See descriptions of definitive tests in the Definitive Drug Testing introductory guidelines. Results indicate the presence of amphetamine. The patient indicates use of lisdexamfetamine, a prescription medication that is metabolized to amphetamine. Illicit drug use is ruled out.

Clinical Example (80325)

A 42-year-old female with post-amputation severe phantom limb pain who is prescribed 20 mg twice per day controlled release oxycodone tests amphetamine qualitative presumptive positive using a direct observation dipstick device. The patient is not prescribed any amphetamines but does admit to recent use of a nonprescription decongestant. Before the prescription refill is issued, a urine specimen is sent to the laboratory to confirm amphetamine(s) present or if presumptive results are false positive.

Description of Procedure (80325)

A qualitative definitive GC/MS analysis for amphetamine and methamphetamine is performed. Any of the instrumental techniques that are defined as definitive may be used. These are high-complexity tests, such as LC-MS/MS or GC/MS. Exact methodology varies by testing facility, but all are instrumental techniques with the ability to specifically identify individual drugs and metabolites, if tested, within a class and rule out interfering drugs and other substances. See descriptions of definitive tests in the Definitive Drug Testing introductory guidelines. Results indicate the presence of amphetamine. The patient indicates use of lisdexamfetamine, a prescription medication that is metabolized to amphetamine. Illicit drug use is ruled out.

Clinical Example (80326)

A 42-year-old female with post-amputation severe phantom limb pain, who is prescribed 20 mg twice per day controlled-release oxycodone, tests amphetamine qualitative presumptive positive using a direct observation dipstick device. The patient is not prescribed any amphetamines but does admit to recent use of a nonprescription decongestant. Before the prescription refill is issued, a urine specimen is sent to the laboratory to confirm amphetamine(s) present or if presumptive results are false positive.

Description of Procedure (80326)

A qualitative definitive GC/MS analysis for amphetamine and methamphetamine is performed. Any of the instrumental techniques that are defined as definitive may be used. These are high-complexity tests, such as LC-MS/MS or GC/MS. Exact methodology varies by testing facility, but all are instrumental techniques with the ability to specifically identify individual drugs and metabolites, if tested, within a class and rule out interfering drugs and other substances. See descriptions of definitive tests in the Definitive Drug Testing introductory guidelines. Results indicate the presence of amphetamine. The patient indicates use of lisdexamfetamine, a prescription medication that is metabolized to amphetamine. Illicit drug use is ruled out.

🩺 Clinical Example (80327)

A physician practicing at a pain management clinic is treating a patient presenting with chronic pain of neuropathic etiology, for which the patient has been prescribed chronic opioid therapy and anticonvulsant/ antidepressant adjuvant medications for several months. The patient also reports symptoms of depression and other signs of testosterone deficiency.

Description of Procedure (80327)

A definitive, quantitative LC-MS/MS analysis is ordered for 12 (code 80328; if 1 or 2 ordered, code 80327) common anabolic steroids. Any of the instrumental techniques that are defined as definitive may be used. These are high-complexity tests, such as LC-MS/MS or GC/MS. Exact methodology varies by testing facility, but all are instrumental techniques with the ability to specifically identify individual drugs and metabolites, if tested, within a class and rule out interfering drugs and other substances. Steroid analysis indicates the use of bolasterone. Patient is advised that the use of this drug is contraindicated with other prescribed medications. Patient is advised to discontinue use of this steroid and is required to undergo more frequent testing as a condition of continued treatment.

🩺 Clinical Example (80328)

A physician practicing at a pain management clinic is treating a patient presenting with chronic pain of neuropathic etiology, for which the patient has been prescribed chronic opioid therapy and anticonvulsant/antidepressant adjuvant medications for several months. The patient also reports symptoms of depression and other signs of testosterone deficiency.

Description of Procedure (80328)

A definitive, quantitative LC-MS/MS analysis is ordered for 12 (code 80328; if 1 or 2 ordered, code 80327) common anabolic steroids. Any of the instrumental techniques that are defined as definitive may be used. These are high complexity tests, such as LC-MS/MS or GC/MS. Exact methodology varies by testing facility, but all are instrumental techniques with the ability to specifically identify individual drugs and metabolites, if tested, within a class and rule out interfering drugs and other substances. Steroid analysis indicates the use of bolasterone. Patient is advised that the use of this drug is contraindicated with other prescribed medications. Patient is advised to discontinue use of this steroid and is required to undergo more frequent testing as a condition of continued treatment.

🩺 Clinical Example (80329)

An 88-year-old male with severe arthritis and mild to moderate dementia is treated with naproxen and hydrocodone but reports increased pain. Before changing medication therapy, physician orders testing for hydrocodone (80361) and naproxen to confirm medication compliance.

⃠=Modifier 51 Exempt   ⊙=Moderate Sedation   ✚=Add-on Code   𝒩=FDA approval pending

Description of Procedure (80329)

A definitive, quantitative LC-MS/MS analysis is ordered for naproxen (code 80350; if more than one analyte was ordered, codes 80330-80331) and hydrocodone. Any of the instrumental techniques that are defined as definitive may be used. These are high-complexity tests, such as LC-MS/MS or GC/MS. Exact methodology varies by testing facility, but all are instrumental techniques with the ability to specifically identify individual drugs and metabolites, if tested, within a class and rule out interfering drugs and other substances. See descriptions of definitive tests in the Definitive Drug Testing introductory guidelines. Results indicate the presence of hydrocodone and absence of naproxen. Patient is advised that he must use both drugs in order to obtain pain relief and reports improved pain control on next visit.

Clinical Example (80330)

An 88-year-old male with severe arthritis and mild to moderate dementia is treated with naproxen and hydrocodone but reports increased pain. Before changing medication therapy, physician orders testing for hydrocodone (80361) and naproxen to confirm medication compliance.

Description of Procedure (80330)

A definitive, quantitative LC-MS/MS analysis is ordered for naproxen (code 80350; if more than one analyte was ordered, codes 80330-80331) and hydrocodone. Any of the instrumental techniques that are defined as definitive may be used. These are high-complexity tests, such as LC-MS/MS or GC/MS. Exact methodology varies by testing facility, but all are instrumental techniques with the ability to specifically identify individual drugs and metabolites, if tested, within a class and rule out interfering drugs and other substances. See descriptions of definitive tests in the Definitive Drug Testing introductory guidelines. Results indicate the presence of hydrocodone and absence of naproxen. Patient is advised that he must use both drugs in order to obtain pain relief and reports improved pain control on next visit.

Clinical Example (80331)

An 88-year-old male with severe arthritis and mild to moderate dementia is treated with naproxen and hydrocodone but reports increased pain. Before changing medication therapy, physician orders testing for hydrocodone (80361) and naproxen to confirm medication compliance.

Description of Procedure (80331)

A definitive, quantitative LC-MS/MS analysis is ordered for naproxen (code 80350; if more than one analyte was ordered, codes 80330-80331) and hydrocodone. Any of the instrumental techniques that are defined as definitive may be used. These are high-complexity tests, such as LC-MS/MS or GC/MS. Exact methodology varies by testing facility, but all are instrumental techniques with the ability to specifically identify individual drugs and metabolites, if tested, within a class and rule out interfering drugs and other substances. See descriptions of definitive tests in the Definitive Drug Testing introductory guidelines. Results indicate the presence of hydrocodone and absence of naproxen. Patient is advised that he must use both drugs in order to obtain pain relief and reports improved pain control on next visit.

Clinical Example (80332)

A 68-year-old male with diabetic neuropathic pain is prescribed duloxetine. Patient reports unresolved pain. Patient scores negative opioid risk. Before changing medication therapy, physician orders testing for duloxetine to confirm medication compliance.

Description of Procedure (80332)

A quantitative, definitive LC-MS/MS analysis for duloxetine and metabolite is performed (code 80332; if more than 1 or 2 drugs ordered, codes 80333-80334). Any of the instrumental techniques that are defined as definitive may be used. These are high-complexity tests, such as LC-MS/MS or GC/MS. Exact methodology varies by testing facility, but all are instrumental techniques with the ability to specifically identify individual drugs and metabolites, if tested, within a class and rule out interfering drugs and other substances. See descriptions of definitive tests in the Definitive Drug Testing introductory guidelines. Results indicate the presence of duloxetine and its primary urinary metabolite. Patient appears to be taking medication as directed. Physician considers hydrocodone for breakthrough pain.

Clinical Example (80333)

A 68-year-old male with diabetic neuropathic pain is prescribed duloxetine. Patient reports unresolved pain. Patient scores negative opioid risk. Before changing medication therapy, physician orders testing for duloxetine to confirm medication compliance.

Description of Procedure (80333)

A quantitative, definitive LC-MS/MS analysis for duloxetine and metabolite is performed (code 80332; if more than 1 or 2 drugs ordered, codes 80333-80334). Any of the instrumental techniques that are defined as definitive may be used. These are high-complexity tests, such as LC-MS/MS or GC/MS. Exact methodology varies by testing facility, but all are instrumental techniques with the ability to specifically identify individual drugs and metabolites, if tested, within a class and rule out interfering drugs and other substances. See descriptions of definitive tests in the Definitive Drug Testing introductory guidelines. Results indicate the presence of duloxetine and its primary urinary metabolite. Patient appears to be taking medication as directed. Physician considers hydrocodone for breakthrough pain.

Clinical Example (80334)

A 68-year-old male with diabetic neuropathic pain is prescribed duloxetine. Patient reports unresolved pain. Patient scores negative opioid risk. Before changing medication therapy, physician orders testing for duloxetine to confirm medication compliance.

Description of Procedure (80334)

A quantitative, definitive LC-MS/MS analysis for duloxetine and metabolite is performed (code 80332; if more than 1 or 2 drugs ordered, codes 80333-80334).

⃠=Modifier 51 Exempt   ⊙=Moderate Sedation   ✚=Add-on Code   𝒩=FDA approval pending

Any of the instrumental techniques that are defined as definitive may be used. These are high-complexity tests, such as LC-MS/MS or GC/MS. Exact methodology varies by testing facility, but all are instrumental techniques with the ability to specifically identify individual drugs and metabolites, if tested, within a class and rule out interfering drugs and other substances. See descriptions of definitive tests in the Definitive Drug Testing introductory guidelines. Results indicate the presence of duloxetine and its primary urinary metabolite. Patient appears to be taking medication as directed. Physician considers hydrocodone for breakthrough pain.

Clinical Example (80335)

A 68-year-old male with diabetic neuropathic pain is prescribed amitriptyline and hydrocodone. Patient reports unresolved pain and requests a stronger opioid. Patient scores positive opioid risk. Before changing medication therapy, physician orders testing for amitriptyline (80335) and opiates (80361) to confirm medication compliance.

Description of Procedure (80335)

A definitive LC-MS/MS analysis for amitriptyline and nortripyline is performed. Any of the instrumental techniques that are defined as definitive may be used. These are high-complexity tests, such as LC-MS/MS or GC/MS. Exact methodology varies by testing facility, but all are instrumental techniques with the ability to specifically identify individual drugs and metabolites, if tested, within a class and rule out interfering drugs and other substances. See descriptions of definitive tests in the Definitive Drug Testing introductory guidelines. Results arc negative for amitriptyline and its primary urinary metabolite, nortriptyline. Use of hydrocodone is confirmed. Patient admits not taking antidepressant medication, amitriptyline hydrochloride, due to unpleasant side effects. Physician takes patient off amitriptyline hydrochloride and prescribes a different antidepressant medication, duloxetine hydrochloride, in its place.

Clinical Example (80336)

A 68-year-old male with diabetic neuropathic pain is prescribed amitriptyline and hydrocodone. Patient reports unresolved pain and requests a stronger opioid. Patient scores positive opioid risk. Before changing medication therapy, physician orders testing for amitriptyline (80335) and opiates (80361) to confirm medication compliance.

Description of Procedure (80336)

A definitive LC-MS/MS analysis for amitriptyline and nortripyline is performed. Any of the instrumental techniques that are defined as definitive may be used. These are high-complexity tests, such as LC-MS/MS or GC/MS. Exact methodology varies by testing facility, but all are instrumental techniques with the ability to specifically identify individual drugs and metabolites, if tested, within a class and rule out interfering drugs and other substances. See descriptions of definitive tests in the Definitive Drug Testing introductory guidelines. Results are negative for amitriptyline and its primary urinary metabolite, nortriptyline. Use of hydrocodone is confirmed. Patient admits not taking antidepressant medication, amitriptyline hydrochloride, due to unpleasant side effects. Physician takes patient off amitriptyline hydrochloride and prescribes a different antidepressant medication, duloxetine hydrochloride, in its place.

Clinical Example (80337)

A 68-year-old male with diabetic neuropathic pain is prescribed amitriptyline and hydrocodone. Patient reports unresolved pain and requests a stronger opioid. Patient scores positive opioid risk. Before changing medication therapy, physician orders testing for amitriptyline (80335) and opiates (80361) to confirm medication compliance.

Description of Procedure (80337)

A definitive LC-MS/MS analysis for amitriptyline and nortripyline is performed. Any of the instrumental techniques that are defined as definitive may be used. These are high-complexity tests, such as LC-MS/MS or GC/MS. Exact methodology varies by testing facility, but all are instrumental techniques with the ability to specifically identify individual drugs and metabolites, if tested, within a class and rule out interfering drugs and other substances. See descriptions of definitive tests in the Definitive Drug Testing introductory guidelines. Results are negative for amitriptyline and its primary urinary metabolite, nortriptyline. Use of hydrocodone is confirmed. Patient admits not taking antidepressant medication, amitriptyline hydrochloride, due to unpleasant side effects. Physician takes patient off amitriptyline hydrochloride and prescribes a different antidepressant medication, duloxetine hydrochloride, in its place.

Clinical Example (80338)

A 68-year-old male is prescribed bupropion by his psychiatrist for depression. Patient reports worsening depression and debilitating side effects, including insomnia. Patient has asked for a different antidepressant medication to treat the insomnia.

Description of Procedure (80338)

A quantitative, definitive LC-MS/MS analysis for hydroxybupropion is performed. Any of the instrumental techniques that are defined as definitive may be used. These are high-complexity tests, such as LC-MS/MS or GC/MS. Exact methodology varies by testing facility, but all are instrumental techniques with the ability to specifically identify individual drugs and metabolites, if tested, within a class and rule out interfering drugs and other substances. See descriptions of definitive tests in the Definitive Drug Testing introductory guidelines. Results indicate the absence of hydroxybupropion, the major urinary metabolite of buproprion. Patient appears not to be using prescribed mediation as directed and may be seeking additional medications due to a previously unrecognized substance abuse disorder. Alternative medication therapy is considered.

Clinical Example (80339)

A 48-year-old female is prescribed carbamazepine by her psychiatrist as part of a multidrug therapy for this patient's psychosis. Worsening symptoms and a history of medication noncompliance suggest the patient is not using her medications as directed. The physician orders testing for the patient's medications, including carbamazepine, in order to explain and treat the new symptoms.

⃠=Modifier 51 Exempt ⊙=Moderate Sedation ✚=Add-on Code ✗=FDA approval pending

Description of Procedure (80339)

A definitive, quantitative LC-MS/MS analysis is ordered for carbamazepine and temazepam (80346). Any of the instrumental techniques that are defined as definitive may be used. These are high-complexity tests, such as LC-MS/MS or GC/MS. Exact methodology varies by testing facility, but all are instrumental techniques with the ability to specifically identify individual drugs and metabolites, if tested, within a class and rule out interfering drugs and other substances. See descriptions of definitive tests in the Definitive Drug Testing introductory guidelines. Results indicate the patient is not using her prescribed carbamezepine but is using temazepam as directed. Patient later reports side effects with carbamazepine. Physician considers alternative medications with fewer side effects.

Clinical Example (80340)

A 48-year-old female is prescribed carbamazepine by her psychiatrist as part of a multidrug therapy for this patient's psychosis. Worsening symptoms and a history of medication noncompliance suggest the patient is not using her medications as directed. The physician orders testing for the patient's medications, including carbamazepine, in order to explain and treat the new symptoms.

Description of Procedure (80340)

A definitive, quantitative LC-MS/MS analysis is ordered for carbamazepine and temazepam (80340). Any of the instrumental techniques that are defined as definitive may be used. These are high-complexity tests, such as LC-MS/MS or GC/MS. Exact methodology varies by testing facility, but all are instrumental techniques with the ability to specifically identify individual drugs and metabolites, if tested, within a class and rule out interfering drugs and other substances. See descriptions of definitive tests in the Definitive Drug Testing introductory guidelines. Results indicate the patient is not using her prescribed carbamezepine but is using temazepam as directed. Patient later reports side effects with carbamazepine. Physician considers alternative medications with fewer side effects.

Clinical Example (80341)

A 48-year-old female is prescribed carbamazepine by her psychiatrist as part of a multidrug therapy for this patient's psychosis. Worsening symptoms and a history of medication noncompliance suggest the patient is not using her medications as directed. The physician orders testing for the patient's medications, including carbamazepine, in order to explain and treat the new symptoms.

Description of Procedure (80341)

A definitive, quantitative LC-MS/MS analysis is ordered for carbamazepine and temazepam (80346). Any of the instrumental techniques that are defined as definitive may be used. These are high-complexity tests, such as LC-MS/MS or GC/MS. Exact methodology varies by testing facility, but all are instrumental techniques with the ability to specifically identify individual drugs and metabolites, if tested, within a class and rule out interfering drugs and other substances. See descriptions of definitive tests in the Definitive Drug Testing introductory guidelines. Results indicate the patient is not using her prescribed carbamezepine but is using temazepam as directed. Patient later reports side effects with carbamazepine. Physician considers alternative medications with fewer side effects.

Clinical Example (80342)

A 32-year-old male with a history of schizophrenia is a new patient. The patient reports his symptoms are not well controlled, confirmed during a psychological evaluation. The physician believes the patient's self-reported medication use is not reliable and orders a battery of tests to determine the patient's current use of anti-psychotic medications.

Description of Procedure (80342)

A definitive, quantitative LC-MS/MS analysis is ordered for the patient's known prescribed medications: clozapine, quetiapine, thorazine, and loxapine. Any of the instrumental techniques that are defined as definitive may be used. These are high-complexity tests, such as LC-MS/MS or GC/MS. Exact methodology varies by testing facility, but all are instrumental techniques with the ability to specifically identify individual drugs and metabolites, if tested, within a class and rule out interfering drugs and other substances. See descriptions of definitive tests in the Definitive Drug Testing introductory guidelines. Results indicate the absence of all prescribed medications, explaining the patient's uncontrolled schizophrenia.

Clinical Example (80343)

A 32-year-old male with a history of schizophrenia is a new patient. The patient reports his symptoms are not well controlled, confirmed during a psychological evaluation. The physician believes the patient's self-reported medication use is not reliable and orders a battery of tests to determine the patient's current use of anti-psychotic medications.

Description of Procedure (80343)

A definitive, quantitative LC-MS/MS analysis is ordered for the patient's known prescribed medications: clozapine, quetiapine, thorazine, and loxapine. Any of the instrumental techniques that are defined as definitive may be used. These are high-complexity tests, such as LC-MS/MS or GC/MS. Exact methodology varies by testing facility, but all are instrumental techniques with the ability to specifically identify individual drugs and metabolites, if tested, within a class and rule out interfering drugs and other substances. See descriptions of definitive tests in the Definitive Drug Testing introductory guidelines. Results indicate the absence of all prescribed medications, explaining the patient's uncontrolled schizophrenia.

Clinical Example (80344)

A 32-year-old male with a history of schizophrenia is a new patient. The patient reports his symptoms are not well controlled, confirmed during a psychological evaluation. The physician believes the patient's self-reported medication use is not reliable and orders a battery of tests to determine the patient's current use of anti-psychotic medications.

Description of Procedure (80344)

A definitive, quantitative LC-MS/MS analysis is ordered for the patient's known prescribed medications: clozapine, quetiapine, thorazine, and loxapine. Any of the instrumental techniques that are defined as definitive may be used. These are high-complexity tests, such as LC-MS/MS or GC/MS. Exact methodology varies by testing facility, but all are instrumental techniques with the ability to

⃠=Modifier 51 Exempt   ⊙=Moderate Sedation   ✚=Add-on Code   𝑵=FDA approval pending specifically identify individual drugs and metabolites, if tested, within a class and rule out interfering drugs and other substances. See descriptions of definitive tests in the Definitive Drug Testing introductory guidelines. Results indicate the absence of all prescribed medications, explaining the patient's uncontrolled schizophrenia.

Clinical Example (80345)

A 58-year-old female with post-accident severe low back pain is prescribed 20 mg controlled release oxycodone twice per day. Initial screen at the physician's office gives a barbiturates qualitative presumptive positive using a direct observation dipstick device. The patient is not prescribed any barbiturates. Before the prescription refill is issued, a urine specimen is sent to the laboratory to confirm barbiturate(s) presence or if presumptive results are false positive.

Description of Procedure (80345)

A definitive GC/MS analysis for five common barbiturates is performed. Any of the instrumental techniques that are defined as definitive may be use. These are high-complexity tests, such as LC-MS/MS or GC/MS. Exact methodology varies by testing facility, but all are instrumental techniques with the ability to specifically identify individual drugs and metabolites, if tested, within a class and rule out interfering drugs and other substances. See descriptions of definitive tests in the Definitive Drug Testing introductory guidelines. Results indicate the presence of butalbital. The patient was able to produce a prescription from another physician who prescribed her the butalbital/acetaminophen/caffeine tablets. The use of this definitive test was necessary to properly identify the drug present. With the source of the barbiturate confirmed, the clinician is able to refill the oxycodone prescription.

Clinical Example (80346)

A 58-year-old female with severe fibromyalgia pain is prescribed 20 mg controlled release oxycodone and 0.5 mg clonazepam twice per day and tests positive for opiates using a qualitative, presumptive direct observation dipstick device. The qualitative dipstick device is negative for benzodiazepines. The patient denies any deviation from dosing instructions for both oxycodone and clonazepam. Before the prescription refill is issued, a urine specimen is sent to the laboratory to confirm the clonazepam metabolite is present or if presumptive results are false negative.

Description of Procedure (80346)

A quantitative, definitive GC/MS analysis for six common benzodiazepines is performed. Any of the instrumental techniques that are defined as definitive may be use. These are high-complexity tests, such as LC-MS/MS or GC/MS. Exact methodology varies by testing facility, but all are instrumental techniques with the ability to specifically identify individual drugs and metabolites, if tested, within a class and rule out interfering drugs and other substances. See descriptions of definitive tests in the Definitive Drug Testing introductory guidelines.

Results indicate the presence of 7-aminoclonazepam, consistent with the use of clonazepam, a benzodiazepine that is not detected using the dipstick device. From these results, the clinician refills the prescription.

Clinical Example (80347)

A 58-year-old female with severe fibromyalgia pain is prescribed 20 mg controlled release oxycodone and 0.5 mg clonazepam twice per day and tests positive for opiates using a qualitative, presumptive direct observation dipstick device. The qualitative dipstick device is negative for benzodiazepines. The patient denies any deviation from dosing instructions for both oxycodone and clonazepam. Before the prescription refill is issued, a urine specimen is sent to the laboratory to confirm the clonazepam metabolite is present or if presumptive results are false negative.

Description of Procedure (80347)

A quantitative, definitive GC/MS analysis for six common benzodiazepines is performed. Any of the instrumental techniques that are defined as definitive may be use. These are high-complexity tests, such as LC-MS/MS or GC/MS. Exact methodology varies by testing facility, but all are instrumental techniques with the ability to specifically identify individual drugs and metabolites, if tested, within a class and rule out interfering drugs and other substances. See descriptions of definitive tests in the Definitive Drug Testing introductory guidelines.

Results indicate the presence of 7-aminoclonazepam, consistent with the use of clonazepam, a benzodiazepine that is not detected using the dipstick device. From these results, the clinician refills the prescription.

Clinical Example (80348)

A 35-year-old male, a new patient, with severe pain from inflammatory bowel disease requests a continuation of buprenorphine transdermal treatment. Patient scores positive on an opioid risk evaluation and admits to past drug abuse with heroin. State guidelines require drug test and PDMP review prior to writing a new prescription for controlled pain medications. In-office qualitative direct optical observation drug screen (dipstick) is negative for buprenorphine, although patient indicates the buprenorphine is providing pain relief. A urine specimen is sent to the laboratory to confirm medication compliance with detection of buprenorphine metabolite.

Description of Procedure (80348)

A definitive LC-MS/MS analysis for buprenorphine and norbuprenorphine is performed. Any of the instrumental techniques that are defined as definitive may be used. These are high-complexity tests, such as LC-MS/MS or GC/MS. Exact methodology varies by testing facility, but all are instrumental techniques with the ability to specifically identify individual drugs and metabolites, if tested, within a class and rule out interfering drugs and other substances. See descriptions of definitive tests in the Definitive Drug Testing introductory guidelines. Buprenorphine (2 ng/ml) and norbuprenorphine (5 ng/ml) are detected by LC-MS/MS. Transdermal buprenorphine is eliminated in low concentrations and generally not detectable with a point-of-care device. Results indicate patient is receiving buprenorphine through the patch, and the buprenorphine prescription is refilled.

Clinical Example (80349)

A 38-year-old male with severe low-back pain is prescribed 20 mg twice per day controlled release oxycodone. Using a direct observation dipstick device, urine tested presumptive positive for marijuana metabolite. The patient is not prescribed medical marijuana but does admit to recent use of nonprescription ibuprofen. Before the prescription refill is issued, a urine specimen is sent to the laboratory to confirm marijuana metabolite presence or if presumptive results are false positive.

Description of Procedure (80349)

A definitive, quantitative LC-MS/MS analysis is ordered for carboxy-THC. Any of the instrumental techniques that are defined as definitive may be used. These are high-complexity tests, such as LC-MS/MS or GC/MS. Exact methodology varies by testing facility, but all are instrumental techniques with the ability to specifically identify individual drugs and metabolites, if tested, within a class and rule out interfering drugs and other substances. See descriptions of definitive tests in the Definitive Drug Testing introductory guidelines. Results are negative for carboxy-THC, indicating the patient was not using marijuana. Illicit drug use is ruled out.

Clinical Example (80350)

A 35-year-old male presents at the emergency department in a severely agitated state, anxious, and with high blood pressure, nausea, and vomiting. Friends reported he had used some type of designer drug, possibly "Spice." A urine specimen is sent to the laboratory to confirm synthetic cannabinoids.

Description of Procedure (80350)

A definitive, quantitative LC-MS/MS analysis is ordered for synthetic cannabinoids. Any of the instrumental techniques that are defined as definitive may be used. These are high-complexity tests, such as LC-MS/MS or GC/MS. Exact methodology varies by testing facility, but all are instrumental techniques with the ability to specifically identify individual drugs and metabolites, if tested, within a class and rule out interfering drugs and other substances. See descriptions of definitive tests in the Definitive Drug Testing introductory guidelines. Results indicate use of the synthetic cannabinoids AM-2201 and JWH-018.

Clinical Example (80351)

A 35-year-old male presents at the emergency department in a severely agitated state, anxious, and with high blood pressure, nausea, and vomiting. Friends reported he had used some type of designer drug, possibly "Spice." A urine specimen is sent to the laboratory to confirm synthetic cannabinoids.

Description of Procedure (80351)

A definitive, quantitative LC-MS/MS analysis is ordered for synthetic cannabinoids. Any of the instrumental techniques that are defined as definitive may be used. These are high-complexity tests, such as LC-MS/MS or GC/MS. Exact methodology varies by testing facility, but all are instrumental techniques with the ability to specifically identify individual drugs and metabolites, if tested, within a class and rule out interfering drugs and other substances. See descriptions of definitive tests in the Definitive Drug Testing introductory guidelines. Results indicate use of the synthetic cannabinoids AM-2201 and JWH-018.

Clinical Example (80352)

A 35-year-old male presents at the emergency department in a severely agitated state, anxious, and with high blood pressure, nausea, and vomiting. Friends reported he had used some type of designer drug, possibly "Spice." A urine specimen is sent to the laboratory to confirm synthetic cannabinoids.

Description of Procedure (80352)

A definitive, quantitative LC-MS/MS analysis is ordered for synthetic cannabinoids. Any of the instrumental techniques that are defined as definitive may be used. These are high-complexity tests, such as LC-MS/MS or GC/MS. Exact methodology varies by testing facility, but all are instrumental techniques with the ability to specifically identify individual drugs and metabolites, if tested, within a class and rule out interfering drugs and other substances. See descriptions of definitive tests in the Definitive Drug Testing introductory guidelines. Results indicate use of the synthetic cannabinoids AM-2201 and JWH-018.

Clinical Example (80353)

A 43-year-old male with post-accident severe low back pain requests continuation of buprenorphine transdermal treatment. Patient scores positive on an opioid risk evaluation and admits to past drug abuse with multiple designer drugs. Patient was counseled 60 days ago for confirmed positive cocaine metabolite. An in-office qualitative direct optical observation drug screen (dipstick) is presumptive positive for cocaine metabolite. A urine specimen is sent to the laboratory to confirm cocaine metabolite presence to establish cause. Once cocaine metabolite presence is confirmed, provider ceases patient relationship and refers patient for substance abuse treatment.

Description of Procedure (80353)

A definitive, quantitative LC-MS/MS analysis is ordered for benzoylecgonine, a cocaine metabolite. Any of the instrumental techniques that are defined as definitive may be used. These are high-complexity tests, such as LC-MS/MS or GC/MS. Exact methodology varies by testing facility, but all are instrumental techniques with the ability to specifically identify individual drugs and metabolites, if tested, within a class and rule out interfering drugs and other substances. See descriptions of definitive tests in the Definitive Drug Testing introductory guidelines. Results are positive for benzoylecgonine, confirming illicit drug use.

Clinical Example (80354)

A 66-year-old female with post-accident severe low-back pain presents for routine office visit for monitoring of fentanyl transdermal treatment. Patient scores negative on an opioid risk evaluation. Patient reports multiple lost patches (x5) over the past month and is not wearing a patch at time of the office visit. Patient explains that a patch was used the previous day. Medication noncompliance and drug diversion are suspected. A urine specimen is sent to the laboratory to assist with verification of patient history and to determine presence of fentanyl and metabolite.

Description of Procedure (80354)

A definitive GC/MS analysis for fentanyl and norfentanyl is performed. Any of the instrumental techniques that are defined as definitive may be used. These are high-complexity tests, such as LC-MS/MS or GC/MS. Exact methodology varies by testing facility, but all are instrumental techniques with the ability to specifically identify individual drugs and metabolites, if tested, within a class and rule out interfering drugs and other substances. See descriptions of definitive tests in the Definitive Drug Testing introductory guidelines. Fentanyl or norfentanyl were not detected, indicating the patient may not be using fentanyl as directed.

Clinical Example (80355)

A 68-year-old male with diabetic neuropathic pain is prescribed gabapentin and oxycodone. Patient reports unresolved pain and requests a stronger opioid. Patient scores positive on an opioid risk evaluation. Before changing medication therapy, physician orders testing for gabapentin and opiates (80361) to confirm medication compliance.

Description of Procedure (80355)

A definitive LC-MS/MS analysis for gabapentin is performed. Any of the instrumental techniques that are defined as definitive may be used. These are high-complexity tests, such as LC-MS/MS or GC/MS. Exact methodology varies by testing facility, but all are instrumental techniques with the ability to specifically identify individual drugs and metabolites, if tested, within a class and rule out interfering drugs and other substances. See descriptions of definitive tests in the Definitive Drug Testing introductory guidelines. Results are negative for gabapentin. Use of oxycodone is confirmed. Patient admits not taking gabapentin due to unpleasant side effects. Physician takes patient off gabapentin and prescribes pregabalin in its place.

Clinical Example (80356)

A 24-year-old male with chronic back pain that is treated with oxycodone tests positive for opiates and oxycodone using a qualitative presumptive, direct-observation dipstick device. Patient scores positive on an opioid risk evaluation but denies any recent drug abuse. State guidelines require drug test and PDMP review prior to issue any prescription for controlled pain medications. A urine specimen is sent to the laboratory to confirm which opiate is actually present (80361 and 80365).

Description of Procedure (80356)

A definitive analysis for 6-acetylmorphine, opiates, and oxycodone is performed. Any of the instrumental techniques that are defined as definitive may be used. These are high-complexity tests, such as LC-MS/MS. Exact methodology varies by testing facility, but all are instrumental techniques with the ability to specifically identify individual drugs and metabolites, if tested, within a class and rule out interfering drugs and other substances. See descriptions of definitive tests in the Definitive Drug Testing introductory guidelines. Results indicate the presence of 6-acetylmorphine (283 ng/ml), morphine (24,382 ng/ml), codeine (352 ng/ml), oxycodone (5231 ng/ml), noroxycodone (6832 ng/ml), and oxymorphone (963 ng/ml), indicating use of heroin and oxycodone. Refer patient for substance abuse treatment.

Clinical Example (80357)

A 19-year-old female is admitted to the emergency department incoherent, delirious, and disoriented. Friends thought she had "taken something" from the veterinary clinic where she was employed. A urine specimen sent to hospital laboratory for qualitative drug screen tested negative, including for amphetamines. The urine specimen is sent to the laboratory to confirm the use of ketamine.

Description of Procedure (80357)

A definitive, quantitative LC-MS/MS analysis for ketamine is performed. Any of the instrumental techniques that are defined as definitive may be used. These are high-complexity tests, such as LC-MS/MS or GC/MS. Exact methodology varies by testing facility, but all are instrumental techniques with the ability to specifically identify individual drugs and metabolites, if tested, within a class and rule out interfering drugs and other substances. See descriptions of definitive tests in the Definitive Drug Testing introductory guidelines. Ketamine was detected. The patient later admitted taking the animal tranquilizer from the clinic where she was employed.

Clinical Example (80358)

A 37-year-old male with severe fibromyalgia pain is prescribed 10 mg methadone orally twice per day. Urine tests are positive for methadone and oxycodone using a presumptive direct-observation dipstick device. Patient scores positive on an opioid risk evaluation. Before the prescription refill is issued, a urine specimen is sent to the laboratory to confirm presence of methadone and oxycodone (80365 and 80358) and to assist with ruling out prescription noncompliance or diversion.

Description of Procedure (80358)

A quantitative, definitive analysis for methadone, methadone metabolite, and oxycodone and metabolites is performed. Any of the instrumental techniques that are defined as definitive may be used. These are high-complexity tests, such as LC-MS/MS or GC/MS. Exact methodology varies by testing facility, but all are instrumental techniques with the ability to specifically identify individual drugs and metabolites, if tested, within a class and rule out interfering drugs and other substances. See descriptions of definitive tests in the Definitive Drug Testing introductory guidelines. Results indicate the presence of methadone (86,000 ng/ml) and the absence of methadone metabolite. The median urinary concentration for patients on methadone is 450 ng/ml. Oxycodone (3260 ng/ml), noroxycodone (4236 ng/ml), and oxymorphone (885 ng/ml) were also identified, but oxycodone was not prescribed. The absence of methadone metabolite and the high level of methadone suggest the patient spiked the urine with methadone. Patient indicates he "borrowed" oxycodone from a neighbor. Refer patient for substance abuse treatment.

Clinical Example (80359)

A 22-year-old female is admitted to the emergency department with the following symptoms: tachycardia, severe hyperthermia, visual hallucinations, and disorientation. The patient seized, lost consciousness, and died soon after admission. Friends thought she had "taken something" during a rave party where the police reported "Ecstasy" had been confiscated. A urine specimen sent to the hospital laboratory for qualitative drug screen tested negative, including amphetamines. The urine specimen is sent to the laboratory to confirm the use of MDMA (3,4-methylene-dioxy-N-methylamphetamine) and related compounds.

Description of Procedure (80359)

A definitive, quantitative LC-MS/MS analysis for MDMA, MDA (3,4-methylene-dioxyamphetamine), and other club drugs is performed. Any of the instrumental techniques that are defined as definitive may be used. These are high-complexity tests, such as LC-MS/MS or GC/MS. Exact methodology varies by testing facility, but all are instrumental techniques with the ability to specifically identify individual drugs and metabolites, if tested, within a class and rule out interfering drugs and other substances. See descriptions of definitive tests in the Definitive Drug Testing introductory guidelines. MDMA and its metabolite MDA were detected.

Clinical Example (80360)

A 24-year-old female, with attention-deficit/hyperactivity disorder and prescribed 60 mg per day controlled-release methylphenidate, tested negative for urine methylphenidate last month. The patient is scheduled for office visit and prescription renewal. There is suspicion that patient may be "diverting" the medication. Before the prescription refill is issued, a urine specimen is sent to the laboratory to confirm if methylphenidate metabolite is present.

Description of Procedure (80360)

A quantitative definitive GC/MS analysis for methylphenidate metabolite (ritalinic acid) is performed. Any of the instrumental techniques that are defined as definitive may be used. These are high-complexity tests, such as LC-MS/MS or GC/MS. Exact methodology varies by testing facility, but all are instrumental techniques with the ability to specifically identify individual drugs and metabolites, if tested, within a class and rule out interfering drugs and other substances. See descriptions of definitive tests in the Definitive Drug Testing introductory guidelines. Results indicate no presence of the methylphenidate metabolite. The patient indicates "friends" had stolen her medication. Further discussion with the patient is warranted prior to issuance of a prescription refill.

Clinical Example (80361)

A 41-year-old female with post-accident severe neck pain is prescribed 5 mg hydrocodone every 4 hours to 6 hours and tested positive for opiates using a qualitative, presumptive, direct-observation dipstick device. Patient scores positive on an opioid-risk evaluation but denies any past drug abuse. State guidelines require drug test and PDMP review prior to issuing any prescription for controlled pain medications. A urine specimen is sent to the laboratory to confirm which opiate is actually present.

Description of Procedure (80361)

A quantitative, definitive GC/MS analysis for six common opiates is ordered. Any of the instrumental techniques that are defined as definitive may be used. These are high-complexity tests, such as LC-MS/MS. Exact methodology varies by testing facility, but all are instrumental techniques with the ability to specifically identify individual drugs and metabolites, if tested, within a class and rule out interfering drugs and other substances. See descriptions of definitive tests in the Definitive Drug Testing introductory guidelines. Results indicate the presence of morphine at 22,352 ng/ml and 150 ng/ml hydromorphone, both consistent with prescription morphine or heroin use. Codeine, hydrocodone, and norhydrocodone were not detected. The quantitative results are above any possible dietary sources of morphine. Patient is considered not compliant because the opiate found was not consistent with the prescribed medication, and the prescribed hydrocodone was not found.

Clinical Example (80362)

A 73-year-old female is prescribed pentazocine for severe arthritis pain. During a routine office visit, the patient indicates she is not getting much relief from using this drug. Patient scores negative on an opioid-risk evaluation and denies any past drug abuse. A urine specimen is sent to the laboratory to confirm the patient is taking the drug as prescribed.

Description of Procedure (80362)

A qualitative, definitive GC/MS analysis for pentazocine is performed. Any of the instrumental techniques that are defined as definitive may be used. These are high-complexity tests, such as LC-MS/MS or GC/MS. Exact methodology varies by testing facility, but all are instrumental techniques with the ability to specifically identify individual drugs and metabolites, if tested, within a class and rule out interfering drugs and other substances. See descriptions of definitive tests in the Definitive Drug Testing introductory guidelines. Results indicate the presence of pentazocine. Patient appears to be taking the drug as prescribed. Physician considers alternative medications.

Clinical Example (80363)

A 73-year-old female is prescribed pentazocine for severe arthritis pain. During a routine office visit, the patient indicates she is not getting much relief from using this drug. Patient scores negative on an opioid-risk evaluation and denies any past drug abuse. A urine specimen is sent to the laboratory to confirm the patient is taking the drug as prescribed.

Description of Procedure (80363)

A qualitative, definitive GC/MS analysis for pentazocine is performed. Any of the instrumental techniques that are defined as definitive may be used. These are high-complexity tests, such as LC-MS/MS or GC/MS. Exact methodology varies by testing facility, but all are instrumental techniques with the ability to specifically identify individual drugs and metabolites, if tested, within a class and rule out interfering drugs and other substances. See descriptions of definitive tests in the Definitive Drug Testing introductory guidelines. Results indicate the presence of pentazocine. Patient appears to be taking the drug as prescribed. Physician considers alternative medications.

Clinical Example (80364)

A 73-year-old female is prescribed pentazocine for severe arthritis pain. During a routine office visit, the patient indicates she is not getting much relief from using this drug. Patient scores negative on an opioid-risk evaluation and denies any past drug abuse. A urine specimen is sent to the laboratory to confirm the patient is taking the drug as prescribed.

Description of Procedure (80364)

A qualitative, definitive GC/MS analysis for pentazocine is performed. Any of the instrumental techniques that are defined as definitive may be used. These are high-complexity tests, such as LC-MS/MS or GC/MS. Exact methodology varies by testing facility, but all are instrumental techniques with the ability to specifically identify individual drugs and metabolites, if tested, within a class and rule out interfering drugs and other substances. See descriptions of definitive tests in the Definitive Drug Testing introductory guidelines. Results indicate the presence of pentazocine. Patient appears to be taking the drug as prescribed. Physician considers alternative medications.

Clinical Example (80365)

A 52-year-old male is on long-term oxycodone (80 mg/day) for unresolved severe pain following spinal surgery. Patient indicates pain has become intolerable and requests additional medications. Patient scores positive on an opioid-risk evaluation but denies any past drug abuse. State guidelines require drug test and PDMP review prior to issuing any prescription for controlled pain medications. A urine specimen is sent to the laboratory to confirm which opiate is actually present.

Description of Procedure (80365)

A quantitative, definitive GC/MS analysis for oxycodone is ordered. Any of the instrumental techniques that are defined as definitive may be used. These are high-complexity tests, such as LC-MS/MS. Exact methodology varies by testing facility, but all are instrumental techniques with the ability to specifically identify individual drugs and metabolites, if tested, within a class and rule out interfering drugs and other substances. See descriptions of definitive tests in the Definitive Drug Testing introductory guidelines. Results indicate the presence of oxycodone and metabolites. Patient is considered compliant. Other long-acting opioid medications and other therapies are evaluated for this patient.

Clinical Example (80366)

A 68-year-old male with diabetic neuropathic pain is prescribed pregabalin and oxycodone. Patient reports unresolved pain and requests a stronger opioid. Patient scores negative on an opioid-risk evaluation. Before increasing the oxycodone dose, physician orders testing for pregabalin (80366) and oxycodone (80365) to confirm medication compliance.

Description of Procedure (80366)

A definitive LC-MS/MS analysis for gabapentin and oxycodone is ordered. Any of the instrumental techniques that are defined as definitive may be used. These are high-complexity tests, such as LC-MS/MS or GC/MS. Exact methodology varies by testing facility, but all are instrumental techniques with the ability to specifically identify individual drugs and metabolites, if tested, within a class and rule out interfering drugs and other substances. See descriptions of definitive tests in the Definitive Drug Testing introductory guidelines. Results are negative for pregabalin and positive for oxycodone. Patient confides not taking pregabalin due to unpleasant side effects. Physician considers alternative medications to avoid use of a higher oxycodone dose.

 Clinical Example (80367)

A 41-year-old female with post-accident severe neck pain is prescribed 5 mg hydrocodone every 4 hours to 6 hours and tests negative for opiates and positive for propoxyphene using a qualitative, presumptive, direct-observation dipstick device. Patient scores positive on an opioid-risk evaluation but denies any past drug abuse. State guidelines require drug test and PDMP review prior to issuing any prescription for controlled pain medications. Because this patient is evaluated as moderate to high risk, a urine specimen is sent to the laboratory to confirm the absence of opiates (80361) and the presence of propoxyphene.

Description of Procedure (80367)

A quantitative, definitive GC/MS analysis for six common opiates and propoxyphene is ordered. Any of the instrumental techniques that are defined as definitive may be used. These are high-complexity tests, such as LC-MS/MS. Exact methodology varies by testing facility, but all are instrumental techniques with the ability to specifically identify individual drugs and metabolites, if tested, within a class and rule out interfering drugs and other substances. See descriptions of definitive tests in the Definitive Drug Testing introductory guidelines. Results indicate the absence of prescribed opiates and the presence of propoxyphene and norpropoxyphene. This indicates the patient has not used the prescribed hydrocodone within 48 hours to 72 hours but has used propoxyphene, an opioid that has not been legally available in the United States since November 2011. Patient is considered noncompliant.

 Clinical Example (80368)

A chronic pain patient is prescribed treatment with opioids and benzodiazepines. The patient presents with significant sedation for which tolerance does not develop. The patient is also obese and has a diagnosis of sleep apnea, which increases the risk for adverse respiratory effects associated with opioids. For this reason, the practitioner is concerned about concurrent use of other sedating agents, particularly zolpidem, promethazine, or antihistamines. Monitoring for zolpidem or other sedative-hypnotics may be indicated in this patient, as increased sedation/respiratory depression may also increase the risk of an adverse respiratory event (eg, respiratory depression).

　　⊘=Modifier 51 Exempt　⊙=Moderate Sedation　✚=Add-on Code　✵=FDA approval pending

Description of Procedure (80368)

A quantitative definitive LC-MS/MS analysis for zolpidem is performed. Any of the instrumental techniques that are defined as definitive may be used. These are high-complexity tests, such as LC-MS/MS or GC/MS. Exact methodology varies by testing facility, but all are instrumental techniques with the ability to specifically identify individual drugs and metabolites, if tested, within a class and rule out interfering drugs and other substances. Results are positive for zolpidem, and it is later determined that the patient has been supplied a sedative-hypnotic by a family member. Patient is advised zolpidem is contraindicated with the other medications prescribed and may be required to do more frequent and comprehensive testing as a condition of treatment.

Clinical Example (80369)

A 42-year-old male with persistent neck pain presents for a routine office visit. Patient reports continued discomfort. Patient scores negative on an opioid-risk evaluation. Drug testing is ordered to confirm compliance with prescribed cyclobenzaprine. A urine sample is sent to the laboratory to assist with verification of patient history.

Description of Procedure (80369)

A quantitative, definitive LC-MS/MS analysis for cyclobenzaprine is performed. Any of the instrumental techniques that are defined as definitive may be used. These are high-complexity tests, such as LC-MS/MS or GC/MS. Exact methodology varies by testing facility, but all are instrumental techniques with the ability to specifically identify individual drugs and metabolites, if tested, within a class and rule out interfering drugs and other substances. See descriptions of definitive tests in the Definitive Drug Testing introductory guidelines. Results indicate the absence of cyclobenzaprine. Patient reports he has not used the drug for the last three days due to the unpleasant side effects. Physician considers alternative medications.

Clinical Example (80370)

A 42-year-old male with persistent neck pain presents for a routine office visit. Patient reports continued discomfort. Patient scores negative on an opioid-risk evaluation. Drug testing is ordered to confirm compliance with prescribed cyclobenzaprine. A urine sample is sent to the laboratory to assist with verification of patient history.

Description of Procedure (80370)

A quantitative, definitive LC-MS/MS analysis for cyclobenzaprine is performed. Any of the instrumental techniques that are defined as definitive may be used. These are high-complexity tests, such as LC-MS/MS or GC/MS. Exact methodology varies by testing facility, but all are instrumental techniques with the ability to specifically identify individual drugs and metabolites, if tested, within a class and rule out interfering drugs and other substances. See descriptions of definitive tests in the Definitive Drug Testing introductory guidelines. Results indicate the absence of cyclobenzaprine. Patient reports he has not used the drug for the last three days due to the unpleasant side effects. Physician considers alternative medications.

Clinical Example (80371)

An 18-year-old male is admitted to the emergency department after ingesting an unknown substance at a pill party. Patient is exhibiting seizures and psychosis and is hyperpyrexic with a rectal temperature of 107.6°F. A urine sample sent to the hospital laboratory for qualitative drug screen tested negative, including for amphetamines. The urine specimen is sent to the laboratory to rule out presence of "bath salts" synthetic stimulants.

Description of Procedure (80371)

A definitive, quantitative LC-MS/MS analysis is ordered for the synthetic stimulants MDVP, mephedrone, and methylone. Any of the instrumental techniques that are defined as definitive may be used. These are high-complexity tests, such as LC-MS/MS or GC/MS. Exact methodology varies by testing facility, but all are instrumental techniques with the ability to specifically identify individual drugs and metabolites, if tested, within a class and rule out interfering drugs and other substances. See descriptions of definitive tests in the Definitive Drug Testing introductory guidelines. Results indicate use of methylone, a synthetic cathinone.

Clinical Example (80372)

A 38-year-old male with severe neurogenic limb pain is prescribed 75 mg controlled-release tapentadol every 4 hours to 6 hours. Patient-history check with the state PDMP reveals history of multiple providers and pharmacies. The pill count is short four days of medication, and the patient avoids answering questions regarding drug abuse. Before the prescription refill is issued, a urine specimen is sent to the laboratory to confirm tapentadol and metabolite presence.

Description of Procedure (80372)

A definitive, quantitative LC-MS/MS analysis is ordered for the tapentadol. Any of the instrumental techniques that are defined as definitive may be used. These are high-complexity tests, such as LC-MS/MS or GC/MS. Exact methodology varies by testing facility, but all are instrumental techniques with the ability to specifically identify individual drugs and metabolites, if tested, within a class and rule out interfering drugs and other substances. See descriptions of definitive tests in the Definitive Drug Testing introductory guidelines. Results are positive for tapentadol and metabolites. Patient appears to be using more drug than is indicated.

Clinical Example (80373)

A 38-year-old male prescribed tramadol for severe neurogenic limb pain complains of poor pain relief and requests a dose increase. The patient is currently receiving a dose of 300 mg/day, close to the maximum recommended dose. To understand the apparent ineffectiveness of this medication and confirm patient medication compliance, a urine sample is sent to the laboratory to confirm the presence of tramadol and its metabolite.

⃠=Modifier 51 Exempt   ⊙=Moderate Sedation   ✛=Add-on Code   ◲=FDA approval pending

Description of Procedure (80373)

A definitive, quantitative LC-MS/MS analysis is ordered for the tramadol and its metabolite. Any of the instrumental techniques that are defined as definitive may be used. These are high-complexity tests, such as LC-MS/MS or GC/MS. Exact methodology varies by testing facility, but all are instrumental techniques with the ability to specifically identify individual drugs and metabolites, if tested, within a class and rule out interfering drugs and other substances. See descriptions of definitive tests in the Definitive Drug Testing introductory guidelines. Results are positive for tramadol at a concentration three times the metabolite. Tramadol is a prodrug that requires conversion to an active metabolite. This result may indicate poor 2D6 metabolic conversion. Physician orders genetic testing to confirm 2D6 polymorphic status of this patient and considers alternative medications that are not dependent on this metabolic pathway.

Clinical Example (80374)

A 42-year-old male with a history of substance abuse is treated with oxycodone for chronic back pain. As a condition of treatment, the patient undergoes definitive, laboratory-based urine drug testing to monitor use of prescribed oxycodone and rule out use of illicit drugs. The latest test revealed the presence of methamphetamine, in addition to the oxycodone prescribed. Stereoisomer analysis is ordered to determine the isomeric composition of the methamphetamine (percentage of d- or l-isomer). The relative amount of these isomers is used to distinguish between medicinal and illicit methamphetamine use.

Description of Procedure (80374)

A quantitative, definitive GC/MS analysis for methamphetamine enantiomers is performed. Any of the instrumental techniques that are defined as definitive may be used. These are high-complexity tests, such as LC-MS/MS or GC/MS. Exact methodology varies by testing facility, but all are instrumental techniques with the ability to specifically identify individual drugs and metabolites, if tested, within a class and rule out interfering drugs and other substances. The isomeric composition was found to be 100% l-methamphetamine. Patient was subsequently found to use selegiline, an antidepressant that is metabolized to l-methamphetamine. Illicit drug use is ruled out.

▶Definitive Drug Classes Listing◀

▶Drugs and metabolites included in each definitive drug class are listed in the Definitive Drug Classes Listing table. This is not a comprehensive list. FDA classification of drugs not listed should be used where possible within the defined drug classes. Any metabolites that are not listed should be categorized with the parent drug. Drugs and metabolites not listed may be reported using codes from the Therapeutic Drug Assay (80150-80299) or Chemistry (82009-84999) sections.◀

DEFINITIVE DRUG CLASSES LISTING

Codes	Classes	Drugs
80320	Alcohol(s)	Acetone, ethanol, ethchlorvynol, ethylene glycol, isopropanol, isopropyl alcohol, methanol
80321-80322	Alcohol Biomarkers	Ethanol conjugates (ethyl glucuronide [ETG], ethyl sulfate [ETS], fatty acid ethyl esters, phosphatidylethanol)
80323	Alkaloids, not otherwise specified	7-Hydroxymitragynine, atropine, cotinine, lysergic acid diethylamide (LSD), mescaline, mitragynine, nicotine, psilocin, psilocybin, scopolamine
80324-80326	Amphetamines	Amphetamine, ephedrinelisdexamphetamine, methamphetamine, phentermine, phenylpropanol-amine, pseudoephedrine
80327-80328	Anabolic steroids	1-Androstenediol, 1-androstenedione, 1-testosterone, 4-hydroxy-testosterone, 6-oxo, 19-norandrostenedione, androstenedione, androstanolone, bolandiol, bolasterone, boldenone, boldione, calusterone, clostebol, danazol, dehy-drochlormethyltestosterone, dihydrotestosterone, drostanolone, epiandrosterone, epitestosterone, fluoxymesterone, furazabol, mestanolone, mester-olone, methandienone, methandriol, methenolone, methydienolone, methyl-1-testosterone, methyl-nortestosterone, methyltestosterone, mibolerone, nandrolone, norbolethone, norclostebol, norethan-drolone, norethindrone, oxabolone, oxandrolone, oxymesterone, oxymetholone, stanozolol, stenbo-lone, tibolone, trenbolone, zeranol
80329-80331	Analgesics, non-opioid	Acetaminophen, diclofenac ibuprofen, ketoprofen, naproxen, oxaprozin, salicylate
80332-80334	Antidepressants, serotonergic class	Citalopram, duloxetine, escitalopram, fluoxetine, fluvoxamine, paroxetine, sertraline
80335-80337	Antidepressants, Tricyclic and other cyclicals	Amitriptyline, amoxapine, clomipramine, demexiptiline, desipramine, doxepin, imipramine, maprotiline, mirtazpine, nortriptyline, protriptyline
80338	Antidepressants, not otherwise specified	Bupropion, desyenlafaxine, isocarboxazid, nefazo-done, phenelzine, selegiline, tranylcypromine, trazodone, venlafaxine
80339-80341	Antiepileptics, not otherwise specified	Carbamazepine, clobazam, diamethadione, ethosuximide, ezogabine, lamotrigine, leveti-racetam, methsuximide, oxcarbazepine, phenytoin, primidone, rufinamide, tiagabine, topiramate, trimethadione, valproic acid, zonisamide

Codes	Classes	Drugs
80342-80344	Antipsychotics, not otherwise specified	Aripiprazole, chlorpromazine, clozapine, fluphenazine, haloperidol, loxapine, mesoridazine, molindone, olanzapine, paliperidone, perphenazine, phenothiazine, pimozide, prochlorperazine, quetiapine, risperidone, trifluoperazine, thiothixene, thoridazine, ziprasidone
80345	Barbiturates	Amobarbital, aprobarbital, butalbital, cyclobarbital, mephobarbital, pentobarbital, phenobarbital, secobarbital, talbutal, thiopental
80346, 80347	Benzodiazepines	Alprazolam, chlordiazepoxide, clonazepam, clorazepate, diazepam, estazolam, flunitrazepam, flurazepam, halazepamlorazepammidazolam, nitrazepam, nordazepam, oxazepam, prazepam, quazepam, temazepam
80348	Buprenorphine	Buprenorphine
80349	Cannabinoids, natural	Marijuana, dronabinol carboxy-THC
80350-80352	Cannabinoids, synthetic	CP-47,497, CP497 C8-homolog, JWH-018 and AM678, JWH-073, JWH-019, JWH-200, JWH-210, JWH-250, JWH-081, JWH-122, HWH-398, AM-2201, AM-694, SR-19 and RCS-4, SR-18 and RCS-8, JWH-203, UR-144, XLR-11, MAM-2201, AKB-48
80353	Cocaine	Benzoylecgonine, cocaethylene, cocaine, ecgonine methyl ester, norcocaine
80354	Fentanyls	Acetylfentanyl, alfentanil, fentanyl, remifentanil, sufentanil
80355	Gabapentin, non-blood	Gabapentin
80356	Heroin metabolite	6-acetylmorphine, acetylcodeine, diacetylmorphine
80368	Hypnotics, sedative (non-benzodiazepines)	See Sedative Hypnotics
80357	Ketamine and Norketamine	Ketamine, norketamine
80358	Methadone	Methadone and EDDP
80359	Methylenedioxyamphetamines	MDA, MDEA, MDMA
80360	Methylphenidate	Methylphenidate, ritalinic acid
80357	Norketamine	See Ketamine
80368	Non-Benzodiazepines	See Hypnotics, sedative
80361	Opiates	Codeine, dihydrocodeine, hydrocodone, hydromorphone, morphine
80362-80364	Opioids and opiate analogs	Butorphanol, desomorphine, dextromethorphan, dextrorphan, levorphanol, meperidine, naloxone, naltrexone, normeperidine, pentazocine
80365	Oxycodone	Oxycodone, oxymorphone
83992	Phencyclidine	Phencyclidine
80366	Pregabalin	Pregabalin
80367	Propoxyphene	Norpropoxyphene, propoxyphene

Codes	Classes	Drugs
80368	Sedative Hypnotics (non-benzodiazepines)	Eszopiclone, zaleplon, zolpidem
80369, 80370	Skeletal muscle relaxants	Baclofen, carisoprodol, cyclobenzaprine, meprobamate, metaxalone, methocarbamol, orphenadrine, tizanidide
80371	Stimulants, synthetic	2C-B, 2C-E, 2C-I, 2C-H, 3TFMPP, 4-methy-lethcathinone, alpha-PVP, benzylpiperazine, bromodragonfly, cathinone, m-CPP, MDPBP, MDPPP, MDPV, mephedrone, methcathinone, methylone, phenethylamines, salvinorin, tryptamines
80372	Tapentadol	Tapentadol
80373	Tramadol	Tramadol

Rationale

The Definitive Drug Classes Listing is a listing of all definitive drugs and metabolites. For coding purposes, a "metabolite" is defined as a derivative of a "parent" drug that may be tested using the same procedure(s). The Definitive Drug Classes Listing may be used to identify common metabolites that are associated with a particular drug class. This gives users the ability to identify the specific definitive testing code(s) that should be used to report the procedure(s) performed. As noted in the guidelines, this listing is not comprehensive. Any metabolites that has not been included in this listing should be categorized with the parent drug (if included in the list) or should be reported with the appropriate therapeutic drug assay (80150-80202) or chemistry (82009-84999) code.

Therapeutic Drug Assays

▶Therapeutic Drug Assays are performed to monitor clinical response to a known, prescribed medication.

The material for examination is whole blood, serum, plasma, or cerebrospinal fluid. Examination is quantitative. Coding is by parent drug; measured metabolites of the drug are included in the code, if performed.◀

80150 Amikacin

▶(80152 has been deleted. To report definitive drug testing for amitryptyline, see 80335, 80336, 80337)◀

▶(80154 has been deleted. To report definitive drug testing for benzodiazepines, see 80346, 80347)◀

▶(80160 has been deleted. To report definitive drug testing for desipramine, see 80335, 80336, 80337)◀

▲**80162** Digoxin; total

●**80163**   free

▶(80166 has been deleted. To report definitive drug testing for doxepin, see 80335, 80336, 80337)◀

#▲**80171**   Gabapentin, whole blood, serum, or plasma

▶(80172 has been deleted. To report definitive drug testing for gold, use 80375)◀

▶(80174 has been deleted. To report testing for imipramine, see 80335, 80336, 80337)◀

▶(80182 has been deleted. To report definitive drug testing for nortriptyline, see 80335, 80336, 80337)◀

▶(80196 has been deleted. To report definitive drug testing for salicylate, see 80329, 80330, 80331)◀

#▲**80164**   Valproic acid (dipropylacetic acid); total

#●**80165**   free

▲**80299**   Quantitation of therapeutic drug, not elsewhere specified

 Rationale

Many of the changes included in the Therapeutic Drug Assay and Chemistry subsections for drug testing have been made to accommodate the addition of the new Drug Assay subsection. These changes include: (1) revisions to guidelines in the Therapeutic Drug Assays subsection to reflect the type of testing and specimen type for which these procedure are intended; (2) the addition of parenthetical notes to direct users to the appropriate definitive drug testing codes to use in place of the deleted codes; and (3) the addition and revision of new and existing code to identify "total" vs "free" testing of metabolites. In addition, see the Drug Assay subsection for additional explanation of the changes to the Therapeutic Drug Assay codes and guidelines.

Evocative/Suppression Testing

80438   Thyrotropin releasing hormone (TRH) stimulation panel; 1 hour

This panel must include the following:

Thyroid stimulating hormone (TSH) (84443 x 3)

80439   2 hour

This panel must include the following:

Thyroid stimulating hormone (TSH) (84443 x 4)

▶(80440 has been deleted. For prolactin, use 84146)◀

Rationale

As part of an effort to ensure that the CPT code set reflects current clinical practice, code 80440 has been deleted due to low utilization.

Duplication/Deletion (Dup/Del): terms that are usually used together with the "/" to refer to molecular testing, which assesses the dosage of a particular genomic region. The region tested is typically of modest to substantial size - from several dozen to several million or more nucleotides. Normal gene dosage is two copies per cell, except for the sex chromosomes (X and Y). Thus, zero or one copy represents a deletion, and three (or more) copies represent a duplication.

Dynamic mutation: polynucleotide (eg, trinucleotide) repeats that are in or associated with genes that can undergo disease-producing increases or decreases in the numbers of repeats within tissues and across generations.

▶***Exome:*** DNA sequences within the human genome that code for proteins (coding regions).◀

▶***Genome:*** The total (nuclear) human genetic content.

Heteroplasmy: The copy number of a variant within a cell; it is expressed as a percent. It reflects the varied distribution and dosage of mutant mitochondria in tissues and organs (mitotic segregation).◀

▶***Mitochondrial DNA (mtDNA):*** DNA located in the mitochondria, which are cytoplasmic organelles involved with energy production. MtDNA contains 37 genes coding for oxidative phosphorylation enzymes, transfer RNAs (tRNAs) and ribosomal RNAs (rRNAs).◀

▶***Nuclear DNA:*** DNA located in the nucleus of a cell, generally packaged in chromosomes.◀

 Rationale

For purposes of accurate CPT reporting and to support the expansion of the Molecular Pathology subsection to include codes that identify genomic sequencing procedures (GSPs) and other molecular multianalyte assays (81410, 81411, 81415-81417, 81420, 81425-81427, 81430-81431, 81435-81436, 81440, 81445-81455, 81460, 81465, and 81470-81471), new definitions have been added to the existing list of definitions within the Molecular Pathology introductory guidelines. Definitions have been added for terms including "exome," "genome," "heteroplasmy," "mitochondrial DNA (MtDNA)," and "nuclear DNA."

Tier 1 Molecular Pathology Procedures

▲**81245**   *FLT3 (fms-related tyrosine kinase 3)* (eg, acute myeloid leukemia), gene analysis; internal tandem duplication (ITD) variants (ie, exons 14, 15)

●**81246**   tyrosine kinase domain (TKD) variants (eg, D835, I836)

Rationale

For reporting fms-related tyrosine kinase 3 (FLT3) gene analysis, molecular pathology Tier 1 code 81245 has been revised as a parent code to report internal tandem duplication (ITD) variants (ie, exons 14, 15). Code 81246 has been established as a child code to report the tyrosine kinase domain (TKD) variants (eg, D835, I836). Analysis of these variants is useful in determining treatment approaches (eg, selection of chemotherapy, aggressiveness of treatment, consideration for stem cell transplant) in patients with diseases such as acute myeloid leukemia.

Clinical Example (81246)

A 55-year-old male presents to his physician complaining of fatigue and easy bruising and is found to have pancytopenia. Bone marrow evaluation reveals acute myeloid leukemia. Bone marrow aspirate is sent to the laboratory for testing for the presence of FLT3 internal tandem duplication (ITD) (reported with code 81245) and D835 mutations.

Description of Procedure (81246)

Extract DNA from a tumor tissue sample. Perform polymerase chain reaction (PCR) assay to detect codon 835 mutations in a background of wild-type DNA by PCR amplification, followed by restriction enzyme digest and capillary gel electrophoresis-based sizing. The pathologist or other qualified health care professional analyzes the results to the established mutation status. The pathologist or other qualified health care professional composes a report that specifies the mutation status of the patient's tumor and includes a comment on the implications of the lower limit of detection of the test relative to the tumor content of the sample. Edit and sign the report and communicate results to appropriate caregivers.

81292 *MLH1 (mutL homolog 1, colon cancer, nonpolyposis type 2)* (eg, hereditary non-polyposis colorectal cancer, Lynch syndrome) gene analysis; full sequence analysis

#●81288   promoter methylation analysis

✏️ Rationale

Molecular pathology Tier 1 code 81288 has been established to report the analysis of the MLH1 gene using promoter methylation. The MLH1 gene is found on chromosome 3 and is linked to diseases such as hereditary nonpolyposis, colorectal cancer, and Lynch syndrome. Lynch syndrome is a group of symptoms that increases cancer risk, including cancers of the colon.

Clinical Example (81288)

A 45-year-old female presented to her physician with a history of unexpected weight loss and lower gastrointestinal (GI) bleeding. A diagnostic workup revealed adenocarcinoma of the colon. The patient underwent a hemicolectomy to remove the tumor. The tumor demonstrated microsatellite instability high (MSI-H), and immunohistochemistry studies revealed a loss of MLH1. MLH1 promoter methylation testing was ordered as part of an evaluation for possible Lynch syndrome.

Description of Procedure (81288)

DNA is extracted from a tumor tissue sample. DNA is treated with sodium bisulfite and PCR is performed using methylation specific primers for MLH1 promoter. The PCR products are analyzed by capillary gel electrophoresis-based size determination. Alternatively, the MLH1 promoter methylation analysis can be done using methylation sensitive multiple ligation-dependent probe amplification (MS-MLPA) kit. The pathologist or other qualified health care professional analyzes the results to establish the promoter methylation status. The pathologist or other qualified health care professional composes a report that specifies the MLH1 promoter methylation status of the patient's tumor and includes a comment on the implications of the lower limit of detection of the test relative to the tumor content of the sample. The report is edited and signed, and the results are communicated to appropriate caregivers.

●81313 *PCA3/KLK3 (prostate cancer antigen 3 [non-protein coding]/kallikrein-related peptidase 3 [prostate specific antigen]) ratio* (eg, prostate cancer)

📝 Rationale

Molecular Pathology Tier 1 code 81313 has been established to report obtaining a PCA3/KLK3 ratio to help physicians and patients make informed decisions about repeat biopsies.

The assay measures the concentration of prostate cancer antigen 3 (PCA3) and kallikrein-related peptidase 3 (KLK3) RNA molecules and calculates the ratio of PCA3 RNA molecules to KLK3 RNA molecules, which is referred to as the "PCA3 Score."

🩺 Clinical Example (81313)

A 57-year-old male with elevated prostate-specific antigen (PSA) and one or more previous negative prostate biopsies was recommended for repeat biopsy by a urologist based on the current standard of care. The PCA3 Assay is used in conjunction with other patient information to aid in the decision for repeat biopsy.

Description of Procedure (81313)

Pre-analytical specimen collection: This is not included in the requested CPT code service. A clinician performs a digital rectal exam (DRE) consisting of three strokes per prostate lobe to release prostate cells into the urinary tract. A first-catch urine specimen (first 20 ml to 30 ml of the urine stream) is collected in a standard urine collection cup to obtain the released prostate cells. The urine specimen is inverted to re-suspend the cells and a 2.5 ml aliquot is transferred to a sample tube that contains a buffered detergent solution. This solution lyses the cells and stabilizes RNA. The sample is shipped to the testing facility under ambient conditions.

At the testing facility, the PCA3 and PSA RNA levels are quantified in separate assays. The following steps are completed: Target RNA molecules are bound to magnetic micro-particles through a target-specific oligonucleotide intermediate. The purified target is then amplified using transcription-mediated amplification (TMA). Detection is performed using the Hybridization Protection Assay (HPA). DNA probes with chemiluminescent labels are bound to the amplicon, then unbound probes were selectively hydrolyzed, and a luminescent signal (measured in relative light units, or RLU) is generated from the bound probe. PCA3 and PSA RNA concentrations (copies/ml) are determined. The ratio of the two values is determined. The PCA3 ratio is used in conjunction with other patient information to aid in the decision for repeat biopsy. A PCA3 ratio value of <25 is associated with a decreased likelihood of a positive biopsy.

Tier 2 Molecular Pathology Procedures

▲**81402**   Molecular pathology procedure, Level 3 (eg, >10 SNPs, 2-10 methylated variants, or 2-10 somatic variants [typically using non-sequencing target variant analysis], immunoglobulin and T-cell receptor gene rearrangements, duplication/deletion variants of 1 exon, loss of heterozygosity [LOH], uniparental disomy [UPD])

▶Chromosome 1p-/19q- (eg, glial tumors), deletion analysis◀

▲**81403**   Molecular pathology procedure, Level 4 (eg, analysis of single exon by DNA sequence analysis, analysis of >10 amplicons using multiplex PCR in 2 or more independent reactions, mutation scanning or duplication/deletion variants of 2-5 exons)

▶*Human erythrocyte antigen gene analyses (eg, SLC14A1 [Kidd blood group], BCAM [Lutheran blood group], ICAM4 [Landsteiner-Wiener blood group], SLC4A1 [Diego blood group], AQP1 [Colton blood group], ERMAP [Scianna blood group], RHCE [Rh blood group, CcEe antigens], KEL [Kell blood group], DARC [Duffy blood group], GYPA, GYPB, GYPE [MNS blood group], ART4 [Dombrock blood group])* (eg, sickle-cell disease, thalassemia, hemolytic transfusion reactions, hemolytic disease of the fetus or newborn), common variants◀

▶*RHD (Rh blood group, D antigen)* (eg, hemolytic disease of the fetus and newborn, Rh maternal/fetal compatibility), deletion analysis (eg, exons 4, 5, and 7, pseudogene)

RHD (Rh blood group, D antigen) (eg, hemolytic disease of the fetus and newborn, Rh maternal/fetal compatibility), deletion analysis (eg, exons 4, 5, and 7, pseudogene), performed on cell-free fetal DNA in maternal blood

(For human erythrocyte gene analysis of RHD, use a separate unit of 81403)◀

▲**81404**   Molecular pathology procedure, Level 5 (eg, analysis of 2-5 exons by DNA sequence analysis, mutation scanning or duplication/deletion variants of 6-10 exons, or characterization of a dynamic mutation disorder/triplet repeat by Southern blot analysis)

▶*MPV17 (MpV17 mitochondrial inner membrane protein)* (eg, mitochondrial DNA depletion syndrome), duplication/deletion analysis◀

▶*PIK3CA (phosphatidylinositol-4,5-bisphosphate 3-kinase, catalytic subunit alpha)* (eg, colorectal cancer), targeted sequence analysis (eg, exons 9 and 20)◀

▲**81405**   Molecular pathology procedure, Level 6 (eg, analysis of 6-10 exons by DNA sequence analysis, mutation scanning or duplication/deletion variants of 11-25 exons, regionally targeted cytogenomic array analysis)

#**81479**   Unlisted molecular pathology procedure

🖎 Rationale

Molecular pathology Tier 2 codes 81402-81404 have been revised to include additional analytes that have been determined to fall under the levels of Tier 2 reporting, and code 81405 has been revised to reflect deleted analytes.

Code 81402 has been revised to include Chromosome 1p-/19q- (eg, glial tumors), deletion analysis.

Code 81403 has been revised to include two additional procedures for RHD, deletion analysis.

Code 81404 has been revised to include two additional analytes, MPV17 and PIK3CA.

Code 81405 has been revised to delete cytogenomic constitutional targeted microarray analysis of the X chromosome and mitochondrial genome deletions, as well as three related cross-references. These deletions were in response to the establishment of codes for genomic sequencing procedures (GSPs) and other molecular multianalyte assays codes (81410, 81411, 81415-81417, 81420, 81425-81427, 81430, 81431, 81435, 81436, 81440, 81445-81455, 81460, 81465, 81470, 81471).

Molecular pathology Tier 2 codes 81400-81408 describe molecular pathology procedures that are not listed in the molecular pathology Tier 1 codes (81161-81383). Tier 2 codes are arranged by level of technical resources and interpretive professional work required. The individual analytes listed under each code (ie, level of procedure) utilize the definitions and coding principles as described in the introduction preceding the molecular pathology Tier 1 codes. The parenthetical examples of methodologies presented near the beginning of each code provide general guidelines used to group procedures for a given level and are not all-inclusive. There are several instructional parenthetical notes, as well as cross-references added throughout this section, to provide additional instruction for the appropriate reporting of these codes.

If the analyte tested is not listed under one of the Tier 2 codes or is not represented by a Tier 1 code, use the unlisted molecular pathology procedure code 81479.

▶Genomic Sequencing Procedures and Other Molecular Multianalyte Assays◀

▶Genomic sequencing procedures (GSPs) and other molecular multianalyte assays GSPs are DNA or RNA sequence analysis methods that simultaneously assay multiple genes or genetic regions relevant to a clinical situation. They may target specific combinations of genes or genetic material, or assay the exome or genome. The technology used for genomic sequencing is commonly referred to as next generation sequencing (NGS) or massively parallel sequencing (MPS). GSPs are performed on nucleic acids from germline or neoplastic samples. Examples of applications include aneuploidy analysis of cell-free circulating fetal DNA, gene panels for somatic alterations in neoplasms, and sequence analysis of the exome or genome to determine the cause of developmental delay. The exome and genome procedures are designed to evaluate the genetic material in totality or near totality. Although commonly used to identify sequence (base) changes, they can also be used to identify copy number, structural changes, and abnormal zygosity patterns. Another unique feature of GSPs is the ability to "re-query" or re-evaluate the sequence data (eg, complex phenotype such as developmental delay is reassessed when new genetic knowledge is attained, or for a separate unrelated clinical indication). The analyses listed below represent groups of genes that are often performed by GSPs; however, the analyses may also be performed by other molecular techniques (polymerase chain reaction [PCR]

⊘=Modifier 51 Exempt ⊙=Moderate Sedation ✚=Add-on Code ⅍=FDA approval pending

methods and microarrays). These codes should be used when the components of the descriptor(s) are fulfilled regardless of the technique used to provide the analysis, unless specifically noted in the code descriptor. When all of the components of the descriptor are not performed, use individual Tier 1 codes, Tier 2 codes, or 81479 (Unlisted molecular pathology procedure).

The assays in this section represent discrete genetic values, properties, or characteristics in which the measurement or analysis of each analyte is potentially of independent medical significance or useful in medical management. In contrast to multianalyte assays with algorithmic analyses (MAAAs), the assays in this section do not represent algorithmically combined results to obtain a risk score or other value, which in itself represents a new and distinct medical property that is of independent medical significance relative to the individual, component test results.◀

▶(For cytogenomic microarray analyses, see 81228, 81229, 81405, 81406)◀

▶(For long QT syndrome gene analyses, see 81280, 81282)◀

●81410   Aortic dysfunction or dilation (eg, Marfan syndrome, Loeys Dietz syndrome, Ehler Danlos syndrome type IV, arterial tortuosity syndrome); genomic sequence analysis panel, must include sequencing of at least 9 genes, including *FBN1, TGFBR1, TGFBR2, COL3A1, MYH11, ACTA2, SLC2A10, SMAD3,* and *MYLK*

●81411   duplication/deletion analysis panel, must include analyses for *TGFBR1, TGFBR2, MYH11, and COL3A1*

●81415   Exome (eg, unexplained constitutional or heritable disorder or syndrome); sequence analysis

+●81416   sequence analysis, each comparator exome (eg, parents, siblings) (List separately in addition to code for primary procedure)

▶(Use 81416 in conjunction with 81415)◀

●81417   re-evaluation of previously obtained exome sequence (eg, updated knowledge or unrelated condition/syndrome)

▶(Do not report 81417 for incidental findings)◀

▶(For exome-wide copy number assessment by microarray, see 81228, 81229)◀

●81420   Fetal chromosomal aneuploidy (eg, trisomy 21, monosomy X) genomic sequence analysis panel, circulating cell-free fetal DNA in maternal blood, must include analysis of chromosomes 13, 18, and 21

●81425   Genome (eg, unexplained constitutional or heritable disorder or syndrome); sequence analysis

+●81426   sequence analysis, each comparator genome (eg, parents, siblings) (List separately in addition to code for primary procedure)

▶(Use 81426 in conjunction with 81425)◀

●81427   re-evaluation of previously obtained genome sequence (eg, updated knowledge or unrelated condition/syndrome)

▶(Do not report 81427 for incidental findings)◀

▶(For genome-wide copy number assessment by microarray, see 81228, 81229)◀

●**81430** Hearing loss (eg, nonsyndromic hearing loss, Usher syndrome, Pendred syndrome); genomic sequence analysis panel, must include sequencing of at least 60 genes, including *CDH23, CLRN1, GJB2, GPR98, MTRNR1, MYO7A, MYO15A, PCDH15, OTOF, SLC26A4, TMC1, TMPRSS3, USH1C, USH1G, USH2A,* and *WFS1*

●**81431** duplication/deletion analysis panel, must include copy number analyses for *STRC* and *DFNB1* deletions *in GJB2 and GJB6 genes*

●**81435** Hereditary colon cancer syndromes (eg, Lynch syndrome, familial adenomatosis polyposis); genomic sequence analysis panel, must include analysis of at least 7 genes, including *APC, CHEK2, MLH1, MSH2, MSH6, MUTYH,* and *PMS2*

●**81436** duplication/deletion gene analysis panel, must include analysis of at least 8 genes, including *APC, MLH1, MSH2, MSH6, PMS2, EPCAM, CHEK2,* and *MUTYH*

●**81440** Nuclear encoded mitochondrial genes (eg, neurologic or myopathic phenotypes), genomic sequence panel, must include analysis of at least 100 genes, including *BCS1L, C10orf2, COQ2, COX10, DGUOK, MPV17, OPA1, PDSS2, POLG, POLG2, RRM2B, SCO1, SCO2, SLC25A4, SUCLA2, SUCLG1, TAZ, TK2,* and *TYMP*

●**81445** Targeted genomic sequence analysis panel, solid organ neoplasm, DNA analysis, 5-50 genes (eg, *ALK, BRAF, CDKN2A, EGFR, ERBB2, KIT, KRAS, NRAS, MET, PDGFRA, PDGFRB, PGR, PIK3CA, PTEN, RET*), interrogation for sequence variants and copy number variants or rearrangements, if performed

▶(For copy number assessment by microarray, use 81406)◀

●**81450** Targeted genomic sequence analysis panel, hematolymphoid neoplasm or disorder, DNA and RNA analysis when performed, 5-50 genes (eg, *BRAF, CEBPA, DNMT3A, EZH2, FLT3, IDH1, IDH2, JAK2, KRAS, KIT, MLL, NRAS, NPM1, NOTCH1*), interrogation for sequence variants, and copy number variants or rearrangements, or isoform expression or mRNA expression levels, if performed

▶(For copy number assessment by microarray, use 81406)◀

●**81455** Targeted genomic sequence analysis panel, solid organ or hematolymphoid neoplasm, DNA and RNA analysis when performed, 51 or greater genes (eg, *ALK, BRAF, CDKN2A, CEBPA, DNMT3A, EGFR, ERBB2, EZH2, FLT3, IDH1, IDH2, JAK2, KIT, KRAS, MLL, NPM1, NRAS, MET, NOTCH1, PDGFRA, PDGFRB, PGR, PIK3CA, PTEN, RET*), interrogation for sequence variants and copy number variants or rearrangements, if performed

▶(For copy number assessment by microarray, use 81406)◀

●**81460** Whole mitochondrial genome (eg, Leigh syndrome, mitochondrial encephalomyopathy, lactic acidosis, and stroke-like episodes [MELAS], myoclonic epilepsy with ragged-red fibers [MERFF], neuropathy, ataxia, and retinitis pigmentosa [NARP], Leber hereditary optic neuropathy [LHON]), genomic sequence, must include sequence analysis of entire mitochondrial genome with heteroplasmy detection

●**81465** Whole mitochondrial genome large deletion analysis panel (eg, Kearns-Sayre syndrome, chronic progressive external ophthalmoplegia), including heteroplasmy detection, if performed

⊘=Modifier 51 Exempt ⊙=Moderate Sedation ✚=Add-on Code 𝒩=FDA approval pending

●**81470** X-linked intellectual disability (XLID) (eg, syndromic and non-syndromic XLID); genomic sequence analysis panel, must include sequencing of at least 60 genes, including *ARX, ATRX, CDKL5, FGD1, FMR1, HUWE1, IL1RAPL, KDM5C, L1CAM, MECP2, MED12, MID1, OCRL, RPS6KA3,* and *SLC16A2*

●**81471** duplication/deletion gene analysis, must include analysis of at least 60 genes, including *ARX, ATRX, CDKL5, FGD1, FMR1, HUWE1, IL1RAPL, KDM5C, L1CAM, MECP2, MED12, MID1, OCRL, RPS6KA3,* and *SLC16A2*

✍ Rationale

Advances in DNA sequencing technology, commonly referred to as next generation sequencing (NGS) or massively parallel sequencing (MPS), are allowing the human genome to be analyzed in complex and diverse ways. Applications of this technology have resulted in new clinical diagnostic procedures that are significantly affecting the practice of medicine.

In response to the changes in clinical practice and the need to provide a reporting mechanism for NGS or MPS procedures, the CPT code set has been expanded to include a new subsection for reporting these analyses called "Genomic Sequencing Procedures and Other Molecular Multianalyte Assays." This new subsection includes introductory guidelines that describe some of the characteristics of GSPs and other molecular multianalyte assays including their unique features, functions, and applications. The introductory guidelines also provide coding advice and instructions for the appropriate reporting of these codes. Finally, the guidelines clarify the methodological differences between GSPs and other molecular multianalyte assays versus multianalyte assays with algorithmic analyses (MAAAs). The new subsection includes 21 new codes that describe disorder-specific multigene assays and multiple cross-references and instructional notes to aid users in reporting these services. The disorder-specific multigene assays included in this subsection are as follows:

■ Aortic dysfunction dilation (81410, 81411)

■ Exome (81415-81417)

■ Fetal chromosomal aneuploidy (81420)

■ Genome (81425-81427)

■ Hearing loss (81430, 81431)

■ Hereditary colon cancer syndromes (81435, 81436)

■ Nuclear encoded mitochondrial genes (81440)

■ Targeted genomic sequence analysis panels (81445-81455)

■ Whole mitochondrial genome (81460, 81465)

■ X-linked intellectual disability (81470, 81471)

For alignment, consistency, and accurate CPT reporting, the Molecular Pathology, Multianalyte Assays with Algorithmic Analyses, and Cytogenetic Studies subsections guidelines were updated to support the establishment of the new Genomic Sequencing Procedures (GSPs) and Other Molecular Multianalyte Assays subsection.

Clinical Example (81410)

A 30-year-old female with mitral valve prolapse and mild aortic dilation is being evaluated for a suspected Marfan-spectrum disorder. A whole-blood sample is submitted for aortic dysfunction or dilation genomic sequencing panel testing, including FBN1, TGFBR1, TGFBR2, COL3A1, MYH11, ACTA2, SLC2A10, SMAD3, and MYLK.

Description of Procedure (81410)

High quality DNA is isolated from the patient's blood sample. DNA targets are enriched by hybrid capture for at least the following genes: FBN1, TGFBR1, TGFBR2, COL3A1, MYH11, ACTA2, SLC2A10, SMAD3, and MYLK. The products undergo massively parallel DNA sequencing of the coding regions and intron/exon boundaries. The pathologist or other qualified health care professional evaluates the reads to identify nucleotide sequence variants. The pathologist or other qualified health care professional composes a report that specifies the patient's mutation status. The report is edited and signed, and the results are communicated to appropriate caregivers.

Clinical Example (81411)

A 30-year-old female with mitral valve prolapse and mild aortic dilation is being evaluated for a suspected Marfan-spectrum disorder. Previous genomic sequencing of related genes did not identify causative mutations. A whole-blood sample is submitted for aortic dysfunction or dilation duplication/deletion panel testing including TGFBR1, TGFBR2, MYH11, and COL3A1.

Description of Procedure (81411)

High quality DNA is isolated from the patient's blood sample. Genomic DNA is hybridized to a targeted microarray for copy number testing for at least the following genes: TGFBR1, TGFBR2, MYH11, and COL3A1. The pathologist or other qualified health care professional evaluates the copy number for each exon. The pathologist or other qualified health care professional composes a report that specifies the patient's duplication/deletion status. The report is edited and signed, and the results are communicated to appropriate caregivers.

Clinical Example (81415)

A 4-year-old male presents with history of developmental delay and recent regression of developmental milestones. Cytogenomic microarray analysis and other laboratory studies do not detect a cause for the patient's condition. Continuing to suspect a heritable disorder, his physician sends a blood sample for whole-exome sequencing.

Description of Procedure (81415)

DNA is extracted, and a genomic library is prepared. The exonic regions of the patient's genome are enriched using a hybrid capture technique. Sequencing of the patient's exome is performed by MPS using sequencing by synthesis chemistry and

⊘=Modifier 51 Exempt   ⊙=Moderate Sedation   ✚=Add-on Code   𝒩=FDA approval pending

paired-end read technology. Alignment is performed, and a table of variants that deviate from the reference sequence is generated, with known polymorphisms and candidate variants identified, and annotation provided.*

*Current guidelines require that variants of interest are confirmed using Sanger sequencing.

Clinical Example (81416)

A sample of blood from a 4-year-old male, who presents with history of developmental delay and recent regression of developmental milestones, is sent for whole-exome sequencing. Blood samples from the mother and father are also sent for whole-exome sequencing to identify the parental or de novo origin of variants identified in the patient.

Description of Procedure (81416)

DNA is extracted, and a genomic library is prepared. The exonic regions of the parents' genomes are enriched using a hybrid capture technique. Sequencing of the parents' exomes is performed by MPS using sequencing by synthesis chemistry and paired-end read technology. Alignment is performed, a table of variants is generated, and variants identified in the patient are compared with parental sequence variants.*

*Current guidelines require that variants of interest are confirmed using Sanger sequencing.

Clinical Example (81417)

A 4-year-old male had whole-exome sequencing performed because of developmental delay and subsequent regression of developmental milestones. Although a number of possible causative variants were identified, no genomic cause for the patient's condition was definitively identified. The patient's condition continued to decline. Two years later, he was noted to have developed profound proximal muscular atrophy. The previously obtained sequence was re-analyzed for relevant variants, in light of potential new information relating to the patient's disorder.

Description of Procedure (81417)

The patient's previous exome sequence was re-annotated to reflect potential new information relevant to the patient's condition.

Clinical Example (81420)

A 40-year-old female, gravida 1, para 0, presents to her OB/GYN for routine prenatal care. Due to advance maternal age, she is at increased risk of fetal aneuploidy. The physician discusses the options of amniocentesis with chromosome analysis as well as a noninvasive prenatal test and counsels the patient of the significance of a positive and a negative test result, including potential follow-up testing. The patient is reluctant to undergo amniocentesis, so the physician requests a noninvasive prenatal screening test. An anticoagulated peripheral blood sample is submitted for fetal chromosomal aneuploidy genomic sequence testing using circulating cell-free fetal DNA in maternal blood. The panel includes analysis of at least chromosomes 13, 18, and 21.

Description of Procedure (81420)

Circulating cell-free (ccf) nucleic acid fragments are extracted from maternal plasma. The ccf DNA is submitted to massively parallel sequence analysis. Sequence information is used to determine chromosomal origins of the fragments and quantify relative amounts of the chromosomes. The pathologist or other qualified health care professional evaluates the results to assess over-representation of chromosome 21 or 18, 13. The pathologist or other qualified health care professional composes a report that specifies the fetal aneuploidy screening findings. The report is edited and signed, and the results are communicated to appropriate caregivers.

Clinical Example (81425)

A 4-year-old male presents with history of developmental delay and recent regression of developmental milestones. Cytogenomic microarray analysis and other laboratory studies do not detect a cause for the patient's condition. Continuing to suspect a heritable disorder, his physician sends a blood sample for whole-genome sequencing.

Description of Procedure (81425)

DNA is extracted, and sequencer-ready DNA fragment libraries are generated. Sequencing of the patient's genome is performed by MPS using sequencing by synthesis chemistry and paired-end read technology. Alignment is performed, and a table of variants that deviate from the reference sequence is generated, with known polymorphisms and candidate variants identified, and annotation provided.*

*Current guidelines require that variants of interest are confirmed using Sanger sequencing.

Clinical Example (81426)

A sample of blood from a 4-year-old male, who presents with history of developmental delay and recent regression of developmental milestones, is sent for whole-genome sequencing. Blood samples from the mother and father are included to identify the parental or de novo origin of variants identified in the patient.

Description of Procedure (81426)

DNA is extracted, and sequencer-ready DNA fragment libraries are generated. Sequencing of the parents' genomes is performed by MPS using sequencing by synthesis chemistry and paired-end read technology. Alignment is performed, a table of variants is generated, and variants identified in the patient are compared with parental sequence variants.*

*Current guidelines require that variants of interest are confirmed using Sanger sequencing.

Clinical Example (81427)

A 4-year-old male had whole-genome sequencing performed because of developmental delay and subsequent regression of developmental milestones. Although a number of possible causative variants were identified, no genomic cause for the

⊘=Modifier 51 Exempt   ⊙=Moderate Sedation   ✚=Add-on Code   ✗=FDA approval pending

patient's condition was definitively identified. The patient's condition continued to decline. Two years later, he was noted to have developed profound proximal muscular atrophy. The previously obtained sequence was re-analyzed for relevant variants, in light of potential new information relating to the patient's disorder.

Description of Procedure (81427)

The patient's previous genome sequence was re-annotated to reflect potential new information relevant to the patient's condition.

Clinical Example (81430)

A 9-month-old male infant has profound, bilateral sensorineural hearing loss, inability to sit upright without support, and no family history of hearing loss. A whole-blood sample is submitted for nonsyndromic hearing loss genomic sequence analysis.

Description of Procedure (81430)

High-quality DNA is isolated from the patient's blood sample. DNA is subjected to PCR amplification for at least 60 genes and must include the following genes: CDH23, CLRN1, GJB2, GPR98, MTRNR1, MYO7A, MYO15A, PCDH15, OTOF, SLC26A4, TMC1, TMPRSS3, USH1C, USH1G, USH2A, and WFS1. The PCR products undergo massively parallel DNA sequencing. The pathologist or other qualified health care professional evaluates the reads to identify nucleotide sequence variants. The pathologist or other qualified health care professional composes a report that specifies the patient's mutation status. The report is edited and signed, and the results are communicated to appropriate caregivers.

Clinical Example (81431)

A 4-year-old female has moderate bilateral hearing loss with an older sister with similar hearing loss and concern for autosomal recessive sensorineural hearing loss. Previous testing by DNA sequencing of the common genes did not identify mutations. A whole-blood sample is submitted for nonsyndromic hearing loss duplication/deletion analysis.

Description of Procedure (81431)

High-quality DNA is isolated from the patient's blood sample. Genomic DNA is hybrized to a targeted microarray for copy number analyses for STRC and DFNB1 deletions in GJB2 and GJB6 genes. The pathologist or other qualified health care professional evaluates the copy number for each exon. The pathologist or other qualified health care professional composes a report that specifies the patient's duplication/deletion status. The report is edited and signed, and the results are communicated to appropriate caregivers.

Clinical Example (81435)

A 40-year-old male with colorectal carcinoma, whose mother died at the age of 30 from colorectal cancer, is being evaluated for a possible hereditary colon cancer syndrome. A whole-blood sample is submitted for hereditary colon cancer genomic sequence panel testing, including APC, EPCAM, CHEK2, MLH1, MSH2, MSH6, MUTYH, and PMS2.

Description of Procedure (81435)

High-quality DNA is isolated from the patient's blood sample. DNA is subjected to PCR amplification for at least the following genes: APC, CHEK2, MLH1, MSH2, MSH6, MUTYH, and PMS2. The PCR products undergo massively parallel DNA sequencing. The pathologist or other qualified health care professional evaluates the reads to identify nucleotide sequence variants. The pathologist or other qualified health care professional composes a report that specifies the patient's mutation status. The report is edited and signed, and the results are communicated to appropriate caregivers.

Clinical Example (81436)

A 40-year-old male with colorectal carcinoma, whose mother died at the age of 30 from colorectal cancer, is being evaluated for a possible hereditary colon cancer syndrome. Previous testing by DNA sequencing of the common genes did not identify any mutations. A whole-blood sample is submitted for hereditary colon cancer duplication/deletion panel testing, including APC, EPCAM, CHEK2, MLH1, MSH2, MSH6, MUTYH, and PMS2.

Description of Procedure (81436)

High-quality DNA is isolated from the patient's blood sample. Genomic DNA is hybridized to a targeted microarray for copy number testing for at least the following genes: APC, EPCAM, CHEK2, MLH1, MSH2, MSH6, MUTYH, and PMS2. The pathologist or other qualified health care professional evaluates the copy number for each exon. The pathologist or other qualified health care professional composes a report that specifies the patient's duplication/deletion status. The report is edited and signed, and the results are communicated to appropriate caregivers.

Clinical Example (81440)

A 10-year-old child with neuropathy, seizures, muscle weakness, and autonomic instability is evaluated for a possible mitochondrial-related disorder. Previous testing by DNA sequencing the mitochondrial genome did not identify any causative mutations. A whole-blood sample is submitted for genomic sequencing of nuclear genes coding for proteins involved in cellular respiration and aerobic metabolism, including BCS1L, C10orf2, COQ2, COX10, DGUOK, MPV17, OPA1, PDSS2, POLG, POLG2, RRM2B, SCO1, SCO2, SLC25A4, SUCLA2, SUCLG1, TAZ, TK2, and TYMP.

Description of Procedure (81440)

High-quality DNA is isolated from the patient's blood sample. DNA targets are enriched by hybrid capture for at least the following genes: BCS1L, C10orf2, COQ2, COX10, DGUOK, MPV17, OPA1, PDSS2, POLG, POLG2, RRM2B, SCO1, SCO2, SLC25A4, SUCLA2, SUCLG1, TAZ, TK2, and TYMP. The products undergo massively parallel DNA sequencing of the coding regions and intron/exon boundaries. The pathologist or other qualified health care professional evaluates the reads to identify nucleotide sequence variants. The pathologist or other qualified health care professional composes a report that specifies the patient's mutation status. The report is edited and signed, and the results are communicated to appropriate caregivers.

⃠=Modifier 51 Exempt   ⊙=Moderate Sedation   ✚=Add-on Code   𝒩=FDA approval pending

Clinical Example (81445)

A 50-year-old female presents with a thyroid nodule. Fine-needle aspiration is performed and sent for evaluation. Initial pathology review showed a follicular lesion of indeterminate diagnosis. Residual tissue is submitted for targeted genomic DNA sequence analysis of a panel of 12 genes known to be important in thyroid cancer.

Description of Procedure (81445)

High-quality DNA is isolated from the patient's tissue and MPS is performed on the tumor DNA looking for mutations in 12 genes (NRAS codons 2, 3; CTNNB1 exon 3; PIK3CA exons 9, 20; BRAF exon 15; RET exons 10 - 13, 15, 16; PTEN exons 5 - 8; HRAS exons 2, 3; KRAS exons 2, 3 TSHR exon 10; AKT1 exon 3; TP53 exons 5-9; and GNAS exons 8, 9). The analytical results are sent to a pathologist or other qualified health care provider for identification of mutations, interpretation and preparation of a written report that specifies the patient's mutation status, which may contain information about diagnosis, prognosis, and patient management to include information about targeted drug therapy.

Clinical Example (81450)

A 55-year-old-male presents with an elevated white blood cell count with 80% blasts, anemia, and thrombocytopenia. The pathologic diagnosis was acute myelogenous leukemia (AML). Cytogenetic studies were normal, stratifying the patient as intermediate risk for survival. Blood is submitted for targeted genomic sequence analysis of a panel of 25 genes known to be informative in patients with AML.

Description of Procedure (81450)

High-quality DNA is isolated from the patient's blood and MPS is performed on the DNA looking for mutations in 25 genes (TET2, ASXL1, DNMT3A, CEBPA, PHF6, WT1, TP53, EZH2, RUNX1, PTEN, FLT3, NPM1, KRAS, NRAS, KIT, IDH1, IDH2, GATA1, NOTCH1, MLL, E2A, IL3, TAL1, NUP214, and EVI1). The analytical results are sent to a pathologist or other qualified health care provider for identification of mutations, interpretation and preparation of a written report that specifies the patient's mutation status, which may contain information about diagnosis, prognosis, and patient management to include information about targeted drug therapy.

Clinical Example (81455)

A 65-year-old male presents with lung and liver lesions. Pathologic evaluation of biopsies of these lesions reveals a poorly differentiated neoplasm of uncertain primary origin. Tumor tissue is submitted for targeted genomic sequence analysis of a panel of 250 genes known to be informative in a broad array of cancers.

Description of Procedure (81455)

High-quality DNA is isolated from the patient's tumor tissue and MPS is performed on the tumor DNA looking for mutations in 250 genes, which may be genomic targets for therapeutic management. The analytical results are sent to a pathologist or other qualified health care provider for identification of mutations, interpretation and preparation of a written report that specifies the patient's mutation status, which may contain information about diagnosis, prognosis, and patient management to include information about targeted drug therapy.

Clinical Example (81460)

A 45-year-old male with neuropathy, seizures, muscle weakness, and autonomic instability is being evaluated for a possible mitochondrial disorder. A family history of relative(s) with similar symptoms suggest maternal inheritance, consistent with a mitochondrial disease. A whole-blood sample is submitted for sequencing the mitochondrial genome, including 37 genes.

Description of Procedure (81460)

High-quality DNA is isolated from the patient's blood sample. DNA is subjected to long-range PCR amplifications covering the entire mitochondrial genome. The PCR products undergo massively parallel DNA sequencing. The pathologist or other qualified health care professional evaluates the reads to identify nucleotide sequence variants and determines whether the variants are homoplasmic or heteroplasmic. The pathologist or other qualified health care professional composes a report that specifies the patient's mutation status. The report is edited and signed, and the results are communicated to appropriate caregivers.

Clinical Example (81465)

A 10-year-old child with progressive external ophthalmoplegia, pigmentary retinopathy, and ataxia is evaluated for Kearns-Sayre syndrome. A whole-blood sample is submitted for large deletion analysis of the mitochondrial genome, including 37 genes.

Description of Procedure (81465)

High-quality DNA is isolated from the patient's blood sample. Genomic DNA is hybridized to a targeted microarray for copy number determination within the 37 mitochondrial genes. The pathologist or other qualified health care professional evaluates the copy number for each exon. The pathologist or other qualified health care professional composes a report that specifies the patient's deletion status. The report is edited and signed, and the results are communicated to appropriate caregivers.

Clinical Example (81470)

A 9-year-old male with intellectual disability and a family history suggestive of an X-linked recessive disorder is evaluated. Previous studies included FMR1 and FMR2 trinucleotide expansion studies and a chromosome X–specific cytogenomic microarray analysis, and all were negative. A whole-blood sample is submitted for sequencing of at least the 60 most common genes known to be associated with intellectual disability on the X chromosome.

Description of Procedure (81470)

High-quality DNA is isolated from the patient's whole blood sample. DNA targets are enriched for at least 60 of the most common genes on the X chromosome associated with intellectual disability. The products undergo massively parallel DNA sequencing of the coding regions and intron/exon boundaries. The pathologist or other qualified health care professional evaluates the reads using software

⃠=Modifier 51 Exempt   ⊙=Moderate Sedation   ✚=Add-on Code   𝄃=FDA approval pending

to identify nucleotide sequence variants compared to a reference database. Using various software and databases, the pathologist or other qualified health care professional then determines if any of the identified variants are likely causative of intellectual disability and composes a report that specifies the patient's mutation status. The report is edited and signed, and the results are communicated to appropriate caregivers.

Clinical Example (81471)

A 9-year-old male with intellectual disability and a family history suggestive of an X-linked recessive disorder is evaluated. Previous studies included FMR1 and FMR2 trinucleotide expansion studies and a cytogenomic microarray analysis and all were negative. A whole-blood sample is submitted for a chromosome X–specific analysis that includes exonic duplication/deletion analysis of at least 60 of the most common genes known to be associated with intellectual disability on the X chromosome.

Description of Procedure (81471)

High-quality DNA is isolated from the patient's whole blood sample. Genomic DNA is then analyzed for copy number changes for at least 60 of the most common genes on the X chromosome associated with intellectual disability. The pathologist or other qualified health care professional uses software to evaluate the copy number status for each exon within each gene. The pathologist or other qualified health care professional then uses relevant databases and literature to determine if an identified exonic copy number change is likely causative of intellectual disability and composes a report that specifies the patient's duplication/deletion status. The report is edited and signed, and the results are communicated to appropriate caregiver.

Multianalyte Assays with Algorithmic Analyses

▶Multianalyte Assays with Algorithmic Analyses (MAAAs) are procedures that utilize multiple results derived from panels of analyses of various types, including molecular pathology assays, fluorescent in situ hybridization assays, and non-nucleic acid based assays (eg, proteins, polypeptides, lipids, carbohydrates). Algorithmic analysis using the results of these assays as well as other patient information (if used) is then performed and typically reported as a numeric score(s) or as a probability. MAAAs are typically unique to a single clinical laboratory or manufacturer. The results of individual component procedure(s) that are inputs to the MAAAs may be provided on the associated laboratory report; however, these assays are not separately reported using additional codes.◀

The format for the code descriptors of MAAAs usually include (in order):

- Disease type (eg, oncology, autoimmune, tissue rejection),

- Material(s) analyzed (eg, DNA, RNA, protein, antibody),

- Number of markers (eg, number of genes, number of proteins),

- Methodology(ies) (eg, microarray, real-time [RT]-PCR, in situ hybridization [ISH], enzyme linked immunosorbent assays [ELISA]),

- Number of functional domains (if indicated),

- Specimen type (eg, blood, fresh tissue, formalin-fixed paraffin embedded),

- Algorithm result type (eg, prognostic, diagnostic),

- Report (eg, probability index, risk score)

▶In contrast to GSPs and other molecular multianalyte assays, the assays in this section represent algorithmically combined results of analyses of multiple analytes to obtain a risk score or other value which in itself represents a new and distinct medical property that is of independent medical significance relative to the individual component test results in clinical context in which the assay is performed.

MAAAs, including those that do not have a Category I code, may be found in Appendix O. MAAAs that do not have a Category I code are identified in Appendix O by a four-digit number followed by the letter "M." The Category I MAAA codes that are included in this subsection are also included in Appendix O. All MAAA codes are listed in Appendix O along with the procedure's proprietary name. In order to report a MAAA code, the analysis performed must fulfill the code descriptor **and**, if proprietary, must be the test represented by the proprietary name listed in Appendix O.◄

When a specific MAAA procedure is not listed below or in Appendix O, the procedure must be reported using the Category I MAAA unlisted code (81599).

These codes encompass all analytical services required (eg, cell lysis, nucleic acid stabilization, extraction, digestion, amplification, hybridization, and detection) in addition to the algorithmic analysis itself. Procedures that are required prior to cell lysis (eg, microdissection, codes 88380 and 88381) should be reported separately.

🖎 Rationale

The Multianalyte Assays with Algorithmic Analyses (MAAAs) guidelines were revised and updated for several reasons. First, the guidelines now reference the addition of the new GSPs and Other Molecular Multianalyte Assays subsection. Second, the guidelines clarify that MAAAs utilize multiple results derived from "panels of analyses" instead of "assays." The updated guidelines also clarify the methodological differences between GSPs and other molecular multianalyte assays versus multianalyte assays with algorithmic analyses. Finally, the MAAA guidelines have been revised to clarify that in order to report an MAAA code, the analysis performed must be specifically described by the MAAA code descriptor and, if proprietary, it must be the test represented by the proprietary name listed in Appendix O of the CPT codebook.

81500   Oncology (ovarian), biochemical assays of two proteins (CA-125 and HE4), utilizing serum, with menopausal status, algorithm reported as a risk score

●81519   Oncology (breast), mRNA, gene expression profiling by real-time RT-PCR of 21 genes, utilizing formalin-fixed paraffin embedded tissue, algorithm reported as recurrence score

(Do not use 81599 for multianalyte assays with algorithmic analyses listed in Appendix O)

⦸=Modifier 51 Exempt   ⊙=Moderate Sedation   ✚=Add-on Code   𝒩=FDA approval pending

Rationale

MAAA code 81519 has been established to report genetic profiling of breast tissue in patients with early-stage invasive breast cancer. This test is used to predict chemotherapy benefit and risk of recurrence.

Clinical Example (81519)

A 60-year-old female with early stage (stage I or II) node-negative, estrogen receptor positive (ER+) invasive breast cancer visits her oncologist two weeks after diagnosis and lumpectomy. The oncologist orders breast cancer assay. The assay is used to analyze the expression of 21 genes to provide a recurrence score unique to this patient. The recurrence score predicts chemotherapy benefit and indicates the 10-year risk of distant recurrence.

Description of Procedure (81519)

The clinician submits a specimen block with the greatest amount/area of invasive breast carcinoma/associated stroma and the least amount of noninvasive mammary epithelium.

Stained slides are prepared from each specimen for pathology review. After confirmation that the sample obtained meets specimen acceptance criteria and macrodissection where necessary, the RNA is extracted from the breast cancer tumor specimen and purified.

The assay analyzes the expression of a 21-gene panel using reverse-transcriptase polymerase chain reaction (RT-PCR). To quantify gene expression, RNA is extracted from formalin-fixed, paraffin-embedded tumor tissue and subjected to DNase I treatment. Total RNA content is measured, and the absence of DNA contamination is verified. Reverse transcription is performed and is followed by quantitative PCR. The expression of each of 16 cancer-related genes is measured in triplicate and then normalized relative to a set of five reference genes, also measured in triplicate. The recurrence score result is calculated from the gene expression results.

Rationale

Many of the changes included in the Therapeutic Drug Assay and Chemistry subsections for drug testing have been made to accommodate the addition of the new Drug Assay subsection. These changes include: (1) revisions to guidelines in the Therapeutic Drug Assays subsection to reflect the type of testing and specimen type for which these procedure are intended; (2) the addition of parenthetical notes to direct users to the appropriate definitive drug testing codes to use in place of the deleted codes; and (3) the addition and revision of new and existing code to identify "total" vs "free" testing of metabolites. In addition, see the Drug Assay subsection for additional explanation of the changes to the Therapeutic Drug Assay codes and guidelines.

▶(82000 has been deleted)◀

▶(82003 has been deleted. For acetaminophen, see 80329, 80330, 80331)◀

▶(82055 has been deleted. For alcohol, any specimen except breath, see 80320, 80321, 80322)◀

82075   Alcohol (ethanol), breath

▶(82101 has been deleted. For alkaloids, use 80323)◀

▶(Amobarbital, use 80345)◀

▶(82145 has been deleted. For amphetamine or methamphetamine, see 80324, 80325, 80326)◀

▶(Aspirin, see acetylsalicylic acid, 80329, 80330, 80331)◀

▶(82205 has been deleted. For barbiturates not elsewhere specified, use 80345)◀

▶(82520 has been deleted. For cocaine or metabolite, use 80353)◀

▶(Cocaine, qualitative analysis, use 80353)◀

▶(Codeine, qualitative analysis, use 80361)◀

Rationale

Parentheticals that direct users to use the appropriate definitive drug testing codes in place of the deleted codes have been added.

▲**82541**   Column chromatography/mass spectrometry (eg, GC/MS, or HPLC/MS), non-drug analyte not elsewhere specified; qualitative, single stationary and mobile phase

▲**82542**   quantitative, single stationary and mobile phase

▲**82543**   stable isotope dilution, single analyte, quantitative, single stationary and mobile phase

▲**82544**   stable isotope dilution, multiple analytes, quantitative, single stationary and mobile phase

▶(For column chromatography/mass spectrometry of drugs or substances, see **Drug Assay** 80300, 80301, 80302, 80303, 80304, 80320-80377, or specific analyte code[s] in the **Chemistry** section)◀

Rationale

Code 82541 (parent code to codes 82542-82544) has been revised to specify "non-drug" analyte in the descriptor. A parenthetical note has been added to direct users to the new codes in the Drug Assay subsection to report column chromatography/mass spectrometry of drugs.

82607   Cyanocobalamin (Vitamin B-12);

82608   unsaturated binding capacity

(Cyclic AMP, use 82030)

82626   Dehydroepiandrosterone (DHEA)

▶(Do not report 82626 in conjunction with 80327, 80328 to identify anabolic steroid testing for testosterone)◀

82638   Dibucaine number

▶(Dichloroethane, use 82441)◀

▶(Dichloromethane, use 82441)◀

▶(82646 has been deleted. For dihydrocodeinone, use 80361)◀

▶(82649 has been deleted. For opiates, use 80361)◀

▶(82651 has been deleted. For anabolic steroids, see 80327, 80328)◀

▶(82654 has been deleted. For dimethadione, see 80339, 80340, 80341)◀

(Dipropylacetic acid, use 80164)

82664   Electrophoretic technique, not elsewhere

▶(82666 has been deleted. For epiandrosterone, see 80327, 80328)◀

82679   Estrone

▶(Ethanol, use 80320)◀

▶(82690 has been deleted. For ethchlorvynol, ethyl alcohol, use 80320)◀

82735   Fluoride

▶(82742 has been deleted. For flurazepam, see 80346, 80347)◀

82951   tolerance test (GTT), 3 specimens (includes glucose)

+ 82952   tolerance test, each additional beyond 3 specimens (List separately in addition to code for primary procedure)

(Use 82952 in conjunction with 82951)

▶(82953 has been deleted)◀

82965   Glutamate dehydrogenase

▶(82975 has been deleted. For glutamine [glutamic acid amide], see 82127, 82128, 82131)◀

82979   Glutathione reductase, RBC

▶(82980 has been deleted)◀

✍ Rationale

As part of an effort to ensure that the CPT code set reflects current clinical practice, codes 82953 and 82975 have been deleted due to low utilization. In addition, consistent with changes made for drug test reporting and accurate reporting of CPT codes, codes 82646, 82649, 82651, 82654, 82666, 82690, 82742, and 82980 have been deleted to support the establishment of the new Drug Assay subsection. In support of these changes, parenthetical notes have been added indicating that the appropriate definitive drug testing codes should be used in place of the deleted codes.

●**83006**   Growth stimulation expressed gene 2 (ST2, Interleukin 1 receptor like-1)

▶(83008 has been deleted)◀

🖉 Rationale

Chemistry code 83006 has been established to report immunoassay measurement of ST2 concentration (growth stimulation expressed gene 2/interleukin 1 receptor-like 1 [IL1RL1]) for risk stratification following congestive heart failure. Previously, the CPT code set did not include a specific code to report the measurement of the suppression of tumorigenicity 2 (ST2) protein.

🩺 Clinical Example (83006)

A 53-year-old male presents with a new heart failure diagnosis with left ventricle ejection fraction (LVEF) of 30%. The patient has a history of ischemic heart disease and multiple prior myocardial infarctions. The patient was treated with multiple medications. The clinician measured the patient's natriuretic peptide to assess the severity of heart failure. After the patient has had a clinical decompensation, the clinician ordered the ST2 Assay to aid in assessing the prognosis of the patient's chronic heart failure.

Description of Procedure (83006)

A sample (human serum, EDTA-plasma, or heparin plasma) is collected using standard collection techniques. Centrifugation and separation of the serum or plasma from the cellular components was performed after sample collection. The sample is then sent to the laboratory for analysis. The ST2 antibody coated wells are numbered and the test kit is equilibrated to room temperature for a minimum of 30 minutes. The wash buffer, streptavidin-HRP conjugate concentrate, controls, standards, and blank are prepared according to the ST2 Assay instructions for use. The patient samples, controls, and blanks are diluted and transferred to a 96-well U-bottom plate. The plate is then incubated for 1 hour ± 5 minutes at 64°-77°F, with shaking at 750 rpm. The incubation mixture is then removed from the incubator and the plate is emptied and washed. The anti-ST2 biotinylated antibody reagent is dispensed into each well and the plate is incubated for an additional 1 hour ± 5 minutes at 64°-77°F. The incubation mixture is removed, emptied, and washed. The working streptavidin-HRP conjugate is dispensed into each well, and the plate is incubated for 30 minutes ± 5 minutes at 64°-77°F. The plate is again removed, emptied, and washed. The tetramethylbenzidine (TMB) reagent is dispensed into each well and incubated for 20 minutes ± 5 minutes at 64°-77°F with shaking at 750 rpm in the dark. The stop solution is then pipetted into each well and mixed gently for 30 seconds. The contents of the well turn from blue to yellow, and the laboratory technician reads the absorbance at 450 nm with a microtiter well reader within 15 minutes of adding the stop solution.

The clinician obtains the results of the assay. Based on the results of the assay, in conjunction with clinical evaluation, the clinician assesses the prognosis of the patient's chronic heart failure.

🖉 Rationale

As part of an effort to ensure that the CPT code set reflects current clinical practice, code 83008 has been deleted due to low utilization.

⊘=Modifier 51 Exempt   ⊙=Moderate Sedation   ✚=Add-on Code   ⋏=FDA approval pending

83020 Hemoglobin fractionation and quantitation; electrophoresis (eg, A2, S, C, and/or F)

83021 chromatography (eg, A2, S, C, and/or F)

▶(For glycosylated [A1c] hemoglobin analysis, by electrophoresis or chromatography, in the absence of an identified hemoglobin variant, use 83036)◀

83026 Hemoglobin; by copper sulfate method, non-automated

83030 F (fetal), chemical

83033 F (fetal), qualitative

83036 glycosylated (A1C)

▶(For glycosylated [A1C] hemoglobin analysis, by electrophoresis or chromatography, in the setting of an identified hemoglobin variant, see 83020, 83021)◀

(For fecal hemoglobin detection by immunoassay, use 82274)

✍ Rationale

In order to reflect current clinical practice and facilitate accurate reporting for glycosylated (A1C) hemoglobin testing, two cross-references following codes 83021 and 83036 were updated. The cross-references now include "electrophoresis" as an additional method for determining hemoglobin variants were updated.

83037 glycosylated (A1C) by device cleared by FDA for home use

83045 methemoglobin, qualitative

83050 methemoglobin, quantitative

(For transcutaneous quantitative methemoglobin determination, use 88741)

83051 plasma

▶(83055 has been deleted)◀

83070 Hemosiderin, qualitative

▶(83071 has been deleted)◀

(HIAA, use 83497)

(High performance liquid chromatography [HPLC], use 82486)

83570 Isocitric dehydrogenase (IDH)
(Isonicotinic acid hydrazide, INH, see code for specific method)

▶(Isopropyl alcohol, use 80320)◀

83633 Lactose, urine, qualitative

▶(83634 has been deleted)◀

✍ Rationale

As part of an effort to ensure that the CPT code set reflects current clinical practice, codes 83055, 83071, and 83634 have been deleted due to low utilization.

83788   Mass spectrometry and tandem mass spectrometry (MS, MS/MS), analyte not elsewhere specified, qualitative, each specimen

83789   Mass spectrometry and tandem mass spectrometry (MS, MS/MS), analyte not elsewhere specified, quantitative, each specimen

▶(For column chromatography/mass spectrometry of drugs or substances, see **Drug Assay** 80300, 80301, 80302, 80303, 80304, 80320-80377, or specific analyte code[s] in the **Chemistry** section)◀

▶(83805 has been deleted. For quantitative testing for meprobamate, see 80369, 80370)◀

▶(83840 has been deleted. For methadone, use 80358)◀

▶(Methamphetamine, see 80324, 80325, 80326)◀

▶(83858 has been deleted. For methsuximide, see 80339, 80340, 80341)◀

▶(Methyl alcohol, use 80320)◀

83864   Mucopolysaccharides, acid, quantitative

▶(83866 has been deleted)◀

▶(83887 has been deleted. For nicotine, use 80323)◀

▶(83925 has been deleted. For opiates, see 80361, 80362, 80363, 80364, or the specific drug [eg, fentanyls, oxycodone])◀

▶(For tissue, see 88342, 88365)◀

▶(Phenobarbital, use 80345)◀

▶(84022 has been deleted. For phenothiazine, see 80342, 80343, 80344)◀

✍ Rationale

Parentheticals have been added to direct users to the appropriate codes to identify: (1) column chromatography/mass spectrometry procedures; (2) methamphetamine; (3) methyl alcohol; and (4) phenobarbitol testing using codes in the Drug Assay section.

In support of the changes for immunohistochemistry procedures, a parenthetical note has also been added to direct users to the appropriate codes for staining procedures.

As part of an effort to ensure that the CPT code set reflects current clinical practice, code 83866 has been deleted due to low utilization. In addition, to accommodate development of new codes for drug testing (located in the Drug Assay section), codes 83805, 83840, 83858, 83887, 83925, and 84022 have also been deleted. The deletion parentheticals following these codes direct users to the appropriate codes to report testing for these analytes.

84126   Porphyrins, feces, quantitative

▶(84127 has been deleted)◀

⊘=Modifier 51 Exempt   ⊙=Moderate Sedation   ✚=Add-on Code   𝑵=FDA approval pending

🖋 Rationale

As part of an effort to ensure that the CPT code set reflects current clinical practice, code 84127 has been deleted due to low utilization.

(Porphyrin precursors, see 82135, 84106, 84110)

(For protoporphyrin, RBC, see 84202, 84203)

84252 Riboflavin (Vitamin B-2)

▶(Salicylates, see 80329, 80330, 80331)◀

🖋 Rationale

A parenthentical has been added to direct users to the appropriate codes for salicylate testing.

84315 Specific gravity (except urine)

(For specific gravity, urine, see 81000-81003)

(Stone analysis, see 82355-82370)

▶(For suppression of growth stimulation expressed gene 2 [ST2] testing, use 83006)◀

🖋 Rationale

A third parenthentical note has been added following code 84315 to direct users to the new code for ST2 testing. For more information see the Rationale for code 83006.

84392 Sulfate, urine

▶(Sulfhemoglobin, use hemoglobin, 83060)◀

🖋 Rationale

In accordance with the deletion of code 83055, the cross-reference parenthetical note for sulfhemoglobin following code 84392 has been revised with the removal of code 83055.

84402 Testosterone; free

84403   total

▶(Do not report 84402, 84403 in conjunction with 80327, 80328 to identify anabolic steroid testing for testosterone)◀

84446 Tocopherol alpha (Vitamin E)

▲**84600** Volatiles (eg, acetic anhydride, diethylether)

▶(For carbon tetrachloride, dichloroethane, dichloromethane, use 82441)◀

▶(For isopropyl alcohol and methanol, use 80320)◀

84999 Unlisted chemistry procedure

▶(For definitive testing of a drug, not otherwise specified, see 80299, 80375, 80376, 80377)◀

Rationale

An exclusionary parenthetical note following code 84403 has been added to exclude the use of codes 84402 and 84403 in conjunction with codes for anabolic steroid testing, which are now identified in the Definitive Drug Testing section. In addition, certain analytes have been removed from the descriptor for code 84600, as these analytes are included in the new Definitive Drug Testing subsection. For alignment, consistency, and accurate reporting of CPT codes, these terms were deleted to support the establishment of the new Drug Assay subsection. Parenthetical notes have been added to direct users to use the appropriate definitive drug testing codes for the noted analytes and procedures that are not otherwise specified.

Transfusion Medicine

▲86900   Blood typing, serologic; ABO

▲86901   Rh (D)

▲86902   antigen testing of donor blood using reagent serum, each antigen test

(If multiple blood units are tested for the same antigen, 86902 should be reported once for each antigen for each unit tested)

▲86904   antigen screening for compatible unit using patient serum, per unit screened

▲86905   RBC antigens, other than ABO or Rh (D), each

▲86906   Rh phenotyping, complete

▶(For human erythrocyte antigen typing by molecular pathology techniques, use 81403)◀

Rationale

To distinguish blood-typing codes 86900-86906 from the RHD gene deletion–analysis and human erythrocyte antigen gene–analyses that have been added to molecular pathology Tier 2 code 81403, codes 86900-86906 have been revised to specify serologic blood-typing procedures. A cross-reference parenthetical note has been added following code 86906 to direct users to report code 81403 for human erythrocyte antigen–typing by molecular pathology techniques.

Microbiology

Presumptive identification of microorganisms is defined as identification by colony morphology, growth on selective media, Gram stains, or up to three tests (eg, catalase, oxidase, indole, urease). Definitive identification of microorganisms is defined as an identification to the genus or species level that requires additional tests (eg, biochemical panels, slide cultures). If additional studies involve molecular probes, nucleic acid sequencing, chromatography, or immunologic techniques, these should be separately coded using 87140-87158, in addition to definitive identification codes. The molecular diagnostic codes (eg, 81161, 81200-81408) are not to be used in combination with or instead of the procedures represented by 87140-87158. For multiple specimens/sites use modifier 59. For repeat laboratory tests performed on the same day, use modifier 91.

▶(87001 has been deleted)◀

✒ Rationale

As part of an effort to ensure that the CPT code set reflects current clinical practice, code 87001 has been deleted due to low utilization.

87003   Animal inoculation, small animal, with observation and dissection

87470   Infectious agent detection by nucleic acid (DNA or RNA); Bartonella henselae and Bartonella quintana, direct probe technique

▲87501   influenza virus, includes reverse transcription, when performed, and amplified probe technique, each type or subtype

▲87502   influenza virus, for multiple types or sub-types, includes multiplex reverse transcription and multiplex amplified probe technique, first 2 types or sub-types

✦▲87503   influenza virus, for multiple types or sub-types, includes multiplex reverse transcription and multiplex amplified probe technique, each additional influenza virus type or sub-type beyond 2 (List separately in addition to code for primary procedure)

✒ Rationale

To maintain consistency among all codes that include the reverse transcription technique, the descriptor for code 87501 has been revised to indicate that reverse transcription is included, when performed. In addition, the descriptors for codes 87502 and 87503 have been revised to indicate that the multiplex amplified probe technique is included to more clearly portray the intended use of these codes.

●87505   gastrointestinal pathogen (eg, Clostridium difficile, E. coli, Salmonella, Shigella, norovirus, Giardia), includes multiplex reverse transcription, when performed, and multiplex amplified probe technique, multiple types or subtypes, 3-5 targets

●87506   gastrointestinal pathogen (eg, Clostridium difficile, E. coli, Salmonella, Shigella, norovirus, Giardia), includes multiplex reverse transcription, when performed, and multiplex amplified probe technique, multiple types or subtypes, 6-11 targets

●87507   gastrointestinal pathogen (eg, Clostridium difficile, E. coli, Salmonella, Shigella, norovirus, Giardia), includes multiplex reverse transcription, when performed, and multiplex amplified probe technique, multiple types or subtypes, 12-25 targets

✒ Rationale

Three new codes (87505, 87506, 87507) have been established to report nucleic acid detection of gastrointestinal pathogens. These qualitative procedures detect multiple pathogens simultaneously, and are performed on patients with symptoms of infectious colitis or gastroenteritis. The new codes reflect that the multiplex amplified probe techique is included, and that multiplex reverse transcription is included, when performed (a procedure that is not necessary when only DNA is assayed). The unit of service for these codes is the number of targets. Code 87505 describes three to five targets, code 87506 describes six to 11 targets, and code 87507 describes 12 to 15 targets.

🩺 Clinical Example (87505)

A patient presents to his or her physician with severe abdominal pain, diarrhea (more than 6 unformed stools), nausea, temperature of 101.2°F, and dehydration persisting more than 24 hours. The physician suspects the patient may have a GI infection. The physician obtains a stool specimen, places it in a transport medium, and sends it to the laboratory for multiplex testing for GI pathogens. (For three to five targets tested, use 87505; for six to 11 targets, use 87506; and for 12 to 25 targets use 87507.)

Description of Procedure (87505)

Upon receipt of the stool specimen, high-quality total nucleic acid is isolated and stored under RNase-free conditions. Multiplexed reverse transcription is used to convert RNA to cDNA followed by PCR-based amplification using primers for multiple gastrointestinal pathogens including bacteria, viruses, and parasites along with a control gene.

🩺 Clinical Example (87506)

A pediatric patient presents to his or her physician with severe abdominal pain, diarrhea (more than 6 unformed stools), nausea, temperature of 101.2°F, and dehydration persisting 24 hours or more. The physician suspects the patient may have a GI infection. The physician obtains a stool specimen, places it in a transport medium, and sends it to the laboratory for multiplex testing for 10 gastrointestinal pathogens.

Description of Procedure (87506)

Upon receipt of the stool specimen, high-quality total nucleic acid is isolated and stored under RNase-free conditions. Multiplexed reverse transcription is used to convert RNA to cDNA followed by PCR-based amplification using primers for multiple gastrointestinal pathogens including bacteria, viruses, and parasites along with a control gene.

🩺 Clinical Example (87507)

A patient presents to his or her physician with severe abdominal pain, diarrhea (more than 6 unformed stools), nausea, temperature of 101.2°F, and dehydration persisting 24 hours or more. The physician suspects the patient may have a GI infection. The physician obtains a stool specimen, places it in a transport medium, and sends it to the laboratory for multiplex testing for 20 gastrointestinal pathogens.

Description of Procedure (87507)

Upon receipt of the stool specimen, high-quality total nucleic acid is isolated and stored under RNase-free conditions. Multiplexed reverse transcription is used to convert RNA to cDNA followed by PCR-based amplification using primers for multiple gastrointestinal pathogens including bacteria, viruses, and parasites along with a control gene.

⊘=Modifier 51 Exempt ⊙=Moderate Sedation ✚=Add-on Code 𝒩=FDA approval pending

#●87623	Human Papillomavirus (HPV), low-risk types (eg, 6, 11, 42, 43, 44)
#●87624	Human Papillomavirus (HPV), high-risk types (eg, 16, 18, 31, 33, 35, 39, 45, 51, 52, 56, 58, 59, 68)

►(When both low-risk and high-risk HPV types are performed in a single assay, use only 87624)◄

#●87625	Human Papillomavirus (HPV), types 16 and 18 only, includes type 45, if performed

►(87620 has been deleted. To report, see 87623, 87624, 87625)◄

►(87621 has been deleted. To report, see 87623, 87624, 87625)◄

►(87622 has been deleted. To report, see 87623, 87624, 87625)◄

Rationale

Codes 87623-87625 have been added to report human papilloma virus (HPV) genotyping to differentiate high- and low-risk HPV types. HPV genotyping should be used in conjunction with or as a follow-up to an abnormal cytology report. HPV codes 87620, 87621, and 87622 have been deleted and replaced with genotyping codes that describe the specific types tested. Low-risk HPV types (eg, 6, 11, 42, 43, 44) should be reported with code 87623, and high-risk HPV types (eg, 16, 18, 31, 33, 35, 39, 45, 51, 52, 56, 58, 59, 68) should be reported with code 87624. Code 87625 should be used to report only HPV types 16 and 18 and includes type 45, if performed. HPV types 16 and 18 (87625) are considered high-risk due to their strong association with cervical cancers. If both low-risk and high-risk HPV types are performed in a single assay, only code 87624 for high-risk genotyping should be reported as indicated in the parenthetical note following code 87624.

Clinical Example (87623)

A patient with recurrent laryngeal papillomatosis has a bronchoscopy, which identifies several tracheal papillomatous growths, which are sampled. Pathology evaluation identifies squamous papillomas with HPV-like changes. Pathology tissue sample is tested for low-risk HPV to assist in determining if intralesional therapy is appropriate.

Description of Procedure (87623)

The patient pathology tissue sample is processed and subjected to HPV genotype-specific detection using real-time PCR technology. Subsequently, the patient is referred back to the attending/treating physician(s) for follow-up.

Clinical Example (87624)

A 33-year-old female presents to her gynecologist for a routine appointment. A liquid-based Pap test was collected with a request for high-risk HPV co-testing.

Description of Procedure (87624)

An aliquot from the liquid-based Pap vial was subjected to HPV genotype-specific detection using real-time PCR technology. A result of positive for high-risk HPV was obtained. Subsequently, the patient is referred back to the attending/treating physician(s) for follow-up.

Clinical Example (87625)

A 33-year-old female presents to her gynecologist for a routine appointment. A Pap test was collected with a request for high-risk HPV co-testing. The Pap test–result was negative for intraepithelial lesion or malignancy and the HPV test–result was positive for high-risk HPV DNA. The gynecologist requested the HPV 16/18 assay to be performed on the liquid-based Pap test sample.

Description of Procedure (87625)

An aliquot from the liquid-based Pap vial was subjected to HPV 16/18 genotype-specific detection using real-time PCR technology. A result of positive for HPV genotype 18 was obtained. Subsequently, the patient is referred back to the attending/treating physician(s) for follow-up. The patient was referred for immediate colposcopic evaluation.

▲87631   respiratory virus (eg, adenovirus, influenza virus, coronavirus, metapneumovirus, parainfluenza virus, respiratory syncytial virus, rhinovirus), includes multiplex reverse transcription, when performed, and multiplex amplified probe technique, multiple types or subtypes, 3-5 targets

▲87632   respiratory virus (eg, adenovirus, influenza virus, coronavirus, metapneumovirus, parainfluenza virus, respiratory syncytial virus, rhinovirus), includes multiplex reverse transcription, when performed, and multiplex amplified probe technique, multiple types or subtypes, 6-11 targets

▲87633   respiratory virus (eg, adenovirus, influenza virus, coronavirus, metapneumovirus, parainfluenza virus, respiratory syncytial virus, rhinovirus), includes multiplex reverse transcription, when performed, and multiplex amplified probe technique, multiple types or subtypes, 12-25 targets

Rationale

For consistency with the new respiratory virus detection codes, the code descriptors of existing codes 87631, 87632, and 87633 have been revised to reflect that multiplex reverse transcription is included, when performed, and that the multiplex amplified probe technique is included.

87802   Infectious agent antigen detection by immunoassay with direct optical observation; Streptococcus, group B

87803   Clostridium difficile toxin A

#●87806   HIV-1 antigen(s), with HIV-1 and HIV-2 antibodies

87804   Influenza

Rationale

Code 87806 has been established to report HIV-1 antigen(s) detection by immunoassay with direct optical observation, with HIV-1 and HIV-2 antibodies. This procedure is performed for the detection of acute HIV infection before the appearance of symptoms.

Clinical Example (87806)

Any patient, male or female, between the ages of 16 and 65 enters an emergency room with certain clinical symptoms (fever, malaise, joint pain, and sore throat)

⊘=Modifier 51 Exempt   ⊙=Moderate Sedation   ✚=Add-on Code   𝒩=FDA approval pending

that could possibly indicate early HIV infection or some other possible diagnosis. Hospital protocol might have patient opt out of testing for HIV. Because Ab-only test would only be able to detect later detection (after formation of Ab) and would most likely show a non-reactive or HIV-negative result for an acute phase infection, especially for a patient at high-risk for HIV, the hospital would likely choose a rapid test with both antigen and antibody capabilities so that both acute and more-established HIV infection could be detected.

Description of Procedure (87806)

The sample collection can be venous whole blood, serum, or plasma collected from patients in tube containing EDTA. A finger stick for whole blood can also be used. The small drop of sample is placed onto the test strip. If sample is whole blood, a chase buffer is added to sample. After 20 minutes the results can be visually read off of a test strip. A hospital performing these tests regularly will have previously validated their control samples using the same methodology described for patient samples.

Cytopathology

88199   Unlisted cytopathology procedure

▶(For electron microscopy, use 88348)◀

 Rationale

In accordance with the deletion of electron microscopy scanning code 88349, the cross-reference parenthetical note following code 88199 (unlisted procedure) has been revised with the removal of code 88349.

Cytogenetic Studies

▶Molecular pathology procedures should be reported using the appropriate code from Tier 1 (81161, 81200-81383), Tier 2 (81400-81408), Genomic Sequencing Procedures and Other Molecular Multianalyte Assays (81410-81471), or Multianalyte Assays with Algorithmic Analyses (81500-81512) sections. If no specific code exists, one of the unlisted codes (81479 or 81599) should be used.◀

 Rationale

For consistency and alignment with the new Genomic Sequencing Procedures (GSPs) and Other Molecular Multianalyte Assays subsection, the cytogenetic studies guidelines were revised to include reference to the GSPs and other molecular multianalyte assays codes (81410-81471).

▶(For immunocytochemistry and immunohistochemistry, use 88342)◀

▶(For detection of enzyme constituents by immunohistochemical or immunocytochemical technique, use 88342)◀

▲88342 Immunohistochemistry or immunocytochemistry, per specimen; initial single antibody stain procedure

(For quantitative or semiquantitative immunohistochemistry, see 88360, 88361)

▶(88343 has been deleted. For multiplex antibody stain procedure, use 88344)◀

#+●88341 each additional single antibody stain procedure (List separately in addition to code for primary procedure)

▶(Use 88341 in conjunction with 88342)◀

▶(For multiplex antibody stain procedure, use 88344)◀

●88344 each multiplex antibody stain procedure

▶(Do not use more than one unit of 88341, 88342, 88344 for each separately identifiable antibody per specimen)◀

▶(Do not report 88341, 88342, 88344 in conjunction with 88360, 88361 unless each procedure is for a different antibody)◀

▶(When multiple separately identifiable antibodies are applied to the same specimen [ie, multiplex antibody stain procedure], use one unit of 88344)◀

▶(When multiple antibodies are applied to the same slide that are not separately identifiable, [eg, antibody cocktails], use 88342, unless an additional separately identifiable antibody is also used, then use 88344)◀

Rationale

The immunohistochemistry/immunocytochemistry codes have been updated to reflect current methodologies. Code 88342 has been revised to allow multiple antibodies that are not separately identifiable to be reported together with a single code. Previously, code 88342 was structured so that each antibody had to be coded separately.

Code 88343 has been deleted and replaced with two new codes (88341, 88344). Code 88341 allows for each additional single antibody stain procedure to be reported separately and should be used in conjunction with parent code 88342. Code 88344 should be reported when multiple separately identifiable antibodies are applied to the same specimen slide. A combination of staining methodologies may be used, and thus, a series of parenthetical instructions have been added to guide the user in the appropriate number of codes to report per specimen.

The difference in the work and technology required in these two different staining methodologies (multiplex antibody staining vs antibody cocktail staining) are significant enough to require separate codes (88341, 88344). Immunohistochemical studies are typically performed singly (ie, single primary antibody used on a single glass slide). However, on occasion multiple primary antibodies can be used on the same tissue/glass slide. When the different antibodies can be differentiated microscopically (eg, by staining location or separate chromogenic detection), the stain is referred to as "multiplex." If the separate antibodies cannot be separately differentiated microscopically, it is referred to as an antibody "cocktail." A combination of staining methodologies may be used, and thus, a series of parenthetical instructions have been added to guide the user in the use of this new series of codes to enable reporting codes multiple times per specimen.

Clinical Example (88341)

After examination of the CD15 immunohistochemical stain on a lymph node of a 25-year-old male with suspected Hodgkin lymphoma, microscopic examination of a CD45 immunohistochemical antibody stain is performed.

Description of Procedure (88341)

Examine positive control tissue known to contain cells that express CD45 to verify that the procedure is working and the stain is optimized. Also examine the negative control to check for nonspecific binding and false positive staining. Microscopically examine the patient sample. Interpret the staining pattern, and determine its significance in its histologic and cellular location.

Clinical Example (88342)

Microscopic examination of a CD15 immunohistochemical antibody stain performed on a lymph node of a 25-year-old male with suspected Hodgkin lymphoma.

Description of Procedure (88342)

Examine positive control tissue known to contain cells that express CD15 to verify that the procedure is working and the stain is optimized. Also examine the negative control to check for nonspecific binding and false positive staining. Microscopically examine the patient sample. Interpret the staining pattern, and determine its significance in its histologic and cellular location.

Clinical Example (88344)

Microscopic examination of an immunohistochemical cocktail of P504S and HMWK (34ßE12) performed on a prostate needle core biopsy from a 66-year-old male with elevated PSA.

Description of Procedure (88344)

Examine positive control tissue known to contain cells that express both the first and second antibody in the cocktail, 34ßE12 and P504S, to verify that the procedure is working and the stain is optimized for both antibodies. Microscopically examine the patient sample. Interpret the staining pattern of the P504S antibody and the 34ßE12 antibody, and determine the significance of their histologic and cellular location.

88348   Electron microscopy, diagnostic

▶(88349 has been deleted. To report, use 88348)◀

✎ Rationale

Code 88349 has been deleted because electron microscopy scanning was an extremely limited clinical service, which could be more appropriately reported with code 88348.

▲**88360**   Morphometric analysis, tumor immunohistochemistry (eg, Her-2/neu, estrogen receptor/progesterone receptor), quantitative or semiquantitative, per specimen, each single antibody stain procedure; manual

▲**88361**   using computer-assisted technology

▶(Do not report 88360, 88361 in conjunction with 88341, 88342, or 88344 unless each procedure is for a different antibody)◀

▶(Morphometric analysis of a multiplex antibody stain should be reported with one unit of 88360 or 88361, per specimen)◀

✎ Rationale

Histomorphometry codes 88360 and 88361 used to report the detection of protein receptors for diagnosing the development of tumor(s) and cancer have been revised to clarify "per specimen, each single antibody stain procedure."

Codes 88360 and 88361 were previously structured to require each antibody to be coded separately; however, they did not reflect current technology, which enables multiple antibodies to be tested per specimen utilizing a manual technique (88360) or computer-assisted technology (88361). Instructional parenthetical notes have been added to clarify the use of these codes for multiplex antibody staining, and an exclusionary parenthetical note has also been added to disallow the use of immunohistochemistry/immunocytochemistry codes 88341, 88342, and 88344 in conjunction with codes 88360 and 88361.

▲**88365**   In situ hybridization (eg, FISH), per specimen; initial single probe stain procedure

#✚●**88364**   each additional single probe stain procedure (List separately in addition to code for primary procedure)

▶(Use 88364 in conjunction with 88365)◀

●**88366**   each multiplex probe stain procedure

▶(Do not report 88365, 88366 in conjunction with 88367, 88368, 88374, 88377 for the same probe)◀

▲**88367**   Morphometric analysis, in situ hybridization (quantitative or semi-quantitative), using computer-assisted technology, per specimen; initial single probe stain procedure

#+ ●88373   each additional single probe stain procedure (List separately in addition to code for primary procedure)

▶(Use 88373 in conjunction with 88367)◀

●88374   each multiplex probe stain procedure

▶(Do not report 88367, 88374 in conjunction with 88365, 88366, 88368, 88377 for the same probe)◀

▲88368   Morphometric analysis, in situ hybridization (quantitative or semi-quantitative), manual, per specimen; initial single probe stain procedure

+ ●88369   each additional single probe stain procedure (List separately in addition to code for primary procedure)

▶(Use 88369 in conjunction with 88368)◀

●88377   each multiplex probe stain procedure

▶(Do not report 88368 or 88377 in conjunction with 88365, 88366, 88367, 88374 for the same probe)◀

(For morphometric in situ hybridization evaluation of urinary tract cytologic specimens, see 88120, 88121)

Rationale

The *in situ* hybridization codes 88365, 88367, and 88368 have been revised and expanded into three separate families of codes that identify: (1) the initial single probe stain procedure (88365, 88367, 88368); (2) each additional single probe stain procedure (88364, 88373, 88369); and (3) each multiplex probe stain procedure (88364, 88374, 88369). Exclusionary parenthetical notes have also been added to each family of codes, as each code is mutually exclusive and cannot be reported in conjunction with one another.

Clinical Example (88364)

A 60-year-old male with a history of lung transplant develops pneumonitis and undergoes transbronchial biopsy. A lung tissue section has been examined for the presence of Epstein-Barr virus (EBV) using in situ hybridization. Another tissue section is examined for cytomegalovirus by in situ hybridization.

Description of Procedure (88364)

Examine positive control tissue known to contain cells that express cytomegalovirus (CMV) to verify that the stain is optimized. Also examine the negative control to check for nonspecific binding and false positive staining. Examine the patient sample by fluorescence microscopy. Interpret the CMV staining pattern, and determine its significance in its histologic and cellular location. Compare the data to current and/or prior specimens and reports. Correlate the findings with the corresponding hematoxylin and eosin (H&E)-stained slide, clinical history, and previous tissue samples and laboratory tests, and report.

Clinical Example (88365)

A 68-year-old male with a history of kidney transplant presents with lymph-adenopathy and undergoes biopsy. A lymphoproliferative process is identified histologically. A stained slide of the lymph node biopsy is analyzed by fluorescence in situ hybridization (FISH) for the presence of EBV-encoded RNAs (EBERs).

Description of Procedure (88365)

Examine positive control tissue known to contain cells that express EBER to verify that the stain is optimized. Also examine the negative control to check for nonspecific binding and false positive staining. Examine the patient sample by fluorescence microscopy. Interpret the EBER staining pattern, and determine its significance in its histologic and cellular location. Compare the data to current and/or prior specimens and reports. Correlate the findings with the corresponding H&E-stained slide, clinical history, and previous tissue samples and laboratory tests, and report.

Clinical Example (88366)

A 67-year-old male with lymphadenopathy presents for biopsy. The lymph node biopsy histologically shows features suggestive of malignant lymphoma. A stained slide is analyzed by FISH for IGH@/BCL2 translocation using DNA probes for both IGH@ and BCL2.

Description of Procedure (88366)

Examine positive control tissue known to contain cells that express probes IGH@ and BCL2 to verify that the stain is optimized for both probes. Examine the patient sample by fluorescence microscopy. Interpret both the IGH@ and BCL2 probes, and determine their significance in their histologic and cellular locations. Compare the data to current and/or prior specimens and reports. Correlate the findings with the corresponding H&E-stained slide, clinical history, and previous tissue samples and laboratory tests, and report.

Clinical Example (88367)

A 60-year-old male presents with a suspected plasma cell dyscrasia. In situ hybridization is performed on a bone marrow specimen to assess for relative kappa light chain mRNA expression using computer assisted technology.

Description of Procedure (88367)

Determine the appropriate areas of tumor to evaluate from review of the H&E-stained slide. Examine positive control tissue known to contain cells that express kappa light chain mRNA to verify that the stain is optimized. Also examine the negative control to check for nonspecific binding and false positive staining. Digitally scan the patient sample using brightfield microscopy, and examine the images. Interpret the kappa mRNA staining pattern and quantification of mRNA signals, and determine their significance in their histologic and cellular locations. Compare the data to current and/or prior specimens and reports. Correlate the findings with the corresponding H&E-stained slide, clinical history, and previous tissue samples and laboratory tests, and report.

⃠=Modifier 51 Exempt   ⊙=Moderate Sedation   ✚=Add-on Code   𝑁=FDA approval pending

Clinical Example (88368)

A 60-year-old male presents with a suspected plasma cell dyscrasia. In situ hybridization is performed on a bone marrow specimen to assess for relative kappa light chain mRNA expression using manual technology.

Description of Procedure (88368)

Determine the appropriate areas of tumor to evaluate from review of the H&E-stained slide. Examine positive control tissue known to contain cells that express kappa light chain mRNA to verify that the stain is optimized. Also examine the negative control to check for nonspecific binding and false positive staining. Then examine the patient sample using brightfield microscopy. Interpret the kappa mRNA staining pattern and quantification of mRNA signals, and determine their significance in their histologic and cellular locations. Compare the data to current and/or prior specimens and reports. Correlate the findings with the corresponding H&E-stained slide, clinical history, and previous tissue samples and laboratory tests, and report.

Clinical Example (88369)

A 60-year-old male presents with a suspected plasma cell dyscrasia. In situ hybridization is performed on a bone marrow specimen to assess for relative lambda light chain mRNA expression using manual technology.

Description of Procedure (88369)

Determine the appropriate areas of tumor to evaluate from review of the H&E-stained slide. Examine positive control tissue known to contain cells that express lambda light chain mRNA to verify that the stain is optimized. Also examine the negative control to check for nonspecific binding and false positive staining. Then examine the patient sample using brightfield microscopy. Interpret the lambda mRNA staining pattern and quantification of mRNA signals, and determine their significance in their histologic and cellular locations. Compare and document the ratios of the lambda and kappa mRNA expression levels. Compare the data to current and/or prior specimens and reports. Correlate the findings with the corresponding H&E-stained slide, clinical history, and previous tissue samples and laboratory tests, and report.

Clinical Example (88373)

A 60-year-old male presents with a suspected plasma cell dyscrasia. In situ hybridization is performed on a bone marrow specimen to assess for relative lambda light chain mRNA expression using computer-assisted technology.

Description of Procedure (88373)

Determine the appropriate areas of tumor to evaluate from review of the H&E-stained slide. Examine positive control tissue known to contain cells that express lambda light chain mRNA to verify that the stain is optimized. Also examine the negative control to check for nonspecific binding and false positive staining. Digitally scan the patient sample using brightfield microscopy, and examine the images. Interpret the lambda mRNA staining pattern and quantification of mRNA signals, and determine their significance in their histologic and cellular locations. Compare and document the ratios of the lambda and kappa mRNA expression levels. Compare the data to current and/or prior specimens and reports. Correlate the findings with the corresponding H&E-stained slide, clinical history, and previous tissue samples and laboratory tests, and report.

Clinical Example (88374)

A 54-year-old female has been diagnosed with invasive ductal carcinoma of the breast. A stained slide of the breast tumor is analyzed by FISH quantifying the copy number of HER2 and centromere 17 (CEP17) signals using computer-assisted technology.

Description of Procedure (88374)

Determine the appropriate areas of tumor to evaluate from review of the H&E-stained slide. Examine positive control tissue known to contain cells that express HER2 and CEP17 to verify that the stain is optimized. Also examine the negative control to check for nonspecific binding and false positive staining. Digitally scan the patient sample using fluorescence microscopy and examine the images. Interpret the HER2 and CEP17 staining pattern and quantification of HER2 and CEP17 signals, and determine their significance in their histologic and cellular locations. Also calculate the HER2:CEP17 ratio. Compare the data to current and/or prior specimens and reports. Correlate the findings with the corresponding H&E-stained slide, clinical history, and previous tissue samples and laboratory tests, and report.

Clinical Example (88377)

A 54-year-old female has been diagnosed with invasive ductal carcinoma of the breast. A stained slide of the breast tumor is analyzed by FISH, quantifying the copy number of the HER2 and CEP17 signals using manual technology.

Description of Procedure (88377)

Determine the appropriate areas of tumor to evaluate from review of the H&E-stained slide. Examine positive control tissue known to contain cells that express HER2 and CEP17 to verify that the stain is optimized. Also examine the negative control to check for nonspecific binding and false positive staining. Then examine the patient sample by fluorescence microscopy. Interpret the HER2 and CEP17 staining pattern and quantification of HER2 and CEP17 signals, and determine their significance in their histologic and cellular locations. Also calculate the HER2:CEP17 ratio. Compare the data to current and/or prior specimens and reports. Correlate the findings with the corresponding H&E-stained slide, clinical history, and previous tissue samples and laboratory tests, and report.

⊘=Modifier 51 Exempt   ⊙=Moderate Sedation   ✚=Add-on Code   ✗=FDA approval pending

Reproductive Medicine Procedures

89335   Cryopreservation, reproductive tissue, testicular

(For cryopreservation of embryo[s], use 89258. For cryopreservation of sperm, use 89259)

▶(For cryopreservation, ovarian tissue, oocytes, use 0058T; for mature oocytes, use 89337; for immature oocytes, use 0357T)◀

●**89337**   Cryopreservation, mature oocyte(s)

▶(For cryopreservation of immature oocyte[s], use 0357T)◀

🖎 Rationale

Previously, the CPT code set did not contain a specific code to report the cryopreservation of mature oocyte(s). Therefore, new code 89337 has been added in the Reproductive Medicine Procedures subsection. In support of the establishment of reproductive medicine code 89337, Category III code 0357T has been established for cryopreservation of immature oocyte(s).

A cross-reference parenthetical note has been added following code 89337 to direct users to code 0357T for the cryopreservation of immature oocyte(s). Preceding code 89337, a cross-reference parenthetical note has been added to instruct users that: (1) Category III code 0058T should be reported for the cryopreservation of ovarian tissue; (2) code 89337 should be reported for the cryopreservation of mature oocytes; and (3) Category III code 0357T should be reported for the cryopreservation of immature oocytes.

🩺 Clinical Example (89337)

A 31-year-old with a breast lump is diagnosed with breast cancer following biopsy. All three hormone receptors are negative. She is single and has never had any children. She is scheduled to undergo chemotherapy, and her oncologist warns her that she may not be able to conceive after treatment. She consults a fertility specialist who states that ovarian stimulation can be performed to harvest some of her oocytes (eggs) prior to chemotherapy. The mature oocytes can be frozen and stored. Once she is healthy and has recovered from her treatments, her embryos can be thawed and fertilized to help her achieve a pregnancy.

Description of Procedure (89337)

After oocyte retrieval, oocytes are maintained in human tubal fluid media for 2 hours. Oocytes are then denuded by enzymatic means and nuclear maturity is assessed. Oocytes suitable for vitrification are transferred to media containing the cryoprotectants: dimethyl sulfoxide (DMSO), ethylene glycol, and sucrose. Oocytes are placed in strips and submerged in liquid nitrogen. Following vitrification, the oocytes are transferred to cryostorage.

Medicine

In the Medicine section, a total of 15 codes were added and 16 codes revised.

The Vaccine, Toxoids subsection includes two new vaccine codes—one for human papillomavirus and one for quadrivalent influenza virus (11V4). The introductory guidelines for the Vaccines, Toxoids subsection were revised to provide: (1) greater specificity to identify each code that may be reported with the vaccine product codes and (2) early announcement of the CPT Editorial Panel's decision to add US vaccine abbreviations to the CPT vaccine product codes 90476-90749.

Throughout the Psychiatry subsections, introductory and exclusionary parenthetical notes have been added to preclude reporting the new adaptive behavior treatment codes in conjunction with other codes in this subsection.

To ensure correct coding of 92270, 92541-92548, several instructional and exclusionary parenthetical notes were added in the Vestibular Function Tests, With Recording (eg, ENG) subsection.

In the Cardiovascular subsection, the Implantable and Wearable Cardiac Device Evaluations introductory guidelines and definitions have been revised to address differences between the subcutaneous implantable defibrillator (S-ICD) procedures and the intravenous implantable cardioverter-defibrillator (ICD) procedures. In addition, new Category I codes for reporting subcutaneous implantable defibrillator procedures have been added and existing codes revised to allow appropriate and consistent reporting.

In the Echocardiography subsection, a new code was added for reporting transesophageal echocardiography during interventional cardiac procedures. New guidelines and parenthetical notes have also been added to provide additional instructions on the appropriate reporting for this new code.

New codes to report bioimpedance spectroscopy (BIS) lymphedema assessment, quantitative carotid initima media thickness and carotid atheroma evaluation, negative pressure wound therapy, and application of topical fluoride varnish have also been added.

Other subsections with changes include Gastroenterology, Ophthalmology, Special Otorhinolaryngologic Services, Neurology and Neuromuscular Procedures, Central Nervous System Assessments/Test (eg, Neuro-Cognitive, Mental Status, Speech Testing), Health and Behavior Assessment/Intervention, and Physical Medicine and Rehabilitation.

Medicine

Vaccines, Toxoids

To assist users to report the most recent new or revised vaccine product codes, the American Medical Association (AMA) currently uses the CPT website, which features updates of CPT Editorial Panel actions regarding these products. Once approved by the CPT Editorial Panel, these codes will be made available for release on a semi-annual (twice a year: July 1 and January 1) basis. As part of the electronic distribution, there is a six-month implementation period from the initial release date (ie, codes released on January 1 are eligible for use on July 1 and codes released on July 1 are eligible for use January 1).

The CPT Editorial Panel, in recognition of the public health interest in vaccine products, has chosen to publish new vaccine product codes prior to approval by the US Food and Drug Administration (FDA). These codes are indicated with the ∕ symbol and will be tracked by the AMA to monitor FDA approval status. Once the FDA status changes to approval, the ∕ symbol will be removed. CPT users should refer to the AMA CPT website (www.ama-assn.org/ama/pub/physician-resources/solutions-managing-your-practice/coding-billing-insurance/cpt/about-cpt/category-i-vaccine-codes.page) for the most up-to-date information on codes with the ∕ symbol.

►Codes 90476-90749 identify the vaccine product **only**. To report the administration of a vaccine/toxoid, the vaccine/toxoid product codes 90476-90749 must be used in addition to an immunization administration code(s) 90460, 90461, 90471, 90472, 90473, 90474. Modifier 51 should not be reported with vaccine/toxoid codes 90476-90749, when reported in conjunction with administration codes 90460, 90461, 90471, 90472, 90473, 90474.◄

If a significantly separately identifiable Evaluation and Management (E/M) service (eg, office or other outpatient services, preventive medicine services) is performed, the appropriate E/M service code should be reported in addition to the vaccine and toxoid administration codes.

To meet the reporting requirements of immunization registries, vaccine distribution programs, and reporting systems (eg, Vaccine Adverse Event Reporting System) the exact vaccine product administered needs to be reported. Multiple codes for a particular vaccine are provided in the CPT codebook when the schedule (number of doses or timing) differs for two or more products of the same vaccine type (eg, hepatitis A, Hib) or the vaccine product is available in more than one chemical formulation, dosage, or route of administration.

The "when administered to" age descriptions included in CPT vaccine codes are not intended to identify a product's licensed age indication. The term "preservative free" includes use for vaccines that contain no preservative and vaccines that contain trace amounts of preservative agents that are not present in a sufficient concentration for the purpose of preserving the final vaccine formulation. The absence of a designation regarding a preservative does not necessarily indicate the presence or absence of preservative in the vaccine. Refer to the product's prescribing information (PI) for the licensed age indication before administering vaccine to a patient.

►Separate codes are available for combination vaccines (eg, DTP-Hib, DTaP-Hib, HepB-Hib). It is inappropriate to code each component of a combination vaccine separately. If a specific vaccine code is not available, the unlisted procedure code should be reported, until a new code becomes available.

The vaccine/toxoid abbreviations listed in codes 90476-90748 reflect the most recent US vaccine abbreviations references used in the Advisory Committee on Immunization Practices (ACIP) recommendations at the time of CPT code set publication. Interim updates to vaccine code descriptors will be made following abbreviation approval by the ACIP on a timely basis via the AMA CPT website (www.ama-assn.org/ama/pub/physician-resources/solutions-managing-your-practice/coding-billing-insurance/cpt/about-cpt/category-i-vaccine-codes.page). The accuracy of the ACIP vaccine abbreviation designations in the CPT code set does not affect the validity of the vaccine code and its reporting function.◄

(For immune globulins, see codes 90281-90399, 96365-96368, 96372-96375 for administration of immune globulins)

90632 Hepatitis A vaccine, adult dosage, for intramuscular use

🖎 Rationale

The third paragraph of the introductory guidelines for the Vaccines, Toxoids sub-section has been revised to provide greater specificity by identifying each code that may be reported with the vaccine product codes to include codes 90460, 90461, and 90471, 90472, 90473, 90474. The website address listed in the introductory language has also been updated to reflect a more direct link to vaccine information on the AMA CPT website. (See the second paragraph of the introductory language.)

A new paragraph has been added to the introductory guidelines to provide the CPT Editorial Panel's decision to add US vaccine abbreviations to CPT vaccine product codes 90476-90749. The transition to include US vaccine abbreviations into the CPT code set will be completed January 1, 2015, and cited on the AMA CPT website (www.ama-assn.org/ama/pub/physician-resources/solutions-managing-your-practice/coding-billing-insurance/cpt/about-cpt/category-i-vaccine-codes.page). Interim updates to vaccine code descriptors will be made following abbreviation approval by the Advisory Committee on Immunization Practices (ACIP) on a timely basis via the AMA CPT website. The accuracy of the ACIP vaccine abbreviation designations in the CPT code set does not affect the validity and reporting function of the vaccine codes.

✷ ●90651 Human Papillomavirus vaccine types 6, 11, 16, 18, 31, 33, 45, 52, 58, nonavalent (HPV), 3 dose schedule, for intramuscular use

🖎 Rationale

A new vaccine product code (90651) has been established for a vaccine that protects against nine (nonavalent) types of Human Papillomavirus (HPV) (6, 11, 16, 18, 31, 33, 45, 52, 58). Currently, code 90650 is used to report two (bivalent) types (16, 18), and code 90649 is used to report four (quadrivalent) types (6, 11, 16, 18). The nonavalent vaccine, once licensed, is expected to be available for administration to healthy females 9 through 26 years of age and healthy males 9 to 15 years of age.

Code 90651 will appear in the CPT codebook with the US Food and Drug Administration (FDA) approval pending symbol (✷). Updates on the FDA status of this code will be reflected on the AMA CPT website under Category I Vaccine

⊘=Modifier 51 Exempt ⊙=Moderate Sedation ✚=Add-on Code ✷=FDA approval pending

Codes (www.ama-assn.org/ama/pub/physician-resources/solutions-managing-your-practice/coding-billing-insurance/cpt/about-cpt/category-i-vaccine-codes.shtml) and in subsequent publications of the CPT codebook. The service associated with the administration of the nonavalent HPV vaccine is reported separately using immunization administration for vaccines/toxoids codes 90460-90474.

🩺 Clinical Example (90651)

A healthy 12-year-old male or female who is not allergic to the ingredients presents for the vaccine. A catch-up vaccination for females up to age 26 and for males up to age 15 would also be common.

Description of Procedure (90651)

The service associated with vaccine administration is reported separately using Immunization Administration for Vaccines/Toxoids codes (90460-90474).

▲90654   Influenza virus vaccine, trivalent (IIV3), split virus, preservative-free, for intradermal use

⚡●90630   Influenza virus vaccine, quadrivalent (IIV4), split virus, preservative free, for intradermal use

✍️ Rationale

A vaccine product code (90630) has been established for a quadrivalent intradermal influenza virus vaccine anticipated to receive US Food and Drug Administration (FDA) approval by the end of 2014 for use in the 2015/2016 influenza season. This vaccine replaces last season's intradermal influenza vaccine reported with trivalent intradermal influenza vaccine code 90654. Code 90630 will appear in the CPT codebook with the FDA approval pending symbol (⚡). Updates on the FDA status of this code will be reflected on the AMA CPT website under Category I Vaccine Codes (www.ama-assn.org/ama/pub/physician-resources/solutions-managing-your-practice/coding-billing-insurance/cpt/about-cpt/category-i-vaccine-codes.shtml) and in subsequent publications of the CPT codebook.

Trivalent vaccine code 90654, which was added to the CPT code set in 2012, has been revised to include "trivalent" in addition to the official Advisory Committee on Immunization Practices (ACIP) abbreviation "IIV3" to differentiate it from new quadrivalent code 90630, which includes the ACIP abbreviation "IIV4." For additional information and status on the use of ACIP abbreviations in CPT vaccine codes, refer to the AMA CPT website under Category I Vaccine Codes (www.ama-assn.org/ama/pub/physician-resources/solutions-managing-your-practice/coding-billing-insurance/cpt/about-cpt/category-i-vaccine-codes.shtml).

Codes 90654 and 90630 are administered intradermally utilizing a pre-filled, single-dose, disposable microinjection system consisting of a small (micro) needle. The antigen content of these vaccines is lower than that of influenza vaccines that are intended for intramuscular delivery and reported with code 90656 (trivalent) and codes 90685 and 90686 (quadrivalent). Both intradermal vaccines (90630, 90654) are preservative-free. The administration of the intradermal influenza split virus vaccines is reported separately using immunization administration for vaccines/toxoids codes 90460-90474.

Clinical Example (90630)

A patient in the recommended age range is seen for routine health maintenance during the appropriate time period and is offered and accepts vaccination to help protect from acquiring an influenza infection.

Description of Procedure (90630)

The service associated with vaccine administration is reported separately using Immunization Administration for Vaccines/Toxoids codes (90460-90474).

▲90721   Diphtheria, tetanus toxoids, and acellular pertussis vaccine and Hemophilus influenza B vaccine (DTaP/Hib), for intramuscular use

▲90723   Diphtheria, tetanus toxoids, acellular pertussis vaccine, hepatitis B, and inactivated poliovirus vaccine (DTaP-HepB-IPV), for intramuscular use

▲90734   Meningococcal conjugate vaccine, serogroups A, C, Y and W-135, quadrivalent, for intramuscular use

Rationale

Editorial revisions have been made to (1) capitalize the letter "t" in the term, "DTaP" in codes 90721 and 90723; (2) lower-case the letter "h" in the term, "hepatitis B" in code 90723; (3) relocate the placement of the word "inactivated" in code 90723; and (4) revise code 90734 to describe a quadrivalent as opposed to a tetravalent vaccine.

Code 90721 has also been revised to change the acronym for diphtheria, tetanus toxoids, and acellular pertussis vaccine and Hemophilus influenza B vaccine to include a slash (/) identifier instead of a dash (-). According to the Centers for Disease Control and Prevention (CDC), a slash (/) indicates products in which active components must be mixed by the user, in contrast to a dash (-), which indicates products in which the active components are supplied in their final (combined) form by the manufacturer. The DTaP/Hib combination product described in code 90721 requires reconstitution of the Hib component, and thus the slash (/) identifier is needed.

Psychiatry

Psychiatry services include diagnostic services, psychotherapy, and other services to an individual, family, or group. Patient condition, characteristics, or situational factors may require services described as being with interactive complexity. Services may be provided to a patient in crisis. Services are provided in all settings of care and psychiatry services codes are reported without regard to setting. Services may be provided by a physician or other qualified health care professional. Some psychiatry services may be reported with **Evaluation and Management Services** (99201-99255, 99281-99285, 99304-99337, 99341-99350) or other services when performed. **Evaluation and Management Services** (99201-99285, 99304-99337, 99341-99350) may be reported for treatment of psychiatric conditions, rather than using **Psychiatry Services** codes, when appropriate.

○=Modifier 51 Exempt   ⊙=Moderate Sedation   ✚=Add-on Code   ✁=FDA approval pending

Hospital care in treating a psychiatric inpatient or partial hospitalization may be initial or subsequent in nature (see 99221-99233).

Some patients receive hospital evaluation and management services only and others receive hospital evaluation and management services and other procedures. If other procedures such as electroconvulsive therapy or psychotherapy are rendered in addition to hospital evaluation and management services, these may be listed separately (eg, hospital care services [99221-99223, 99231-99233] plus electroconvulsive therapy [90870]), or when psychotherapy is done, with appropriate code(s) defining psychotherapy services.

Consultation for psychiatric evaluation of a patient includes examination of a patient and exchange of information with the primary physician and other informants such as nurses or family members, and preparation of a report. These services may be reported using consultation codes (see **Consultations**).

▶(Do not report 90785-90899 in conjunction with 90839, 90840, 0364T, 0365T, 0366T, 0367T, 0373T, 0374T)◀

Interactive Complexity

+ 90785   Interactive complexity (List separately in addition to the code for primary procedure)

(Use 90785 in conjunction with codes for diagnostic psychiatric evaluation [90791, 90792], psychotherapy [90832, 90834, 90837], psychotherapy when performed with an evaluation and management service [90833, 90836, 90838, 99201-99255, 99304-99337, 99341-99350], and group psychotherapy [90853])

(Do not report 90785 in conjunction with 90839, 90840, or in conjunction with E/M services when no psychotherapy service is also reported)

▶(Do not report 90785 in conjunction with 90839, 90840, 0364T, 0365T, 0366T, 0367T, 0373T, 0374T)◀

Psychiatric Diagnostic Procedures

Psychiatric diagnostic evaluation is an integrated ...

Codes 90791, 90792 are used for the diagnostic assessment(s) or reassessment(s), if required, and do not include psychotherapeutic services. Psychotherapy services, including for crisis, may not be reported on the same day.

▶(Do not report 90791-90899 in conjunction with 90839, 90840, 0364T, 0365T, 0366T, 0367T, 0373T, 0374T)◀

90791   Psychiatric diagnostic evaluation

90792   Psychiatric diagnostic evaluation with medical services

▶(Do not report 90791 or 90792 in conjunction with 99201-99337, 99341-99350, 99366-99368, 99401-99444, 0368T, 0369T, 0370T, 0371T)◀

OTHER PSYCHOTHERAPY

90846   Family psychotherapy (without the patient present)

90847   Family psychotherapy (conjoint psychotherapy) (with patient present)

►(Do not report 90846, 90847 in conjunction with 0368T, 0369T, 0370T, 0371T)◄

90849   Multiple-family group psychotherapy

90853   Group psychotherapy (other than of a multiple-family group)

(Use 90853 in conjunction with 90785 for the specified patient when group psychotherapy includes interactive complexity)

►(Do not report 90853 in conjunction with 0372T)◄

OTHER PSYCHIATRIC SERVICES OR PROCEDURES

90887   Interpretation or explanation of results of psychiatric, other medical examinations and procedures, or other accumulated data to family or other responsible persons, or advising them how to assist patient

►(Do not report 90887 in conjunction with 0368T, 0369T, 0370T, 0371T)◄

✍️ Rationale

An exclusionary parenthetical has been added to the introductory guidelines to the Psychiatry section and an exclusionary parenthetical in the Psychiatric Diagnostic Procedures subsection has been revised to instruct users not to report psychiatry service codes 90785-90899 with the new Category III adaptive behavior treatment codes (0364T, 0365T, 0366T, 0367T, 0373T, and 0374T). In addition, new and revised exclusionary parenthetical notes have been added following codes 90785, 90792, 90847, 90853, and 90887 to further instruct users not to report these codes in conjunction with new adaptive behavior treatment codes 0364T-0374T.

Gastroenterology

91110   Gastrointestinal tract imaging, intraluminal (eg, capsule endoscopy), esophagus through ileum, with interpretation and report

►(Do not report 91110 in conjunction with 91111, 0355T)◄

(Visualization of the colon is not reported separately)

(Append modifier 52 if the ileum is not visualized)

91111   Gastrointestinal tract imaging, intraluminal (eg, capsule endoscopy), esophagus with interpretation and report

►(Do not report 91111 in conjunction with 91110, 0355T)◄

(For measurement of gastrointestinal tract transit times or pressure using wireless capsule, use 91112)

⊘=Modifier 51 Exempt   ⊙=Moderate Sedation   ✚=Add-on Code   ⑉=FDA approval pending

🖎 Rationale

🖎 Rationale

In support of new colon capsule endoscopy code 0355T, an exclusionary parenthetical note has been added following code 91110 indicating that codes 91110 and 0355T should not be reported together. Code 0355T has also been added to the exclusionary note following esophageal capsule endoscopy code 91111 indicating that codes 91111 and 0355T should not be reported together. Finally, code 91111 was added to the exclusionary note following code 91110 to clarify that codes 91110 and 91111 should not be reported together for consistency with the exclusionary note following code 91111.

Other Procedures

●91200   Liver elastography, mechanically induced shear wave (eg, vibration), without imaging, with interpretation and report

🖎 Rationale

Code 91200 has been established to identify liver elastography performed via a mechanically induced shear wave technique (eg, vibration). The procedure includes interpretation and report but does not include imaging. Measuring the stiffness in the liver via elastography is one of a number of methods used to identify the presence of conditions, such as advanced fibrosis and cirrhosis of the liver in patients with chronic liver disease (CLD).

🩺 Clinical Example (91200)

A 55-year-old male presents for further evaluation of liver disease secondary to hepatitis C. Physical findings are unremarkable. Laboratory studies show abnormal liver enzymes (ie, aminotransferase levels twice the upper limits of normal), and the platelet count is borderline low. Physician schedules patient for liver elastography by mechanically induced shear wave to assess presence of cirrhosis prior to starting antiviral therapy.

Description of Procedure (91200)

Review the test results. Convert each shear wave speed value to its calculated equivalent stiffness value and the median stiffness value. Quantify the variability of stiffness values across the 10 measurements. Correlate the stiffness measurement with the fibrosis stage. Come to a diagnosis by comparing and correlating the results with clinical, biological, and morphological parameters of liver disease. Dictate a report for the medical record.

Special Ophthalmological Services

92081   Visual field examination, unilateral or bilateral, with interpretation and report; limited examination (eg, tangent screen, Autoplot, arc perimeter, or single stimulus level automated test, such as Octopus 3 or 7 equivalent)

92082   intermediate examination (eg, at least 2 isopters on Goldmann perimeter, or semiquantitative, automated suprathreshold screening program, Humphrey suprathreshold automatic diagnostic test, Octopus program 33)

92083   extended examination (eg, Goldmann visual fields with at least 3 isopters plotted and static determination within the central 30°, or quantitative, automated threshold perimetry, Octopus program G-1, 32 or 42, Humphrey visual field analyzer full threshold programs 30-2, 24-2, or 30/60-2)

        (Gross visual field testing (eg, confrontation testing) is a part of general ophthalmological services and is not reported separately)

        ▶(For visual field assessment by patient activitated data transmission to a remote surveillance center, see 0378T, 0379T)◀

✍ Rationale

A parenthetical note has been added following code 92083 directing users to Category III codes 0378T and 0379T to report visual field self-monitoring assessment up to 30 days. For more information, see the Rationale for codes 0378T and 0379T.

●**92145**   Corneal hysteresis determination, by air impulse stimulation, unilateral or bilateral, with interpretation and report

✍ Rationale

Category III code 0181T has been replaced with code 92145, which describes corneal hysteresis determination by air impulse stimulation. This test has achieved Category I status, as the clinical utility has been established and usage has grown since it was first implemented in CPT 2007 as a Category III code. The code descriptor for corneal hysteresis determination has been changed since its original placement in the Category III section, as it now describes a test performed on a single eye or both eyes (eg, unilateral or bilateral).

🩺 Clinical Example (92145)

A 50-year-old male with a family history of glaucoma, elevated intraocular pressure, central corneal thickness of 545 microns, and normal visual fields is being evaluated for glaucoma.

Description of Procedure (92145)

Instruct the patient to look at a target, and the operator triggers the measurement. Then reposition the patient, and measure the second eye. The physician then reviews the data, correlates the findings with other information if necessary, and generates an interpretation and report.

OTHER SPECIALIZED SERVICES

92270   Electro-oculography with interpretation and report

▶(For vestibular function tests with recording, see 92540, 92541, 92542, 92543, 92544, 92545, 92546, 92547, 92548)◀

▶(Do not report 92270 in conjunction with 92540, 92541, 92542, 92543, 92544, 92545, 92546, 92547, 92548)◀

▶(To report saccadic eye movement testing with recording, use 92700)◀

✐ Rationale

The American Medical Association/Specialty Society Relative Value Scale (RVS) Update Committee (RUC) identified electro-oculography code 92270 and vestibular function testing (VNG) codes 92541-92548 as high-volume growth codes. As a result, instructional and exclusionary parenthetical notes have been added following code 92270 to ensure the correct reporting of code 92270, which has been miscoded instead of or in addition to the VNG codes. In some cases code 92270 might be reported for eye movement recordings, which is not the intended purpose of this code.

Special Otorhinolaryngologic Services

92507   Treatment of speech, language, voice, communication, and/or auditory processing disorder; individual

▶(Do not report 92507 in conjunction with 0364T, 0365T, 0368T, 0369T)◀

92508   group, 2 or more individuals

▶(Do not report 92508 in conjunction with 0366T, 0367T, 0372T)◀

92511   Nasopharyngoscopy with endoscope (separate procedure)

▶(Do not report 92511 in conjunction with 43197, 43198)◀

✐ Rationale

Exclusionary parenthetical notes have been added following codes 92507 and 92508 precluding the use of these codes in conjunction with the new Category III adaptive behavior treatment codes 0364T-0372T.

Also, in accordance with the changes to the digestive system endoscopy codes, an exclusionary parenthetical note has been added following nasopharyngoscopy code 92511 indicating that code 92511 should not be reported with flexible transnasal esophagoscopy codes 43197 and 43198.

Vestibular Function Tests, With Recording (eg, ENG)

92540   Basic vestibular evaluation, includes spontaneous nystagmus test with eccentric gaze fixation nystagmus, with recording, positional nystagmus test, minimum of 4 positions, with recording, optokinetic nystagmus test, bidirectional foveal and peripheral stimulation, with recording, and oscillating tracking test, with recording

▶(Do not report 92540 in conjunction with 92270, 92541, 92542, 92544, 92545)◀

92541   Spontaneous nystagmus test, including gaze and fixation nystagmus, with recording

▶(Do not report 92541 in conjunction with 92270, 92540 or the set of 92542, 92544, and 92545)◀

92542   Positional nystagmus test, minimum of 4 positions, with recording

▶(Do not report 92542 in conjunction with 92270, 92540 or the set of 92541, 92544, and 92545)◀

92543   Caloric vestibular test, each irrigation (binaural, bithermal stimulation constitutes 4 tests), with recording

▶(Do not report 92543 in conjunction with 92270)◀

92544   Optokinetic nystagmus test, bidirectional, foveal or peripheral stimulation, with recording

▶(Do not report 92544 in conjunction with 92270, 92540 or the set of 92541, 92542, and 92545)◀

92545   Oscillating tracking test, with recording

▶(Do not report 92545 in conjunction with 92270, 92540 or the set of 92541, 92542, and 92544)◀

92546   Sinusoidal vertical axis rotational testing

▶(Do not report 92546 in conjunction with 92270)◀

+ 92547   Use of vertical electrodes (List separately in addition to code for primary procedure)

(Use 92547 in conjunction with 92540-92546)

(For unlisted vestibular tests, use 92700)

▶(Do not report 92547 in conjunction with 92270)◀

92548   Computerized dynamic posturography

▶(Do not report 92548 in conjunction with 92270)◀

🖉 Rationale

The American Medical Association/Specialty Society RUC identified electro-oculography code 92270 and vestibular function testing (VNG) codes 92541-92548 as high-volume growth codes. As a result, instructional and exclusionary parenthetical notes have been added and/or revised following codes 92541-92548 to ensure the correct reporting of code 92270, which has been miscoded instead of or in addition to the VNG codes. In some cases, code 92270 might be reported for eye movement recordings, which is not the intended purpose of this code.

⊘=Modifier 51 Exempt   ⊙=Moderate Sedation   ✚=Add-on Code   ✓=FDA approval pending

Cardiovascular

Implantable and Wearable Cardiac Device Evaluations

►Cardiac device evaluation services are diagnostic medical procedures using in-person and remote technology to assess device therapy and cardiovascular physiologic data. Codes 93260, 93261, 93279-93299 describe this technology and technical/professional and service center practice. Codes 93260, 93261, 93279-93292 are reported per procedure. Codes 93293, 93294, 93295, 93296 are reported no more than **once** every 90 days. Do not report 93293, 93294, 93295, 93296, if the monitoring period is less than 30 days. Codes 93297, 93298 are reported no more than **once** up to every 30 days. Do not report 93297-93299, if the monitoring period is less than 10 days.

A service center may report 93296 or 93299 during a period in which a physician or other qualified health care professional performs an in-person interrogation device evaluation. The same individual may not report an in-person and remote interrogation of the same device during the same period. Report only remote services when an in-person interrogation device evaluation is performed during a period of remote interrogation device evaluation. A period is established by the initiation of the remote monitoring or the 91st day of a pacemaker or implantable defibrillator monitoring or the 31st day of an implantable loop recorder (ILR) or implantable cardiovascular monitor (ICM) monitoring, and extends for the subsequent 90 or 30 days respectively, for which remote monitoring is occurring. Programming device evaluations and in-person interrogation device evaluations may not be reported on the same date by the same individual. Programming device evaluations and remote interrogation device evaluations may both be reported during the remote interrogation device evaluation period.◄

For monitoring by wearable devices, see 93224-93272.

►ECG rhythm derived elements are distinct from physiologic data, even when the same device is capable of producing both. ICM device services are always separately reported from implantable defibrillator services. When ILR data is derived from an implantable defibrillator or pacemaker, do not report ILR services with pacemaker or implantable defibrillator services.

Do not report 93268-93272 when performing 93260, 93261, 93279-93289, 93291-93296, or 93298-93299. Do not report 93040, 93041, 93042 when performing 93260, 93261, 93279-93289, 93291-93296, or 93298-93299.

The pacemaker and implantable defibrillator interrogation device evaluations, peri-procedural device evaluations and programming, and programming device evaluations may not be reported in conjunction with pacemaker or implantable defibrillator device and/or lead insertion or revision services by the same individual.

The following definitions and instructions apply to codes 93260, 93261, 93279-93299.◄

Attended surveillance: the immediate availability of a remote technician to respond to rhythm or device alert transmissions from a patient, either from an implanted or wearable monitoring or therapy device, as they are generated and transmitted to the remote surveillance location or center.

►***Device, single lead:*** a pacemaker or implantable defibrillator with pacing and sensing function in only one chamber of the heart or a subcutaneous electrode.

Device, dual lead: a pacemaker or implantable defibrillator with pacing and sensing function in only two chambers of the heart.

Device, multiple lead: a pacemaker or implantable defibrillator with pacing and sensing function in three or more chambers of the heart.◄

Electrocardiographic rhythm derived elements: elements derived from recordings of the electrical activation of the heart including, but not limited to heart rhythm, rate, ST analysis, heart rate variability, T-wave alternans.

►**Implantable cardiovascular monitor (ICM):** an implantable cardiovascular device used to assist the physician in the management of non-rhythm related cardiac conditions such as heart failure. The device collects longitudinal physiologic cardiovascular data elements from one or more internal sensors (such as right ventricular pressure, left atrial pressure, or an index of lung water) and/or external sensors (such as blood pressure or body weight) for patient assessment and management. The data are stored and transmitted by either local telemetry or remotely to an Internet-based file server or surveillance technician. The function of the ICM may be an additional function of an implantable cardiac device (eg, implantable defibrillator) or a function of a stand-alone device. When ICM functionality is included in an implantable defibrillator device or pacemaker, the ICM data and the implantable defibrillator or pacemaker, heart rhythm data such as sensing, pacing, and tachycardia detection therapy are distinct and, therefore, the monitoring processes are distinct.

Implantable defibrillator: two general categories of implantable defibrillators exist: transvenous implantable pacing cardioverter-defibrillator (ICD) and subcutaneous implantable defibrillator (SICD). An implantable pacing cardioverter-defibrillator device provides high-energy and low-energy stimulation to one or more chambers of the heart to terminate rapid heart rhythms called tachycardia or fibrillation. Implantable pacing cardioverter-defibrillators also have pacemaker functions to treat slow heart rhythms called bradycardia. In addition to the tachycardia and bradycardia functions, the implantable pacing cardioverter-defibrillator may or may not include the functionality of an implantable cardiovascular monitor or an implantable loop recorder. The subcutaneous implantable defibrillator uses a single subcutaneous electrode to treat ventricular tachyarrhythmias. Subcutaneous implantable defibrillators differ from transvenous implantable pacing cardioverter-defibrillators in that subcutaneous implantable defibrillators do not provide antitachycardia pacing or chronic pacing. For subcutaneous implantable defibrillator device evaluation, see 93260, 93261.

Implantable loop recorder (ILR): an implantable device that continuously records the electrocardiographic rhythm triggered automatically by rapid and slow heart rates or by the patient during a symptomatic episode. The ILR function may be the only function of the device or it may be part of a pacemaker or implantable defibrillator device. The data are stored and transmitted by either local telemetry or remotely to an Internet-based file server or surveillance technician. Extraction of data and compilation or report for physician or qualified health care professional interpretation is usually performed in the office setting.

Interrogation device evaluation: an evaluation of an implantable device such as a cardiac pacemaker, implantable defibrillator, implantable cardiovascular monitor, or implantable loop recorder. Using an office, hospital, or emergency room instrument or via a remote interrogation system, stored and measured information about the lead(s) when present, sensor(s) when present, battery and the implanted device function, as well as data collected about the patient's heart rhythm and heart rate is retrieved. The retrieved information is evaluated to determine the current programming of the device and to evaluate certain aspects of the device function such as battery voltage, lead impedance, tachycardia detection settings, and rhythm treatment settings.◄

⊘=Modifier 51 Exempt   ☉=Moderate Sedation   ✚=Add-on Code   𝒩=FDA approval pending

The components that must be evaluated for the various types of implantable cardiac devices are listed below. (The required components for both remote and in-person interrogations are the same.)

Pacemaker: Programmed parameters, lead(s), battery, capture and sensing function and heart rhythm.

▶*Implantable defibrillator:* programmed parameters, lead(s), battery, capture and sensing function, presence or absence of therapy for ventricular tachyarrhythmias and underlying heart rhythm.◀

Implantable cardiovascular monitor: Programmed parameters and analysis of at least one recorded physiologic cardiovascular data element from either internal or external sensors.

Implantable loop recorder: Programmed parameters and the heart rate and rhythm during recorded episodes from both patient initiated and device algorithm detected events, when present.

▶*Interrogation device evaluation (remote):* a procedure performed for patients with pacemakers, implantable defibrillators, or implantable loop recorders using data obtained remotely. All device functions, including the programmed parameters, lead(s), battery, capture and sensing function, presence or absence of therapy for ventricular tachyarrhythmias (for implantable defibrillators) and underlying heart rhythm are evaluated.◀

The components that must be evaluated for the various types of implantable cardiac devices are listed below. (The required components for both remote and in person interrogations are the same.)

Pacemaker: Programmed parameters, lead(s), battery, capture and sensing function, and heart rhythm.

▶*Implantable defibrillator:* Programmed parameters, lead(s), battery, capture and sensing function, presence or absence of therapy for ventricular tachyarrhythmias, and underlying heart rhythm.◀

Implantable cardiovascular monitor: Programmed parameters and analysis of at least one recorded physiologic cardiovascular data element from either internal or external sensors.

Implantable loop recorder: Programmed parameters and the heart rate and rhythm during recorded episodes from both patient-initiated and device algorithm detected events, when present.

Pacemaker: an implantable device that provides low energy localized stimulation to one or more chambers of the heart to initiate contraction in that chamber.

▶*Peri-procedural device evaluation and programming:* an evaluation of an implantable device system (either a pacemaker or implantable defibrillator) to adjust the device to settings appropriate for the patient prior to a surgery, procedure, or test. The device system data are interrogated to evaluate the lead(s), sensor(s), and battery in addition to review of stored information, including patient and system measurements. The device is programmed to settings appropriate for the surgery, procedure, or test, as required. A second evaluation and programming are performed after the surgery, procedure, or test to provide settings appropriate to the post procedural situation, as required. If one performs both the pre- and post-evaluation and programming service, the appropriate code, either 93286 or 93287, would be reported two times. If one performs the pre-surgical service and a separate individual performs the post-surgical service, each reports either 93286 or 93287 only one time.◀

Physiologic cardiovascular data elements: data elements from one or more internal sensors (such as right ventricular pressure, left atrial pressure or an index of lung water) and/or external sensors (such as blood pressure or body weight) for patient assessement and management. It does not include ECG rhythm derived data elements.

▶*Programming device evaluation (in person):* a procedure performed for patients with a pacemaker, implantable defibrillator, or implantable loop recorder. All device functions, including the battery, programmable settings and lead(s), when present, are evaluated. To assess capture thresholds, iterative adjustments (eg, progressive changes in pacing output of a pacing lead) of the programmable parameters are conducted. The iterative adjustments provide information that permits the operator to assess and select the most appropriate final program parameters to provide for consistent delivery of the appropriate therapy and to verify the function of the device. The final program parameters may or may not change after evaluation.◀

The programming device evaluation includes all of the components of the interrogation device evaluation (remote) or the interrogation device evaluation (in person), and it includes the selection of patient specific programmed parameters depending on the type of device.

The components that must be evaluated for the various types of programming device evaluations are listed below. (See also required interrogation device evaluation [remote and in person] components above.)

Pacemaker: Programmed parameters, lead(s), battery, capture and sensing function, and heart rhythm. Often, but not always, the sensor rate response, lower and upper heart rates, AV intervals, pacing voltage and pulse duration, sensing value, and diagnostics will be adjusted during a programming evaluation.

▶*Implantable defibrillator:* Programmed parameters, lead(s), battery, capture and sensing function, presence or absence of therapy for ventricular tachyarrhythmias and underlying heart rhythm. Often, but not always, the sensor rate response, lower and upper heart rates, AV intervals, pacing voltage and pulse duration, sensing value, and diagnostics will be adjusted during a programming evaluation. In addition, ventricular tachycardia detection and therapies are sometimes altered depending on the interrogated data, patient's rhythm, symptoms, and condition.◀

Implantable loop recorder: Programmed parameters and the heart rhythm during recorded episodes from both patient initiated and device algorithm detected events. Often, but not always, the tachycardia and bradycardia detection criteria will be adjusted during a programming evaluation.

Transtelephonic rhythm strip pacemaker evaluation: service of transmission of an electrocardiographic rhythm strip over the telephone by the patient using a transmitter and recorded by a receiving location using a receiver/recorder (also commonly known as transtelephonic pacemaker monitoring). The electrocardiographic rhythm strip is recorded both with and without a magnet applied over the pacemaker. The rhythm strip is evaluated for heart rate and rhythm, atrial and ventricular capture (if observed) and atrial and ventricular sensing (if observed). In addition, the battery status of the pacemaker is determined by measurement of the paced rate on the electrocardiographic rhythm strip recorded with the magnet applied.

93279   Programming device evaluation (in person) with iterative adjustment of the implantable device to test the function of the device and select optimal permanent programmed values with analysis, review and report by a physician or other qualified health care professional; single lead pacemaker system

(Do not report 93279 in conjunction with 93286, 93288)

⃠=Modifier 51 Exempt   ⊙=Moderate Sedation   ✚=Add-on Code   𝒩=FDA approval pending

93280   dual lead pacemaker system

(Do not report 93280 in conjunction with 93286, 93288)

93281   multiple lead pacemaker system

(Do not report 93281 in conjunction with 93286, 93288)

▲**93282**   single lead transvenous implantable defibrillator system

►(Do not report 93282 in conjunction with 93260, 93287, 93289, 93745)◄

▲**93283**   dual lead transvenous implantable defibrillator system

(Do not report 93283 in conjunction with 93287, 93289)

▲**93284**   multiple lead transvenous implantable defibrillator system

(Do not report 93284 in conjunction with 93287, 93289)

#●**93260**   implantable subcutaneous lead defibrillator system

►(Do not report 93260 in conjunction with 93261, 93282, 93287)◄

►(Do not report 93260 in conjunction with pulse generator and lead insertion or repositioning codes 33240, 33241, 33262, 33270, 33271, 33272, 33273)◄

93285   implantable loop recorder system

(Do not report 93285 in conjunction with 33282, 93279-93284, 93291)

93286   Peri-procedural device evaluation (in person) and programming of device system parameters before or after a surgery, procedure, or test with analysis, review and report by a physician or other qualified health care professional; single, dual, or multiple lead pacemaker system

(Report 93286 once before and once after surgery, procedure, or test, when device evaluation and programming is performed before and after surgery, procedure, or test)

(Do not report 93286 in conjunction with 93279-93281, 93288)

▲**93287**   single, dual, or multiple lead implantable defibrillator system

(Report 93287 once before and once after surgery, procedure, or test, when device evaluation and programming is performed before and after surgery, procedure, or test)

►(Do not report 93287 in conjunction with 93260, 93261, 93282, 93283, 93284, 93289)◄

93288   Interrogation device evaluation (in person) with analysis, review and report by a physician or other qualified health care professional, includes connection, recording and disconnection per patient encounter; single, dual, or multiple lead pacemaker system

(Do not report 93288 in conjunction with 93279-93281, 93286, 93294, 93296)

▲**93289**   single, dual, or multiple lead transvenous implantable defibrillator system, including analysis of heart rhythm derived data elements

►(For monitoring physiologic cardiovascular data elements derived from an implantable defibrillator, use 93290)◄

►(Do not report 93289 in conjunction with 93261, 93282, 93283, 93284, 93287, 93295, 93296)◄

#●93261   implantable subcutaneous lead defibrillator system

▶(Do not report 93261 in conjunction with 93260, 93287, 93289)◀

▶(Do not report 93261 in conjunction with pulse generator and lead insertion or repositioning codes 33240, 33241, 33262, 33270, 33271, 33272, 33273)◀

93290   implantable cardiovascular monitor system, including analysis of 1 or more recorded physiologic cardiovascular data elements from all internal and external sensors

(For heart rhythm derived data elements, use 93289)

(Do not report 93290 in conjunction with 93297, 93299)

93291   implantable loop recorder system, including heart rhythm derived data analysis

(Do not report 93291 in conjunction with 33282, 93288-93290, 93298, 93299)

93292   wearable defibrillator system

(Do not report 93292 in conjunction with 93745)

93293   Transtelephonic rhythm strip pacemaker evaluation(s) single, dual, or multiple lead pacemaker system, includes recording with and without magnet application with analysis, review and report(s) by a physician or other qualified health care professional, up to 90 days

(Do not report 93293 in conjunction with 93294)

(For in person evaluation, see 93040, 93041, 93042)

(Report 93293 only once per 90 days)

93294   Interrogation device evaluation(s) (remote), up to 90 days; single, dual, or multiple lead pacemaker system with interim analysis, review(s) and report(s) by a physician or other qualified health care professional

(Do not report 93294 in conjunction with 93288, 93293)

(Report 93294 only once per 90 days)

▲93295   single, dual, or multiple lead implantable defibrillator system with interim analysis, review(s) and report(s) by a physician or other qualified health care professional

(For remote monitoring of physiologic cardiovascular data elements derived from an ICD, use 93297)

(Do not report 93295 in conjunction with 93289)

(Report 93295 only once per 90 days)

▲93296   single, dual, or multiple lead pacemaker system or implantable defibrillator system, remote data acquisition(s), receipt of transmissions and technician review, technical support and distribution of results

(Do not report 93296 in conjunction with 93288, 93289, 93299)

(Report 93296 only once per 90 days)

Rationale

Category III codes 0319T-0328T have been deleted and replaced with Category I codes 33270-33273, 93260, 93261, and 93644 to report subcutaneous implantable defibrillator (S-ICD) procedures. The S-ICD system is an entirely subcutaneous system designed to avoid the need for the placement of sensing and therapy electrodes within or on the heart. Codes 93282, 93283, 93284, 93287, 93289, 93295, and 93296 have been revised to enable the appropriate reporting of S-ICD procedures. Guidelines and definitions that apply to codes 93260, 93261, and 93279-93299 have also been revised to address differences between S-ICD procedures and transvenous implantable cardioverter–defibrillator (ICD) procedures.

Clinical Example (93260)

A 65-year-old male with ischemic cardiomyopathy and a left ventricular ejection fraction (LVEF) of 28% had an S-ICD implanted. The patient tells his cardiologist that he "fainted" without palpitations, warning, or feeling a shock. The physician requests a programming device evaluation to assess device, battery, and lead function and subsequently performs programming adjustments to the device's rate cutoff and diagnostic parameters based upon the patient's interrogated data.

Description of Procedure (93260)

Verbal consent is obtained from the patient. The patient is connected to a single or multi-lead electrocardiographic (ECG) recording system, and a communication link is established between the device and the programmer.

A full interrogation of the stored device parameters is performed with assessment and recording of the current rhythm. A detailed analysis of the retrieved stored tachyarrhythmia episode and recorded rhythm data is performed. The lead impedance is measured, and measurement information used to identify any integrity issues with the existing lead and determination of appropriate settings. The sensing-threshold data is obtained by recording the signal from the ventricular chamber and utilizing iterative (stepwise) adjustment and identification of the appropriate ICD sensing level.

After detailed analysis of the data is performed, the appropriateness of the initial programmed antitachycardia parameters and therapies are evaluated relative to the patient's clinical status and, if indicated, the device's programing is also altered at this time.

Clinical Example (93261)

A 66-year-old patient with history of nonsustained ventricular tachycardia treated with an S-ICD system is followed with interrogation device evaluations (in person). The patient presents to the clinic for in-person follow up to assess device function.

Description of Procedure (93261)

Interrogate the information from the device by telemetric communication, and either print for review or review on the programmer or computer monitor. Critically review the interrogated data with assessment of the appropriateness of the function of device, safety of the current programmed parameters, and to assess whether the device function is normal. Also review the following data: presenting

EGM for appropriateness or presence of arrhythmia and appropriate sensing; stored episodes of data for appropriate sensing, appropriate magnet reversion, and noise reversions; alerts generated from the device; battery voltage and impedance, lead impedance, and sensed electrogram voltage amplitude for each lead; counters of events; stored episodes of sensed events, including arrhythmias, ectopic beats, and nonsustained and sustained arrhythmias. Note the frequency, rate, and duration.

Echocardiography

▶Code 93355 is used to report transesophageal echocardiography (TEE) services during transcatheter intracardiac therapies. Code 93355 is reported once per intervention and only by an individual who is not performing the interventional procedure. Code 93355 includes the work of passing the endoscopic ultrasound transducer through the mouth into the esophagus, when performed by the individual performing the TEE, diagnostic transesophageal echocardiography and ongoing manipulation of the transducer to guide sizing and/or placement of implants, determination of adequacy of the intervention, and assessment for potential complications. Real-time image acquisition, measurements, and interpretation of image(s), documentation of completion of the intervention, and final written report are included in this code.

A range of intracardiac therapies may be performed with TEE guidance. Code 93355 describes TEE during advanced transcatheter structural heart procedures (eg, transcatheter aortic valve replacement [TAVR], left atrial appendage closure [LAA], or percutaneous mitral valve repair).

See 93313 for separate reporting of the probe insertion by a physician other than the physician performing the TEE.◀

⊙**93312**   Echocardiography, transesophageal, real-time with image documentation (2D) (with or without M-mode recording); including probe placement, image acquisition, interpretation and report

▶(Do not report 93312 in conjunction with 93355)◀

⊙**93313**   placement of transesophageal probe only

(93313 may not be reported in conjunction with 93355 by the same individual)

▶(The same individual may not report 93313 in conjunction with 93355)◀

⊙**93314**   image acquisition, interpretation and report only

▶(Do not report 93314 in conjunction with 93355)◀

⊙**93315**   Transesophageal echocardiography for congenital cardiac anomalies; including probe placement, image acquisition, interpretation and report

▶(Do not report 93315 in conjunction with 93355)◀

⊙**93316**   placement of transesophageal probe only

▶(Do not report 93316 in conjunction with 93355)◀

⊙**93317**   image acquisition, interpretation and report only

▶(Do not report 93317 in conjunction with 93355)◀

⊘=Modifier 51 Exempt   ⊙=Moderate Sedation   ✚=Add-on Code   ⩘=FDA approval pending

⊙**93318**   Echocardiography, transesophageal (TEE) for monitoring purposes, including probe placement, real time 2-dimensional image acquisition and interpretation leading to ongoing (continuous) assessment of (dynamically changing) cardiac pumping function and to therapeutic measures on an immediate time basis

▶(Do not report 93318 in conjunction with 93355)◄

+**93320**   Doppler echocardiography, pulsed wave and/or continuous wave with spectral display (List separately in addition to codes for echocardiographic imaging); complete

(Use 93320 in conjunction with 93303, 93304, 93312, 93314, 93315, 93317, 93350, 93351)

▶(Do not report 93320 in conjunction with 93355)◄

+**93321**   follow-up or limited study (List separately in addition to codes for echocardiographic imaging)

(Use 93321 in conjunction with 93303, 93304, 93308, 93312, 93314, 93315, 93317, 93350, 93351)

▶(Do not report 93321 in conjunction with 93355)◄

+**93325**   Doppler echocardiography color flow velocity mapping (List separately in addition to codes for echocardiography)

(Use 93325 in conjunction with 76825, 76826, 76827, 76828, 93303, 93304, 93308, 93312, 93314, 93315, 93317, 93350, 93351)

▶(Do not report 93325 in conjunction with 93355)◄

●**93355**   Echocardiography, transesophageal (TEE) for guidance of a transcatheter intracardiac or great vessel(s) structural intervention(s) (eg, TAVR, transcathether pulmonary valve replacement, mitral valve repair, paravalvular regurgitation repair, left atrial appendage occlusion/closure, ventricular septal defect closure) (peri-and intra-procedural), real-time image acquisition and documentation, guidance with quantitative measurements, probe manipulation, interpretation, and report, including diagnostic transesophageal echocardiography and, when performed, administration of ultrasound contrast, Doppler, color flow, and 3D

▶(To report placement of transesophageal probe by separate physician, use 93313)◄

▶(Do not report 93355 in conjunction with 76376, 76377, 93312, 93313, 93314, 93315, 93316, 93317, 93318, 93320, 93321, 93325)◄

🖎 Rationale

Code 93355 has been established to report transesophageal echocardiography (TEE) during interventional cardiac procedures. This code is different from the existing TEE codes, which do not adequately define the additional levels of complexity needed for interventional procedures. New guidelines and parenthetical notes have also been added to provide additional instruction on the appropriate reporting of code 93355. The parenthetical notes following codes 93314, 93315, 93316, 93317, 93318, 93320, 93321, and 93325 are reciprocal exclusionary notes that have been added to maintain consistency with the exclusionary parenthetical notes in the CPT code set.

Clinical Example (93355)

A 66-year-old female with remote mantle irradiation for Hodgkin lymphoma and two previous coronary artery bypass graft operations presents with severe symptomatic aortic stenosis. She is not a surgical aortic valve replacement candidate due to a porcelain aorta. She is referred for transcatheter aortic valve replacement via a transfemoral approach with TEE.

Description of Procedure (93355)

Following initiation of general anesthesia, place the TEE probe (esophageal intubation) by the echocardiographer. Advance the transducer to the esophagus. Perform a complete diagnostic examination. Acquire digital images for subsequent transfer and archival storage. Perform transgastric left ventricular imaging at 0° (short-axis view), 90° (two-chamber view), and 120° (long-axis view). Assess inferior vena cava size and responsiveness. Withdraw the transducer to the mid-esophagus. Again image the left ventricle in the four-chamber view (0° to 30°), two-chamber view (90°), and long-axis view (120° to 140°). Next interrogate the cardiac valves with two-dimensional (2D) imaging, color Doppler, and spectral Doppler, including the tricuspid valve (multiple views from 0° to 30°), the mitral valve (multiple views from 0° to 140°), the aortic valve (long axis at 120° and short axis at 45°), and the pulmonic valve (60°). Next image additional cardiac and great vessel structures, including the ascending aorta (multiple views from 80° to 120°), the proximal pulmonary artery to the bifurcation (0°, high transesophageal view), the left atrial appendage (multiple views from 0° to 150°, including pulsed Doppler assessment of emptying velocities), the atrial septum (including color Doppler interrogation and 2D imaging with an intravenous injection of agitated saline to exclude patent foramen ovale), the pericardial space (to exclude pericardial effusion), the inferior and superior vena cava, the descending thoracic aorta and aortic arch, and the pulmonary veins (2D, spectral Doppler, and color Doppler flow). In addition to standard complete diagnostic imaging as detailed above, perform repeated 2D and three-dimensional (3D) measurements of the aortic annulus to aid in proper valve size selection. To minimize risk of subsequent coronary occlusion, measure the annulus to coronary ostia distances. Assess the ascending aorta for protruding atheroma, which may increase risk of aortic injury during valve deployment, and exclude mobile/protruding plaque in the aortic arch to help assess risk of periprocedural stroke. Prior to balloon valvuloplasty, use TEE to guide balloon position. During subsequent aortic valve deployment, use TEE to confirm correct prosthetic valve positioning. Immediately following deployment, use TEE to confirm adequate position and function and to exclude complications, including but not limited to: prosthesis misplacement; central or paravalvular aortic regurgitation; mitral regurgitation secondary to aortic prosthesis impingement on the anterior mitral leaflet or distortion of the subvalvular mitral apparatus by the delivery system; new left ventricular wall motion abnormalities (due to coronary occlusion); pericardial tamponade (due to cardiac rupture or perforation); or aortic root dissection, rupture, or hematoma.

Cardiac Catheterization

⊙⊘**93451**   Right heart catheterization including measurement(s) of oxygen saturation and cardiac output, when performed

(Do not report 93451 in conjunction with 93453, 93456, 93457, 93460, 93461)

▶(Do not report 93451 in conjunction with 0345T for diagnostic left and right heart catheterization procedures intrinsic to the valve repair procedure)◄

⊙**93452**   Left heart catheterization including intraprocedural injection(s) for left ventriculography, imaging supervision and interpretation, when performed

(Do not report 93452 in conjunction with 93453, 93458-93461)

⊙**93453**   Combined right and left heart catheterization including intraprocedural injection(s) for left ventriculography, imaging supervision and interpretation, when performed

(Do not report 93453 in conjunction with 93451, 93452, 93456-93461)

▶(Do not report 93453 in conjunction with 0345T for diagnostic left and right heart catheterization procedures intrinsic to the valve repair procedure)◄

⊙**93454**   Catheter placement in coronary artery(s) for coronary angiography, including intraprocedural injection(s) for coronary angiography, imaging supervision and interpretation;

▶(Do not report 93453, 93454 in conjunction with 0345T for coronary angiography intrinsic to the valve repair procedure)◄

⊙**93455**   with catheter placement(s) in bypass graft(s) (internal mammary, free arterial, venous grafts) including intraprocedural injection(s) for bypass graft angiography

⊙⊘**93456**   with right heart catheterization

▶(Do not report 93456 in conjunction with 0345T for diagnostic left and right heart catheterization procedures intrinsic to the valve repair procedure)◄

⊙**93457**   with catheter placement(s) in bypass graft(s) (internal mammary, free arterial, venous grafts) including intraprocedural injection(s) for bypass graft angiography and right heart catheterization

⊙**93458**   with left heart catheterization including intraprocedural injection(s) for left ventriculography, when performed

⊙**93459**   with left heart catheterization including intraprocedural injection(s) for left ventriculography, when performed, catheter placement(s) in bypass graft(s) (internal mammary, free arterial, venous grafts) with bypass graft angiography

⊙**93460**   with right and left heart catheterization including intraprocedural injection(s) for left ventriculography, when performed

⊙**93461**   with right and left heart catheterization including intraprocedural injection(s) for left ventriculography, when performed, catheter placement(s) in bypass graft(s) (internal mammary, free arterial, venous grafts) with bypass graft angiography

▶(Do not report 93461 in conjunction with 0345T for diagnostic left and right heart catheterization procedures intrinsic to the valve repair procedure)◄

⊙+93462 Left heart catheterization by transseptal puncture through intact septum or by transapical puncture (List separately in addition to code for primary procedure)

(Use 93462 in conjunction with 93452, 93453, 93458, 93459, 93460, 93461, 93582, 93653, 93654)

(Do not report 93462 in conjunction with 93656)

▶(Do not report 93462 in conjunction with 0345T unless transapical puncture is performed)◀

Rationale

In support of new code 0345T for percutaneous transcatheter mitral valve repair, reciprocal exclusionary parenthetical notes have been added following codes 93451, 93454, 93456, 93461, and 93462 to maintain consistency with the exclusionary parenthetical notes in the CPT code set.

INJECTION PROCEDURES

⊙+93563 Injection procedure during cardiac catheterization including imaging supervision, interpretation, and report; for selective coronary angiography during congenital heart catheterization (List separately in addition to code for primary procedure)

⊙+93564   for selective opacification of aortocoronary venous or arterial bypass graft(s) (eg, aortocoronary saphenous vein, free radial artery, or free mammary artery graft) to one or more coronary arteries and in situ arterial conduits (eg, internal mammary), whether native or used for bypass to one or more coronary arteries during congenital heart catheterization, when performed (List separately in addition to code for primary procedure)

▶(Do not report 93563, 93564 in conjunction with 0345T for coronary angiography intrinsic to the valve repair procedure)◀

Rationale

In support of new code 0345T for percutaneous transcatheter mitral valve repair, a reciprocal exclusionary parenthetical note has been added following code 93564 to maintain consistency with the exclusionary parenthetical notes in the CPT code set.

Intracardiac Electrophysiological Procedures/Studies

⊙93640 Electrophysiologic evaluation of single or dual chamber pacing cardioverter-defibrillator leads including defibrillation threshold evaluation (induction of arrhythmia, evaluation of sensing and pacing for arrhythmia termination) at time of initial implantation or replacement;

⊙93641   with testing of single or dual chamber pacing cardioverter-defibrillator pulse generator

(For subsequent or periodic electronic analysis and/or reprogramming of single or dual chamber pacing cardioverter-defibrillators, see 93282, 93283, 93289, 93292, 93295, 93642)

⊙▲93642 Electrophysiologic evaluation of single or dual chamber transvenous pacing cardioverter-defibrillator (includes defibrillation threshold evaluation, induction of arrhythmia, evaluation of sensing and pacing for arrhythmia termination, and programming or reprogramming of sensing or therapeutic parameters)

⊘=Modifier 51 Exempt ⊙=Moderate Sedation ✚=Add-on Code 𝑁=FDA approval pending

⊙●**93644**   Electrophysiologic evaluation of subcutaneous implantable defibrillator (includes defibrillation threshold evaluation, induction of arrhythmia, evaluation of sensing for arrhythmia termination, and programming or reprogramming of sensing or therapeutic parameters)

▶(Do not report 93644 in conjunction with 33270 at the time of subcutaneous implantable defibrillator device insertion)◀

▶(For subsequent or periodic electrophysiologic evaluation of a subcutaneous implantable defibrillator device, see 93260, 93261)◀

🖎 Rationale

Category III codes 0319T-0328T have been deleted and replaced with Category I codes 33270-33273, 93260, 93261, and 93644 to report S-ICD procedures. The S-ICD system is an entirely subcutaneous system designed to avoid the need for the placement of sensing and therapy electrodes within or on the heart. Code 93644 describes the electrophysiologic evaluation of an S-ICD and includes any necessary defibrillation threshold evaluation, induction of arrhythmia, sensing for arrhythmia termination, and programming or reprogramming of sensing or therapeutic parameters. Code 93642 has been revised to enable the appropriate reporting of an S-ICD procedure. The instructional parenthetical note following code 93644 has been added to identify that subsequent or periodic electrophysiologic evaluation of an S-ICD device should be reported with codes 93260 and 93261. In addition, an exclusionary parenthetical note has been added following code 93644 to exclude the reporting of code 93644 in conjunction with code 33270 at the time of the S-ICD system insertion.

🩺 Clinical Example (93644)

A 55-year-old male with existent S-ICD has multiple appropriate shocks for ventricular tachycardia (VT) and is now placed on an antiarrhythmic medication. He is referred for defibrillator threshold testing, as there is concern for an increased threshold with the antiarrhythmic medication.

Description of Procedure (93644)

Deep sedation is induced prior to induction of ventricular fibrillation through the device. Using the two sensing electrodes, or by either of the sensing electrodes or the pulse generator, cardiac rhythm is detected. The S-ICD system automatically selects an appropriate vector for rhythm detection and avoiding double QRS counting and T-wave oversensing. The feature analysis and rate detection are used to sort rhythm type and determine the need for therapy, once the signals have been validated as free of noise and double detection. A conditional discrimination zone that incorporates a feature extraction technique can be programmed between the rates of 170 and 240 beats per minute to distinguish supraventricular tachycardia from ventricular tachycardia, and to avoid inappropriate treatment of the former. Following capacitor charging, ventricular tachyarrhythmia will be reconfirmed to avoid the delivery of shocks for nonsustained ventricular tachyarrhythmias. The defibrillator threshold testing of the device will be evaluated with the use of 65-J shocks to ensure an energy margin of safety.

93701   Bioimpedance-derived physiologic cardiovascular analysis

▶(For bioelectrical impedance analysis whole body composition, use 0358T. For left ventricular filling pressure indirect measurement by computerized calibration of the arterial waveform response to Valsalva, use 93799)◀

●**93702**   Bioimpedance spectroscopy (BIS), extracellular fluid analysis for lymphedema assessment(s)

▶(For bioelectrical impedance analysis whole body composition, use 0358T)◀

▶(For bioimpedance-derived physiological cardiovascular analysis, use 93701)◀

Rationale

Code 93702 has been established to report bioimpedance spectroscopy (BIS) lymphedema assessment for extracellular fluid analysis. BIS is intended to assess and monitor patients at risk of subclinical, Stage 0 lymphedema, prior to the presence of visible signs and symptoms. BIS makes it possible to document a standardized and objective quantitative measurement for the presence of the impairment or to assess the patient's response to lymphedema treatment. This is achieved through the establishment of a presurgical baseline followed by periodic surveillance during the period of the highest incidence.

In support of the establishment of code 93702, Category III BIS code 0239T has been deleted.

A reciprocal parenthetical note has been added following code 93702 to direct users to report code 93701 for bioimpedance-derived physiological cardiovascular analysis.

In support of the establishment of Category III code 0358T for bioelectrical impedance analysis, reciprocal parenthetical notes have been added following codes 93701 and 93702 to direct users to report code 0358T for bioelectrical impedance analysis whole body composition.

Clinical Example (93702)

A 50-year-old female with stage III breast cancer who has had a modified radical mastectomy has a BIS assessment to evaluate lymphedema.

Description of Procedure (93702)

The patient is placed in the examination room and her vital signs are obtained. Following the patient's removal of her shoes, socks, watches, bracelets, anklets, and any metal from her pockets, she is instructed to lie supine on a nonconductive examination table with feet shoulder width apart with her hands by her side. A towel or sheet is placed between her legs or between the arms and torso in order to prevent skin-to-skin contact, and anatomical landmarks are cleaned with an alcohol swab where the electrodes are then placed on each arm and the right ankle. Her demographic information and dominant and at-risk limb information is entered into the device. The color-coded leads from the device are attached to the appropriate drive and the sense tab locations on the electrodes. After ensuring proper lead placement, a measurement of the right arm is taken. The graphic representation of the reading presented on the device is analyzed for quality and then either accepted or rejected, and if rejected, followed with performance of a new more accurate measurement. Once all measurements and assessments have been performed, analyzed, and accepted, the color-coded leads are removed from the electrodes and repositioned for measurement of the left arm with a repeat of the measurement capture and analysis procedure, as described above. The measurement results of the two accepted measurements are calculated and stored on the device. The leads and electrodes are then removed from the skin.

After uploading results from the device into the analysis software provided, the physician then interprets the data provided in the printed report, including analysis of the results from any previous readings and baseline measurement(s), and provides a written plan in the chart regarding diagnosis and treatment. The care plan is dictated to address any early signs of lymphedema or signs of progression. The plan is then communicated to the patient.

Noninvasive Vascular Diagnostic Studies

Cerebrovascular Arterial Studies

▶Code 93895 includes the acquisition and storage of images of the common carotid arteries, carotid bulbs, and internal carotid arteries bilaterally with quantification of intima media thickness (common carotid artery mean and maximal values) and determination of presence of atherosclerotic plaque. When any of these elements are not obtained, use 0126T.◀

93880   Duplex scan of extracranial arteries; complete bilateral study

▶(Do not report 93880 in conjunction with 93895, 0126T)◀

93882   unilateral or limited study

▶(Do not report 93882 in conjunction with 93895, 0126T)◀

●**93895**   Quantitative carotid intima media thickness and carotid atheroma evaluation, bilateral

▶(Do not report 93895 in conjunction with 93880, 93882, 0126T)◀

✍ Rationale
Code 93895 has been established to report carotid intima media thickness (CIMT) and carotid atheroma evaluation. This code includes the acquisition and storage of images of the common carotid arteries, carotid bulbs, and internal carotid arteries with quantification of intima media thickness and determination of presence of atherosclerotic plaque. New guidelines have been added to clarify that if any of these elements are not obtained, the Category III code 0126T for common carotid intima-media thickness study should be reported instead. An exclusionary parenthetical note has also been added precluding the use of code 93895 with codes 93880, 93882, and 0126T. In addition, exclusionary parenthetical notes have been added following codes 93880 and 93882 restricting their use with new code 93895 and Category III code 0126T.

Clinical Example (93895)

A 62-year-old female without symptoms of heart disease presents for evaluation of cardiovascular risk factors. The patient's father died from a myocardial infarction at age 50. She no longer smokes, adheres to a healthy diet, and exercises infrequently. Body mass index is 32 kg/m². Blood pressure is 133/82 mm Hg on an antihypertensive medication. Lipid profile shows total cholesterol of 226 mg/dL; triglycerides 179 mg/dL; HDL-C 42 mg/dL; and LDL-C 148 mg/dL. Fasting glucose is 96 mg/dL. High-sensitivity C-reactive protein is 1.8 gm/dL. The calculated 10-year Framingham Risk Score is 6%. A CIMT/plaque survey is requested to refine the patient's cardiovascular risk assessment and thereby assist the physician with decision making on the selection and intensity of risk-reducing therapies.

Description of Procedure (93895)

Following image acquisition, as the first step of image analysis, review all images of the bilateral carotid arteries, obtained from multiple views, and of multiple sites (far wall common carotid artery, bulb, and internal carotid artery) for image quality and study completeness. Images include those for atherosclerosis survey and CIMT quantitative assessment.

Atherosclerosis Survey: Perform a detailed survey of obtained images for the presence or absence of focal atherosclerotic plaque, within an operational definition of 1.5X surrounding CIMT. Measure focal plaque dimensions, when present, to confirm area of interest meets definition of focal plaque. Expertise is required to avoid errors from image noise or artifact from acoustic shadowing.

CIMT Quantitation: Conduct a quantitative assessment of CIMT within the far wall of the distal common carotid artery within all images from the bilateral carotid arteries. Ensure proper identification of the distal portion of the common carotid artery for the assessment. Following identification of the carotid bulb, use either manual or semiautomatic (computer assisted with manual override) methods. Trace both luminal-intimal and media-adventitial borders over an appropriate length of the carotid wall (minimum 1 cm). Expertise is required for manual interpolation of border delineation. Recorded values of wall thickness include the mean and maximum CIMT for both the right and left carotid arteries (averaged across all angles of insonation).

Archive images detailing evaluation of atherosclerosis and quantitation of intima-media thickness (IMT) and any technical annotations. Compare the CIMT for this patient to databases of population stratified by age, gender, and ethnicity, in addition to ensuring comparability of imaging methods used in the assessment. This may be performed in lookup tables provided by the American Society of Echocardiography. Determine a revised cardiovascular risk assessment for the patient by using computer-based risk calculators such as those provided by the Atherosclerosis Risk in Communities study. Data required include quantitative cardiovascular risk variables, CIMT, and the presence or absence of atherosclerotic plaque.

Electromyography

Needle electromyographic (EMG) procedures include the interpretation of electrical waveforms measured by equipment that produces both visible and audible components of electrical signals recorded from the muscle(s) studied by the needle electrode.

Use 95870 or 95885 when four or fewer muscles are tested in an extremity. Use 95860-95864 or 95886 when five or more muscles are tested in an extremity.

Use EMG codes (95860-95864 and 95867-95870) when no nerve conduction studies (95907-95913) are performed on that day. Use 95885, 95886, and 95887 for EMG services when nerve conduction studies (95907-95913) are performed in conjunction with EMG on the same day.

Report either 95885 or 95886 once per extremity. Codes 95885 and 95886 can be reported together up to a combined total of four units of service per patient when all four extremities are tested.

►Report 95887 once per anatomic site (ie, cervical paraspinal muscle[s], thoracic paraspinal muscle[s], lumbar paraspinal muscle[s], chest wall muscle[s], and abdominal wall muscle[s]). Use 95887 for a unilateral study of the cranial nerve innervated muscles (excluding extra-ocular and larynx); when performed bilaterally, 95887 may be reported twice.

Use 95887 when a study of the cervical paraspinal muscle(s), or the lumbar paraspinal muscle(s) is performed with no corresponding limb study (95885 or 95886) on the same day.◄

►(For needle electromyography of anal or urethral sphincter, use 51785)◄

►(For non-needle electromyography of anal or urethral sphincter, use 51784)◄

►(For needle electromyography of larynx, use 95865)◄

►(For needle electromyography of hemidiaphragm, use 95866)◄

►(For needle electromyography of extra-ocular muscles, use 92265)◄

95860   Needle electromyography; 1 extremity with or without related paraspinal areas

#+95887   Needle electromyography, non-extremity (cranial nerve supplied or axial) muscle(s) done with nerve conduction, amplitude and latency/velocity study (List separately in addition to code for primary procedure)

(Use 95887 in conjunction with 95907-95913)

(Do not report 95887 in conjunction with 95867-95870, 95905)

✍ Rationale

The electromyography guidelines have been revised to clarify that the needle electromyography non-extremity code 95887 is intended to be reported only once per anatomic site, identifying a list of the various anatomic sites. The guidelines also instruct the users to report code 95887 for a unilateral study of the cranial nerve innervated muscles, and, if performed bilaterally, that code 95887 may be reported twice. The guidelines further explain when a study of the cervical paraspinal muscle(s) or the lumbar paraspinal muscle(s) is performed with no corresponding limb study (95885 or 95886) on the same day, it is appropriate to report code 95887.

In support of these revisions, instructional parenthetical notes have been added following the electromyography guidelines to direct users to the appropriate codes to identify various electromyography procedures.

▶Ischemic Muscle Testing and Guidance for Chemodenervation◀

+ 95873 Electrical stimulation for guidance in conjunction with chemodenervation (List separately in addition to code for primary procedure)

🖉 Rationale

The heading for the chemodenervation and muscle testing codes has been revised to clarify that the guidance activity for the chemodenervation services does not apply to ischemic muscle testing.

Neurostimulators, Analysis-Programming

▶(For implantation of neurostimulator electrodes, see 43647, 43881, 61850-61870, 63650-63655, 64553-64580. For revision or removal of neurostimulator electrodes, see 43648, 43882, 61880, 63661-63664, 64585)◀

95970 Electronic analysis of implanted neurostimulator pulse generator system (eg, rate, pulse amplitude, pulse duration, configuration of wave form, battery status, electrode selectability, output modulation, cycling, impedance and patient compliance measurements); simple or complex brain, spinal cord, or peripheral (ie, cranial nerve, peripheral nerve, sacral nerve, neuromuscular) neurostimulator pulse generator/transmitter, without reprogramming

95971 simple spinal cord, or peripheral (ie, peripheral nerve, sacral nerve, neuromuscular) neurostimulator pulse generator/transmitter, with intraoperative or subsequent programming

▲95972 complex spinal cord, or peripheral (ie, peripheral nerve, sacral nerve, neuromuscular) (except cranial nerve) neurostimulator pulse generator/transmitter, with intraoperative or subsequent programming, up to 1 hour

🖉 Rationale

The parenthetical note preceding code 95970 has been revised to remove reference to deleted code 61875. Also, neurostimulator code 95972 has been revised to more accurately define the time component to include the phrase, "up to 1 hour."

◯=Modifier 51 Exempt   ⊙=Moderate Sedation   +=Add-on Code   𝓝=FDA approval pending

Central Nervous System Assessments/Tests (eg, Neuro-Cognitive, Mental Status, Speech Testing)

The following codes are used to report the services provided during testing of the cognitive function of the central nervous system. The testing of cognitive processes, visual motor responses, and abstractive abilities is accomplished by the combination of several types of testing procedures. It is expected that the administration of these tests will generate material that will be formulated into a report. A minimum of 31 minutes must be provided to report any per hour code. Services 96101, 96116, 96118 and 96125 report time as face-to-face time with the patient and the time spent interpreting and preparing the report.

(For development of cognitive skills, see 97532, 97533)

(For mini-mental status examination performed by a physician, see **Evaluation and Management** services codes)

▶(Do not report 96101-96125 in conjunction with 0364T, 0365T, 0366T, 0367T, 0373T, 0374T)◀

96101 Psychological testing (includes psychodiagnostic assessment of emotionality, intellectual abilities, personality and psychopathology, eg, MMPI, Rorschach, WAIS), per hour of the psychologist's or physician's time, both face-to-face time administering tests to the patient and time interpreting these test results and preparing the report

▲**96110** Developmental screening (eg, developmental milestone survey, speech and language delay screen), with scoring and documentation, per standardized instrument

▶(For an emotional/behavioral assessment, use 96127)◀

●**96127** Brief emotional/behavioral assessment (eg, depression inventory, attention-deficit/hyperactivity disorder [ADHD] scale), with scoring and documentation, per standardized instrument

▶(For developmental screening, use 96110)◀

Rationale

Code 96127 has been established to report the administration of a standardized behavioral and emotional assessment instrument (eg, depression inventory, attention-deficit/hyperactivity disorder [ADHD] scale) primarily for, but not limited to, children and adolescents. This assessment serves as a mechanism to identify emotional and behavioral conditions that previously may have been underestimated and/or undetected in any age population.

The individual administering the assessment explains the purpose of the instrument to the patient and/or family member and explains the response choices, scores the instrument, records the results, and delivers the results to the physician. The professional interprets the results in the context of the patient's clinical history, explains the results to the patient and/or family member, and includes the results and interpretation in the patient's medical record.

Code 96110 has been revised to better distinguish it from code 96127. The assessment described in code 96110 also utilizes an instrument, with its focus not on behavioral or emotional status, but on identification of childhood and adolescent developmental levels (eg, fine and gross motor skills, cognitive level, receptive/expressive and pragmatic language abilities, neuropsychological areas [attention, memory, executive functions] and social interaction abilities). An instructional parenthetical note has been added following code 96110 to direct users to report code 96127 for emotional and behavioral assessments. Likewise, a parenthetical note has been added following code 96127 to reference developmental screening code 96110.

In addition, an exclusionary parenthetical note has been added following the introductory guidelines for the Central Nervous System Assessments/Tests section to instruct users not to report codes 96101-96125 with new Category III adaptive behavior treatment codes 0364T-0367T, 0373T, and 0374T. For more information, see the Rationale for codes 0364T-0367T, 0373T, and 0374T.

Clinical Example (96127)

An 8-year-old male presents with a history of short attention span, inability to sit through a meal at home, and impulsive comments and actions. He has a six-month history of irritability, angry outbursts, and refusal to cooperate at home and in his school classroom. A parent version of a behavior assessment system for children is administered to his mother and scored. The medical provider explains the results to the mother and notes results in the medical record. A teacher's version of the behavioral assessment tool is sent to the child's teacher for additional input and a follow-up appointment is scheduled to review the teacher's responses and discuss diagnosis and treatment options.

Description of Procedure (96127)

The administration and scoring of the brief standardized behavioral/emotional assessment instrument is performed by a qualified health care professional. This individual explains the purpose of the instrument to the patient (if self-reported) and/or family member and explains the response choices. When the brief instrument is completed, the qualified health care professional scores the instrument, records the results on the form, and delivers the results to the physician.

Health and Behavior Assessment/Intervention

Health and behavior assessment procedures are used to identify the psychological, behavioral, emotional, cognitive, and social factors important to the prevention, treatment, or management of physical health problems.

The focus of the assessment is not on mental health but on the biopsychosocial factors important to physical health problems and treatments. The focus of the intervention is to improve the patient's health and well-being utilizing cognitive, behavioral, social, and/or psychophysiological procedures designed to ameliorate specific disease-related problems.

⊘=Modifier 51 Exempt ⊙=Moderate Sedation ✦=Add-on Code 𝒩=FDA approval pending

Codes 96150-96155 describe services offered to patients who present with primary physical illnesses, diagnoses, or symptoms and may benefit from assessments and interventions that focus on the biopsychosocial factors related to the patient's health status. These services do not represent preventive medicine counseling and risk factor reduction interventions.

For patients that require psychiatric services (90785-90899) as well as health and behavior assessment/intervention (96150-96155), report the predominant service performed. Do not report 96150-96155 in conjunction with 90785-90899 on the same date.

Evaluation and Management services codes (including Counseling Risk Factor Reduction and Behavior Change Intervention [99401-99412]), should not be reported on the same day.

(For health and behavior assessment and/or intervention performed by a physician or other qualified health care professional who may report evaluation and management services, see **Evaluation and Management** or **Preventive Medicine** services codes)

▶(Do not report 96150, 96151, 96152, 96153, 96154, 96155 in conjunction with 0364T, 0365T, 0366T, 0367T, 0373T, 0374T)◀

96150   Health and behavior assessment (eg, health-focused clinical interview, behavioral observations, psychophysiological monitoring, health-oriented questionnaires), each 15 minutes face-to-face with the patient; initial assessment

Rationale

An exclusionary parenthetical note has been added to the end of the introductory guidelines for the Health and Behavior Assessment/Intervention section to instruct users not to use adaptive behavior treatment codes 0364T, 0365T, 0366T, 0367T, 0373T, and 0374T with health and behavior assessment procedure codes 96150-96155. For more information, see the Rationale for codes 0364T, 0365T, 0366T, 0367T, 0373T, and 0374T.

Hydration, Therapeutic, Prophylactic, Diagnostic Injections and Infusions, and Chemotherapy and Other Highly Complex Drug or Highly Complex Biologic Agent Administration

Therapeutic, Prophylactic, and Diagnostic Injections and Infusions (Excludes Chemotherapy and Other Highly Complex Drug or Highly Complex Biologic Agent Administration)

96372   Therapeutic, prophylactic, or diagnostic injection (specify substance or drug); subcutaneous or intramuscular

▶(For administration of vaccines/toxoids, see 90460, 90461, 90471, 90472)◀

(Report 96372 for non-antineoplastic hormonal therapy injections)

(Report 96401 for anti-neoplastic nonhormonal injection therapy)

(Report 96402 for anti-neoplastic hormonal injection therapy)

(Do not report 96372 for injections given without direct physician or other qualified health care professional supervision. To report, use 99211. Hospitals may report 96372 when the physician or other qualified health care professional is not present)

(96372 does not include injections for allergen immunotherapy. For allergen immunotherapy injections, see 95115-95117)

Rationale

The parenthetical note following code 96372 has been editorially revised by eliminating codes 96365 and 96366 for intravenous (IV) infusion procedures, and adding codes 90460 and 90461 for immunization injection procedures to indicate only immunization procedures within the note. This change is a technical correction as this was the original intent of the parenthetical note.

Physical Medicine and Rehabilitation

Therapeutic Procedures

97140 Manual therapy techniques (eg, mobilization/ manipulation, manual lymphatic drainage, manual traction), 1 or more regions, each 15 minutes

97150 Therapeutic procedure(s), group (2 or more individuals)

(Report 97150 for each member of group)

(Group therapy procedures involve constant attendance of the physician or other qualified health care professional [ie, therapist], but by definition do not require one-on-one patient contact by the same physician or other qualified health care professional)

(For manipulation under general anesthesia, see appropriate anatomic section in **Musculoskeletal System**)

(For osteopathic manipulative treatment [OMT], see 98925-98929)

▶(Do not report 97150 in conjunction with 0366T, 0367T, 0372T)◀

97530 Therapeutic activities, direct (one-on-one) patient contact (use of dynamic activities to improve functional performance), each 15 minutes

97532 Development of cognitive skills to improve attention, memory, problem solving (includes compensatory training), direct (one-on-one) patient contact, each 15 minutes

▶(Do not report 97532 in conjunction with 0364T, 0365T, 0368T, 0369T)◀

Rationale

Exclusionary parenthetical notes have been added following codes 97150 and 97532 to restrict their use in conjunction with the new Category III adaptive behavior treatment codes 0364T-0372T.

⊘=Modifier 51 Exempt ⊙=Moderate Sedation ✚=Add-on Code ✗=FDA approval pending

Active Wound Care Management

▲97605   Negative pressure wound therapy (eg, vacuum assisted drainage collection), utilizing durable medical equipment (DME), including topical application(s), wound assessment, and instruction(s) for ongoing care, per session; total wound(s) surface area less than or equal to 50 square centimeters

▲97606   total wound(s) surface area greater than 50 square centimeters

●97607   Negative pressure wound therapy, (eg, vacuum assisted drainage collection), utilizing disposable, non-durable medical equipment including provision of exudate management collection system, topical application(s), wound assessment, and instructions for ongoing care, per session; total wound(s) surface area less than or equal to 50 square centimeters

●97608   total wound(s) surface area greater than 50 square centimeters

    ▶(Do not report 97607, 97608 in conjunction with 97605, 97606)◀

Rationale

Two codes (97607 and 97608) have been established to report negative pressure wound therapy (eg, vacuum-assisted drainage collection) utilizing disposable, non-durable medical equipment (DME), including the provision of an exudate management collection system, topical application(s), wound assessment, and instructions for ongoing care. These codes are for the treatment of wounds with a total wound surface area of either less than or equal to 50 sq cm, and for wounds with a surface area greater than 50 sq cm. The dressing is included and should not be reported separately.

As a result, codes 97605 and 97606 have been revised to include the phrase "durable medical equipment (DME)" to distinguish between these codes and new codes 97607 and 97608, which are intended to report non-durable medical equipment (DME).

An exclusionary parenthetical note has been added to preclude the reporting of codes 97607 and 97608 with codes 97605 and 97606.

Clinical Example (97607)

A male patient presents with a diabetic foot ulcer of the heel that measures 2.0 x 1.8 x 0.8 cm. The base of the wound is clean and red and has minimal necrotic tissue. Negative pressure wound therapy using a disposable mechanical wound care system is applied.

Description of Procedure (97607)

Thoroughly clean the wound and periwound area. Ensure adequate hemostasis has been achieved. Prior to foam placement, protect tendons, ligaments, blood vessels, nerves, and organs, when present. Apply skin protectant to periwound area. Assess wound dimensions and pathology, including the presence of undermining or tunnels. Cut dressing to dimensions that will allow the foam to be placed gently into the wound without overlapping intact skin. Place a drape to cover the foam dressing. Place the adhesive face down over foam, and apply drape to cover foam and intact skin, avoiding placement over bony prominences or within creases in the tissue. Place pump strap and pump, and connect to the dressing tube. Secure excess tubing to prevent interference with patient mobility. Pull pump activation tab to begin negative pressure therapy, and inspect system for leaks and proper function.

Clinical Example (97608)

A female patient presents with a venous ulcer of the right anterior leg that measures 10.2 x 6.8 x 1.2 cm. The base of the wound is clean and red and has minimal necrotic tissue. Negative pressure wound therapy using a disposable mechanical wound care system is applied.

Description of Procedure (97608)

Thoroughly clean the wound and periwound area. Ensure adequate hemostasis has been achieved. Prior to foam placement, protect tendons, ligaments, blood vessels, nerves, and organs, when present. Apply skin protectant to periwound area. Assess wound dimensions and pathology, including the presence of undermining or tunnels. Cut dressing to dimensions that will allow the foam to be placed gently into the wound without overlapping intact skin. Place a drape to cover the foam dressing. Place the adhesive face down over foam, and apply drape to cover foam and intact skin, avoiding placement over bony prominences or within creases in the tissue. Place pump strap and pump, and connect to the dressing tube. Secure excess tubing to prevent interference with patient mobility. Pull pump activation tab to begin negative pressure therapy, and inspect system for leaks and proper function.

Other Services and Procedures

99183   Physician or other qualified health care professional attendance and supervision of hyperbaric oxygen therapy, per session

(Evaluation and Management services and/or procedures [eg, wound debridement] provided in a hyperbaric oxygen treatment facility in conjunction with a hyperbaric oxygen therapy session should be reported separately)

●**99184**   Initiation of selective head or total body hypothermia in the critically ill neonate, includes appropriate patient selection by review of clinical, imaging and laboratory data, confirmation of esophageal temperature probe location, evaluation of amplitude EEG, supervision of controlled hypothermia, and assessment of patient tolerance of cooling

▶(Do not report 99184 more than once per hospital stay)◀

Rationale

Codes 99481 and 99482 have been deleted and replaced with code 99184, which combines both selective head and total body hypothermia of neonates into a single description that includes all of the service components required of this procedure, including the review of clinical, imaging, and laboratory data;

○=Modifier 51 Exempt   ⊙=Moderate Sedation   ✚=Add-on Code   ⊅=FDA approval pending

confirmation of esophageal temperature probe location; evaluation of amplitude electroencephalography (EEG); supervision of controlled hypothermia; and assessment of patient tolerance of cooling. The refinement of the neonatal hypothermia service, as described in code 99184, was necessary for the AMA/Specialty Society RUC to assign an appropriate work value. The location of this code in the CPT code set has also been changed from the Evaluation and Management section to a more accurate placement in the Medicine section. Code 99184 represents a single service that may be reported only once per hospital stay, as captured in the parenthetical note following code 99184. Hypothermia services are considered as separately reported services from initial inpatient and subsequent inpatient neonatal critical care codes 99468 and 99469.

 Clinical Example (99184)

A 2-hour-old critically ill term neonate born with severe in utero hypoxemia and admitted to a neonatal intensive care unit (NICU) receives head or total body cooling after meeting objective criteria.

Description of Procedure (99184)

After evaluating the radiograph, confirm the position of the esophageal temperature probe. Initiate total body or selective head cooling. Under the physician's direction, the patient is cooled to a core temperature of 91.8°F to 95°F and maintained at this temperature. The patient may be continued on the amplitude integrated EEG, which the physician interprets, looking for evidence of seizures. Perform neurologic function tests (eg, Sarnat scores) every four hours. Continuously monitor cooling and temperature and make recommendations for adjustments to keep core temperatures within the ordered range.

●**99188**   Application of topical fluoride varnish by a physician or other qualified health care professional

 Rationale

Code 99188 is used to report the application of topical fluoride varnish by a physician or other qualified health care professional for the prevention of dental caries (cavities). This code is intended for use only by a physician or other qualified health care professional and only for patients that are at high risk for caries.

 Clinical Example (99188)

A 24-month-old patient who is at risk for dental caries receives a topical application of fluoride varnish to the teeth from a physician or other qualified health care professional.

Description of Procedure (99188)

Dry the first quadrant of the mouth with gauze, and apply the fluoride varnish with a brush to cover every surface of the teeth. Continue for all four quadrants of the mouth.

Category II Codes

Category II codes remain important for claims-based performance measures reporting. Changes for 2015 include the: (1) revision to code 3125F and addition of code 3126F for esophageal biopsy reporting; (2) addition of two codes (3775F and 3776F) for identification of adenoma and other neoplasm detection; (3) revision of the Esophageal Biopsies with a Diagnosis of Barrett's Esophagus that also include a Statement on Dysplasia[9] measure; and (4) addition of a new footnote to identify a measure developed by the American College of Gastroenterology (ACG), the American Gastroenterological Assocation (AGA), and the American Society for Gastrointestinal Endoscopy (ASGE).

Go to www.ama-assn.org/ama/pub/physician-resources/ solutions-managing-your-practice/coding-billing-insurance/cpt/ about-cpt/category-ii-codes.page? for the Alphabetical Clinical Topics Listing (or Alphabetical Listing).

Category II Codes

▶[12]American College of Gastroenterology (ACG), www.gi.org; American Gastroenterological Association (AGA), www.gastro.org; and American Society for Gastrointestinal Endoscopy (ASGE), www.asge.org.◀

✍ Rationale

A new footnote has been added to the CPT code set. The reference directs users to the American College for Gastroenterology (ACG), the American Gastroenterological Association (AGA),and the American Society for Gastgrointestinal Endoscopy (ASGE) websites to obtain information to access the specific measures represented by the codes included within the code set.

Diagnostic/Screening Processes or Results

3120F   12-Lead ECG Performed (EM)[5]

     ▶(Code 3125F has been deleted)◀

●**3126F**   Esophageal biopsy report with a statement about dysplasia (present, absent, or indefinite, and if present, contains appropriate grading) (PATH)[9]

✍ Rationale

Code 3126F should be used to report a new measure, which has been written as a revision to a measure that has been deleted for 2015. Deleted code 3125F was originally used to identify reporting esophageal biopsies with a diagnosis of Barrett's Esophagus with a statement on dysplasia. However, the numerator of the measure was updated to reflect the addition of a statement regarding appropriate upgrading if dysplasia is present. As a result, a new measure—Esophageal Biopsies with a Diagnosis of Barrett's Esophagus that also includes a Statement on Dysplasia[9] (Revised Measure)—has been included within the Alphabetical Clinical Topics Listing. To accommodate the change noted within the new measure, code 3126F was developed in order to report compliance with the new measure. In order to identify the appropriate exclusions for the measure, exclusion and reporting instructions have been included online to direct user to report code 3125F with modifier 1P.

●**3775F**   Adenoma(s) or other neoplasm detected during screening colonoscopy (SCADR)[12]

●**3776F**   Adenoma(s) or other neoplasm not detected during screening colonoscopy (SCADR)[12]

✍ Rationale

Codes 3775F and 3776F should be used to report detection of adenomas or other neoplasms during colonoscopy screening (or lack of detection of adenomas). These codes should be used within the new measure set and measure listing of Screening Colonoscopy Adenoma Rate Detection[13] reported within the new Screening Colonoscopy Adenoma Detection Rate (SCADR). This measure is used to determine whether a patient age 50 or older has had at least one adenoma or other colorectal cancer precursor detection during a screening colonoscopy. Code 3775F should be used to identify the detection of an adenoma or other neoplasm during screening colonoscopy, while code 3776F should be used when an adenoma is not detected. Note that medical exclusions for this measure do exist when no adenoma or other colorectal cancer precursor is detected. As a result of medical exclusions, the reporting instructions have indicated that modifier 1P should be used in conjunction with code 3776F to identify the exclusion circumstance.

Category III Codes

Changes that have been made to the Category III section include the addition of 39 codes, revision of 6 codes, and deletion of 26 codes.

In accordance with CPT guidelines for archiving Category III codes, three codes and related parenthetical notes have been deleted for 2015. The remaining 23 deleted Category III codes have been converted to Category I codes, including deletion of related codes from the Subcutaneous Implantable Defibrillator System subsection.

The other additions to Category III include three new subsections, guidelines, and 16 codes for the assessment and treatment in the Adaptive Behavior subsection.

Category III Codes

0058T   Cryopreservation; reproductive tissue, ovarian

     ▶(0059T has been deleted)◀

     ▶(For cryopreservation of mature oocyte(s), use 89337. For cryopreservation of immature oocyte(s), use 0357T)◀

#●0357T   immature oocyte(s)

     ▶(For cryopreservation of mature oocyte(s), use 89337)◀

Rationale

In correlation with the establishment of new code 89337 to report cryopreservation of mature oocyte(s), Category III code 0357T has been established to report cryopreservation of immature oocyte(s).

Code 0059T has been deleted and a parenthetical note about the deletion was added. Previously, code 0059T was used to report cryopreservation for oocyte(s).

A cross-reference note has been added following code 0375T with instructions to use code 89337 to report cryopreservation of mature oocytes(s). Preceding code 0357T, a cross-reference note has been added to direct users to report code 89337 for cryopreservation of mature oocytes and code 0375T for cryopreservation of immature oocytes.

Clinical Example (0357T)

A 33-year-old is diagnosed with acute leukemia. Her oncologist tells her she needs to begin chemotherapy and radiation as soon as possible. She is told that she may not able to conceive after completing her treatments. She wants to preserve her ability to conceive. A fertility specialist states that there is not adequate time to perform ovarian stimulation and recover mature oocytes. The physician offers to retrieve some of her oocytes (eggs) from intermediate-sized follicles. The oocytes recovered will be immature, and these can be frozen for her use in the future when she is disease-free. She is counseled that freezing of immature oocytes and in-vitro maturation of oocytes are considered experimental at this time.

Description of Procedure (0357T)

After oocyte retrieval, maintain oocytes in human tubal fluid media for 2 hours. Denude oocytes by enzymatic means, and assess nuclear maturity. Transfer oocytes suitable for vitrification to media containing the cryoproectants dimethyl sulfoxide (DMSO), ethylene glycol, and sucrose. Place oocytes in strips, and submerge them in liquid nitrogen. Following vitrification, transfer the oocytes to cryostorage.

     ▶(0073T has been deleted. To report, use 77385)◀

Rationale

Category III code 0073T. which represented compensator-based beam modulation treatment delivery, has been deleted. A deletion parenthetical cross-reference note directing users to code 77385 has been added.

▲**0075T** Transcatheter placement of extracranial vertebral artery stent(s), including radiologic supervision and interpretation, open or percutaneous; initial vessel

✚▲**0076T** each additional vessel (List separately in addition to code for primary procedure)

(Use 0076T in conjunction with 0075T)

►(When the ipsilateral extracranial vertebral arteriogram (including imaging and selective catheterization) confirms the need for stenting, then 0075T and 0076T include all ipsilateral extracranial vertebral catheterization, all diagnostic imaging for ipsilateral extracranial vertebral artery stenting, and all related radiologic supervision and interpretation. If stenting is not indicated, then the appropriate codes for selective catheterization and imaging should be reported in lieu of 0075T or 0076T)◄

✎ Rationale

Category III codes 0075T and 0076T have been revised to specify that these codes should be used to report vertebral artery stenting. Previously included intrathoracic common carotid artery stenting will now be reported with the new Category I code 37218.

In addition, an instructional parenthetical note has been added following code 0076T to provide instructions for the appropriate reporting of these codes.

►(0092T has been deleted)◄

►(For cervical arthroplasty procedure on three or more levels, use 0375T)◄

✎ Rationale

In support of the revision of code 22856 and the establishment of codes 22858 and 0375T to report cervical arthroplasty procedures and the recently adopted concept of permanence principle, which dictates that new code numbers should be established if a revision alters the meaning of the code, code 0092T has been deleted. An instructional parenthetical note has been added to direct the user to use code 0375T for cervical arthroplasty procedure on three or more levels.

0126T Common carotid intima-media thickness (IMT) study for evaluation of atherosclerotic burden or coronary heart disease risk factor assessment

►(Do not report 0126T in conjunction with 93880, 93882, 93895)◄

►(For bilateral quantitative carotid intima media thickness and carotid atheroma evaluation that includes all required elements, use 93895)◄

✎ Rationale

In support of the establishment of code 93895, an instructional parenthetical note directing users to report code 93895 for bilateral quantitative carotid intima media thickness and carotid atheroma evaluation has been added following code 0126T.

In addition, an exclusionary parenthetical note following code 0126T has been added to preclude reporting code 0126T in conjunction with codes 93880, 93882, 93895 (noninvasive vascular diagnostic studies).

►(0181T has been deleted. To report, use 92145)◄

⃠=Modifier 51 Exempt ⊙=Moderate Sedation ✚=Add-on Code ⩘=FDA approval pending

✍ Rationale

In support of the establishment of code 92145 to report corneal hysteresis determination by air impulse stimulation, code 0181T has been deleted. A parenthetical note was added directing users to code 92145.

▲0191T Insertion of anterior segment aqueous drainage device, without extraocular reservoir, internal approach, into the trabecular meshwork; initial insertion

#✢●0376T   each additional device insertion (List separately in addition to code for primary procedure)

▶(Use 0376T in conjunction with 0191T)◀

#▲0253T Insertion of anterior segment aqueous drainage device, without extraocular reservoir, internal approach, into the suprachoroidal space

✍ Rationale

Category III codes 0191T and 0253T for insertion of aqueous drainage devices to relieve intraocular pressure (IOP) associated with glaucoma have been revised to accommodate new Category III code 0376T to describe the additional work of inserting additional drainage devices into the trabecular meshwork. Code 0191T now describes the insertion of a single stent, while code 0376T is an add-on code, which should be used in conjunction with code 0191T for insertion of each additional stent beyond the first implanted stent. The work (eg, patient preparation, incision, and closing of the wound) associated with the initial procedure (0191T) is not captured in the add-on code 0376T.

To accommodate the addition of code 0376T, code 0253T has been revised to be a stand-alone code in order to further delineate the location of the implant into the suprachoroidal space vs into the trabecular meshwork.

🩺 Clinical Example (0376T)

A 65-year-old female presents with a history of open angle glaucoma. The patient has been treated with topical hypotensive medication, and her IOP remains uncontrolled. In order to achieve the desired IOP reduction without major incisional surgery, the surgeon implants two trabecular meshwork microstents in the same intraoperative session on the same date of service.

Description of Procedure (0376T)

Create a small, temporal clear corneal incision. Use viscoelastic to deepen the anterior chamber. Inspect the angle with a goniolens. Locate the trabecular meshwork, a narrow (150-micron) circumferential band of tissue that drains aqueous humor from the anterior chamber. Use viscoelastic to clear any blood from the implantation site. Introduce the inserter into the anterior chamber and, under gonioscopy, advance it to the trabecular meshwork. Implant the first stent into the trabecular meshwork, and withdraw the inserter. Advance a second inserter loaded with a second stent through the same wound. Implant the second stent into the trabecular meshwork, and withdraw the inserter. Flush the anterior chamber of any refluxed blood, irrigate it with balanced salt solution (BSS) to remove all viscoelastic, and inflate it with BSS as needed to achieve physiologic pressure.

▶(0197T has been deleted. To report, use 77387)◀

✍ Rationale

Category III code 0197T, which represented intra-fraction localization and tracking of target or patient motion during radiation therapy, has been deleted. A deletion parenthetical note directing users to code 77387 has been added.

▶(0199T has been deleted)◀

▶(For tremor measurement with accelerometer(s) and/or gyroscope(s), use 95999)◀

✍ Rationale

In accordance with CPT guidelines for archiving Category III codes, code 0199T has been deleted for CPT 2015. Code 0199T was used to report tremor measurement with accelerometer(s) and/or gyroscope(s). A deletion parenthetical note directing users to unlisted code 95999 has been added.

⊙▲**0200T** Percutaneous sacral augmentation (sacroplasty), unilateral injection(s), including the use of a balloon or mechanical device, when used, 1 or more needles, includes imaging guidance and bone biopsy, when performed

⊙▲**0201T** Percutaneous sacral augmentation (sacroplasty), bilateral injections, including the use of a balloon or mechanical device, when used, 2 or more needles, includes imaging guidance and bone biopsy, when performed

▶(Do not report 0200T, 0201T in conjunction with 20225 when performed at the same level)◀

0202T Posterior vertebral joint(s) arthroplasty (eg, facet joint[s] replacement), including facetectomy, laminectomy, foraminotomy, and vertebral column fixation, injection of bone cement, when performed, including fluoroscopy, single level, lumbar spine

▶(Do not report 0202T in conjunction with 22511, 22514, 22840, 22851, 22857, 63005, 63012, 63017, 63030, 63042, 63047, 63056 at the same level)◀

✍ Rationale

In correlation with the addition of the new comprehensive codes for percutaneous vertebral augmentation of the thoracic and lumbar areas, codes 0200T and 0201T have been revised to include imaging guidance and bone biopsy to align with the services included in the new comprehensive augmentation codes. As a result, an exclusionary parenthetical note has been added restricting the use of codes 0200T and 0201T in addition to code 20225 (bone biopsy) when performed at the same level, as this procedure is now included in these codes. The exclusionary parenthetical note following code 0202T has also been revised to include the new code numbers for percutaneous lumbar vertebroplasty (22511) and percutaneous lumbar augmentation (22514).

0213T Injection(s), diagnostic or therapeutic agent, paravertebral facet (zygapophyseal) joint (or nerves innervating that joint) with ultrasound guidance, cervical or thoracic; single level

(To report bilateral procedure, use 0213T with modifier 50)

⊘=Modifier 51 Exempt ⊙=Moderate Sedation ✚=Add-on Code 𝒩=FDA approval pending

+ 0214T   second level (List separately in addition to code for primary procedure)

▶(Use 0214T in conjunction with 0213T)◀

(To report bilateral procedure, use 0214T with modifier 50)

+ 0215T   third and any additional level(s) (List separately in addition to code for primary procedure)

(Do not report 0215T more than once per day)

▶(Use 0215T in conjunction with 0213T, 0214T)◀

(To report bilateral procedure, use 0215T with modifier 50)

0216T   Injection(s), diagnostic or therapeutic agent, paravertebral facet (zygapophyseal) joint (or nerves innervating that joint) with ultrasound guidance, lumbar or sacral; single level

(To report bilateral procedure, use 0216T with modifier 50)

+ 0217T   second level (List separately in addition to code for primary procedure)

▶(Use 0217T in conjunction with 0216T)◀

(To report bilateral procedure, use 0217T with modifier 50)

+ 0218T   third and any additional level(s) (List separately in addition to code for primary procedure)

(Do not report 0218T more than once per day)

▶(Use 0218T in conjunction with 0216T, 0217T)◀

(If injection(s) are performed using fluoroscopy or CT, see 64490-64495)

(To report bilateral procedure, use 0218T with modifier 50)

Rationale

Three inclusionary parenthetical notes have been added and revised within the paravertebral spinal nerve injection codes in the Category III code section (0213T-0218T). The parenthetical instructions are editorial and have been inserted to direct the appropriate use of the add-on codes included for these services. The add-on code families listed in this section are intended to be used together in a "progressive" fashion to denote the appropriate service(s) performed (ie, the codes are "additive" and build on each other to note the number of levels of injections provided).

▶(0226T has been deleted. To report, use 46601)◀

▶(0227T has been deleted. To report, use 46607)◀

Rationale

High-resolution anoscopy (HRA) codes 0226T and 0227T have been deleted and converted to Category I codes 46601 and 46607. Instructional notes have been added to direct users to the new codes.

▶(0239T has been deleted. To report, use 93702)◀

✍ Rationale

In accordance with the conversion of Category III code 0239T to Category I code 93702, code 0239T has been deleted, and a cross-reference note has been added to direct users to the new Category I code for bioimpendance spectroscopy (BIS) lymphedema assessment for extracellular fluid analysis.

▶(0245T, 0246T, 0247T, 0248T have been deleted. To report, see 21811, 21812, 21813)◀

✍ Rationale

In accordance with the conversion of Category III codes 0245T-0248T to Category I codes 21811-21813, codes 0245T-0248T have been deleted, and a cross-reference note has been added to direct users to the new Category I codes for internal fixation of rib fracture. Because the amount of work is more amenable to three codes instead of four, only three codes have been established.

▶(0260T, 0261T have been deleted. To report, use 99184)◀

✍ Rationale

The parenthetical note for deleted codes 0260T and 0261T has been updated to direct users to code 99184 for total body hypothermia of neonates procedures.

⊙0301T   Destruction/reduction of malignant breast tumor with externally applied focused microwave, including interstitial placement of disposable catheter with combined temperature monitoring probe and microwave focusing sensocatheter under ultrasound thermotherapy guidance

▶(Do not report 0301T in conjunction with 76641, 76642, 76942, 76998, 77600, 77605, 77610, 77615)◀

✍ Rationale

In accordance with the establishment of codes 76641 and 76642 to report complete and limited breast ultrasound examination, the exclusionary parenthetical note following code 0301T has been revised to preclude these services.

Subcutaneous Implantable Defibrillator System

▶(0319T, 0320T, 0321T, 0322T, 0323T, 0324T, 0325T, 0326T, 0327T, 0328T have been deleted. To report, see 33240, 33241, 33262, 33270, 33271, 33272, 33273, 93260, 93261, 93644)◀

✍ Rationale

Category III codes 0319T-0328T related to subcutaneous implantable defibrillator procedures have been deleted and replaced with Category I codes 33270-33273, 93261, 93260, and 93644.

▶(0334T has been deleted)◀

▶(To report percutaneous/minimally invasive [indirect visualization] arthrodesis of the sacroiliac joint with image guidance, use 27279)◀

✍️ Rationale

Category III code 0334T has been deleted and replaced with Category I code 27279 to describe minimally invasive sacroiliac joint arthrodesis. A cross-reference note has been added to direct users to the new Category I code 27279 to report percutaneous/minimally invasive (indirect visualization) arthrodesis of the sacroiliac joint with image guidance.

⊙●**0340T** Ablation, pulmonary tumor(s), including pleura or chest wall when involved by tumor extension, percutaneous, cryoablation, unilateral, includes imaging guidance

▶(Do not report 0340T in conjunction with 76940, 77013, 77022)◀

✍️ Rationale

Code 0340T has been established to report percutaneous ablation of pulmonary tumors performed within the chest wall or pleura (when the tumor has extended into these structures), which also includes the imaging procedure when imaging is performed. This procedure inherently includes ultrasound guidance (76940), computed tomographic imaging guidance (77013), and magnetic resonance guidance (77022). To exemplify this, an exclusionary parenthetical note has been included following the code to exclude reporting these imaging procedures in conjunction with the ablation procedure.

🩺 Clinical Example (0340T)

A 68-year-old male with a history of large right renal cell carcinoma treated by a surgical partial nephrectomy presents several years later with an enlarging lingular metastasis and is referred for percutaneous cryoablation treatment for the enlarging pulmonary nodule.

Description of Procedure (0340T)

Prepare and drape the patient in sterile fashion. Administer intravenous conscious sedation. Perform imaging for localization/targeting purposes.

Utilizing intermittent computer tomographic (CT) fluoroscopy, place a 17-gauge cryoablation needle into the lingular nodule from an anterior approach. Place two additional 17-gauge cryoablation needles, approximately 1.5 cm apart, to allow for complete tumor coverage by ice. Initiate the cryoablation procedure with activation of the 3 cryoneedles simultaneously with 3 minutes of freeze, 3 minutes thaw, 7 minutes freeze, 3 minutes thaw, 12 minutes freeze, and 10 minutes thaw. Monitor the location and dimensions of the ice-ball coverage with noncontrast CT imaging approximately every 2 to 5 minutes throughout the freeze cycles. Remove the cryoneedles following the final thaw without further complications. Wake the patient from anesthesia and send him to the recovery room in stable condition. Postablation images demonstrate surrounding ground glass and airspace consolidation without pneumothorax.

🖋 Rationale

Code 0341T has been established to report quantitative pupillometry with interpretation and report, unilateral and bilateral. Pupillometery offers noninvasive technique to provide measures of pupil diameter and responses to light.

🩺 Clinical Example (0341T)

A 12-year-old male with congenital central hypoventilation syndrome is referred for evaluation of his autonomic system function using quantitative pupillary testing.

Description of Procedure (0341T)

A physician or trained technician operates the portable handheld pupillometers. Perform the test when the patient is fully awake and initiate the test after a minimum of 1 minute adaptation to a completely dark and quiet room. Separately record the pupil response to a fixed amount and duration of light for a 5-second duration in each eye. Hold the device in front of the eye and start recording by holding down a single button (recording is stopped when button is released). The recording lasts 5 seconds in duration and includes delivery of a flash of light. The pupillometer measures pupil diameter with ± 0.1 mm accuracy and sampling rate every 0.33 seconds. Each monocular measurement includes the following: maximum dark-adapted pupil diameter (max); minimum pupil diameter (min) after light exposure, latency, percentage of pupil constriction (delta), average constriction (ACV), and dilation (ADV); and time to redilate to 75% of maximum pupil diameter (T75).

Specific responsibilities of the qualified health care professional include interpretation of the test results in context of the patient condition (including review of medical history/medications); documentation of the results; and communication with the patient/family and referring health care professional.

●0342T   Therapeutic apheresis with selective HDL delipidation and plasma reinfusion

🖋 Rationale

Category III code 0342T has been added as a new code and should be used to report therapeutic apheresis performed with selective high-density lipoprotein (HDL) delipidation and plasma reinfusion. Therapeutic apheresis modifies a component of the patient's blood (ie, alpha HDL or αHDL) and converts it into another form (ie, pre-beta HDL or preβ HDL). The converted blood component is then reinfused into the patient.

This procedure differs from apheresis services because apheresis is a continuous procedure, which separates blood components that are not returned to the body (the separation of the blood compenent is the therapeutic treatment). Therapeutic apheresis with selective HDL delipidation separates blood components (ie, alpha HDL) with the intent of changing that component into beta HDL, which is then used to accomplish the treatment.

Clinical Example (0342T)

A 58-year-old male currently on lipid-lowering medication presents to the emergency room with acute chest pain. He is admitted to the hospital and treated for acute coronary syndrome. After discharge, he is referred for HDL delipidation therapy.

Description of Procedure (0342T)

Obtain patient's plasma by therapeutic aphereisis. Introduce the patient's plasma into the HDL delipidation system, where it is treated. Store the HDL-delipidated plasma in an intravenous bag. Reinfuse the HDL delipidated plasma into the patient via an infusion pump for, approximately 1 hour. Observe the patient for 30 minutes after completion of his infusion, and then release him from the clinic.

▶Fluoroscopy (76000, 76001) and radiologic supervision and interpretation are inherent to the transcatheter mitral valve repair (TMVR) procedure and are not separately reportable. Diagnostic cardiac catheterization (93451, 93452, 93453, 93454, 93455, 93456, 93457, 93458, 93459, 93460, 93461, 93530, 93531, 93532, 93533) should **not** be reported with transcatheter mitral valve repair 0345T for:

- Contrast injections, angiography, roadmapping, and/or fluoroscopic guidance for the transcatheter mitral valve repair (TMVR),

- Left ventricular angiography to assess mitral regurgitation, for guidance of TMVR, or

- Right and left heart catheterization for hemodynamic measurements before, during, and after TMVR for guidance of TMVR.

Diagnostic right and left heart catheterization (93451, 93452, 93453, 93456, 93457, 93458, 93459, 93460, 93461, 93530, 93531, 93532, 93533), and diagnostic coronary angiography (93454, 93455, 93456, 93457, 93458, 93459, 93460, 93461, 93563, 93564) not inherent to the TMVR, may be reported with 0345T, appended with modifier 59 if:

1. No prior study is available and a full diagnostic study is performed, or

2. A prior study is available, but as documented in the medical record:

   a. There is inadequate visualization of the anatomy and/or pathology, or

   b. The patient's condition with respect to the clinical indication has changed since the prior study, or

   c. There is a clinical change during the procedure that requires new evaluation.

Percutaneous coronary interventional procedures may be reported separately, when performed.

Other cardiac catheterization services may be reported separately, when performed for diagnostic purposes not intrinsic to the TMVR.

When transcatheter ventricular support is required, the appropriate code may be reported with the appropriate ventricular assist device (VAD) procedure (33990, 33991, 33992, 33993) or balloon pump insertion (33967, 33970, 33973).◀

▶(0343T has been deleted. To report, use 33418)◀

▶(0344T has been deleted. To report, use 33419)◀

●**0345T** Transcatheter mitral valve repair percutaneous approach via the coronary sinus

▶(For transcatheter mitral valve repair percutaneous approach including transseptal puncture when performed, see 33418, 33419)◄

▶(Do not report 0345T in conjunction with 93451, 93452, 93453, 93456, 93457, 93458, 93459, 93460, 93461 for diagnostic left and right heart catheterization procedures intrinsic to the valve repair procedure)◄

▶(Do not report 0345T in conjunction with 93453, 93454, 93563, 93564 for coronary angiography intrinsic to the valve repair procedure)◄

Rationale

Category III codes 0343T and 0344T have been converted to Category I codes 33418 and 33419 to report implantation of endovascular transcatheter prostheses for mitral valve repair. Parenthetical notes have been added to direct users to codes 33418 and 33419. For more information, see Rationales for codes 33418 and 33419. Category III code 0345T has been established to report transcatheter mitral valve repair using a percutaneous approach, while other cardiac catheterization services not intrinsic to code 0345T may be reported separately, when performed for diagnostic purposes only. New guidelines have also been added to clarify the reporting needs of these services. To further clarify the intent of this code, three parenthetical notes have been added to clarify the reporting of these services. The first parenthetical note directs the users to report new Category I codes 33418 and 33419 for transcatheter mitral valve repair percutaneous approach, including transseptal puncture. The second parenthetical note is an exclusionary note that has been added to restrict the use of code 0345T with diagnostic left and right heart catheterization procedures intrinsic to the valve repair procedure. The third parenthetical note, which is also an exclusionary parenthetical, has been added to restrict the use of code 0345T with other cardiac catheterization procedures for coronary angiography intrinsic to the valve repair procedure.

Clinical Example (0345T)

A 61-year-old female with ischemic cardiomyopathy presents with progressive shortness of breath and New York Heart Association Class III heart failure symptoms. Echocardiography reveals an enlarged left ventricle, severely depressed left ventricular function with an ejection fraction of 26%, and moderately severe (3+) mitral regurgitation. She is considered to be high risk for surgical therapy for her mitral regurgitation. She does not currently have coronary artery obstructions requiring revascularization. She is on optimal medical therapy for her heart failure and mitral regurgitation.

Description of Procedure (0345T)

Anesthesiologist administers general anesthesia. A separate provider performs echocardiographic imaging with transthoracic echocardiography, which is separately reported. Echocardiographer (who reports echocardiographic services separately) obtains preprocedure transesophageal echocardiography (TEE) images of the mitral valve and individual leaflets with focus on the mechanism of mitral regurgitation and the characteristics of the regurgitant jet. Perform key

⊘=Modifier 51 Exempt ⊙=Moderate Sedation ✛=Add-on Code 𝒩=FDA approval pending

measurements, such as quantitative assessment of mitral regurgitation (vena contracta, effective regurgitant orifice area, and jet area/left atrial area). Obtain right internal jugular (RIJ) vein access. Obtain arterial access from the femoral or radial artery. Give patient anticoagulant and check the activated clotting time (ACT) level at the appropriate time interval to obtain ACT >200 seconds. Continuously check the ACT every 30 minutes to verify the patient is therapeutically anticoagulated. Anticoagulant is readministered during the procedure, as needed.

Perform coronary angiography of the left circumflex artery to provide a baseline appearance of the vessel (not separately reported). In addition, perform extended imaging to visualize the coronary venous anatomy (venous follow-through) to assess the character of the coronary sinus/great cardiac vein and to aid in engagement of the coronary sinus. This is done in a left anterior oblique view, typically with caudal or cranial angulation. Full, diagnostic coronary angiography is reported separately when it meets the criteria established in the introductory language.

Load an angled catheter through a larger bore delivery catheter, and advance this combination over a wire from the RIJ and directed toward the coronary sinus. Using the venous follow-through image of the coronary sinus as a road map, use the angled catheter to catch the opening of the coronary sinus. Advance the wire through the coronary sinus into the terminal branch of the great cardiac vein. Advance the catheter over the wire to the distal aspect of the great cardiac vein. Telescope the delivery catheter over the angled catheter into position, and remove the wire and angled catheter. Carefully de-air the delivery catheter. Advance a marker catheter through the delivery catheter to its tip. Move the image intensifier to a right anterior oblique with caudal angulation, and perform left coronary arteriography to establish the relationship of the circumflex coronary artery with the great cardiac vein (demarcated by the delivery and marker catheters). Perform venography of the cardiac vein and coronary sinus to assist in sizing the device. Move the image intensifier to a left anterior oblique with caudal angulation, and perform left coronary arteriography followed by venography. Assess the length of usable vein. If there is insufficient vein length, remove the marker catheter, and re-insert the wire and angled catheter to further advance the delivery catheter up to the anterior interventricular vein. Provided there is optimal length, assess vein characteristics for optimal placement of the device. This assessment includes the size of the vein, curvature of the vein, tapering characteristics, presence of side branches, and the relationship with the circumflex coronary artery. Make vein measurements at the intervals within the intended placement of the device, using the marker catheter as a scaling device. Select an appropriate length device.

Advance the device through the delivery sheath to the coronary sinus, and using the markings from the venogram, carefully position the device. Perform coronary artery injections as necessary to assist in optimal placement, and de-sheath the distal aspect of the device by withdrawing the delivery sheath. Perform left coronary angiography to ensure no compromise of the left circumflex. Position the proximal aspect of the device aided by injection in the side arm of the delivery catheter to identify the ostium of the coronary sinus and/or echo assessment of mitral regurgitation improvement. Once the desired location is achieved, again perform coronary arteriography to look for coronary artery compromise. If compromise of the circumflex coronary artery is seen, recapture the device. Perform left coronary angiography to ensure resolution of the circumflex compromise. Perform angiography of the vein to ensure patency. Using the same techniques, place a new delivery catheter slightly proximal to the first attempt, and use less tension in an attempt to modify the mitral annulus without compromising the left circumflex. If repeat left coronary angiography shows no compromise of the circumflex, exchange the left coronary catheter for a right coronary catheter, and perform right coronary angiography (report separately). The echocardiographer performs transthoracic echo imaging of mitral regurgitation with quantitative assessment. If this demonstrates appropriate reduction in mitral regurgitation, release the device.

Constantly monitor the patient's arterial pressure, electrocardiogram (EKG) waveforms, and oxygen saturation throughout the procedure. Right heart catheterization is typically repeated to assess intracardiac hemodynamics, including cardiac output, pulmonary arterial pressure, and pulmonary capillary wedge pressure. Review images to ensure no additional views are required before leaving the procedure suite. Close the groin site per physician and institutional practices. Reverse anesthesia, and extubate the patient as appropriate. Hypertension, hypotension, bleeding, and oxygen desaturation are potential complications; treat with medications and/or oxygen as needed during the procedure. Transfer the patient to the recovery suite for additional monitoring.

+ ●0346T   Ultrasound, elastography (List separately in addition to code for primary procedure)

▶(Use 0346T in conjunction with 76536, 76604, 76700, 76705, 76770, 76775, 76830, 76856, 76857, 76870, 76872, 76881, 76882)◀

✍ Rationale

Code 0346T has been established as an add-on code to identify the use of elastography with ultrasound procedures to describe the added work of measuring tissue displacement using probe compression to differentiate malignant from benign masses. As an add-on code, 0346T is intended to be used in conjunction with base-imaging procedures codes 76536, 76604, 76700, 76705, 76770, 76775, 76830, 76856, 76857, 76870, 76872, 76881, 76882, as noted in the parenthetical note following code 0346T.

Clinical Example (0346T)

A 50-year-old female presents with an abnormal mammogram showing a mass in the left breast. Ultrasound shows the mass to be hypo-echoic. Ultrasound elastography is performed.

Description of Procedure (0346T)

Physician performs breast elastography that includes qualitative visual assessment of change in lesion appearance with application of elastography; application of qualitative B-mode color imaging; and/or measurement of the lesion pre- and post-elastography. Documents elastographic images and data with B-mode, cine clips, and/or quantitative worksheets; analyzes elastographic information to determine

⊘=Modifier 51 Exempt ⊙=Moderate Sedation ✚=Add-on Code ✄=FDA approval pending

stiffness of lesion; and reviews elastographic information with other imaging information (such as B-mode and color Doppler exams [reported separately]) to form assessment of malignancy; and dictates the report for medical record.

● **0347T**   Placement of interstitial device(s) in bone for radiostereometric analysis (RSA)

● **0348T**   Radiologic examination, radiostereometric analysis (RSA); spine, (includes cervical, thoracic and lumbosacral, when performed)

● **0349T**   upper extremity(ies), (includes shoulder, elbow, and wrist, when performed)

● **0350T**   lower extremity(ies), (includes hip, proximal femur, knee, and ankle, when performed)

✎ Rationale

Category III code 0347T has been established to report placement of interstitial device(s) for radiostereometric analysis (RSA). One or more interstitial device(s) is implanted for the purpose of enhanced visualization using planar radiographs and/or RSA.

Three Category III codes, 0348T, 0349T, 0350T, have been established to report radiologic examination, RSA of the spine, upper extremities, and lower extremities. These codes have been structured into specific anatomic sites: supine, upper and lower extremities.

RSA is the simultaneous taking of two planar X rays from two points of view, and in combination with a superimposed calibration cage, provides the ability to image, measure, and locate bones and structures in three dimensions (3D). After acquiring the pair of radiographs, the images are processed using a software that determines the precise locations of interstitial device(s) in 3D space with an accuracy as high as 50 micrometers to 70 micrometers. This same processing step also typically involves the determination of the distance and potential movement of bones relative to one another and/or implants relative to bone. A written report with graphic display is produced for physician interpretation and clinical decision making.

🩺 Clinical Example (0347T)

A 67-year-old female presents with a five-year history of degenerative osteoarthritis of the left hip. Conservative management is ineffective; daily living activities are severely limited. Patient has moderate osteopenia, with increasing risk of implant stability post total hip arthroplasty (THA). The patient undergoes placement of interstitial devices to be used for future RSA.

Description of Procedure (0347T)

After all of the bone cuts/preparations associated with THA have been completed, the surgeon implants seven, 1.0-mm interstitial device(s) in the acetabulum and seven, 1.0-mm interstitial device(s) in the proximal femur (14 total) using a cannulated surgical instrument specifically designed to penetrate bone and insert the tantalum spheres. The interstitial device(s) are placed in a dispersion pattern that broadly registers the bone, providing a high precision frame of reference for RSA imaging.

Clinical Example (0348T)

A 62-year-old female presents with a ten-year history of degenerative disc disease (DDD) of the lumbar spine (L4-L5) that has caused progressive disability and increasing pain. Conservative management is ineffective and the pain is adversely impacting daily living activities. The patient underwent lumbar fusion with a titanium cage with the markers placed in the adjacent vertebrae at the time of spine surgery. The patient has moderate degenerative loss of bone mass and is at higher risk for implant migration. She now undergoes postoperative ragiographic imaging for RSA to monitor stability.

Description of Procedure (0348T)

RSA exams are performed during regular patient follow-up visits in an imaging room outfitted with an RSA imaging system. Postoperatively, and at 6 weeks and 3 months, the patient has one RSA exam performed (two simultaneous X rays/ sources, resulting in two images), and two RSA exams performed at 6, 12, and 24 months (two pairs of RSA images, one set in flexion and one set in extension). After the patient's RSA exam, the RSA images are analyzed by a trained technician with specialized hardware and software to determine: the positions of the interstitial device(s) and/or prostheses in 3D space, and the changes in relative position of bones, anatomical structures, and prostheses of interest. The RSA data is provided to the physician for interpretation and diagnosis (for example, evidence of fusion of adjacent vertebrae based on comparison of RSA images in flexion and extension).

Clinical Example (0349T)

A 58-year-old male presents with a five-year history of degenerative osteoarthritis of the right shoulder. Conservative management is ineffective; daily living activities are severely limited. Patient undergoes total shoulder replacement; the markers are placed in the glenoid and humerus. He now undergoes postoperative radiographic imaging for RSA to monitor stability.

Description of Procedure (0349T)

RSA exams are performed during the standard follow-up visits for primary shoulder arthroplasty in an imaging room outfitted with an RSA imaging system. The patient is positioned (supine) and RSA exam is performed, one or more pairs of RSA images are obtained (two simultaneous X rays, resulting in two images). After the RSA exam, one or more pairs of RSA images are analyzed by a trained technician with specialized hardware and software for determination of the marker positions and/or prostheses in 3D space, and determination of changes in relative position of bones, anatomical structures, and prostheses of interest. The RSA data are provided to the physician for interpretation and diagnosis (for example, stability of glenoid component with respect to the glenoid).

Clinical Example (0350T)

A 72-year-old female presents with a five-year history of degenerative osteoarthritis of the left hip. Conservative management is ineffective; daily living activities are severely limited. Patient has moderate osteopenia, increasing risk of implant

⊘=Modifier 51 Exempt   ⊙=Moderate Sedation   ✚=Add-on Code   ⅄=FDA approval pending

stability post–total hip arthroplasty. The patient undergoes primary total hip arthroplasty; the markers are placed in the acetabulum and proximal femur. She now undergoes postoperative radiographic imaging for RSA to monitor stability.

Description of Procedure (0350T)

RSA exams are performed during the standard follow-up visits for total hip arthroplasty in an imaging room outfitted with an RSA imaging system. The patient is positioned (supine) and RSA exam is performed, obtaining one or more pairs of RSA images (two simultaneous X rays, resulting in two images). After the patient's RSA exam, one or more pairs of RSA images are analyzed by a trained technician with specialized hardware and software for determination of the marker positions and/or prostheses in 3D space and determination of changes in relative position of bones, anatomical structures, and prostheses of interest. The RSA data are provided to the physician for interpretation and diagnosis (for example, stability of an acetabular cup with respect to the acetabulum).

●**0351T**   Optical coherence tomography of breast or axillary lymph node, excised tissue, each specimen; real-time intraoperative

●**0352T**   interpretation and report, real-time or referred

▶(Do not report 0352T in conjunction with 0351T, when performed by the same physician)◀

●**0353T**   Optical coherence tomography of breast, surgical cavity; real-time intraoperative

▶(Report 0353T once per session)◀

●**0354T**   interpretation and report, real-time or referred

▶(Do not report 0354T in conjunction with 0353T, when performed by the same physician)◀

🖎 Rationale

Four Category III codes, 0351T, 0352T, 0353T, and 0354T, have been established to report optical coherence tomography of the breast. Codes 0351T, 0352T describe optical coherence tomography of the breast or axillary lymph node, excised tissue, including each specimen with real-time interpretation and report. Codes 0353T and 0354T differ from codes 0351T and 0352T in that they describe the optical coherence tomography of the breast, including the surgical cavity, real-time intraoperative and interpretation and report.

Codes 0351T, 0352T, 0353T, and 0354T describe the interpretation and report of optical coherence tomography images during breast surgery. These procedures employ microscopic cross-sectional imaging of excised specimen(s) and tissue at the surgical site. During surgery, a real-time imaging method is required to intraoperatively assess these structures, in order to inform surgical decisions and reduce the likelihood of repeat surgery after postoperative histopathology examination.

Exclusionary parenthetical notes have been added to restrict the use of these codes, when performed by the same physician. In addition, an instructional parenthetical note has been added to indicate that code 0353T should be reported once per session.

Clinical Example (0351T)

A 67-year-old female with no family history of breast cancer presents for partial mastectomy (lumpectomy or breast conserving surgery) of needle biopsy-proven invasive ductal carcinoma of the left breast with a 20% ductal carcinoma in situ component. During surgery, a real-time imaging method is required to intraoperatively assess the surgical margins to reduce the likelihood of repeat surgery after postoperative histopathology.

Description of Procedure (0351T)

Place the excised specimen on a surgical tray in the sterile field for imaging. Using the imaging system software, open a new patient case and enter patient-specific information. Place the sterile handheld optical coherence tomography probe in contact with one of the six surgical margins of the breast tissue or axillary lymph node specimen to begin scanning. Scan the sterile handheld probe across the surface of the specimen, and acquire representative images by pressing a foot pedal. Repeat scanning for the five remaining surgical margins on the breast tissue specimen. Capture at least four, and typically ten or more, images of each surgical margin or lymph node, providing comprehensive cross-sectional views. Annotate the images with comments, and save them.

Clinical Example (0352T)

A 67-year-old female with no family history of breast cancer presents for partial mastectomy (lumpectomy or breast conserving surgery) of needle biopsy-proven invasive ductal carcinoma of the left breast with a 20% ductal carcinoma in situ component. The surgeon excises breast tissue or axillary lymph node specimens and real-time optical coherence tomography images of the specimen are acquired. Surgery is paused pending intraoperative interpretation and report of the images by the pathologist to determine the presence of suspicious tissue.

Description of Procedure (0352T)

While the surgery is paused, the pathologist reviews the images from each breast tissue or axillary lymph node specimen margin to determine the presence of suspicious tissue. Each image (2 mm x 10 mm in size, approximately 10 μm resolution) is displayed on the screen with associated annotations; the coloration (grayscale or false color), intensity mapping (log or linear scale), brightness, and contrast are adjusted for optimal viewing. The pathologist interprets the images and records findings indicating whether suspicious tissue is present, and if detected, the suspicious tissue size and distance to surface. This process is repeated for all surgical margins or lymph nodes. Findings are reported to the surgeon.

Clinical Example (0353T)

A 67-year-old female with no family history of breast cancer presents for partial mastectomy (lumpectomy or breast conserving surgery) of needle biopsy-proven invasive ductal carcinoma of the left breast with a 20% ductal carcinoma in situ component. During surgery, real-time optical coherence tomography images of the excised breast tissue specimen are interpreted by the pathologist and the presence of suspicious tissue is identified at the medial margin. A real-time imaging method is required to intraoperatively assess the medial aspect of the surgical cavity to confirm the presence of suspicious tissue and localize the area for re-excision.

Ø=Modifier 51 Exempt   ⊙=Moderate Sedation   ✚=Add-on Code   ✗=FDA approval pending

Description of Procedure (0353T)

Place the sterile handheld optical coherence tomography probe in contact with the medial surgical cavity aspect to begin scanning. Scan the sterile handheld probe across the surgical cavity, and acquire additional representative images by pressing a foot pedal. Capture at least four, and typically ten or more, images of the medial surgical cavity aspect, providing comprehensive cross-sectional views. Annotate the images with comments, and save them.

Clinical Example (0354T)

A 67-year-old female with no family history of breast cancer presents for partial mastectomy (lumpectomy or breast conserving surgery) of needle biopsy-proven invasive ductal carcinoma of the left breast with a 20% ductal carcinoma *in situ* component. The surgeon excises a breast tissue specimen and real-time optical coherence tomography images of the specimen are interpreted by the pathologist who identifies suspicious tissue at the medial margin. The surgeon performs additional scanning and image acquisition at the medial aspect of the surgical cavity. Surgery is paused pending intraoperative interpretation and report of the images by the pathologist to confirm the presence of suspicious tissue and localize the area for re-excision.

Description of Procedure (0354T)

While the surgery is paused, the pathologist reviews the images from the surgical cavity aspect to confirm the presence of suspicious tissue and localize the area for re-excision. Each image (2 mm x 10 mm in size, approximately 10 μm resolution) is displayed on the screen with associated annotations; the coloration (grayscale or false color), intensity mapping (log or linear scale), brightness, and contrast are adjusted for optimal viewing. The pathologist interprets the images, comparing the images to those from the corresponding specimen margin, and records findings indicating whether suspicious tissue is present, and if detected, the suspicious tissue size, distance to surface, and location. Findings are reported to the surgeon.

●0355T   Gastrointestinal tract imaging, intraluminal (eg, capsule endoscopy), colon, with interpretation and report

▶(Use 0355T for imaging of distal ileum, when performed)◀

▶(Do not report 0355T in conjunction with 91110, 91111)◀

Rationale

Code 0355T has been established to report intraluminal colon imaging, also known as colon capsule endoscopy. Colon capsule endoscopy is used in the assessment of conditions, such as gastrointestinal bleeding, iron-deficiency anemia, altered bowel habits, abdominal pain, inflammatory bowel disease, and diarrhea. It is also used in colorectal cancer screening and in patients with personal and/or family history of colon cancer and polyps. Colon capsule endoscopy is often performed in instances when a colonoscopy using a scope is performed but the procedure cannot be completed due to unforeseen circumstances. To perform capsule endoscopy, the capsule is administered to the patient and the recording device is activated. The images are recorded on a device worn by the patient.

At the conclusion of the recording period, the images are downloaded for subsequent review by the physician. The capsule is not retrieved and is subsequently eliminated. Code 0355T should be reported for capsule imaging of the distal ileum, when performed. It is important to note that capsule endoscopic imaging of the esophagus and ileum should be reported with code 91110, and imaging limited to the esophagus should be reported using code 91111. As such, capsule endoscopy of the colon should not be reported using either code 91110 or 91111, and code 0355T should not be reported with codes 91110 and 91111.

Clinical Example (0355T)

A 60-year-old patient presents with abdominal discomfort and occult blood in the stool. A colonoscopy was performed, but the scope could not be advanced beyond the hepatic flexure into the right side of the colon. The patient was referred for intraluminal gastrointestinal (GI) tract imaging of the colon for diagnostic evaluation.

Description of Procedure (0355T)

Give the patient the capsule endoscope to swallow, and provide him or her with instructions for activities, meals, and return time. The patient remains in the delivery setting until the capsule passes into the small bowel, usually about 45 minutes to 60 minutes. Once the capsule has transferred into the small bowel, the data recorder will alert the patient to drink a booster regimen that improves the capsule's propulsion through the GI tract. After the booster is taken, the patient can leave the clinical setting and return home.

●0356T   Insertion of drug-eluting implant (including punctal dilation and implant removal when performed) into lacrimal canaliculus, each

Rationale

Category III code 0356T has been added for implantation and removal of a drug-eluting device into and from the lacrimal punctum. Code 0356T includes both the initial device insertion and any subsequent devices implanted, including the removal of the existing device. A nondrug containing lacrimal punctum implant, which is used on a permanent or semi-permanent basis to close the lacrimal punctum to treat dry eyes, is described in code 68761. An exclusionary parenthetical note following code 68761 has been added to distinguish the use of these related devices.

Clinical Example (0356T)

A 60-year-old male is seen for glaucoma. A drug-eluting implant is inserted in the punctum for control of IOP.

Description of Procedure (0356T)

The physician numbs the punctal area and dilates it to prepare for insertion. The physician then uses an applicator or forceps to insert the drug-eluting implant through the punctum into the canaliculus. For removal, the physician may flush the residual drug-eluting material down the canaliculus or express it up through the punctum.

⊘=Modifier 51 Exempt   ⊙=Moderate Sedation   ✚=Add-on Code   ⋂=FDA approval pending

●0358T Bioelectrical impedance analysis whole body composition assessment, supine position, with interpretation and report

▶(For bioimpedance-derived physiological cardiovascular analysis, use 93701)◀

▶(For bioimpedance spectroscopy (BIS), use 93702)◀

 Rationale

Category III code 0358T has been established to report bioelectrical impedance analysis for whole body composition assessment in the supine position and with interpretation and report.

Bioelectrical impedance analysis provides whole body composition tissue and fluid measurements.

A parenthetical note has been added to instruct users to report code 93701 for bioimpedance-derived physiological analysis. In accordance with the establishment of code 93702, to report bioimpedance spectroscopy (BIS), a reciprocal parenthetical note has also been added.

 Clinical Example (0358T)

A 45-year-old overweight but otherwise healthy female presents for her annual office visit with her physician. Bioelectrical impedance analysis (BIA) is performed to differentiate excess body fat from fluid retention.

Description of Procedure (0358T)

The patient is placed supine, the tetrapolar electrode sites are cleaned with an alcohol pad, and electrodes are applied on the foot, ankle, middle finger, and wrist. The BIA device measures resistance and reactance, whose values, along with height, weight, age, and gender are entered into the body composition equation software, and the results are available immediately. An interpretation and report is created by the physician or qualified health care professional.

▶Adaptive Behavior Assessments◀

▶**Behavior identification assessment** (0359T) conducted by the physician or other qualified health care professional includes a detailed behavioral history, patient observation, administration of standardized and non-standardized tests, and structured guardian/caregiver interview to identify and describe deficient adaptive or maladaptive behaviors (eg, impaired social skills and communication deficits, destructive behaviors, and additional functional limitations secondary to maladaptive behaviors). Code 0359T also includes the physician's or other qualified health care professional's interpretation of results and development of plan of care, which may include further observational or exposure behavioral follow-up assessment(s) (0360T, 0361T, 0362T, 0363T), discussion of findings and recommendations with the primary guardian(s)/caregiver(s), and preparation of report.

Observational behavioral follow-up assessment (0360T, 0361T) is administered by a technician under the direction of a physician or other qualified health care professional. The physician or other qualified health care professional may or may not be on site during the face-to-face assessment process. Codes 0360T and 0361T include the physician's or other qualified health care professional's interpretation of results, discussion of findings and recommendations with the primary caregiver(s), and preparation of report.

Codes 0360T and 0361T describe services provided to patients who present with specific destructive behavior(s) (eg, self-injurious behavior, aggression, property destruction) or behavioral problems secondary to repetitive behaviors or deficits in communication or social relatedness. These assessments include use of structured observation and/or standardized and non-standardized tests to determine levels of adaptive behavior. Areas assessed may include cooperation, motivation, visual understanding, receptive and expressive language, imitation, requests, labeling, play and leisure, and social interactions. Specific destructive behavior(s) assessments include structured observational testing to examine events, cues, responses, and consequences associated with the behavior(s).

Exposure behavioral follow-up assessment (0362T, 0363T) is administered by the physician or other qualified health care professional with the assistance of one or more technicians. Codes 0362T and 0363T include the physician's or other qualified health care professional's interpretation of results, discussion of findings and recommendations with the primary caregiver(s), and preparation of report.

The typical patients for 0362T and 0363T include patients with one or more specific severe destructive behavior(s) (eg, self-injurious behavior, aggression, property destruction). Specific severe destructive behavior(s) are assessed using structured testing to examine events, cues, responses, and consequences associated with the behavior(s).

Codes 0362T and 0363T include exposing the patient to a series of social and environmental conditions associated with the destructive behavior(s). Assessment methods include using testing methods designed to examine triggers, events, cues, responses, and consequences associated with the aforementioned maladaptive behavior(s). This assessment is completed in a structured, safe environment.

Codes 0360T, 0361T, 0362T, and 0363T are reported following 0359T based on the time that the patient is face-to-face with one or more technician(s). Only count the time of one technician when two or more are present. Codes 0360T, 0361T, 0362T, and 0363T are reported per the CPT Time–Rule (eg, a unit of time is attained when the mid-point is passed). See table below. The time reported with 0360T, 0361T, 0362T, and 0363T is over a single day and is not cumulative over a longer period.◀

▶(Do not report 0359T, 0360T, 0361T, 0362T, 0363T in conjunction with 90785-90899, 96101-96125, 96150, 96151, 96152, 96153, 96154, 96155 on the same date)◀

▶(For psychiatric diagnostic evaluation, see 90791, 90792)◀

▶(For speech evaluations, see 92521, 92522, 92523, 92524)◀

▶(For occupational therapy evaluation, see 97003, 97004)◀

▶(For medical team conference, see 99366, 99367, 99368)◀

▶(For health and behavior assessment/intervention, see 96150, 96151, 96152, 96153, 96154, 96155)◀

▶(For neurobehavioral status exam, use 96116)◀

▶(For neuropsychological testing, use 96118)◀

⊘=Modifier 51 Exempt   ⊙=Moderate Sedation   ✚=Add-on Code   ☌=FDA approval pending

CPT Time–Rule for Face-to-Face Technician Time: Codes 0360T, 0361T, 0362T, 0363T	
Time	CPT Code(s)
Less than 16 min	Not reportable
16-45 min	0360T or 0362T
46-75 min	0360T and 0361T or 0362T and 0363T
Each additional increment up to 30 min	Additional 0361T or 0363T

●0359T **Behavior identification assessment,** by the physician or other qualified health care professional, face-to-face with patient and caregiver(s), includes administration of standardized and non-standardized tests, detailed behavioral history, patient observation and caregiver interview, interpretation of test results, discussion of findings and recommendations with the primary guardian(s)/caregiver(s), and preparation of report

●0360T **Observational behavioral follow-up assessment,** includes physician or other qualified health care professional direction with interpretation and report, administered by one technician; first 30 minutes of technician time, face-to-face with the patient

+●0361T each additional 30 minutes of technician time, face-to-face with the patient (List separately in addition to code for primary service)

▶(Use 0361T in conjunction with 0360T)◀

●0362T **Exposure behavioral follow-up assessment,** includes physician or other qualified health care professional direction with interpretation and report, administered by physician or other qualified health care professional with the assistance of one or more technicians; first 30 minutes of technician(s) time, face-to-face with the patient

+●0363T each additional 30 minutes of technician(s) time, face-to-face with the patient (List separately in addition to code for primary procedure)

▶(Use 0363T in conjunction with 0362T)◀

▶(0362T, 0363T are reported based on a single technician's face-to-face time with the patient and not the combined time of multiple technicians)◀

▶(Do not report 0359T, 0360T, 0361T, 0362T, 0363T in conjunction with 90785-90899, 96101-96125, 96150, 96151, 96152, 96153, 96154, 96155)◀

✍ Rationale

A series of Category III codes (0359T-0363T) and guidelines and instructional notes have been added for adaptive behavior assessment services provided to patients of any age with deficient adaptive or maladaptive behaviors including, but not limited to, patients who present with autism spectrum disorders (ASDs) or other diagnoses or conditions (eg, developmental disabilities, head trauma). These codes were posted to AMA CPT website (www.ama-assn.org/go/cpt) in January and March of 2014, with an implementation date of July 1, 2014.

Code 0359T, the first code in the assessment code series, describes the initial assessment to identify deficient adaptive or maladaptive behaviors (eg, impaired social skills and communication deficits, destructive behaviors, and additional functional limitations secondary to maladaptive behaviors), including the development of plan of care. Code 0359T may be reported for the assessment required for early intensive behavioral intervention (EIBI). The service described in code 0359T will be typically reported only once, regardless of the number of hours or days, within a defined treatment period necessary to complete the assessment.

Four codes have been established for behavioral follow-up assessments (0360T, 0361T, 0362T, 0363T) to describe assessments that enable the physician or other qualified health care professional to finalize or fine-tune the baseline results and plan of care, which were initiated in the behavior identification assessment (0359T).

Codes 0360T and 0361T are used to report follow-up assessments that require patient observation and the presence of one technician directed by a physician or other qualified health care professional, who may be located off-site. Codes 0362T and 0363T are used to report follow-up assessments that are less frequently performed and require manipulation of the patient's environment. Codes 0362T and 0363T are provided by a team of technicians and require direct (on-site) direction by a physician or other qualified health care professional due to the high intensity of the patient's severe destructive behavior(s).

The follow-up assessments (0360T, 0361T, 0362T, 0363T) are services administered on a single calendar day based on 30-minute increments of technician time face-to-face with the patient. Often these assessments must be repeated over multiple days, usually during a one-month period of time. A table has been developed to assist in selection of the follow-up assessment codes based on the time concepts already established in CPT (see the discussion of Time on page xv of the *CPT 2015* Professional Edition).

Parenthetical notes in the adaptive behavior assessment section provide instructions on the use of add-on codes 0361T, and 0363T, when expanded time is spent, and to denote that assessment codes 0360T, 0361T, 0362T, and 0363T should not be reported with codes 90785-90899, 96101-96125, 96150, 96151, 96152, 96153, 96154, and 96155.

Clinical Example (0359T)

A preschool-age male is brought in by his parents for an office assessment. The patient has been diagnosed with ASD and has limited and tangential speech, poor eye contact, repetitive motor movements, tantrums with unexpected change in routine, and ritualistic play. He does not respond to gestures or his name and has almost no imitative behavior.

Description of Procedure (0359T)

The physician or other qualified health care professional reviews medical records, including reports of prior assessments and obtains a patient history from the boy's parents. Observe the patient and administer a structured behavior interview to the parents. Review and interpret the data, and discuss recommendations for treatment and possible further assessment with the parents. Prepare a report that includes procedures and instructions for a technician to conduct direct-observational assessments of specific adaptive skills and problem behaviors.

⃠=Modifier 51 Exempt ⊙=Moderate Sedation ✚=Add-on Code 𝒩=FDA approval pending

Clinical Example (0360T)

A home assessment for a pre-teen female diagnosed with Rett syndrome and stereotyped movement disorder with self-injurious behavior (SIB). The patient lacks functional communication (both verbal and nonverbal), functional hand usage, play skills, and has frequent SIB (head hitting and finger biting).

Description of Procedure (0360T)

The physician or other qualified health care professional instructs technician in conducting: (1) a preference assessment to identify effective reinforcers for the patient; (2) a series of structured assessments to establish baselines and determine the best prompting strategies to promote functional communication, hand usage, and play skills; and (3) a series of naturalistic observations to collect data on the frequency of SIB and to identify antecedents and consequences that are significantly correlated with the behavior using conditional probabilities. The technician records the patient responses. The physician or other qualified health care professional interprets the data, prepares a report, and discusses findings and recommendations with the parents.

Clinical Example (0361T)

A home assessment for a pre-teen female diagnosed with Rett syndrome and stereotyped movement disorder with SIB. The patient lacks functional communication (both verbal and nonverbal), functional hand usage, play skills, and has frequent SIB (head hitting and finger biting).

Description of Procedure (0361T)

The physician or other qualified health care professional instructs technician in conducting: (1) a preference assessment to identify effective reinforcers for the patient; (2) a series of structured assessments to establish baselines and determine the best prompting strategies to promote functional communication, hand usage, and play skills; and (3) a series of naturalistic observations to collect data on the frequency of SIB and to identify antecedents and consequences that are significantly correlated with the behavior using conditional probabilities. The technician records the patient responses. The physician or other qualified health care professional interprets the data, prepares a report, and discusses findings and recommendations with the parents.

Clinical Example (0362T)

An adolescent male, who is diagnosed with ASD, severe intellectual disability, stereotyped movement disorder, and severe SIB is referred to a specialized day-treatment program for a controlled functional analysis of his severe SIB and aggressive behavior. He does not speak, and caregivers feed, dress, and bath him because his SIB interferes with these activities. His SIB occurs more than 50 times per hour and includes hitting his head against objects, hitting his head with his hands, forcefully throwing himself to the ground, and self-biting his hands and arms. The patient acts aggressively against his caregivers (eg, hitting and biting). The family is unable to take him into the community (eg, church, restaurant) or travel (eg, vacation, visit relatives) due to these behaviors. He requires constant supervision by at least one, and often two, adults.

Description of Procedure (0362T)

The physician or other qualified health care professional instructs and directs technicians in assessment to determine the specific role of attention and escape/avoidance/free choice activity/internal consequence in maintaining each destructive behavior. Record patient responses on laptop computers. Summarize daily the accumulated data in graphical form with modifications of assessment based on these data. The physician or other qualified health care professional interprets the data on a daily basis, prepares a report, and discusses findings and recommendations with the parents.

Clinical Example (0363T)

An adolescent male, who is diagnosed with ASD, severe intellectual disability, stereotyped movement disorder, and severe SIB is referred to a specialized day-treatment program for a controlled functional analysis of his severe SIB and aggressive behavior. He does not speak, and caregivers feed, dress, and bath him because his SIB interferes with these activities. His SIB occurs more than 50 times per hour and includes hitting his head against objects, hitting his head with his hands, forcefully throwing himself to the ground, and self-biting his hands and arms. The patient acts aggressively against his caregivers (eg, hitting and biting). The family is unable to take him into the community (eg, church, restaurant) or travel (eg, vacation, visit relatives) due to these behaviors. He requires constant supervision by at least one, and often two, adults.

Description of Procedure (0363T)

The physician or other qualified health care professional instructs and directs technicians in assessment to determine the specific role of attention and escape/avoidance/free choice activity/internal consequence in maintaining each destructive behavior. Record patient responses on laptop computers. Summarize daily the accumulated data in graphical form with modifications of assessment based on these data. The physician or other qualified health care professional interprets the data on a daily basis, prepares a report, and discusses findings and recommendations with the parents.

►Adaptive Behavior Treatment◄

►Adaptive behavior treatment codes 0364T, 0365T, 0366T, 0367T, 0368T, 0369T, 0370T, 0371T, 0372T, 0373T, 0374T describe services provided to patients who present with deficient adaptive or maladaptive behaviors (eg, impaired social skills and communication, destructive behaviors, or additional functional limitations secondary to maladaptive behaviors). Specific target problems and treatment goals are based on results of previous assessments (see 0359T, 0360T, 0361T, 0362T, 0363T).

Adaptive behavior treatment by protocol and group adaptive behavior treatment by protocol are administered by a technician face-to-face with one patient (0364T, 0365T), or two or more patients (0366T, 0367T) under the direction of a physician or other qualified health care professional, utilizing a behavioral intervention protocol designed in advance by the physician or other qualified health care

Ⓢ=Modifier 51 Exempt   ⊙=Moderate Sedation   ✚=Add-on Code   ⁄=FDA approval pending

professional, who may or may not provide direct supervision during the face-to-face therapy. Do not report 0366T, 0367T if the group is larger than eight patients.

Adaptive behavior treatment with protocol modification (0368T, 0369T) is administered by a physician or other qualified health care professional face-to-face with a single patient. The physician or other qualified health care professional resolves one or more problems with the protocol and may simultaneously instruct a technician and/or guardian(s)/caregiver(s) in administering the modified protocol. Physician or other qualified health care professional instruction to the technician without the patient present is not reported separately.

Family adaptive behavior treatment guidance and multiple-family group adaptive behavior treatment guidance are administered by a physician or other qualified health care professional face-to-face with guardian(s)/caregiver(s), without the presence of a patient, and involve identifying problem behaviors and deficits and teaching guardian(s)/caregiver(s) of one patient (0370T) or multiple patients (0371T) to utilize treatment protocols designed to reduce maladaptive behaviors and/or skill deficits. Do not report 0371T if the group is larger than eight patients.

Adaptive behavior treatment social skills group (0372T) is administered by a physician or other qualified health care professional face-to-face with multiple patients, focusing on social skills training and identifying and targeting individual patient social deficits and problem behaviors. The physician or other qualified health care professional monitors the needs of individual patients and adjusts the therapeutic techniques during the group, as needed. Services to increase target social skills may include modeling, rehearsing, corrective feedback, and homework assignments. In contrast to adaptive behavior treatment by protocol techniques (0364T, 0365T, 0366T, 0367T), adjustments required in social skills group setting are made in real time rather than for a subsequent service. Do not report 0372T if the group is larger than eight patients.

Codes 0364T, 0365T, 0366T, 0367T, 0368T, 0369T, 0372T may include services involving patient interaction with other individuals, including other patients. Report group services (0366T, 0367T, 0372T) only for patients who are participating in the interaction in order to meet their own individual treatment goals.◄

● **0364T**   Adaptive behavior treatment by protocol, administered by technician, face-to-face with one patient; first 30 minutes of technician time

✚ ● **0365T**   each additional 30 minutes of technician time (List separately in addition to code for primary procedure)

       ►(Use 0365T in conjunction with 0364T)◄

       ►(Do not report 0364T, 0365T in conjunction with 90785-90899, 92507, 96101-96155, 97532)◄

● **0366T**   Group adaptive behavior treatment by protocol, administered by technician, face-to-face with two or more patients; first 30 minutes of technician time

✚ ● **0367T**   each additional 30 minutes of technician time (List separately in addition to code for primary procedure)

       ►(Use 0367T in conjunction with 0366T)◄

       ►(Do not report 0366T, 0367T if the group is larger than eight patients)◄

       ►(Do not report 0366T, 0367T in conjunction with 90785-90899, 92508, 96101-96155, 97150)◄

●0368T   Adaptive behavior treatment with protocol modification administered by physician or other qualified health care professional with one patient; first 30 minutes of patient face-to-face time

+ ●0369T   each additional 30 minutes of patient face-to-face time (List separately in addition to code for primary procedure)

    ▶(Use 0369T in conjunction with 0368T)◀

    ▶(Do not report 0368T, 0369T in conjunction with 90791, 90792, 90846, 90847, 90887, 92507, 97532)◀

●0370T   Family adaptive behavior treatment guidance, administered by physician or other qualified health care professional (without the patient present)

●0371T   Multiple-family group adaptive behavior treatment guidance, administered by physician or other qualified health care professional (without the patient present)

    ▶(Do not report 0371T when the families of more than eight patients are participants)◀

    ▶(Do not report 0370T, 0371T in conjunction with 90791, 90792, 90846, 90847, 90887)◀

●0372T   Adaptive behavior treatment social skills group, administered by physician or other qualified health care professional face-to-face with multiple patients

    ▶(Do not report 0372T if the group is larger than eight patients)◀

    ▶(Do not report 0372T in conjunction with 90853, 92508, 97150)◀

Rationale

A series of Category III codes (0364T, 0365T, 0366T, 0367T, 0368T, 0369T), guidelines, and instructional notes have been added for adaptive behavior treatment, adaptive behavior treatment guidance (0370T, 0371T), and adaptive behavior treatment social skills group (0372T) to describe services intended to address a patient's specific target problems and treatment goals as defined in previous assessments (see Rationale for codes 0359T-0363T). Adaptive behavior treatment is based on principles including analysis and alteration of contextual events and motivating factors, stimulus-consequence strategies and replacement behavior, and monitoring of outcome metrics.

Goals of adaptive behavior treatment may include reduction of repetitive and aberrant behavior and improved communication and social functioning. Adaptive behavior skill tasks are often broken into small measurable units, and each skill is practiced repeatedly until the patient masters it.

The adaptive behavior treatment codes (0364T, 0365T, 0366T, 0367T, 0368T, 0369T) are services administered on a single calendar day based on 30-minute increments of technician time face-to-face with the patient. The frequency of these services varies depending on the number of target problems and treatment goals. For example, the typical early intensive behavioral intervention (EIBI) patient with 15 or more treatment targets may require 25 hours of treatment per week during a defined treatment period. The same time rules applied to the assessment codes also apply to the codes for adaptive behavior treatment by protocol (0364T, 0357T), group adaptive behavior treatment by protocol (0358T, 0367T), and adaptive behavior treatment with protocol modification (0368T, 0369T).

Codes 0364T and 0365T are intended to report skill training delivery to patients by a technician. For example, a technician providing skill training to a patient may introduce small, incremental changes to the patient's expected routine and deliver a reinforcer each time the patient appropriately tolerates a given stimulus change. This service is repeated over a defined period until the patient can gradually tolerate variations in his or her daily activities without poor emotional response. The physician or other qualified health care professional directs the treatment by designing the sequence of stimulus and response procedures, analyzing the technician-recorded progress data, and judging whether the use of the protocol is producing adequate progress.

Codes 0366T and 0367T are intended to report skill training delivered to a patient with ASD or another condition, who could benefit from skill training in a group of peers, typically with similar issues. For example, the technician assists the patient in playing a game that requires group interaction by simple turn-taking. The amount of time and complexity of turn-taking of each participant are gradually increased. The technician administers reinforcers, error-correction procedures, or other consequences based on the patients' level of participation. The physician or other qualified health care professional analyzes technician-recorded progress data to assist the technician in adhering to the protocol and judges whether the use of the protocol is producing adequate progress.

Codes 0368T and 0369T are intended to report adaptive behavior treatment with protocol modification, not administered by a technician, but delivered by a physician or other qualified health care professional face-to-face with a single patient. The service may include demonstration of the new or modified protocol to a technician, guardian(s), and/or caregiver(s). For example, codes 0368T and 0369T will include treatment services provided to a patient experiencing regression of behavioral targets that were previously met. A modified treatment protocol is administered by the qualified health care professional to demonstrate to a technician/guardian/caregiver how to apply modified protocol(s), with the goal of regaining the patient's lost targets.

Parenthetical notes in the adaptive behavior treatment section that are applicable to codes 0364T, 0365T, 0366T, 0367T, 0368T, 0369T have been established to: (1) instruct the use of add-on codes 0365T, 0367T, 0369T, when expanded treatment time is spent; (2) provide a list of exclusionary codes that cannot be reported in conjunction with the adaptive behavior treatment codes; and (3) denote that the group adaptive behavior treatment codes 0366T and 0367T may not be reported, if the group is larger than eight patients.

Codes 0370T and 0371T are intended to report guidance services provided to guardian(s)/caregiver(s) of one patient (0370T) or multiple patients (0371T) to utilize treatment protocols designed to reduce maladaptive behaviors and/or skill deficits. These services are provided by a physician or other qualified health care professional face-to-face with guardian(s)/caregiver(s), without the presence of a patient. The guidance services (0370T, 0371T) are untimed codes, which are to be reported once per session, regardless of the amount of time spent with the guardian(s)/caregiver(s).

Parenthetical notes after codes 0370T and 0371T have been established to provide a list of exclusionary codes that cannot be reported in conjunction with codes 0370T and 0371T, namely, codes 90791, 90792, 90846, 90847, 90887, and to denote that the group adaptive behavior treatment code 0371T may not be reported, if the group is larger than eight patients.

Code 0372T is intended to report adaptive behavior treatment administered by a physician or other qualified health care professional to patients in a social skills group. The physician or other qualified health care professional monitors the needs of individual patients and adjusts the therapeutic techniques in real-time to address targeted social deficits and problem behaviors utilizing various techniques (eg, modeling, rehearsing, corrective feedback). Each participant is given specific measurable goals to contribute to the success of their treatment goals. Code 0372T should only be reported for patients who are participating in the interaction in order to meet their own individual treatment goals.

Parenthetical notes after code 0372T have been established to provide a list of exclusionary codes that cannot be reported in conjunction with code 0372T, namely, codes 90853, 92508, 97150, and to denote that the group adaptive behavior treatment code 0372T may not be reported, if the group is larger than eight patients.

Clinical Example (0364T)

Home visit for a 4-year-old female with high functioning autism. Patient has considerable language but poor social understanding and skills, perseverative speech regarding one or two preferred topics, and poor emotional regulation with rage and crying with deviation from rigid routines and subject topics. She has been taught by therapists in a treatment center to tolerate various small changes in daily routines in simulation situations using a shaping and stimulus fading desensitization process, but generalization to home has been poor.

Description of Procedure (0364T)

Technician participates in normally occurring daily routines at home, assisting the patient to transfer learned abilities to tolerate disruptions in routines during naturally occurring activities. Disruptions in expected routines are briefly introduced in small steps along a stimulus generalization gradient, and minimal responses of tolerating the disruption are rewarded. In a series of larger steps, more intrusive changes in routines are faded into preferred activities into her normal daily activities until she is able to tolerate approximations of typical daily activities without tantrums. The qualified health care professional designs the overall sequence of stimulus and response fading procedures and analyzes technician-recorded progress data to assist the technician in adhering to the protocol and judges whether use of the protocol is producing adequate progress.

Clinical Example (0365T)

Home visit for a 4-year-old female with high functioning autism. Patient has considerable language but poor social understanding and skills, perseverative speech regarding one or two preferred topics, and poor emotional regulation with rage and crying with deviation from rigid routines and subject topics. She has been taught

⊘=Modifier 51 Exempt ⊙=Moderate Sedation ✚=Add-on Code 𝒩=FDA approval pending

by therapists in a treatment center to tolerate various small changes in daily routines in simulation situations using a shaping and stimulus fading desensitization process, but generalization to home has been poor.

Description of Procedure (0365T)

Technician participates in normally occurring daily routines at home, assisting the patient to transfer learned abilities to tolerate disruptions in routines during naturally occurring activities. Disruptions in expected routines are briefly introduced in small steps along a stimulus generalization gradient, and minimal responses of tolerating the disruption are rewarded. In a series of larger steps, more intrusive changes in routines are faded into preferred activities into her normal daily activities until she is able to tolerate approximations of typical daily activities without tantrums. The qualified health care professional designs the overall sequence of stimulus and response fading procedures and analyzes technician-recorded progress data to assist the technician in adhering to the protocol and judges whether use of the protocol is producing adequate progress.

Clinical Example (0366T)

Treatment center social skills group visit for 7-year-old female with moderate to high functioning autism. Patient is verbal and has emerging social skills as a result of one-to-one therapy designed to teach basic communication and social interactions. The group also includes a 5-year-old male and a 6-year-old female with similar deficits.

Description of Procedure (0366T)

The technician targets the patient's missing skills making it possible for her to tolerate social intrusions by her peers, taking turns, and perspective-taking through differential reinforcement of skills previously taught one-to-one but now applying them to a social context approximating more normal daily activities. The qualified health care professional has analyzed each of the social tasks before the group begins and designs graded levels of social participation (such as taking turns), such that the patient is able to succeed with minimal participation (eg, takes one turn in a relatively less-preferred game) and allows the peer to take a turn. The amount of time and complexity of turn taking and increasingly preferred activities are gradually increased (which the patient is more reluctant to interrupt). The technician orally prompts patient cooperation and provides tangible and social rewards for compliance. The qualified health care professional analyzes technician-recorded progress data to assist the technician in adhering to the protocol and judges whether use of the protocol is producing adequate progress.

Clinical Example (0367T)

Treatment center social skills group visit for 7-year-old female with moderate to high functioning autism. Patient is verbal and has emerging social skills as a result of one-to-one therapy designed to teach basic communication and social interactions. The group also includes a 5-year-old male and a 6-year-old female with similar deficits.

Description of Procedure (0367T)

The technician targets the patient's missing skills making it possible for her to tolerate social intrusions by her peers, taking turns, and perspective-taking through differential reinforcement of skills previously taught one-to-one but now applying them to a social context approximating more normal daily activities. The qualified health care professional has analyzed each of the social tasks before the group begins and designs graded levels of social participation (such as taking turns), such that the patient is able to succeed with minimal participation (eg, takes one turn in a relatively less-preferred game) and allows the peer to take a turn. The amount of time and complexity of turn taking and increasingly preferred activities are gradually increased (which the patient is more reluctant to interrupt). The technician orally prompts patient cooperation and provides tangible and social rewards for compliance. The qualified health care professional analyzes technician-recorded progress data to assist the technician in adhering to the protocol and judges whether use of the protocol is producing adequate progress.

 ### Clinical Example (0368T)

Office visit for a 5-year-old male with moderate to severe autism with the patient's grandparents. The patient had begun to show improvements in his language and social skills at home as a result of one-to-one intensive behavior therapy but seems to have reached a plateau in skill development over the past month, associated with a grandparent now living with the family.

Description of Procedure (0368T)

The qualified health care professional modifies the protocol, incorporating grandparent into language and social activities in place of the parent to increase generalization to grandparent. (Expect patient's initial level of involvement with the grandparent to be very low but gradual increase is anticipated as his interactions become more natural and less contrived.) The qualified health care professional administers a set of daily routine skills incorporating the modified protocol to include grandparent with additional real-time adjustments as needed. The qualified health care professional demonstrates to the grandparent and a technician how to administer the modified protocol to facilitate the desired behavior from the child.

Clinical Example (0369T)

Office visit for a 5-year-old male with moderate to severe autism with the patient's grandparents. The patient had begun to show improvements in his language and social skills at home as a result of one-to-one intensive behavior therapy but seems to have reached a plateau in skill development over the past month, associated with a grandparent now living with the family.

Description of Procedure (0369T)

The qualified health care professional modifies the protocol, incorporating grandparent into language and social activities in place of the parent to increase generalization to grandparent. (Expect patient's initial level of involvement with the grandparent to be very low but gradual increase is anticipated as his interactions become more natural and less contrived.) The qualified health care

⊘=Modifier 51 Exempt   ☉=Moderate Sedation   ✚=Add-on Code   𝑵=FDA approval pending professional administers a set of daily routine skills incorporating the modified protocol to include grandparent with additional real-time adjustments as needed. The qualified health care professional demonstrates to the grandparent and a technician how to administer the modified protocol to facilitate the desired behavior from the child.

Clinical Example (0370T)

Office visit for parents of a 6-year-old male with severe autistic disorder and epilepsy. The patient communicates some using icon cards and has frequent episodes of striking his head with fists and against hard surfaces. Communication-skill treatment to date resulted in reduced self-injury when therapists are present but not when the patient is alone with parents.

Description of Procedure (0370T)

Qualified health care professional teaches parents skills to prompt and reinforce their child's use of alternative communication strategies for making requests in natural home environments to promote generalization of therapist-taught skills. Qualified health care professional has determined that a combination of a pictorial request card and a gesture effectively indicates to parents the desire to stop an activity (eg, a card with a "stop" sign) and a "break" manual sign. (A second card resembles a hand with a finger motioning toward the child in a "come here" gesture with the word "HELP" printed on it.) The caregivers are taught to honor the "stop" and "help" requests when they occur, which rewards the child for his communication attempts.

Clinical Example (0371T)

Office multiple-family group visit for parents of a 3-year-old male recently diagnosed with autistic disorder who has pervasive hyperactivity and no functional play, social skills, or language. Parents seek training on how to manage his hyperactive and disruptive behavior and encourage appropriate play, social, and language skills.

Description of Procedure (0371T)

The qualified health care professional reviews homework from the preceding multiple-family group session. Next, the qualified health care professional asks parents to identify one of their own child's problems (eg, whining to get attention) regarding a particular behavioral skill concept and requests evaluation by other parents, to assist each participant to understand the concept when applied to different situations. The qualified health care professional models a specific behavioral skill that involves applying that concept (eg, prompting use of spoken communication instead of attending to whining). Parents role-play the same skill, and other group participants make constructive suggestions with the qualified health care professional providing corrective feedback. The qualified health care professional ends the group session by summarizing the main points, answering questions, and giving parents a homework assignment to practice the newly learned behavioral skill.

Clinical Example (0372T)

Office group visit for a 13-year-old female with ASD who has above-average intelligence and a B+ grade average at school and is isolated from peers due to poor social skills and odd behavior. She has difficulty recognizing emotions of others and often annoys her peers because she tells the same joke over and over and talks incessantly about comic-book heroes.

Description of Procedure (0372T)

The qualified health care professional begins the group session by asking each group member to briefly discuss two social encounters with peers that occurred since the last session, one that went well and one that did not. The qualified health care professional uses this information to then develop a group activity in which the members have the opportunity to practice the activities from the encounters that went well and to problem solve the activities that did not go well. The qualified health care professional assists the group members to identify the cues that were interpreted correctly and incorrectly. Each participant is asked to identify a specific measurable goal of success. The qualified health care professional adjusts the level of assistance (eg, prompts) and feedback given to each member based on his or her skill level and ongoing progress in the group. The qualified health care professional ends the group session by summarizing the behavioral treatment principles that were addressed, answering questions, and giving each member of the group an individualized homework assignment to practice a particular social skill.

▶Exposure Adaptive Behavior Treatment With Protocol Modification◀

▶Codes 0373T and 0374T describe services provided to patients with one or more specific severe destructive behaviors (eg, self-injurious behavior, aggression, property destruction), with direct supervision by a physician or other qualified health care professional that requires two or more technicians face-to-face with the patient for safe treatment. Technicians elicit behavioral effects of exposing the patient to specific environmental conditions and treatments. Technicians record all occurrences of targeted behaviors. The physician or other qualified health care professional reviews and analyzes data and refines the therapy using single-case designs; ineffective components are modified or replaced until discharge goals are achieved (eg, reducing destructive behavior by at least 90%, generalizing the treatment effects across caregivers and settings, or maintaining the treatment effects over time). The therapy is conducted in a structured, safe environment. Precautions may include environmental modifications and/or protective equipment for the safety of the patient or the technicians.◀

●0373T   Exposure adaptive behavior treatment with protocol modification requiring two or more technicians for severe maladaptive behavior(s); first 60 minutes of technicians' time, face-to-face with patient

✚●0374T   each additional 30 minutes of technicians' time face-to-face with patient (List separately in addition to code for primary procedure)

     ▶(Use 0374T in conjunction with 0373T)◀

    ⊘=Modifier 51 Exempt   ⊙=Moderate Sedation   ✚=Add-on Code   ⅍=FDA approval pending

►(0373T, 0374T are reported based on a single technician's face-to-face time with the patient and not the combined time of multiple technicians)◄

►(Do not report 0373T, 0374T in conjunction with 90785-90899, 96101-96155)◄

📎 Rationale

Two Category III codes (0373T, 0374T), guidelines, and instructional notes have been added for exposure adaptive behavior treatment directed by physician or other qualified health care professional and delivered by a team of technicians. This treatment is staged to train patients in utilizing appropriate alternative responses under the environmental contexts that typically evoke problem behavior. Exposure adaptive behavior treatment addresses one or more specific severe destructive behaviors (eg, SIB, aggression, property destruction). These services are typically provided in intensive outpatient, day treatment, or inpatient facilities within a safe environment (eg, padded rooms). Protective gear is also typically used during treatment to safeguard the technicians and patient from destructive behavior. In reporting codes 0373T and 0374T, only the face-to-face time spent by one technician during a single session of sequential time may be counted. Although the physician or other qualified health care professional is on site, he or she may be directing 5-10 other similar treatments simultaneously. The complexity of the exposure adaptive behavior treatment codes (0373T and 0374T) is addressed by the increased time designation (60 minutes) and the use of multiple technicians.

Parenthetical notes in the adaptive behavior treatment section applicable to codes 0373T and 0374T have been established to: (1) instruct the use of add-on code 0374T in conjunction with code 0373T when expanded treatment time is spent; (2) provide a list of exclusionary codes that cannot be reported in conjunction with codes 0373T and 0374T, namely codes 90785-90899, 96101-96155; and (3) denote that the exposure adaptive behavior treatment codes 0373T and 0374T are reported based on a single technician's face-to-face time with the patient and not the combined time of multiple technicians.

🩺 Clinical Example (0373T)

Treatment center visit for a 13-year-old female with Cornelia de Lange syndrome, severe intellectual disability, and stereotyped movement disorder referred for severe SIB and aggression. Her speech is limited to short, two- to three-word utterances, and she requires constant supervision from an adult due to her limited adaptive skills and severe problem behavior. The patient was placed in a group home last year due to her family's inability to manage the problem behaviors at home, and she is now at risk of losing that placement. A controlled functional analysis showed that her SIB and aggression served to gain adult attention and escape from nonpreferred tasks. These results indicate that the patient should receive a function-based behavioral intervention in which she is taught to use appropriate replacement responses (eg, functional communication) under the environmental conditions that have typically evoked problem behavior.

Description of Procedure (0373T)

Three technicians work with the patient in a padded room according to a qualified health care professional–designed protocol. One collects continuous real-time data on her SIB, aggression, and communication responses; a second technician stands closely behind the patient and blocks her attempts at SIB; while the third technician uses modeling and differential reinforcement to teach the patient to request attention using a short phrase ("Play, please"). This functional communication response first taught in a padded-treatment room is intended to be initiated and then systematically generalized across different technicians and settings at a subsequent session. The technicians adhere to the qualified health care professional protocol design including the overall sequence of training and generalization procedures and progress determinations to enable judgment on whether the protocol is producing adequate response The technician records all results and provides data to the qualified health care professional, who is present on-site to analyze the collected data.

Clinical Example (0374T)

Treatment center visit for a 13-year-old female with Cornelia de Lange syndrome, severe intellectual disability, and stereotyped movement disorder referred for severe SIB and aggression. Her speech is limited to short, two- to three-word utterances, and she requires constant supervision from an adult due to her limited adaptive skills and severe problem behavior. The patient was placed in a group home last year due to her family's inability to manage the problem behaviors at home, and she is now at risk of losing that placement. A controlled functional analysis showed that her SIB and aggression served to gain adult attention and escape from nonpreferred tasks. These results indicate that the patient should receive a function-based behavioral intervention in which she is taught to use appropriate replacement responses (eg, functional communication) under the environmental conditions that have typically evoked problem behavior.

Description of Procedure (0374T)

Three technicians work with the patient in a padded room according to a qualified health care professional–designed protocol. One collects continuous real-time data on her SIB, aggression, and communication responses; a second technician stands closely behind the patient and blocks her attempts at SIB; while the third technician uses modeling and differential reinforcement to teach the patient to request attention using a short phrase ("Play, please"). This functional communication response first taught in a padded-treatment room is intended to be initiated and then systematically generalized across different technicians and settings at a subsequent session. The technicians adhere to the qualified health care professional protocol design including the overall sequence of training and generalization procedures and progress determinations to enable judgment on whether the protocol is producing adequate response The technician records all results and provides data to the qualified health care professional, who is present on-site to analyze the collected data.

●0375T Total disc arthroplasty (artificial disc), anterior approach, including discectomy with end plate preparation (includes osteophytectomy for nerve root or spinal cord decompression and microdissection), cervical, three or more levels

▶(Do not report 0375T in conjunction with 22851, 22856, 22858 when performed at the same level)◀

Rationale

The recently adopted concept of permanence principle has been applied to code 0092T, which has been renumbered as code 0375T, in order to adhere to health information technology (HIT) standards. The concept of permanence principle dictates that new code numbers should be established, if a revision alters the meaning of the code. Code 0375T is a stand-alone code that is intended for a cervical arthroplasty procedure on three or more levels, which differs from code 0092T. Code 0092T was an add-on code that was used for each additional interspace, but it is no longer the reporting mechanism for total disc cervical arthroplasty procedures. Instead, codes 22856 and 22858 should be reported for arthroplasty procedures that are performed up to two levels. And, code 0375T is intended for three or more levels, which should not be used in conjunction with Category I codes 22856 and 22858, when performed at the same level. Instructions for the use of code 0375T have also been included in a new exclusionary parenthetical following the code, which precludes its use with codes 22851, 22856, and 22858, when performed at the same level.

Clinical Example (0375T)

A 37-year-old female presents with right-sided cervical radicular pain refractory to multimodality conservative therapy. Examination shows findings of nerve root compression with cervical motion, C6 and C7 radiculopathy on neurologic examination along with a magnetic resonance imaging (MRI) scan showing a C5-6 disc with focal right paracentral disc herniation and/or associated osteophyte formation with C6 foraminal and canal compromise, and C6-7 para central or right sided foraminal compression from either herniated disc or disc osteophyte causing compression of the C7 nerve root.

Description of Procedure (0375T)

Patient undergoes an anterior cervical discectomy, osteophytectomy at both C5-6 and C6-7 and implantation of a C5-6 and C6-7 total disc arthroplasty. Make a skin incision, and use sharp and blunt dissection to dissect between the carotid sheath laterally and the esophagus and trachea medially, exposing the prevertebral space. Identify vertebral level using fluoroscopy, and dissect the edges of the longus coli muscles, and elevate them from the vertebral bodies. Insert self-retaining retractors beneath the edge of the longus coli. Incise the disc space, and remove the disc material with curettes and rongeurs to the posterior longitudinal ligament. Introduce disc space distractor pins into the C5 and C6 vertebral bodies, apply the distractor, and open up the space with end plates parallel to each other. Drape the operating microscope in sterile fashion, and bring it into the field. The remainder of the procedure is performed utilizing standard microdissection techniques. Open and resect the posterior ligament. Identify the disc herniation, and remove it from the epidural space decompressing the nerve root. Use a micro Kerrison punch and/or the high-speed air-powered drill to perform a foramentomy on both sides to remove uncovertebral osteophytes. Achieve hemostasis, and remove the cartilaginous end plate, sparing the bone. Introduce the implant trial into the disc space between the uncinate processes. Confirm the trial to be appropriately sized, and locate it utilizing anteroposterior (AP) and lateral plane fluoroscopy. Introduce a drill guide over the implant trial, and create tracts in the inferior and superior end plates, and clean of bone debris. Remove the trial, and insert the final implant into the tracts previously cut and tapped into position. Use fluoroscopy to confirm position in AP and lateral projections, and make adjustments as necessary. The procedure is repeated at C6-7. Introduce disc space distractor pins into the C6 and C7 vertebral bodies, apply the distractor, and open up the space with end plates parallel to each other. Drape the operating microscope in sterile fashion, and bring it into the field. The remainder of the procedure is performed utilizing standard microdissection techniques. Open and resect the posterior ligament. Identify the disc herniation, and remove it from the epidural space decompressing the nerve root. Use a micro Kerrison punch and/or the high-speed air powered drill to perform a foramentomy on both sides to remove uncovertebral osteophytes. Achieve hemostasis, and remove the cartilaginous end plate, sparing the bone. Introduce the implant trial into the disc space between the uncinate processes. Confirm the trial to be appropriately sized and located utilizing AP and lateral plane fluoroscopy. Introduce a drill guide over the implant trial, and create tracts in the inferior and superior end plates, and clean of bone debris. Remove the trial, and insert the final implant into the tracts previously cut and tapped into position. Use fluoroscopy to confirm position in AP and lateral projections, and make adjustments as necessary. Check alignment of additional prosthesis with the initial level prosthesis. Achieve hemostasis, remove the retractors, and close the incision in layers and place a sterile dressing.

●**0377T**   Anoscopy with directed submucosal injection of bulking agent for fecal incontinence

▶(Do not report 0377T in conjunction with 46600)◀

Rationale

Code 0377T has been established to report anoscopy with submucosal injection of bulking agent for patients with fecal incontinence. Code 0377T should not be reported with anoscopy code 46600 and the bulking agent should be reported separately.

Clinical Example (0377T)

A 60-year-old female with fecal incontinence has failed conservative treatment such as dietary change and pharmacotherapy. She undergoes submucosal injection of a bulking agent.

Description of Procedure (0377T)

Position patient left lateral or prone after pre-treatment enema. Efface the patient's buttocks. Perform a visual inspection of the perineum. Perform digital rectal examination. Place a lubricated (including topical anesthetic) anoscope in the anal canal. Rotate the anoscope 180° and the remove the obturator. Perform visual inspection. Withdraw the anoscope so that the dentate line is identified. Provide

⊘=Modifier 51 Exempt   ⊙=Moderate Sedation   ✚=Add-on Code   ✗=FDA approval pending

four injections (posterior, left lateral, anterior, and right lateral) and perform this slowly to avoid stress on the Luer-lock connection and to allow the tissue to adapt to the injected gel. Under direct vision, the mucosa is penetrated, approximately 5 mm proximal to the dentate line. Advance the needle an additional 5 mm at approximately 30° to the axis of the rectum. If the patient indicates pain at the puncture, the injection site should be adjusted a few mm in the cephalic direction. If the puncture is painless, 1 ml of bulking agent is injected in the deep submucosal layer. After injection, keep the needle in position for 15-30 seconds to minimize leakage of bulking agent. Repeat the injection at the remaining three injection sites. Use a new needle for each syringe and injection site. After completion of the 4 injections, extract the anoscope, and the patient typically remains at rest for approximately 60 minutes. If no bleeding or other treatment-related symptoms are observed during this time, discharge the patient (from facility or office) with diet, activity, and necessary medications and instructions.

●**0378T**   Visual field assessment, with concurrent real time data analysis and accessible data storage with patient initiated data transmitted to a remote surveillance center for up to 30 days; review and interpretation with report by a physician or other qualified health care professional

●**0379T**   technical support and patient instructions, surveillance, analysis, and transmission of daily and emergent data reports as prescribed by a physician or other qualified health care professional

Rationale

Two new Category III codes (0378T, 0379T) have been added to report visual field assessment up to 30 days.

For the assessment, the patient transmits daily test-data to a monitoring center (eg, independent diagnostic testing facility [IDTF]) for storage into a secured database, and a technician with physician or other qualified heath care oversees analyzes the data and prepares a report. The attending physician or other qualified health care professional reviews the report and interprets the results.

Code 0378T describes the professional component of the physician or other qualified health care professional review and interpretation of the 30-day recordings and monthly report received from the monitoring center. Code 0379T describes the technical component of the device set-up and patient instructions for daily testing and transmission with technical-staff support and preparation of monthly summary reports, under the direction of a physician or other qualified health care professional.

Clinical Example (0378T)

A 69-year-old patient presents with intermediate age-related macular degeneration in both eyes, age-related eye disease study (AREDS) category 3, visual acuity 20/25 in the right eye and 20/32 in the left eye.

Description of Procedure (0378T)

Upon order by a physician or other qualified health care professional, the patient receives a personalized monitoring device, set to test the visual fields of one or two eyes as prescribed. The patient tests the eyes daily as prompted by the application. The test results are securely transmitted to a secured database, where the data are stored and analyzed by the technical staff of the monitoring center and accessible by the prescribing physician or other qualified health care professional. A summary report is prepared monthly by the technical staff of the monitoring center and sent to the prescribing physician or other qualified health care provider for review and interpretation. In the case of a change in patient's visual field status, an emergent notification is immediately sent to the prescribing physician or other qualified health care professional who reviews the test results and recommends further management, as clinically appropriate. In the event of low testing frequency, the monitoring center's staff will contact the patient to encourage testing and provide technical support and will notify the prescribing physician or other qualified health care professional of the patient's reduced testing frequency.

Clinical Example (0379T)

A 69-year-old patient presents with intermediate age-related macular degeneration in both eyes, AREDS category 3, visual acuity 20/25 in the right eye and 20/32 in the left eye.

Description of Procedure (0379T)

Upon order by a physician or other qualified health professional, the patient receives a personalized monitoring device. The visual field device is delivered to the patient's home by the monitoring center. At the home, the device is personalized remotely including patient instructions and technical support by the monitoring center technical staff and set to test one or two eyes as prescribed by ordering physician. The patient tests the eyes daily as prompted by the application. The test results are securely transmitted to a secured monitoring center database, where the data is stored and analyzed by the technical staff with oversight by the supervising physician of the monitoring center. Daily test results are accessible by the prescribing physician or other qualified health care professional. A summary report is prepared monthly by the technical staff of the monitoring center and sent for review and interpretation to the prescribing physician or other qualified health care professional. In the case of a change in patient's visual field status, an emergent notification is immediately sent by the monitoring center staff to the prescribing physician or other qualified health care professional who reviews the test results and recommends further management, as clinically appropriate. In the event of low testing frequency, the monitoring center's staff will contact the patient to encourage testing and provide technical support and will notify the prescribing physician or other qualified health care professional of the patient's reduced testing frequency.

●0380T Computer-aided animation and analysis of time series retinal images for the monitoring of disease progression, unilateral or bilateral, with interpretation and report

Rationale

Code 0380T should be used to report computer-aided animation and analysis of time series retinal images to monitor the disease progression (glaucoma or other structural damage) in the eye. It may be performed for one or both eyes and includes the interpretation and report for the service. In this procedure, a series of digital images of the optic nerve are taken over time. The images are loaded into

⊘=Modifier 51 Exempt   ⊙=Moderate Sedation   ✚=Add-on Code   ⟋=FDA approval pending

a computer, which enables the creation of an animated view of the nerve to evaluate the progression of structural damage, as well as an interpretation and report for the animated images. Because the same code may be reported for unilateral or bilateral procedures, code 0380T may only be reported once to identify bilateral provision of the service.

Clinical Example (0380T)

A 53-year-old male has been followed for several years as a glaucoma suspect with automated visual fields and fundus photographs. The series of images acquired over time is uploaded and analyzed.

Description of Procedure (0380T)

The physician or other qualified health care professional locates images for review. Perform a computer-aided analysis to create an animated view of the optic nerve for evaluation of structural damage progression. Perform the animation interpretation and prepare a report.

Appendix O

For 2015, Appendix O has been updated to include a revision to the introductory language, addition of one new Category I Multianalyte Assays with Algorithmic Analyses (MAAA) code (81519) and three new Administrative MAAA codes (0006M, 0007M, 0008M), and a deletion of one code (0005M).

Appendix O

Multianalyte Assays with Algorithmic Analyses

The following list includes a set of administrative codes for Multianalyte Assays with Algorithmic Analyses (MAAA) procedures that by their nature are typically unique to a single clinical laboratory or manufacturer.

Multianalyte Assays with Algorithmic Analyses (MAAAs) are procedures that utilize multiple results derived from assays of various types, including molecular pathology assays, fluorescent in situ hybridization assays and non-nucleic acid based assays (eg, proteins, polypeptides, lipids, carbohydrates). Algorithmic analysis using the results of these assays as well as other patient information (if used) is then performed and reported typically as a numeric score(s) or as a probability. MAAAs are typically unique to a single clinical laboratory or manufacturer. The results of individual component procedure(s) that are inputs to the MAAAs may be provided on the associated laboratory report, however these assays are not reported separately using additional codes.

The list includes a proprietary name and clinical laboratory or manufacturer in the first column, an alpha-numeric code in the second column and code descriptor in the third column. The format for the code descriptor usually includes (in order):

- Disease type (eg, oncology, autoimmune, tissue rejection),

- Chemical(s) analyzed (eg, DNA, RNA, protein, antibody),

- Number of markers (eg, number of genes, number of proteins),

- Methodology(s) (eg, microarray, real-time [RT]-PCR, in situ hybridization [ISH], enzyme linked immunosorbent assays [ELISA]),

- Number of functional domains (if indicated),

- Specimen type (eg, blood, fresh tissue, formalin-fixed paraffin embedded),

- Algorithm result type (eg, prognostic, diagnostic),

- Report (eg, probability index, risk score).

MAAA procedures that have been assigned a Category I code are noted in the list below and additionally listed in the Category I MAAA section (81500-81599). The Category I MAAA section introductory language and associated parenthetical instruction(s) should be used to govern the appropriate use for Category I MAAA codes. If a specific MAAA procedure has not been assigned a Category I code, it is indicated as a four-digit number followed by the letter M.

▶When a specific MAAA procedure is not included in either the list below or in the Category I MAAA section, report the analysis using the Category I MAAA unlisted code (81599). The codes below are specific to the assays identified in Appendix O by proprietary name. In order to report a MAAA code, the analysis performed must fulfill the code descriptor **and**, if proprietary, must be the test represented by the proprietary name listed in Appendix O. When an analysis is performed that may potentially fall within a specific descriptor, however the proprietary name is not included in the list below, the MAAA unlisted code (81599) should be used.◄

Additions in this section may be released tri-annually via the AMA CPT website to expedite dissemination for reporting. The list will be published annually in the CPT codebook. Go to www.ama-assn.org/go/cpt for the most current listing.

These administrative codes encompass all analytical services required for the algorithmic analysis (eg, cell lysis, nucleic acid stabilization, extraction, digestion, amplification, hybridization and detection) in addition to the algorithmic analysis itself. Procedures that are required prior to cell lysis (eg, microdissection, codes 88380 and 88381) should be reported separately.

The codes in this list are provided as an administrative coding set to facilitate accurate reporting of MAAA services. The minimum standard for inclusion in this list is that an analysis is generally available for patient care. The AMA has not reviewed procedures in the administrative coding set for clinical utility. The list is not a complete list of all MAAA procedures.

Proprietary Name and Clinical Laboratory or Manufacturer	Alpha-Numeric Code	Code Descriptor
Administrative Codes for Multianalyte Assays with Algorithmic Analyses (MAAA)		
HCV FibroSURE™, LabCorp	0001M	Infectious disease, HCV, six biochemical assays (ALT, A2-macroglobulin, apolipoprotein A-1, total bilirubin, GGT, and haptoglobin) utilizing serum, prognostic algorithm reported as scores for fibrosis and necroinflammatory activity in liver
ASH FibroSURE™, LabCorp	0002M	Liver disease, ten biochemical assays (ALT, A2-macroglobulin, apolipoprotein A-1, total bilirubin, GGT, haptoglobin, AST, glucose, total cholesterol and triglycerides) utilizing serum, prognostic algorithm reported as quantitative scores for fibrosis, steatosis and alcoholic steatohepatitis (ASH)
NASH FibroSURE™, LabCorp	0003M	Liver disease, ten biochemical assays (ALT, A2-macroglobulin, apolipoprotein A-1, total bilirubin, GGT, haptoglobin, AST, glucose, total cholesterol and triglycerides) utilizing serum, prognostic algorithm reported as quantitative scores for fibrosis, steatosis and nonalcoholic steatohepatitis (NASH)
ScoliScore™ Transgenomic	0004M	Scoliosis, DNA analysis of 53 single nucleotide polymorphisms (SNPs), using saliva, prognostic algorithm reported as a risk score
	(0005M has been deleted, use 81507)	—
HeproDX™, GoPath Laboratories, LLC	● 0006M	Oncology (hepatic), mRNA expression levels of 161 genes, utilizing fresh hepatocellular carcinoma tumor tissue, with alpha-fetoprotein level, algorithm reported as a risk classifier
NETest (Wren Laboratories, LLC)	● 0007M	Oncology (gastrointestinal neuroendocrine tumors), real-time PCR expression analysis of 51 genes, utilizing whole peripheral blood, algorithm reported as a nomogram of tumor disease index

Prosigna Breast Cancer Assay (NanoString Technologies)	● 0008M	Oncology (breast), mRNA analysis of 58 genes using hybrid capture, on formalin-fixed paraffin-embedded (FFPE) tissue, prognostic algorithm reported as a risk score

Category I Codes for Multianalyte Assays with Algorithmic Analyses (MAAA)

Risk of Ovarian Malignancy Algorithm (ROMA)™, Fujirebio Diagnostics	81500	Oncology (ovarian), biochemical assays of two proteins (CA-125 and HE4), utilizing serum, with menopausal status, algorithm reported as a risk score
OVA1™, Vermillion, Inc.	81503	Oncology (ovarian), biochemical assays of five proteins (CA-125, apoliproprotein A1, beta-2 microglobulin, transferrin, and pre-albumin), utilizing serum, algorithm reported as a risk score
Pathwork® Tissue of Origin Test, Pathwork Diagnostics	81504	Oncology (tissue of origin), microarray gene expression profiling of >2000 genes, utilizing formalin-fixed paraffin embedded tissue, algorithm reported as tissue similarity scores
PreDx Diabetes Risk Score™, Tethys Clinical Laboratory	81506	Endocrinology (type 2 diabetes), biochemical assays of seven analytes (glucose, HbA1c, insulin, hs-CRP, adoponectin, ferritin, interleukin 2-receptor alpha), utilizing serum or plasma, algorithm reporting a risk score
Harmony™ Prenatal Test, Ariosa Diagnostics	81507	Fetal aneuploidy (trisomy 21, 18, and 13) DNA sequence analysis of selected regions using maternal plasma, algorithm reported as a risk score for each trisomy
No proprietary name and clinical laboratory or manufacturer. Maternal serum screening procedures are well established procedures and are performed by many labs throughout the country. The concept of prenatal screens has existed and evolved for over ten years and is not exclusive to any one facility.	81508	Fetal congenital abnormalities, biochemical assays of two proteins (PAPP-A, hCG [any form]), utilizing maternal serum, algorithm reported as a risk score
	81509	Fetal congenital abnormalities, biochemical assays of three proteins (PAPP-A, hCG [any form], DIA), utilizing maternal serum, algorithm reported as a risk score
	81510	Fetal congenital abnormalities, biochemical assays of three analytes (AFP, uE3, hCG [any form]), utilizing maternal serum, algorithm reported as a risk score
	81511	Fetal congenital abnormalities, biochemical assays of four analytes (AFP, uE3, hCG [any form], DIA) utilizing maternal serum, algorithm reported as a risk score (may include additional results from previous biochemical testing)
	81512	Fetal congenital abnormalities, biochemical assays of five analytes (AFP, uE3, total hCG, hyperglycosylated hCG, DIA) utilizing maternal serum, algorithm reported as a risk score
Oncotype DX® (Genomic Health)	● 81519	Oncology (breast), mRNA, gene expression profiling by real-time RT-PCR of 21 genes, utilizing formalin-fixed paraffin embedded tissue, algorithm reported as recurrence score
	81599	Unlisted multianalyte assay with algorithmic analysis

Rationale

Appendix O has been updated to include three Administrative MAAA codes (0006M, 0007M, 0008M) and one new Category 1 MAAA code (81519). Refer to the introductory guidelines for specific guidance on how to accurately report or assign new codes, as well as the specific requirements for inclusion in the Administrative Code List or as a Category 1 code.

To correlate with the revisions to the MAAA introductory guidelines, Appendix O's introductory guidelines have also been revised to clarify that in order to report an MAAA code, the analysis performed must be specifically described by the MAAA code descriptor and, if proprietary, the test must be represented by the proprietary name listed in Appendix O.

⊘=Modifier 51 Exempt   ⊙=Moderate Sedation   ✚=Add-on Code   𝒩=FDA approval pending

Tabular Review of the Changes

Evaluation and Management

Inpatient Neonatal Intensive Care Services and Pediatric and Neonatal Critical Care Services

Inpatient Neonatal and Pediatric Critical Care

Section/Code	Added	Deleted	Revised	Grammatical Revision
99481		X		
99482		X		

Care Management Services

Chronic Care Management Services

Section/Code	Added	Deleted	Revised	Grammatical Revision
99490	X			

Complex Chronic Care Management Services

Section/Code	Added	Deleted	Revised	Grammatical Revision
99487			X	
99488		X		
99489			X	

Advance Care Planning

Section/Code	Added	Deleted	Revised	Grammatical Revision
99497	X			
99498	X			

Anesthesia

Thorax (Chest Wall and Shoulder Girdle)

Section/Code	Added	Deleted	Revised	Grammatical Revision
00452		X		

Spine and Spinal Cord

Section/Code	Added	Deleted	Revised	Grammatical Revision
00622		X		
00634		X		

Surgery

Musculoskeletal System

General

Introduction or Removal

Section/Code	Added	Deleted	Revised	Grammatical Revision
20600			X	
20604	X			
20605			X	
20606	X			
20610			X	
20611	X			

Other Procedures

Section/Code	Added	Deleted	Revised	Grammatical Revision
20982			X	
20983	X			

Neck (Soft Tissues) and Thorax

Fracture and/or Dislocation

Section/Code	Added	Deleted	Revised	Grammatical Revision
21800		X		
21810		X		
21811	X			
21812	X			
21813	X			

Spine (Vertebral Column)

Percutaneous Vertebroplasty and Vertebral Augmentation

Section/Code	Added	Deleted	Revised	Grammatical Revision
22510	X			
22511	X			
22512	X			
22513	X			
22514	X			
22515	X			

Section/Code	Added	Deleted	Revised	Grammatical Revision
Percutaneous Augmentation and Annuloplasty				
22520		X		
22521		X		
22522		X		
22523		X		
22524		X		
22525		X		
Spinal Instrumentation				
22856			X	
22858	X			
Pelvis and Hip Joint				
Arthrodesis				
27279	X			
27280			X	
Femur (Thigh Region) and Knee Joint				
Introduction or Removal				
27370			X	
Application of Casts and Strapping				
Body and Upper Extremity				
29020		X		
29025		X		
Removal or Repair				
29715		X		
Cardiovascular System				
Heart and Pericardium				
Pacemaker or Implantable Defibrillator				
33215			X	
33216			X	

⃠=Modifier 51 Exempt   ⊙=Moderate Sedation   ✚=Add-on Code   ⁄⁄=FDA approval pending

Section/Code	Added	Deleted	Revised	Grammatical Revision
33217			X	
33218			X	
33220			X	
33223			X	
33224			X	
33225			X	
33230			X	
33231			X	
33240			X	
33241			X	
33243			X	
33244			X	
33249			X	
33262			X	
33263			X	
33264			X	
33270	X			
33271	X			
33272	X			
33273	X			

Heart (Including Valves) and Great Vessels

| 33332 | | X | | |

Cardiac Valves

33418	X			
33419	X			
33472		X		

Section/Code	Added	Deleted	Revised	Grammatical Revision
Extracorporeal Membrane Oxygenation or Extracorporeal Life Support Services				
33946	X			
33947	X			
33948	X			
33949	X			
33951	X			
33952	X			
33953	X			
33954	X			
33955	X			
33956	X			
33957	X			
33958	X			
33959	X			
33962	X			
33963	X			
33964	X			
33965	X			
33966	X			
33969	X			
33984	X			
33985	X			
33986	X			
33987	X			
33988	X			
33989	X			
Cardiac Assist				
33960		X		
33961		X		

⃠=Modifier 51 Exempt   ⊙=Moderate Sedation   ✚=Add-on Code   ✗=FDA approval pending

Section/Code	Added	Deleted	Revised	Grammatical Revision
Arteries and Veins				
Fenestrated Endovascular Repair of the Visceral and Infrarenal Aorta				
34839	X			
Vascular Injection Procedures				
36469		X		
Hemodialysis Access, Intervascular Cannulation for Extracorporeal Circulation, or Shunt Insertion				
36822		X		
Transcatheter Procedures				
37215			X	
37216			X	
37217			X	
37218	X			
Endovascular Revascularization (Open or Percutaneous, Transcatheter)				
37236			X	
37237			X	
Digestive System				
Salivary Gland and Ducts				
Repair				
42508		X		
Esophagus				
Endoscopy				
43180	X			
43194			X	
43197			X	
43215			X	
43216			X	
43247			X	
43250			X	

Section/Code	Added	Deleted	Revised	Grammatical Revision
Repair				
43350		X		
Intestines (Except Rectum)				
Endoscopy, Small Intestine				
44360			X	
44363			X	
Endoscopy, Stomal				
44380			X	
44381	X			
44383		X		
44384	X			
44385			X	
44386			X	
44388			X	
44390			X	
44391			X	
44392			X	
44393		X		
44397		X		
44401	X			
44402	X			
44403	X			
44404	X			
44405	X			
44406	X			
44407	X			
44408	X			
Other Procedures				
44799			X	

⊘=Modifier 51 Exempt   ⊙=Moderate Sedation   ✚=Add-on Code   ✗=FDA approval pending

Section/Code	Added	Deleted	Revised	Grammatical Revision
Colon and Rectum				
Endoscopy				
45330			X	
45332			X	
45333			X	
45334			X	
45337			X	
45339		X		
45340			X	
45345		X		
45346	X			
45347	X			
45349	X			
45350	X			
45355		X		
45378			X	
45379			X	
45380			X	
45381			X	
45382			X	
45383		X		
45384			X	
45385			X	
45386			X	
45387		X		
45388	X			
45389	X			
45390	X			
45391			X	

Section/Code	Added	Deleted	Revised	Grammatical Revision
45392			X	
45393	X			
45398	X			
Other Procedures				
45399	X			

Anus

Endoscopy

46600			X	
46601	X			
46607	X			

Liver

Other Procedures

47383	X			

Urinary System

Bladder

Vesical Neck and Prostate

52441	X			
52442	X			

Nervous System

Skull, Meninges, and Brain

Injection, Drainage, or Aspiration

61055			X	

Craniectomy or Craniotomy

61334		X		
61440		X		
61470		X		
61490		X		
61542		X		

⃠=Modifier 51 Exempt ⊙=Moderate Sedation ✚=Add-on Code ✗=FDA approval pending

Section/Code	Added	Deleted	Revised	Grammatical Revision
Surgery of Skull Base				
61609		X		
Neurostimulators (Intracranial)				
61875		X		
Repair				
62116		X		

Spine and Spinal Cord

Section/Code	Added	Deleted	Revised	Grammatical Revision
Injection, Drainage, or Aspiration				
62284			X	
62302	X			
62303	X			
62304	X			
62305	X			

Extracranial Nerves, Peripheral Nerves, and Autonomic Nervous System

Section/Code	Added	Deleted	Revised	Grammatical Revision
Introduction/Injection of Anesthetic Agent (Nerve Block), Diagnostic or Therapeutic				
64486	X			
64487	X			
64488	X			
64489	X			
Transection or Avulsion				
64752		X		
64761		X		
Neurorrhaphy				
64870		X		

Eye and Ocular Adnexa

Anterior Segment

Section/Code	Added	Deleted	Revised	Grammatical Revision
Anterior Sclera				
66165		X		
66179	X			

Section/Code	Added	Deleted	Revised	Grammatical Revision
66180			X	
66184	X			
66185			X	

Ocular Adnexa

Extraocular Muscles

67399			X	

Auditory System

Middle Ear

Introduction

69400		X		
69401		X		
69405		X		

Radiology

Diagnostic Radiology (Diagnostic Imaging)

Spine and Pelvis

72291		X		
72292		X		

Gastrointestinal Tract

74291		X		

Diagnostic Ultrasound

Chest

76641	X			
76642	X			
76645		X		

Ultrasonic Guidance Procedures

76950		X		

  ⊘=Modifier 51 Exempt   ⊙=Moderate Sedation   ✚=Add-on Code   ✗=FDA approval pending

Section/Code	Added	Deleted	Revised	Grammatical Revision
Breast, Mammography				
77061	X			
77062	X			
77063	X			
Bone/Joint Studies				
77082		X		
77085	X			
77086	X			
Radiation Oncology				
Medical Radiation Physics, Dosimetry, Treatment Devices, and Special Services				
77305		X		
77306	X			
77307	X			
77310		X		
77315		X		
77316	X			
77317	X			
77318	X			
77326		X		
77327		X		
77328		X		
Radiation Treatment Delivery				
77385	X			
77386	X			
77387	X			
77401			X	
77402			X	
77403		X		

Section/Code	Added	Deleted	Revised	Grammatical Revision
77404		X		
77406		X		
77407			X	
77408		X		
77409		X		
77411		X		
77412			X	
77413		X		
77414		X		
77416		X		
77418		X		
77421		X		

Pathology and Laboratory

Organ or Disease-Oriented Panels

80100		X		
80101		X		
80102		X		
80103		X		
80104		X		

Drug Assay

Presumptive Drug Class Screening

Drug Class List B

80300	X			
80301	X			
80302	X			
80303	X			
80304	X			

⊘=Modifier 51 Exempt   ⊙=Moderate Sedation   ✚=Add-on Code   ✚=FDA approval pending

Section/Code	Added	Deleted	Revised	Grammatical Revision
Definitive Drug Testing				
80320	X			
80321	X			
80322	X			
80323	X			
80324	X			
80325	X			
80326	X			
80327	X			
80328	X			
80329	X			
80330	X			
80331	X			
80332	X			
80333	X			
80334	X			
80335	X			
80336	X			
80337	X			
80338	X			
80339	X			
80340	X			
80341	X			
80342	X			
80343	X			
80344	X			
80345	X			
80346	X			
80347	X			

Section/Code	Added	Deleted	Revised	Grammatical Revision
80348	X			
80349	X			
80350	X			
80351	X			
80352	X			
80353	X			
80354	X			
80355	X			
80356	X			
80357	X			
80358	X			
80359	X			
80360	X			
80361	X			
80362	X			
80363	X			
80364	X			
80365	X			
80366	X			
80367	X			
80368	X			
80369	X			
80370	X			
80371	X			
80372	X			
80373	X			
80374	X			
80375	X			
80376	X			
80377	X			

⊘=Modifier 51 Exempt   ⊙=Moderate Sedation   ✚=Add-on Code   ✗=FDA approval pending

Section/Code	Added	Deleted	Revised	Grammatical Revision
Therapeutic Drug Assays				
80152		X		
80154		X		
80160		X		
80162			X	
80163	X			
80164			X	
80165	X			
80166		X		
80171			X	
80172		X		
80174		X		
80182		X		
80196		X		
80299			X	
Evocative/Suppression Testing				
80440		X		
Molecular Pathology				
Tier 1 Molecular Pathology Procedures				
81245			X	
81246	X			
81288	X			
81313	X			
Tier 2 Molecular Pathology Procedures				
81402			X	
81403			X	
81404			X	
81405			X	

Section/Code	Added	Deleted	Revised	Grammatical Revision
Genomic Sequencing Procedures and Other Molecular Multianalyte Assays				
81410	X			
81411	X			
81415	X			
81416	X			
81417	X			
81420	X			
81425	X			
81426	X			
81427	X			
81430	X			
81431	X			
81435	X			
81436	X			
81440	X			
81445	X			
81450	X			
81455	X			
81460	X			
81465	X			
81470	X			
81471	X			
Multianalyte Assays with Algorithmic Analyses				
81519	X			
Chemistry				
82000		X		
82003		X		
82055		X		

    =Modifier 51 Exempt ⊙=Moderate Sedation ✚=Add-on Code ⲁ=FDA approval pending

Section/Code	Added	Deleted	Revised	Grammatical Revision
82101		X		
82145		X		
82205		X		
82520		X		
82541			X	
82542			X	
82543			X	
82544			X	
82646		X		
82649		X		
82651		X		
82654		X		
82666		X		
82690		X		
82742		X		
82953		X		
82975		X		
82980		X		
83006	X			
83008		X		
83055		X		
83071		X		
83634		X		
83805		X		
83840		X		
83858		X		
83866		X		
83887		X		
83925		X		

Section/Code	Added	Deleted	Revised	Grammatical Revision
84022		X		
84127		X		
84600			X	

Transfusion Medicine

Section/Code	Added	Deleted	Revised	Grammatical Revision
86900			X	
86901			X	
86902			X	
86904			X	
86905			X	
86906			X	

Microbiology

Section/Code	Added	Deleted	Revised	Grammatical Revision
87001		X		
87501			X	
87502			X	
87503			X	
87505	X			
87506	X			
87507	X			
87620		X		
87621		X		
87622		X		
87623	X			
87624	X			
87625	X			
87631			X	
87632			X	
87633			X	
87806	X			

⊘=Modifier 51 Exempt   ⊙=Moderate Sedation   ✚=Add-on Code   ✎=FDA approval pending

Section/Code	Added	Deleted	Revised	Grammatical Revision
Surgical Pathology				
88341	X			
88342			X	
88343		X		
88344	X			
88349		X		
88360			X	
88361			X	
88364	X			
88365			X	
88366	X			
88367			X	
88368			X	
88369	X			
88373	X			
88374	X			
88377	X			
Reproductive Medicine Procedures				
89337	X			

Medicine

Section/Code	Added	Deleted	Revised	Grammatical Revision
Vaccines, Toxoids				
90630	X			
90651	X			
90654			X	
90721			X	
90723			X	
90734			X	

Section/Code	Added	Deleted	Revised	Grammatical Revision
Gastroenterology				
Other Procedures				
91200	X			
Ophthalmology				
Special Ophthalmological Services				
92145	X			
Cardiovascular				
Implantable and Wearable Cardiac Device Evaluations				
93260	X			
93261	X			
93282			X	
93283			X	
93284			X	
93287			X	
93289			X	
93295			X	
93296			X	
Echocardiography				
93355	X			
Intracardiac Electrophysiological Procedures/Studies				
93642			X	
93644	X			
Noninvasive Physiologic Studies and Procedures				
93702	X			
Noninvasive Vascular Diagnostic Studies				
Cerebrovascular Arterial Studies				
93895	X			

⊘=Modifier 51 Exempt ⊙=Moderate Sedation ✚=Add-on Code 𝒩=FDA approval pending

Section/Code	Added	Deleted	Revised	Grammatical Revision
Neurology and Neuromuscular Procedures				
Neurostimulators, Analysis-Programming				
95972			X	
Central Nervous System Assessments/Tests (eg, Neuro-Cognitive, Mental Status, Speech Testing)				
96110			X	
96127	X			
Physical Medicine and Rehabilitation				
Active Wound Care Management				
97605			X	
97606			X	
97607	X			
97608	X			
Other Services and Procedures				
99184	X			
99188	X			

Category II Codes

Patient History				
1040F			X	

Diagnostic/Screening Processes or Results				
3125F		X		
3126F	X			
3775F	X			
3776F	X			

Section/Code	Added	Deleted	Revised	Grammatical Revision

Category III Codes

Section/Code	Added	Deleted	Revised	Grammatical Revision
0059T		X		
0073T		X		
0075T			X	
0076T			X	
0092T		X		
0181T		X		
0191T			X	
0197T		X		
0199T		X		
0200T			X	
0201T			X	
0226T		X		
0227T		X		
0239T		X		
0245T		X		
0246T		X		
0247T		X		
0248T		X		
0253T			X	
0357T	X			
0376T	X			

Subcutaneous Implantable Defibrillator System

Section/Code	Added	Deleted	Revised	Grammatical Revision
0319T		X		
0320T		X		
0321T		X		
0322T		X		
0323T		X		
0324T		X		

⊘=Modifier 51 Exempt   ⊙=Moderate Sedation   ✚=Add-on Code   ✗=FDA approval pending

Section/Code	Added	Deleted	Revised	Grammatical Revision
0325T		X		
0326T		X		
0327T		X		
0328T		X		
0334T		X		
0340T	X			
0341T	X			
0342T	X			
0343T		X		
0344T		X		
0345T	X			
0346T	X			
0347T	X			
0348T	X			
0349T	X			
0350T	X			
0351T	X			
0352T	X			
0353T	X			
0354T	X			
0355T	X			
0356T	X			
0358T	X			

Section/Code	Added	Deleted	Revised	Grammatical Revision
Adaptive Behavior Assessments				
0359T	X			
0360T	X			
0361T	X			
0362T	X			
0363T	X			
Adaptive Behavior Treatment				
0364T	X			
0365T	X			
0366T	X			
0367T	X			
0368T	X			
0369T	X			
0370T	X			
0371T	X			
0372T	X			
Exposure Adaptive Behavior Treatment With Protocol Modification				
0373T	X			
0374T	X			
0375T	X			
0377T	X			
0378T	X			
0379T	X			
0380T	X			